THE
SOUTH
THE BEAUTIFUL
COOKBOOK

AUTHENTIC RECIPES FROM THE AMERICAN SOUTH

Crawfish Étouffée (recipe page 99)

AUTHENTIC RECIPES FROM THE AMERICAN SOUTH

THE SOUTH
THE BEAUTIFUL COOKBOOK

RECIPES BY
MARA REID ROGERS

TEXT BY
JIM AUCHMUTEY

GENERAL EDITOR
SUSAN PUCKETT

FOOD PHOTOGRAPHY BY
PHILIP SALAVERRY

SCENIC PHOTOGRAPHY BY
MELISSA FARLOW AND RANDY OLSON

HarperCollinsPublishers

First published in USA 1996
by Collins Publishers San Francisco
1160 Battery Street, San Francisco, CA 94111 USA
HarperCollins Web Site: http://www.harpercollins.com

Produced by Weldon Owen Inc.
814 Montgomery Street, San Francisco, CA 94133 USA
Phone (415) 291-0100   Fax (415) 291-8841

Weldon Owen Inc.:
Chairman: Kevin Weldon
President: John Owen
General Manager: Stuart Laurence
Co-Editions Director: Derek Barton, Tarji Mickelson
Associate Publisher: Anne Dickerson
Project Coordinator: Genevieve Morgan
Assistant Editor: Hannah Rahill
Copyeditor: Desne Border
Proofreaders: Sharilynn Hovind, Sharon Silva,
    Suzanne Sherman
Indexer: Ken Dellapenta
Designer: Tom Morgan, Blue Design
Design Assistants: Brenda Rae Eno, Jennifer Peterson
Illustrations: Diana Reiss Koncar
Map Illustrations: Kenn Backhaus
Photographer: Philip Salaverry
Prop Stylist: Amy Glenn
Food Stylist: Sue White
Photographer Assistants: Shayne O'Neill, Sarah Gummere
Prop Stylist Assistants: Christina Ecklund, Tony Huerta
Primary Food Stylist Assistant: Susan Sheinkopf
Food Stylist Assistants: Dan Becker, Kim Komely,
    Jennifer Spiegel
Southern Food Consultant: Anne Byrn

Library of Congress Cataloging-in-Publication Data
The South the beautiful cookbook : authentic recipes from
the American South / recipes by Mara Reid Rogers ; text by
Jim Auchmutey ; food photography by Philip Salaverry ;
scenic photography by Randy Olson.
p.   cm.
Includes index.
ISBN 0-00-225196-5
1. Cookery, American--Southern style.
2. Southern States--Social life and customs--1865–
I. Rogers, Mara Reid.   II. Auchmutey, Jim.
III. Salaverry, Philip.   IV. Olson, Randy.
TX715.2.S68S68   1996
641.5975--dc20   95-39078
                          CIP

Manufactured by Toppan Printing Co., Hong Kong
Printed in Hong Kong
A Weldon Owen Production

Endpapers: Spanish moss drapes from the limbs of oak trees.

*Pages 2–3: Fourth of July flags sail from the veranda of the
American Queen steamboat in New Orleans, Louisiana.*

*Right: A guide illuminates the curtained entrance to one of the
many secret tunnels that make up the underground railroad at
Slave Haven in Memphis, Tennessee. Thousands of runaway
slaves took refuge in an intricate network of sympathetic
homes as they traveled north to freedom.*

*Pages 8–9: Moonshine Loaf Cakes with Whiskey Glaze
(recipe page 234)*

*Pages 12–13: An avenue of Virginia live oak trees dating
from the late seventeenth century lines the entrance to the Oak
Alley Plantation in Vacherie, Louisiana.*

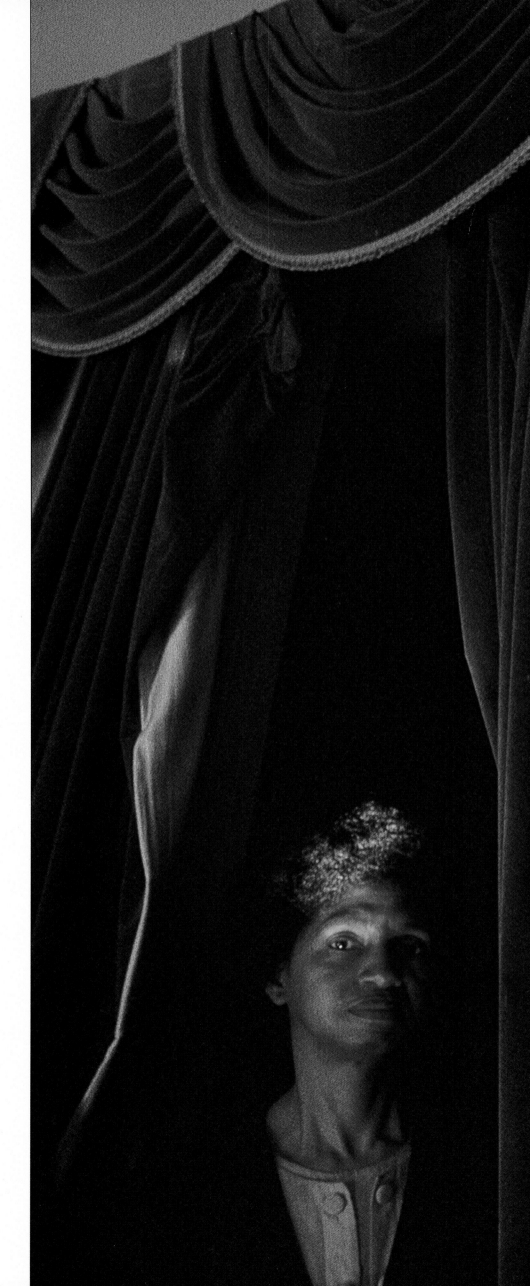

The Okefenokee swamp in Georgia and Florida is a vast wilderness of wetlands providing refuge for resident wildlife and migratory birds. In the early days, the Seminoles named the place Ecunnau Finacau, *or Land of Trembling Earth, because the floating peat that forms it barely supports a person's weight.*

CONTENTS

Historians consider the American Civil War to be the single most defining historical event in the South, perhaps the nation. Memorabilia from those bloody years abound at the Smith-McDowell House Museum in Ashville, North Carolina.

INTRODUCTION

The South has been called the closest thing in the United States to a nation within a nation. It is the only region that fought to become a separate nation, of course, but the differences run much deeper. The South stands apart even today, decades after the passing of legal segregation, the coming of air-conditioning and the in-migration of millions of outlanders. Southerners have expressed their distinctive culture in many ways, from their music to their stories to the manner in which they behave, but no expression strikes closer to the heart than the great folk art of Southern food.

When Americans speak of down-home cooking, more often than not they mean Southern. Savor the thought of the region's most famous dishes: pan-fried chicken, greens and pot likker, catfish and hush puppies, pecan pie and peach ice cream. The very names evoke images of family reunions and church dinners on the grounds, a preacher blessing the bounty before the elbows commence to flying.

Yet Southern cooking is far more than Aunt Bea's Sunday dinner in Mayberry, North Carolina. It's also the polyglot conversation of gumbo, the Old World sophistication of a Huguenot torte, the New South inventiveness of roasted squab on sweet potato spoon bread with sour cherry compote. Southern cooking is in fact much more diverse than is widely thought. But then, so is the South.

Generations of journalists and academics have felled many a pulpwood tree trying to explain what constitutes the South. Is it the states that seceded from the Union? Is it wherever the preferred second-person plural pronoun is y'all? Is it any town where you can order grits for breakfast without raising an eyebrow?

There are many places to draw the cultural equivalent of the line Mason and Dixon surveyed in 1763 (the Maryland-Pennsylvania border, incidentally). For the purposes of this book, the South comprises the eleven states of the Confederacy, minus Texas (increasingly a world unto itself), plus West Virginia and Kentucky (what's the use of being Southern without mint juleps?).

It is a vast and varied land of foggy mountains, undulating hills, scrubby coastal plains, mysterious swamps, subtropical shorelines and alluvial flatlands so fertile the chocolaty dirt looks edible. More than sixty million Americans–almost a quarter of the nation's population–call the region home. They are the product of an ethnic stewpot that has been simmering for centuries and has cooked down to something as spicy as a Cajun might conjure.

The South's first cooks were the Native Americans who had the land to themselves before Europeans splashed ashore in the 1500s. The Powhatans of the Chesapeake Bay, the Cherokees of Appalachia, the Creeks of Georgia, the Natchez and Choctaws and

Shiloh National Military Park and Cemetery was the site of one of the most gruesome battles in American history. During the Civil War, the North and South together experienced more than 23,000 casualties here.

Chickasaws of the Mississippi plain—the indigenous peoples of the South left more than place names; they left a food heritage.

Early accounts make it clear that Southern natives were far from culinary primitives. They ate well, maybe better than the average European. They took game from the forest, fish from the sea, nuts and fruits from the wilderness, and they took advantage of the warm climate to become accomplished farmers. Sir Walter Raleigh's colonists in North Carolina were impressed by the tidy rows of beans and maize the Croatan people tended. Among the foods the natives shared with the settlers were pecans, corn bread and filé, a powder made from sassafras leaves that was used as a gumbo thickener. History also records that it was the Powhatans who showed the Jamestown settlers how to soak and dehull corn and then grind it into something they called rockahominy, the Algonquin word for parched corn. Southerners come to know it as hominy grits.

The Spanish explorers who preceded the English brought many foods that would become Southern standards. Starting with Hernando de Soto's expedition in 1539, conquistadores introduced the natives to oranges, peaches, pigs, chickens and sugarcane. Yet Spanish cooking left little impact, probably because the Spanish were more interested in looking for gold than in looking to set down roots. One of the few Southern specialties with Spanish bloodlines is jambalaya, the paellalike dish whose name may derive from the Spanish word *jamón* or the French *jambon*, which both mean ham.

During the Civil War, North Carolina was the last state to secede. Nevertheless, it sent 125,000 men to fight for the Confederacy and lost more soldiers by the war's end than any other Southern state.

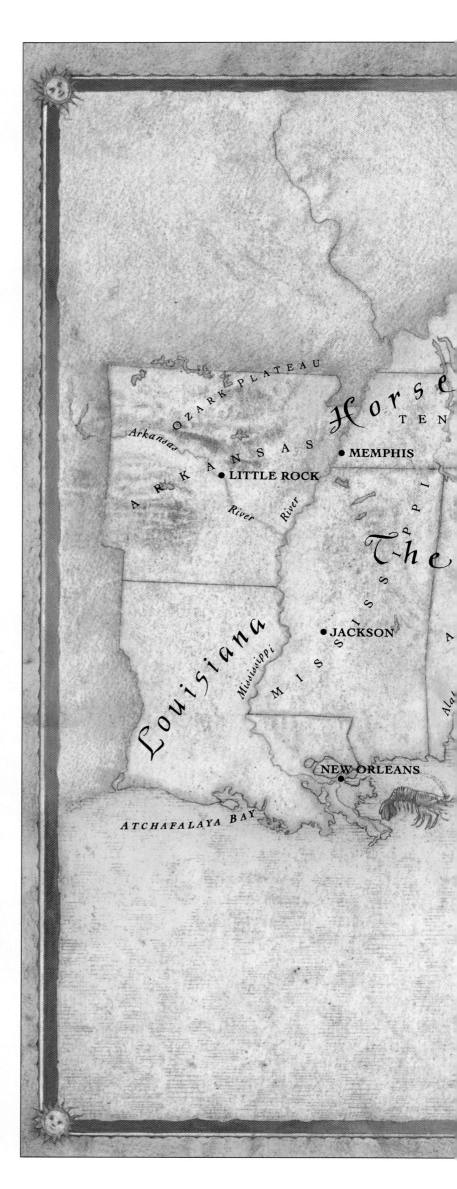

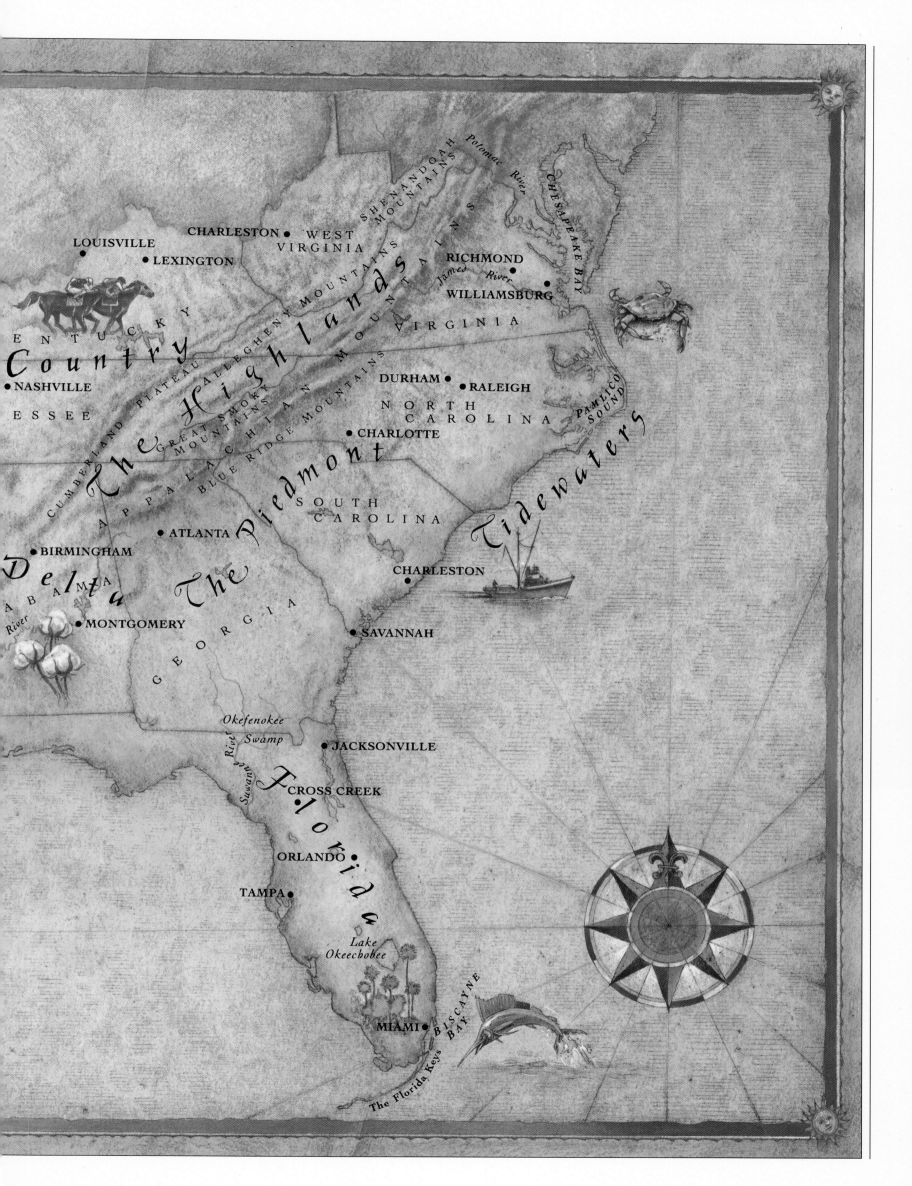

LOUISVILLE

CHARLESTON • WEST
VIRGINIA

RICHMOND

LEXINGTON

WILLIAMSBURG

SHENANDOAH
MOUNTAINS

Potomac River

CHESAPEAKE BAY

James River

VIRGINIA

K E N T U C K Y

Country

The Highlands

A L L E G H E N Y M O U N T A I N S

C U M B E R L A N D P L A T E A U

A P P A L A C H I A N M O U N T A I N S

• NASHVILLE

T E N N E S S E E

G R E A T S M O K Y M O U N T A I N S

B L U E R I D G E M O U N T A I N S

DURHAM •   • RALEIGH

N O R T H
C A R O L I N A

PAMLICO SOUND

• CHARLOTTE

The Piedmont

Tidewaters

S O U T H
C A R O L I N A

• ATLANTA

• BIRMINGHAM

Delta

A L A B A M A

River

• MONTGOMERY

G E O R G I A

CHARLESTON

SAVANNAH

Okefenokee Swamp

Suwannee River

• JACKSONVILLE

CROSS CREEK

Florida

ORLANDO •

TAMPA •

Lake Okeechobee

MIAMI •   BISCAYNE BAY

The Florida Keys

Diners watch boats glide into the harbor at Key West, Florida. Steamships from Havana once docked at this pier, which juts out into the Gulf of Mexico.

The French are another matter. Though they introduced few foods to the New World, they left a definitive legacy in their colony of Louisiana. French explorers had tested the southern edges of the continent for decades, but they didn't dig in until the founding of Mobile and New Orleans in the early 1700s. Their rich cuisine helped make New Orleans the nation's first great restaurant city. Meanwhile, the Acadians brought their French Canadian culture to the bayous of southern Louisiana after they were expelled from Nova Scotia by the English in the 1760s. They married the traditions of hearty French country cooking with the abundant shellfish of the wetlands and created one of America's most popular cuisines, Cajun.

As enlivening as the Latin influences were, the dominant strains of Southern cooking—indeed, Southern life—came from the British Isles and Africa. In 1619,

only twelve years after the English settled Jamestown, the first black Africans appeared in Virginia as indentured servants. Slavery soon flourished, and the two cultures—white and black—entwined, despite a cruel social order that would scar the South for centuries to come.

Ignorant of the foods of the strange new world, the English almost starved at first. They came by necessity to appreciate corn, squash and other native staples. To these they added their livestock, their fruits (chief among them, apples) and a taste for pies and puddings that grew into the notorious Southern sweet tooth.

By the 1700s the British colonies of the South were developing a plantation economy based on cheap labor and extensive cultivation of single cash crops. Virginia had tobacco, South Carolina rice, Louisiana sugarcane, and the whole Southern Tier eventually blossomed with cotton. Out of this almost medieval culture sprang one of the region's defining legends: Southern hospitality.

It was no myth. The handful of wealthy planters atop antebellum society lived for the chance to show off their good fortune. You can almost see the jaws drop as you read visitors' accounts of feasts at Westover, Drayton Hall, Shadows-on-the-Teche and other plantation manors. The Southerner who perhaps best embodied the spirit was Thomas Jefferson, who entertained so often and so well at his Virginia estate, Monticello, that he died $40,000 in debt. Hospitality, Jefferson's overseer wrote, "almost ate him out of house and home."

The formidable cooks responsible for this embarrassment of riches were almost always African slaves, and they knew how to use seasonings in a way the British would never dream of. Despite deadly, cramped conditions aboard slave ships, the Africans managed to bring with them some of the foods most identified with the South: okra, peanuts, watermelons, black-eyed peas. Slave cooks should be considered the unsung heroes of Southern food, for while they prepared fancy food for the Big House, they created for themselves a peasant cuisine built around corn bread, vegetables and the less exalted parts of the pig. Yeoman whites ate much the same diet.

The cataclysms of the Civil War and Reconstruction did much to merge these high and low traditions, at

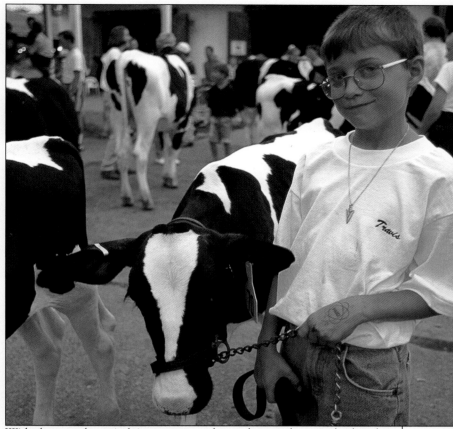

With sheep and cow judging contests, a horse show and carnival rides, the Mason County Fair brings festive revelry to Mt. Pleasant, West Virginia.

The Cajun culture in Louisiana maintains its own musical and culinary traditions. This Cajun musician plays his accordion in Montegut, Louisiana.

As Victorian rationalist Sir William Archer once said, "The South is by a long way the most simply and sincerely religious country I ever was in." Here, a Baptist pastor enters his church in Nutbush, Tennessee.

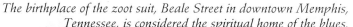

The birthplace of the zoot suit, Beale Street in downtown Memphis, Tennessee, is considered the spiritual home of the blues.

least from a culinary standpoint. When you're as poor for as long as the South was, almost every belly at some point gets filled with "low-down cornpone," as Mark Twain called it.

It should come as no surprise then, that Southerners have sometimes seemed rather ambivalent about their native cookery. When the region finally started to prosper after World War II, Southerners were quite capable of acting a little ashamed of all that hominy and hog meat, as if it were, like the outhouse, a reminder of hard times and backward ways. The writer Calvin Trillin noticed this phenomenon in Atlanta during the early 1970s. Proud Atlantans would point him to the latest revolving restaurant with pseudo-Continental cuisine when all he wanted was a good mess of greens.

There was also the undeniable fact that much of what passed for Southern cooking in restaurants was a deep-fried caricature. To a large extent, Southern food has always been a phenomenon of the home. Those lucky enough to be invited into a private residence invariably ate better than those who had to rely on the blue plate special at Granny's Kountry Kitchen. Surveying the roadside offerings in 1949, Atlanta newspaperman Ralph McGill wrote, "Southern cooking has been perverted by slatterns with a greasy skillet." Many outsiders viewed this oversalted, overfried, overcooked corruption as typical of the region's viands. The image probably reached its nadir in the famously eccentric diet of Elvis Presley, who seemed to live on fried banana-and-peanut-butter sandwiches and vegetables cooked down to a mush only a botanist could identify.

Thankfully, recent years have seen a movement to reclaim Southern cooking and celebrate it as the authentic regional cuisine it is. Acclaimed chefs such as Ben Barker of Durham, Elizabeth Terry of Savannah and Frank Stitt III of Birmingham have rediscovered traditional dishes and added contemporary flourishes.

Cookbook authors like Edna Lewis of Virginia, James Villas of North Carolina and Nathalie Dupree of Georgia have championed classic Southern cooking, stressing the freshest local ingredients in season. Many of today's Southern chefs have also found ways to reduce fat and salt without compromising "sumption," as black cooks used to call flavor.

The result is a full-blown revival. Today, when visitors to Atlanta ask about the hot new restaurants, they're likely to be steered toward establishments serving New Southern fare. Catfish, collard greens and good old grits are turning up on some of the region's choicest menus.

There is an old Southern saying that goes, Every dog has its day.

Somebody say grace; Southern cooking is having its day.

The glistening white sand beach of Gulf Shores is Alabama's toehold on the Gulf of Mexico.

Deep South

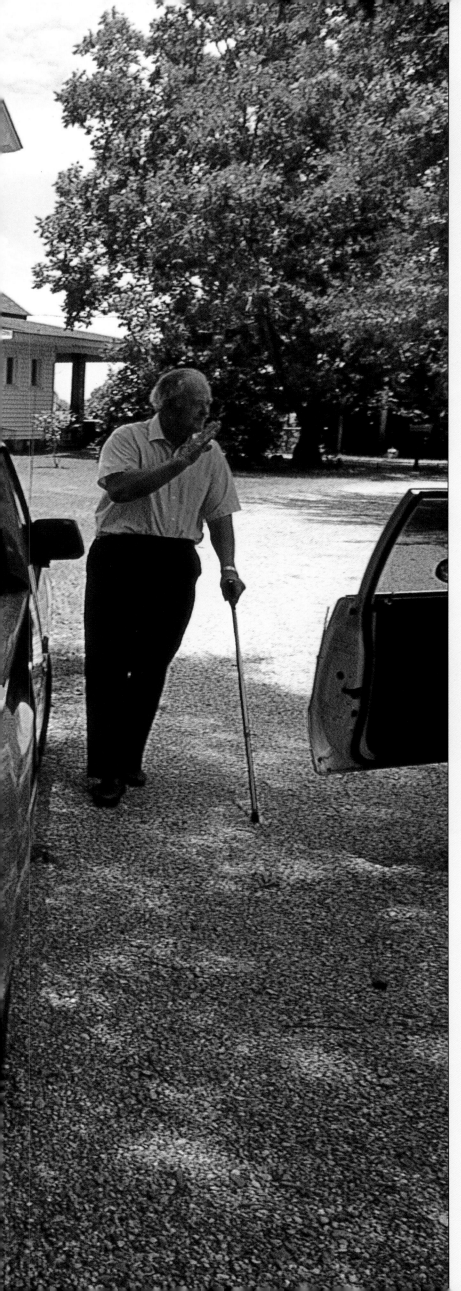

THE DELTA

Gulf of Mexico

DEEP SOUTH

Think of Dixie. A hoop-skirted belle flirts with her beau on the veranda of a white-columned plantation house. A work-shirted man with a guitar sings plaintively on the porch of a gray tar-paper shack. The fertile land they share slumbers under a soft blanket of cotton that almost glows beneath the moonlight.

Thanks to generations of pulp novelists and Tin Pan Alley songwriters, these are the mental postcards most people have of the Deep South. While the images indeed are based on fact, the full picture is more complicated—and just as captivating. In this history-haunted land, the novelist William Faulkner wrote, "The past isn't dead. It isn't even past."

The same could be said of the repast.

The Deep South, the heart of the old plantation belt, stretches westward from Georgia to Alabama, Mississippi and Arkansas, from the peanut fields of the Wiregrass to the pine woods of the Gulf coastal plain to the hardwood hills of the upland to the rich, flat floodplain of the Mississippi River. It is a humid hothouse of geography suited for growing things, for the one crop above all that knitted the land's culture and led its people into a romantically tragic history: cotton.

Long before cotton, a thriving native population of Mississippian Indians lived in city-states clustered around burial mounds along the river valleys. The

Previous pages: A local resident enjoys a bowl of piping-hot jambalaya on the front porch of the General Store in Lorman, Mississippi. Left: A farmer in Tylertown, Mississippi, sells homegrown watermelons from the back of his truck.

The historic Quapaw Quarter of Little Rock, Arkansas, is known for its handsome collection of Greek Revival and Victorian structures.

Creeks of Georgia and Alabama and the Choctaws and Natchez of Mississippi grew corn, squash and beans, and hunted deer and other game. Their way of life began to unravel when the first Europeans came in the 1500s carrying smallpox, yellow fever and a world of other diseases for which the natives had no defense. More than half had died of illness by the time of the American Revolution.

Shortly afterward, a new way of life appeared on the eastern horizon. Eli Whitney, a New Englander visiting Georgia in 1793, invented a machine to separate cotton fiber from seeds, a task that until then had been done slowly and painfully by hand. The cotton gin changed everything. Cotton became the South's primary crop. More African slaves were imported to work the fields. And because cotton rapidly depleted the soil, the South's agricultural frontier pushed west as farmers abandoned

the played-out fields of the Carolinas for the virgin earth of Alabama and Mississippi.

Great plantations were carved out of the bottomlands along meandering rivers with mellifluous Native American names: Alabama, Tombigbee, Arkansas, Yazoo. The wealthiest planters built mansions with Greek porticos and imitated the lavish hospitality of their kinsfolk in Virginia and South Carolina. The Mississippi River port of Natchez came to symbolize the new cotton aristocracy. Natchez had more millionaires per capita than any other city in the antebellum United States, and they lived large in a matchless collection of architectural confections filled with the latest European furnishings. Visiting a nearby plantation before the Civil War, diarist William Howard Russell described "a profusion of dishes—grilled fowl, prawns, eggs and ham, fish from New Orleans, potted salmon from England, preserved meats from France, claret, iced water, coffee and tea, varieties of hominy, mush, and African vegetable preparations."

The vast majority of white Mississippians were dirt farmers and could only dream of such a life. The other half of the state's population had even less; they were slaves.

Cotton accounts for the most striking aspect of the Deep South's human geography. African Americans have always made up a large percentage of the populace. Mississippi was majority black well into the 1900s, and it remains the only state where more than a third of the citizenry descends from Africa. The racial balance of the Deep South flavors everything from its politics to its music to its cooking.

The slaves who cooked for the planters prepared a stripped-down version of the same cuisine for themselves. They supplemented their rations of cornmeal and salt pork with greens, sweet potatoes and other vegetables they cultivated or picked wild. They also caught catfish and hunted squirrel and other small game, especially opossum. Underprivileged white farmers ate much the same way.

The Civil War destroyed slavery, but it did not destroy the old order, which reappeared more or less in the institution of sharecropping. Blacks and whites alike were now free to farm somebody else's land for a portion of the crop. The ironic result: the Deep South, heart of the

moonlight-and-magnolias ideal of Southern gentility, became home to the region's worst poverty and hunger. Nowhere was the contrast more dramatic than the storied Misssssippi Delta—"the most Southern place on Earth," as historian James Cobb called it.

The Delta is not the actual delta of the Mississippi River. The name refers instead to the land between the Mississippi and Yazoo rivers in the northwestern part of the state—an alluvial plain as wide as sixty miles, running north from Vicksburg two hundred miles to the bluffs of Memphis. Ages of silt-rich floodwaters made the Delta one of the world's most fecund expanses and gave it an unrelenting levelness that can seem like a heat mirage. Watching a tractor work these fields is like watching a ship inch across the far horizon.

The Delta is one of the few places in the South where the landed gentry still calls themselves planters. It is also one of the few places where the elite entertain in the grand old fashion. The cotillion, the harvest ball and the debutante party live on here, along with the many finger foods and potables associated with the social whirl. The Delta still knows how to make planter's punch.

But the planters are not how the world best knows the Delta. It is known above all for the musical language blacks created out of their hardship: the blues. At the roadhouses and juke joints where people gathered to

Each year, thousands of tourists visit Elvis "The King of Rock and Roll" Presley's grave in Paradise Garden at his Graceland estate outside of Memphis, Tennessee.

listen, certain foods came to be associated with the hard-edged sound. Fried catfish, of course, and chitlins, the breaded and fried small intestines of a hog. But the food that danced with the blues most often was, and still is, barbecue, particularly pork ribs. When large numbers of black Southerners started moving north during World War I, they took their music and barbecue and the other cooking that came to be called soul food, and transformed whole neighborhoods into Little Dixies. Alabamians gravitated toward Cleveland and Detroit. Arkansans and Mississippians lit out for Chicago. The rib shacks that send their sweet smoke across the south side of that city have their roots, like the blues, in Mississippi.

Today, as always, the best cooking in the Deep South is preserved in private homes. A few restaurants have won acclaim for their New Southern cooking, most notably the Highlands Bar & Grill in Birmingham, Alabama. For the most part, though, the Deep South's taste buds are as conservative as its politics. *Southern Living,* the ultrapopular regional magazine based in Birmingham, rediscovers this from time to time when its food editors, who by no means see themselves as trendsetters, get their wrists slapped by their readers. One woman phoned wanting to know why the magazine was getting so carried away with yogurt.

The most noteworthy thing about food in the Deep South is how little it has changed over the years. True, cooks here as elsewhere use less fat and salt these days.

The 1991 cookbook of the Jackson, Mississippi, Junior League features considerably lighter dishes than its 1977 predecessor. Yet the classics endure. At bed-and-breakfast inns in Natchez, they still serve cheese grits. In Memphis, they still make a convincing claim to being the pork barbecue capital of the world. On front porches in Alabama, they still snap beans and then cook them with fatback. And in Mississippi they still fry catfish—though the lowly fish has gone from something caught with a cane pole to a major aquacultural commodity.

Rich and poor, black and white, city and country, the people of the Deep South share their proudly traditional cooking even if they don't share many other things. It's part of them, like the climate and their eloquently remembered past.

Willie Morris captured the sentiment well in his memoir *North Toward Home* when he described how he found a taste of his native Mississippi in Harlem one New Year's Day with two expatriate black writers from the South, Al Murray and Ralph Ellison: "[We] congregated for an unusual feast: bourbon, collard greens, black-eyed peas, ham hocks and corn bread—a kind of ritual for all of us. Where else in the East but in Harlem could a Southern white boy greet the New Year with the good-luck food he had had as a child, and feel at home as he seldom had thought he could in the Cave?"

The Cave? That's just Deep Southern for New York City.

Dense morning fog lifts slowly off a road outside Poplarville, Mississippi.

Known as "Father of the Blues," William Christopher (W. C.) Handy was born in the small town of
Florence, Tennessee, in 1873. His epic talent has made him famous in cities as far afield as Chicago,
St. Louis and Memphis. This is his Knights of Pythian band outfit.

29

APPETIZERS, SALADS & DRINKS

Peanuts are widely grown throughout the South; the revered nut makes its way into a number of creative recipes.

APPETIZERS, SALADS & DRINKS

One of the most pernicious ideas ever foisted upon the South is the meteorological concept of "heat index." As if it weren't bad enough that thermometers from Savannah to Shreveport regularly violate 95°, weather forecasters had to dream up something to make things sound worse. It may be 96° in Montgomery, but thanks to the heat index and its factoring of humidity, it *feels* like 106°. That's nice to know.

Thin, crisp benne wafers are a favorite treat concocted in Southern kitchens.

Climate definitely affects the way Southerners eat. In the dog days of summer, when haze and discomfort hang over the land, heavy foods don't suit every taste. The South has evolved a wealth of lighter fare—salads, appetizers, finger foods—that commonly appears at receptions and ladies' luncheons. Cheese straws, sausage balls, pickled shrimp and the like aren't so much diet food as pick-a-little food.

But the most obvious response to the heat is the region's unslakable thirst. Southerners have probably created or customized more distinctive drinks than the rest of the states put together. It was Kentucky, of course, that sired bourbon, America's chief contribution to the world of distilled spirits as well as the chief ingredient in the South's most potent cooler, the mint julep.

The Southern contribution to the world of carbonated soft drinks is even more impressive. Most people know that an Atlanta pharmacist formulated Coca-Cola in the 1880s. Fewer know that Coke's archrival, Pepsi-Cola, also has Southern roots: Caleb D. Bradham, a pharmacist in New Bern, North Carolina, created it in 1896. Other well-known drinks that originated in the thirsty Southland include Royal Crown Cola (concocted in 1933 in Columbus, Georgia), Gatorade (1965, Gainesville, Florida) and Dr. Pepper (1885, Waco, Texas—though named for a Dr. Charles K. Pepper of Rural Retreat, Virginia).

The most popular Southern drink, however, comes in a pitcher instead of a bottle. Other Americans regard iced tea as a warm-weather drink. Not down here. Southern-

Previous pages: Clockwise from top left: Champagne Peach Cup (recipe page 54–55), Oyster and Andouille Pastries (recipe page 51), Pecan-Smoked Trout Spread (recipe page 51), Pimento Cheese (recipe page 38)

ers guzzle iced tea whether it's January or July. To save labor, some restaurants serve it in quart jars so they won't have to keep refilling the standard-sized glasses. Many Southerners prefer their tea presweetened (sugar melts better in a warm brew) and would rather drink water than sweeten their tea cold at the table.

No one knows exactly who first thought of iced tea. Food historians have credited a vendor at the 1904 St. Louis World's Fair with bringing the drink to a wider audience. But Southern cookbooks mentioned it decades earlier. The magic ingredient—ice—was being manufactured commercially in New Orleans as early as the 1860s. "Iced tea is too pure and natural a creation not to have been invented as soon as tea, ice and hot weather crossed paths," wrote Southern historian John Egerton, speculating that if the inventor were known, he or she might have a statue in the French Quarter like Andrew Jackson.

As elsewhere, Southerners also enjoy salads as a way of eating light during warm weather. But they have different notions of what constitutes a salad. Until recent years, lettuce played an insignificant role in the Southern diet (this despite the efforts of Thomas Jefferson, who sent lettuce seeds from France back to Monticello). Southerners usually thought of salads as something sweet, maybe with fruit, like ambrosia. Congealed salads became particularly popular after the spread of gelatin mixes and refrigeration in the early 1900s.

Salads of all kinds were a specialty at the Southern institution of the ladies' luncheon. At the tearooms that once dotted downtowns across the region, white-gloved shoppers and socializers chatted over chicken salad, frozen fruit salad and other chilled offerings. It was a ritual of womanhood, as Mildred Huff Coleman remembered in her *Frances Virginia Tea Room Cookbook*. After she had graduated from the seventh grade in Carrollton, Georgia,

The star of Key lime pie, Florida's Key limes are smaller, rounder and more yellow than limes found in other tropical climates.

Coleman and a classmate donned gloves, high heels and white dresses over starched crinolines, and boarded a bus for Atlanta, where the finest tearoom in town, the Frances Virginia, presided over Peachtree Street. Once there, they broke with tradition and decided not to order fried chicken because *children* ate fried chicken. They ordered shrimp salad. The waitress smiled and said, "That's what many other ladies eat, too."

Most of the tearooms are gone today, but the cool, light dishes they favored survive in countless kitchens and lunch counters. Styles change. Heat doesn't.

The proprietor of the Corners Bed and Breakfast prepares a tray of appetizers for his guests. The Vicksburg, Mississippi, mansion is on the National Register of Historic Places.

The South

AMBROSIA

The word ambrosia *is commonly defined as the food of the Greek and Roman gods. The dish "ambrosia" is a very traditional Southern salad that, in its purest form, consists of sliced oranges and grated coconut. I surmise that this dish was thus named because it was often served on special holiday occasions that fell during the winter months, when fresh fruit would be most welcome. A dish with such a perfumelike scent would indeed be food for the gods. There are many deviations from the basic recipe, depending on the convention of the region in which it is prepared. I have tasted versions that use pineapple, others with bananas. Sometimes the coconut will be fresh, other times toasted. Though Ambrosia is considered a salad and served as such, it often makes an appearance on Southern dessert tables, too. Maraschino cherries are customarily used as garnish, but fresh cherries can be substituted. If the oranges you use for this recipe are not sweet, sift some confectioners' (icing) sugar lightly over each layer of orange sections before sprinkling with coconut.*

6 large navel oranges
2 cups (8 oz/250 g) sweetened shredded coconut
fresh or maraschino cherries, stemmed and halved (and pitted if fresh), and fresh mint leaves for garnish (optional)

Ambrosia

✳ Peel and section the oranges, removing and discarding the white membrane.
✳ In a decorative glass bowl or straight-sided trifle dish, arrange a layer of orange sections. Sprinkle the oranges with a layer of coconut. Repeat, alternating orange sections and coconut until all have been used. Cover the bowl tightly with plastic wrap and refrigerate to allow the flavors to blend, about 2 hours.
✳ To serve, garnish with a decorative pattern of cherry halves and mint leaves, if desired. Serve chilled.

SERVES 6

Virginia

SALAD OF MIXED GARDEN GREENS WITH MONTICELLO DRESSING

Thomas Jefferson loved salads and usually served them with dinner at Monticello. He grew nineteen varieties of lettuce and also took an interest in developing benne (sesame) oil as a salad dressing substitute for imported olive oil. In an 1808 letter he wrote: "The African negroes brought over to Georgia a seed which they called Beni, & the botanists Sesamum. I lately received a bottle of the oil, which was eaten with sallad by various companies. all agree it is equal to the olive oil. a bushel of seed yields 3 gallons of oil. I propose to cultivate it for my own use at least."

This recipe for salad with Monticello Dressing is adapted from The American Heritage Cookbook. *While the original recipe does not list weights for the heads of lettuces, rest assured that you will have enough to feed a large crowd in true Jeffersonian style. Don't dress any extra greens. Save for later use by rolling them in damp paper towels and refrigerating to keep crisp.*

1 head Bibb lettuce, about 6 oz (185 g)
1 bunch watercress, about 4 oz (125 g)
1 head Belgian endive, about 3 oz (90 g)
1 head iceberg lettuce, about 8 oz (250 g)
1 head chicory, about 6 oz (185 g)
tender spinach leaf sprigs, about 5 oz (155 g)
1 tablespoon chopped chives or green (spring) onions

FOR THE MONTICELLO DRESSING:

2 small cloves garlic, crushed through a garlic press
2 teaspoons salt
1 teaspoon freshly ground white pepper
⅔ cup (5 fl oz/160 ml) olive oil
⅔ cup (5 fl oz/160 ml) light-colored sesame oil
⅔ cup (5 fl oz/160 ml) tarragon vinegar or white wine vinegar

✳ In a basin or large bowl, wash the salad greens in ice water, drain and pat completely dry. Tear into bite-sized pieces, wrap in paper towels and place in the refrigerator to crisp.
✳ To make the dressing, combine the garlic, salt, pepper, olive oil, sesame oil and vinegar in a 1-qt (1-l) jar or bottle. Cover tightly and shake well.
✳ To serve, in a large salad bowl combine the crisped greens, spinach sprigs and chives or green onions. Toss with the Monticello Dressing and serve at once.

SERVES 16; MAKES 2 CUPS (16 FL OZ/500 ML) DRESSING

Top to bottom: Salad of Mixed Garden Greens with Monticello Dressing, Roasted Corn and Boiled Peanut Salad

Atlanta, Georgia

ROASTED CORN AND BOILED PEANUT SALAD

Though chef Joe Scully of Atlanta's Indigo Coastal Grill hails from New Jersey, he's open to experimenting with Southern ingredients. For instance, he takes advantage of boiled peanuts' legumelike qualities by combining them with corn kernels and other ingredients in this intriguing salad. (Black beans, kidney beans or black-eyed peas could be used in place of the peanuts.) If you don't wish to boil your own peanuts, you can find them canned in some markets, but drain, rinse and drain again before using canned peanuts in this recipe. If cilantro has too strong a flavor for your taste, opt for basil or parsley. If you like, serve this salad with sliced fresh tomatoes.

2 ears of yellow corn, husks and silks removed
1 cup (6 oz/185 g) shelled Boiled Peanuts (see page 48)
½ cup (3 oz/90 g) finely chopped sweet onion
¼ cup (1½ oz/40 g) finely chopped red bell pepper (capsicum)
¼ cup (1½ oz/40 g) finely chopped green bell pepper (capsicum)
1 tablespoon minced garlic
1 tablespoon minced fresh cilantro (fresh coriander)
¼ cup (2 fl oz/60 ml) olive oil
3 tablespoons apple cider vinegar
salt and freshly ground pepper to taste

❈ Prepare a medium-hot, indirect fire in a charcoal grill and oil the grill rack. Cover and grill the corn about 5–6 inches from the ash-covered coals, for 15 minutes, turning the ears every 3–4 minutes. Remove the corn from the grill, let cool and then cut the kernels off. In a large mixing bowl, combine the corn kernels, peanuts, onion, bell peppers, garlic and cilantro. Set aside.
❈ In a small glass measuring cup, whisk together the oil and vinegar. Pour over corn mixture, add salt and pepper and stir to combine. Cover and refrigerate for at least 1 hour until chilled. Serve cold.

SERVES 6

Top to bottom: Mojito, Conch Fritters with Mango-Mustard Dipping Sauce

MOJITO

The Mojito is probably one of the most refreshing drinks to grace a glass. Based on mint and sugar, this Cuban-style mint julep can also be made with yerba buena, a cousin of spearmint, which is less sweet and has a slightly bitter aftertaste. The Mojito's effervescence is due to a splash of club soda, thus leading to the origin of its name—the Spanish verb mojar, *meaning to wet or moisten. This recipe was shared by Steven Raichlen, author of* Miami Spice.

16 mint or yerba buena leaves
¼ cup (2 oz/60 g) sugar, or to taste
6 tablespoons (3 fl oz/90 ml) fresh lime juice, about 2 limes
6 tablespoons (3 fl oz/90 ml) white rum
4 cups (17 oz/530 g) ice cubes
4 cups (32 fl oz/1 l) club soda
4 sprigs fresh mint or yerba buena for garnish

❀ Place the leaves of mint or yerba buena in a 2-qt (2-l) glass pitcher. Add the sugar and, using a wooden spoon, bruise the leaves to release the aromatic oil. Add the lime juice and rum and stir until the sugar has dissolved.
❀ Add half of the ice cubes to the pitcher and stir. Place the remaining ice cubes in 4 glasses. Add the club soda to the rum mixture and stir. Taste and add more sugar, if desired. Pour the rum mixture into the ice-filled glasses and garnish with sprigs of mint or yerba buena.

SERVES 4

Florida Keys

CONCH FRITTERS WITH MANGO-MUSTARD DIPPING SAUCE

Long before it was baptized Margaritaville, Key West was known to natives and tourists alike as the Conch Republic. The name, a reference to the spirit of offshore independence found in the Keys, comes from the big pink shell with the little white mollusk inside. Floridians have been making spicy fritters from its meat for years.

FOR THE FRITTERS:

8 oz (250 g) conch meat, foot and orange
    fin removed
1 tablespoon fresh lemon juice
¼ cup (1 oz/30 g) finely minced onion
¼ cup (1 oz/30 g) minced red bell
    pepper (capsicum)
1 clove garlic, crushed through a garlic press
1 teaspoon dried dill
1 teaspoon salt
¼ teaspoon ground cayenne pepper
1 egg, lightly beaten
¾ cup (6 fl oz/180 ml) milk
1 cup (5 oz/155 g) all-purpose (plain) flour
1 teaspoon baking powder
vegetable oil for frying
sprigs of fresh dill for garnish (optional)

FOR THE DIPPING SAUCE:

1 ripe mango, about 1½ lb (750 g), peeled and cut into
    medium dice
½ cup (4 fl oz/125 ml) mayonnaise
2 tablespoons Dijon-style mustard
½–1 teaspoon hot pepper sauce
1 tablespoon fresh lemon juice

❊ Thinly slice the conch meat and then dice. In a food processor fitted with the metal blade or in a blender, process the conch meat until finely minced, using a rubber spatula to scrape down the sides of the bowl. Transfer the conch to a nonreactive medium bowl, add the lemon juice and toss to coat. Cover with plastic wrap and refrigerate for 30 minutes to tenderize.
❊ Add the onion, bell pepper, garlic, dill, salt, cayenne, egg and milk to the conch mixture and stir until blended. Set aside.
❊ In a large bowl, combine the flour and baking powder. Make a well in the center of the flour mixture and slowly add the conch mixture, stirring until well blended into a thick batter. Cover and refrigerate for 1 hour.
❊ Meanwhile, to make the sauce, in a food processor fitted with the metal blade or in a blender, combine the mango, mayonnaise, mustard, hot pepper sauce and lemon juice and process until completely smooth. Transfer to a small serving bowl, cover and set aside at room temperature while frying the fritters.
❊ Preheat an oven to 200°F (93°C).
❊ In a large saucepan over medium heat, pour the oil to a depth of 1 in (2.5 cm) and heat to 325°F (165°C) on a deep-fry thermometer. Working in batches, drop a few table-spoonfuls of conch batter into the hot oil. Fry, turning frequently with a slotted spoon, until the fritters are golden brown and cooked through, 3–5 minutes. Drain on paper towels. Repeat with the remaining batter, keeping the fritters warm in the oven until all are ready to serve. Serve immediately with the dipping sauce. Garnish with fresh dill sprigs, if desired.

MAKES 12–14 FRITTERS, 1½ CUPS (12 FL OZ/375 ML) SAUCE

The South

CHEESE COINS

Celebrity and Southern food authority Nathalie Dupree makes this "pick-up food" in the traditional form of strips, so once baked, they look like flat "straws." The following recipe is adapted from Dupree's book Southern Memories, *but here these delicious edibles are shaped like coins rather than straws. In this easy version you simply form the cheese-studded dough into logs, chill until firm, then slice and bake. Use a high-quality imported aged Parmesan. No salt is needed in this dough because of the salty Parmesan and Cheddar cheeses and the lightly salted butter. (However, if you use unsalted butter you might add a pinch.) Store up to 3 months in the freezer.*

8 oz (250 g) Parmesan cheese, finely grated
8 oz (250 g) sharp Cheddar cheese, shredded
1 cup (8 oz/250 g) salted butter, at room temperature
3¼–3½ cups (16–17 oz/515–550 g) all-purpose (plain) flour
½–1 teaspoon ground cayenne pepper

❊ In a large mixing bowl, using an electric mixer on medium-low speed, beat together the cheeses and butter until well combined. Fold in 2 cups (10 oz/315 g) of the flour and the cayenne and beat on low speed until combined.
❊ Transfer the dough to a lightly floured work surface. Knead in the remaining flour. When well combined, form the dough into 3 logs, 12–14 in (30–35 cm) long and about 1½ in (4 cm) in diameter. Wrap in waxed paper or plastic wrap and refrigerate at least 2 hours.
❊ Preheat an oven to 375°F (190°C). Lightly coat three 15-by-13½-in (38-by-34-cm) baking sheets with vegetable cooking spray.
❊ Unwrap the chilled logs and slice into rounds ¼ in (6 mm) thick. Place on baking sheets and bake on the middle oven rack until golden brown, about 8–10 minutes, reducing the oven temperature a bit if they begin to brown too quickly. Remove to a wire rack to cool completely. Store in an airtight container.

MAKES ABOUT 9 DOZEN CHEESE COINS

Cheese Coins

Charleston, South Carolina

CHARLESTON TEA PLANTATION WEDDING PUNCH

This recipe is from Ann Fleming of the Charleston Tea Plantation in South Carolina, located on a tiny barrier island 20 miles from historic Charleston. Not only can you visit the plantation, but you can mail-order their tea (see Mail Order Sources). Theirs is the only tea grown in the United States—a tradition revived after nearly a century. This recipe makes a deep amber punch that's quite refreshing.

2 cups (16 fl oz/500 ml) brewed black tea, chilled
2 cups (16 fl oz/500 ml) apple juice, chilled
1 cup (8 fl oz/250 ml) unsweetened pineapple juice, chilled
4 cups (32 fl oz/1 l) club soda
ice cubes
orange slices, lemon slices and fresh mint sprigs for garnish

❀ In a large punch bowl, combine the tea, apple juice and pineapple juice. Cover and refrigerate until ready to serve.
❀ To serve, add the club soda and ice cubes and stir. Garnish with the orange and lemon slices and mint sprigs.

SERVES 8–10

South Carolina

POTTED SHRIMP

This recipe for combining shrimp with butter, seasonings and cream is an example of the English colonial influence on the Southeast. The English love to pot cheeses—no doubt the settlers along coastal South Carolina were delighted to find such lovely shrimp to preserve in the same manner. To serve, spread on melba toast squares, toasted French baguette slices or crackers and garnish with parsley.

1 qt (1 l) water
¼ cup (2 fl oz/60 ml) dry white wine
⅛ teaspoon plus ¼ teaspoon salt
pinch of freshly ground black pepper
1 bay leaf
8 oz (250 g) shrimp (prawns)
1 clove garlic, peeled
¼ cup (2 oz/60 g) unsalted butter, at room temperature
¼ teaspoon ground mace
⅛ teaspoon freshly ground white pepper
⅛ teaspoon ground cayenne pepper
⅛ teaspoon ground allspice
2–3 tablespoons light (single) cream, or as needed

❀ In a large, heavy saucepan over medium heat, combine the water, wine, the ⅛ teaspoon salt, black pepper and bay leaf and bring to a boil. Reduce the heat to low and add the shrimp. Simmer, stirring occasionally, until the shrimp curl and turn pink and opaque throughout, 3–4 minutes. Immediately drain the shrimp in a colander and rinse to cool them under cold running water. Remove and discard the bay leaf. Peel and devein the shrimp (see glossary).
❀ Engage the motor of a food processor fitted with the metal blade and drop the garlic down the feed tube to mince. Turn off the food processor. Add the shrimp, butter, mace, the ¼ teaspoon salt, white pepper, cayenne and allspice. Process until smooth, using a rubber spatula to scrape down the sides of the bowl. Pulse in enough cream to make a spreadable consistency. Spoon the shrimp mixture into a ramekin, cover tightly with plastic wrap and refrigerate for 24 hours. Serve at room temperature.

SERVES 4

Louisville, Kentucky

BENEDICTINE SPREAD

Jennie Benedict, a caterer and restaurateur in Louisville at the turn of the century, was renowned for her tea lunches and light sandwiches. The following spread was one of her creations. Serve on crackers or finger sandwiches or as a dip thinned with a little lowfat sour cream, alongside a tray of crudités. Lowfat sour cream may be substituted for the mayonnaise. This spread is at its best when made the same day as serving.

1 cucumber, peeled, seeded and grated
1 cup (8 oz/250 g) cream cheese, at room temperature
3 tablespoons grated yellow onion
1 tablespoon mayonnaise, or as needed
½ teaspoon salt
½ teaspoon hot pepper sauce
thin cucumber slices, left whole or julienned, for garnish
    (see glossary)

❀ Gently squeeze the grated cucumber to remove excess moisture. In a small mixing bowl, combine the grated cucumber, cream cheese, onion, mayonnaise, salt and hot pepper sauce and stir until smooth. Adjust consistency with a little more mayonnaise, if desired. Cover with plastic wrap and refrigerate to allow flavors to blend, about 2 hours.
❀ Transfer the spread to a serving bowl and garnish the outer edge of the bowl with a ring of overlapping cucumber slices. Alternatively, spread on individual crackers and garnish with julienned cucumbers. Serve at once.

MAKES ABOUT 1½ CUPS (12 OZ/375 G)

The South

PIMENTO CHEESE

You might call Pimento Cheese the pâté of the South. More than merely a sandwich filling, this spicy, comforting spread is also frequently used as a topping for canapés. Simply fill a pastry bag fitted with a large rosette tip, pipe the spread onto toast squares and top with an X made from 2 strips of pimiento. This spread is best when made 1 day ahead of serving.

8 oz (250 g) sharp yellow Cheddar cheese
8 oz (250 g) sharp white Cheddar cheese
7 oz (220 g) jarred pimientos (sweet peppers), drained
    (liquid reserved) and finely chopped
2 tablespoons liquid from jarred pimientos
⅓ cup (3 fl oz/80 ml) reduced-fat mayonnaise
2 tablespoons fresh lemon juice
1 tablespoon Worcestershire sauce
2 or 3 dashes of hot pepper sauce, or to taste
salt to taste

❀ Using a food processor fitted with a large-holed shredding disk or the coarse side of a cheese grater, shred both Cheddar cheeses.
❀ In a food processor fitted with the metal blade or in a blender, combine the shredded cheeses, pimientos, pimiento liquid, mayonnaise, lemon juice and Worcestershire sauce. Process until the mixture is a well-blended, spreadable consistency, using a rubber spatula to scrape down the sides of the bowl, about 3 minutes. Add the hot pepper sauce and salt. Cover and refrigerate for up to 3 days. Serve at room temperature.

MAKES ABOUT 3 CUPS (24 OZ/750 G) *Photograph pages 30–31*

Top to bottom: Charleston Tea Plantation Wedding Punch, (clockwise from top) Potted Shrimp, Benedictine Spread

SWEET VINEGAR COLESLAW

Among the South's great flavormates are barbecue and coleslaw. This favored rendition—a sweet but tangy combination of shredded cabbage and onion—provides the perfect foil to smoky meats or stews. It also is a welcome addition to another Southern favorite, the vegetable plate. This salad is best made the day of serving.

2 green bell peppers (capsicums), seeded and finely chopped
1 large head green cabbage, about 3 lb (1.5 kg), cored
   and shredded

2 yellow onions, finely chopped
4 carrots, grated
¾ cup (6 oz/185 g) sugar
¼ cup (2 fl oz/60 ml) vegetable oil
¼ cup (2 fl oz/60 ml) apple cider vinegar
2 tablespoons Dijon-style mustard
1 teaspoon salt, or to taste
½ teaspoon freshly ground pepper
½ teaspoon celery seeds
thinly sliced red bell pepper (capsicum) rings for garnish

Georgia

GEORGIA CAVIAR

The base of this popular Southern salad is not beluga but black-eyed peas. This dish actually improves with age, so it can be made up to 2 days ahead of serving. For an elegant presentation, line individual salad plates or a large platter with Bibb lettuce leaves, mound with "caviar" and garnish with julienned red bell pepper. Or serve it as a dip, with tortilla chips or pita triangles.

3 cups (21 oz/660 g) fresh, frozen or canned black-eyed peas
⅓ cup (1½ oz/45 g) minced green bell pepper (capsicum)
⅓ cup (1½ oz/45 g) minced red bell pepper (capsicum)
2 tablespoons minced jalapeño pepper (see glossary)
¼ cup (1½ oz/45 g) minced yellow onion
3 cloves garlic, minced
3 tablespoons red wine vinegar
¼ cup (2 fl oz/60 ml) olive oil or vegetable oil
salt to taste

❉ If using fresh or frozen black-eyed peas, place in a large saucepan, add cold water to cover, place over medium heat and bring to a boil. Reduce the heat to low and simmer, stirring occasionally, until the peas are just tender, about 15 minutes. Drain the peas and let cool to room temperature. If using canned black-eyed peas, simply drain in a colander and rinse under cold running water.
❉ In a large mixing bowl, combine the black-eyed peas, green and red bell peppers, jalapeño pepper, onion and garlic.
❉ In a small bowl, whisk together the vinegar, oil and salt until well blended. Pour the dressing over the black-eyed pea mixture and stir gently until the peas are well coated with the dressing. Cover and refrigerate until ready to serve. Stir to redistribute and serve chilled.

SERVES 8

Savannah, Georgia

WATERCRESS SLAW

This version of coleslaw has a wonderful herbal flavor. The recipe was contributed by Jane H. Long, owner of a carryout food shop, The Easy Way Out, in Atlanta, Georgia, where she showcases the fancier dishes of Low Country cuisine that mirror her vision of a comfortably elegant lifestyle. This recipe uses cultivated watercress, which is milder in flavor than wild watercress (also called "creasies" or field cress). The latter grows in the South around the edges of lakes, rivers and streams.

1 head green cabbage, about 2 lb (1 kg), cored and shredded
4 green (spring) onions, including tender green tops, thinly sliced
1 cup (1 oz/30 g) loosely packed stemmed watercress
1 red bell pepper (capsicum), seeded and julienned
1 cup (8 fl oz/250 ml) mayonnaise
1 cup (8 oz/250 g) sour cream
¼ cup (2 fl oz/60 ml) rice wine vinegar
½ cup (4 oz/125 g) prepared horseradish
1 tablespoon sugar
salt to taste

❉ In a large nonreactive bowl, combine the cabbage, green onions, watercress and most of the bell pepper, reserving a few strips for garnish.
❉ In a small bowl, whisk together the mayonnaise, sour cream, vinegar, horseradish, sugar and salt. Pour the dressing over the cabbage mixture and toss to coat. Cover and refrigerate for 1 hour. Stir to redistribute just before serving. Garnish with the reserved julienned bell pepper strips and serve chilled.

SERVES 8–10

Clockwise from left: Sweet Vinegar Coleslaw, Georgia Caviar, Watercress Slaw

❉ In a large nonreactive serving bowl, combine the chopped bell peppers, cabbage, onions and carrots and set aside.
❉ In a small nonreactive saucepan over medium heat, combine the sugar, oil and vinegar. Add the mustard, salt, pepper and celery seeds and stir until well blended. Bring to a boil and then remove from the heat.
❉ Pour the hot dressing over the cabbage mixture and toss until well blended and evenly coated with dressing. Let cool to room temperature, then cover with plastic wrap and refrigerate for 2 hours before serving to allow the flavors to blend.
❉ To serve, garnish with thinly sliced red bell pepper rings, if desired. Serve chilled or at room temperature.

SERVES 8–12

Atlanta, Georgia

TOASTED ALMOND CHICKEN SALAD AND FROZEN FRUIT SALAD LUNCHEON

Generations of Atlantans once made the pilgrimage downtown to shop at Rich's department store. For many—particularly ladies—the fondest part of the ritual was lunch at the legendary Magnolia Room restaurant. The store has closed, but the memories linger: the Atlanta-Journal Constitution counts this among its most requested recipes.

FOR THE CHICKEN SALAD:

3½ lb (1.75 kg) skinless, boneless chicken
   breast halves
1½ cups (12 fl oz/375 ml) mayonnaise
7 celery ribs, cut into small dice
½ cup (4 oz/125 g) pickle relish
1 teaspoon freshly ground white pepper
salt to taste

FOR THE FROZEN FRUIT SALAD:

8 oz (250 g) cream cheese, at room temperature
½ cup (2 oz/60 g) confectioners' (icing) sugar
⅓ cup (3 fl oz/80 ml) mayonnaise
2 teaspoons vanilla extract (essence)
8¼ oz (255 g) canned sliced peaches, drained
½ cup (2 oz/60 g) maraschino cherries, drained,
   stemmed and halved
30 oz (940 g) canned fruit cocktail, drained
8 oz (250 g) canned crushed pineapple, drained
2 cups (3½ oz/105 g) miniature marshmallows
½ cup (4 fl oz/125 ml) heavy (double) cream,
   whipped to stiff peaks

FOR SERVING:

Bibb lettuce leaves
½ cup (2 oz/60 g) sliced (flaked) almonds, toasted
   (see glossary)
whipped cream, whole maraschino or fresh
   cherries and orange slices for garnish (optional)

❋ To make the chicken salad, in a Dutch oven over medium heat, place the chicken breasts with water to cover and bring to a boil. Reduce the heat to low and simmer until the chicken is tender and cooked throughout, with no pink remaining, 20–30 minutes. Drain the chicken and transfer to a plate to cool completely. Slice the cooled chicken crosswise into bite-sized strips.

❋ In a large bowl, combine the mayonnaise, celery, pickle relish and pepper. Fold in the chicken strips and salt. Cover with plastic wrap and refrigerate until chilled, about 4 hours.

❋ To make the fruit salad, line 16 muffin cups with paper muffin liners. Place the cream cheese in a medium bowl and, using an electric mixer on medium speed, beat for 1 minute. While continuing to beat, gradually add the confectioners' sugar, then the mayonnaise until well blended and smooth. Beat in the vanilla extract. Using a rubber spatula, fold in the peaches, cherry halves, fruit cocktail, pineapple, marshmallows and the whipped cream. Spoon

⅓ cup (3 oz/90 g) of the fruit mixture into each of the prepared muffin cups, smoothing the surface. Freeze until hard, about 4 hours. Remove from the freezer 15 minutes before serving, but do not allow to get soft.

❋ To serve, line each of 16 individual salad plates with lettuce leaves. Spoon a mound of the chicken salad on each plate and sprinkle each mound with an equal amount of the almonds. Peel the paper liners from the frozen fruit salads and discard. Place one frozen fruit salad alongside each mound of chicken salad. Garnish the frozen fruit salad with whipped cream and a cherry and fresh orange slices, if desired. Serve at once.

SERVES 16

Florida

JELLIED LEMON-PINEAPPLE-GRAPEFRUIT SALAD RING

Old-fashioned jellied salad rings are pretty and easy to prepare, and the fact that they can be made ahead with a wide range of fruit choices is a big advantage. The subtle, monochromatic hues of this recipe, inspired by one from an old Florida cookbook, make this salad very elegant. To set the gelatin properly, use only canned fruits, reserving their juices for another use.

FOR THE SALAD:

2 packages (3 oz/90 g each), lemon-flavored gelatin powder
2 cups (16 fl oz/500 ml) boiling water
2 cups (16 fl oz/500 ml) cold water
20 oz (625 g) canned pineapple chunks packed in
   fruit juice, drained
16 oz (500 g) canned white grapefruit sections packed
   in fruit juice, drained
sprigs of fresh flat-leaf (Italian) parsley for garnish

FOR THE SAUCE:

1⅓ cups (11 fl oz/345 ml) lowfat mayonnaise
⅔ cup (5 fl oz/160 ml) frozen white grapefruit juice
   concentrate, thawed

❋ Lightly coat the inside and rim of a 2-qt (2-l) ring mold with vegetable cooking spray.

❋ To make the salad, in a large heatproof bowl, combine the gelatin and the boiling water and stir until the gelatin has completely dissolved. Then stir in the cold water until well blended. Pour into the prepared mold and cover tightly with plastic wrap. Refrigerate until the gelatin is partially set, 1½–2 hours. Stir in the pineapple and grapefruit until well blended. Smooth the surface, cover again and refrigerate until completely set and firm, about 4 hours.

❋ Meanwhile, to make the sauce, in a small bowl, combine the mayonnaise and grapefruit concentrate and whisk until well blended. Cover and refrigerate until ready to serve.

❋ Just before serving, invert the mold onto a serving plate. To unmold, wrap a hot, wet kitchen towel over the inverted mold for about 2 minutes. Gently lift the mold to release the salad ring. If needed, repeat the hot towel process to release the ring completely.

❋ To serve, spoon the sauce into the center of the ring and garnish with the parsley. Serve chilled, drizzling some of the sauce over each serving.

SERVES 4–6

Top to bottom: Jellied Lemon-Pineapple-Grapefruit Salad Ring, Toasted Almond Chicken Salad and Frozen Fruit Salad Luncheon

Top to bottom: Hearts of Palm Salad, West Indies Salad

WEST INDIES SALAD

This recipe is loosely adapted from Jeanne Voltz and Caroline Stuart's book The Florida Cookbook. *Though this elegant crabmeat salad was originally created at Bayley's Steak House on Mobile Bay in Alabama, recipes for it abound in neighboring states as well. The following version is more ornate than the original.*

1 lb (500 g) fresh-cooked crabmeat, picked over
   to remove cartilage and shell fragments
4 green (spring) onions, including tender green tops,
   thinly sliced
¼ cup (1½ oz/45 g) minced yellow or red bell
   pepper (capsicum)
¼ cup (2 fl oz/60 ml) white wine vinegar
¼ cup (2 fl oz/60 ml) olive oil or vegetable oil
¼ cup (2 fl oz/60 ml) ice water
½ teaspoon salt
¼ teaspoon freshly ground white pepper

2 dashes of hot pepper sauce
2 bunches watercress
2 cups (12 oz/375 g) cherry tomatoes, quartered
sprigs of watercress for garnish

❃ In a medium nonreactive bowl, place the crabmeat. Using a fork, fluff, but do not cut, the crabmeat to separate it into bite-sized pieces. Add the onions, bell pepper, vinegar, oil, ice water, salt, white pepper and hot pepper sauce. With the fork, stir gently until well blended, then fluff again. Cover tightly with plastic wrap and refrigerate for 6 hours to allow the flavors to blend.

❃ When ready to serve, drain off most of the liquid in the bowl, leaving just enough to keep the salad moist. Gently toss the salad with a fork to fluff and redistribute.

❃ To serve, line individual salad plates with a bed of watercress leaves. Place a mound of the crabmeat salad on each watercress bed, surround with cherry tomato quarters and garnish with a watercress sprig. Serve chilled at once.

SERVES 6

Florida

HEARTS OF PALM SALAD

Marjorie Kinnan Rawlings has called swamp cabbage—commercially known as hearts of palm—the "greatest of Florida vegetables." But she hesitated recommending it for eating, for fear that the state's tropical palm groves would be destroyed if demand were to grow. Hearts of palm are the white cores of sabal palms, Florida's state tree. Because the trees on public lands are protected, about the only way to savor them fresh is if they are harvested on your own property. Fortunately, canned hearts of palm (usually from Brazil) make a satisfactory substitute. In this recipe, the smooth, tender-crisp cylinders are sliced into rounds and combined with other complementary Florida flavors, including citrus and avocados. In Cross Creek Cookery, Rawlings writes that the local bears apparently appreciate the flavor of this food: In the bear region west of the St. Johns River, palms are found slashed to their roots and the hearts torn out as though by giant forks.

¼ cup (2 fl oz/60 ml) mayonnaise
3 tablespoons frozen orange juice concentrate, thawed
3 tablespoons white wine vinegar
1 tablespoon vegetable oil
1 teaspoon sugar
Bibb lettuce leaves
14 oz (440 g) canned hearts of palm, drained and sliced into thin rounds
11 oz (345 g) canned mandarin orange segments, drained
2 avocados
2 green (spring) onions, including tender green tops, thinly sliced
3 tablespoons finely chopped oil-cured black olives
¼ cup (1 oz/30 g) coarsely chopped pecans, toasted (see glossary)

❈ In a small bowl, combine the mayonnaise, orange juice concentrate, vinegar, oil and sugar and whisk until well blended. Transfer to a nonreactive airtight container, cover and refrigerate up to 24 hours or until ready to use.
❈ To prepare the salad, line 6 individual salad plates with a bed of Bibb lettuce leaves. Divide the palm heart rounds evenly among the plates and top evenly with the mandarin orange segments.
❈ Just before serving, cut each avocado in half and remove and discard the pits. Using a small melon baller, scoop out as many avocado balls as possible from each avocado half and distribute evenly among the salad plates. Drizzle the salads with half of the dressing and sprinkle with even amounts of the green onions, olives and chopped pecans. Pass the remaining dressing.

SERVES 6

South Carolina

PICKLED SHRIMP

Gray shrimp caught along the coasts of Georgia and South Carolina are cooked and tossed with a fragrant mix of lemon, herbs and spices—double the recipe for great cocktail-party fare.

1½ lb (750 g) shrimp (prawns)
1 cup (3½ oz/105 g) thinly sliced white onion
½ cup (¾ oz/20 g) finely chopped fresh parsley
½ cup (¾ oz/20 g) finely chopped fresh chives
¼ cup (2 fl oz/60 ml) fresh lemon juice
1¼ cups (10 fl oz/310 ml) vegetable oil
½ cup (4 fl oz/125 ml) apple cider vinegar
¼ cup (2 oz/60 g) sugar
2 cloves garlic, minced
1 teaspoon salt, or to taste
½ teaspoon whole peppercorns
½ teaspoon whole allspice
½ teaspoon whole cloves
4 thin lemon slices
2 bay leaves

❈ Fill a medium nonreactive saucepan with lightly salted water and bring to a boil over high heat. Add the shrimp all at once and cook until they curl and turn pink and opaque throughout, about 3 minutes. Immediately drain the shrimp in a colander and rinse to cool them under cold running water. Peel and devein the shrimp (see glossary).
❈ Using the same saucepan over low heat, combine the onion, parsley, chives, lemon juice, oil, vinegar, sugar, garlic, salt, peppercorns, allspice and cloves. Cook, stirring until the sugar has dissolved, about 2 minutes.
❈ In a medium heatproof nonreactive jar or bowl, place the shrimp and pour the hot marinade mixture over them. Tuck the lemon slices and bay leaves down the sides of the jar or bowl and let cool to room temperature. Tightly cover the jar or bowl with plastic wrap and refrigerate for 3 hours. Uncover, stir to redistribute the marinade, tightly recover and refrigerate for 3–5 hours longer, or until the shrimp take on the flavor of the marinade.
❈ To serve, strain the shrimp, discarding the marinade, and remove and discard the peppercorns, allspice, cloves, lemon slices and bay leaves. Arrange the shrimp on a serving platter and serve at once.

SERVES 6

Pickled Shrimp

South Carolina

BENNE WAFERS

Benne is the West African word for sesame seeds, which are grown in the South Carolina Low Country. It is believed that Africans aboard the slave ships brought sesame seeds to this country for good luck. Benne seeds are used to make biscuits, cookies and candies. Charleston cooks are famous for their sweet benne cookies, but there is also this savory version that yields small, thick, flavorful wafers with a texture similar to that of shortbread. If you don't want to bake them all at once, wrap the dough tightly in plastic wrap and refrigerate for up to 2 days.

1¼ cups (5 oz/155 g) benne (sesame) seeds
2⅓ cups (12 oz/375 g) all-purpose (plain) flour
1½ teaspoons salt
½ teaspoon ground cayenne pepper
½ cup (4 oz/125 g) unsalted butter, chilled
½ cup (4 oz/125 g) lard, chilled
¼ cup (2 fl oz/60 ml) ice water, or as needed

❋ Preheat an oven to 350°F (180°C). To toast the benne seeds, spread them on a baking sheet and bake, stirring frequently and spreading them evenly, until toasted light golden brown, 7–10 minutes. Set aside to cool.
❋ Lower the oven temperature to 300°F (150°C).
❋ In a medium bowl, sift together the flour, salt and cayenne. Add the butter and lard and, using a pastry blender, 2 knives or a fork, cut in until it resembles small peas. Add the toasted benne seeds and mix until well blended. Gradually add the ice water and combine until the dough just comes together, adding up to 1 tablespoon more ice water if needed. Gather the dough into a ball and divide in half.
❋ On a lightly floured work surface, roll out half the dough ¼ in (6 mm) thick. Cut into rounds using a 1-in (2.5-cm) diameter round cookie cutter and flouring between each cut. Using a floured metal spatula, carefully transfer the rounds to ungreased baking sheets, placing them ½ in (12 mm) apart. Repeat with the remaining half of the dough.
❋ Bake on the middle oven rack until the wafers are a pale tan color and lightly browned underneath, 30–35 minutes. Transfer the baking sheets to a wire rack to cool. (The wafers are too fragile to remove from the baking sheets until they are completely cool.) Store the cooled wafers in an airtight container between layers of waxed paper at room temperature for up to 2 weeks.

MAKES ABOUT 14 DOZEN WAFERS

Georgia

SPICY PECANS

Pecans come from a tree known to botanists as the Illinois hickory. Maybe it should be the Georgia hickory. While the tree thrives across the Deep South, Georgia produces far more pecans than any other state. From pecan pie to pecan-crusted trout, there's no shortage of ideas on how to use them. This is one of the simplest.

1½ teaspoons seasoning salt, garlic salt or herb salt
½ teaspoon ground cumin
½ teaspoon curry powder
2 cups (8 oz/250 g) pecan halves
1 tablespoon unsalted butter, cut into small pieces

❋ Preheat an oven to 275°F (135°C).
❋ In a small cup or ramekin, combine the seasoning, garlic

or herb salt and spices and stir until well blended.
❋ Spread the pecan halves in a shallow baking pan. Dot with the butter. Bake on the middle oven rack, about 10 minutes, until toasted completely but not darkened. Sprinkle with the seasoning mixture and stir, tossing lightly to coat the pecans evenly. Continue to bake until the pecans are deep brown and fragrant but not burned, 5–8 minutes longer.
❋ Transfer to paper towels to cool. Serve at room temperature.

MAKES 2 CUPS (8 OZ/250 G)

Florida Keys

KOKOMO

This award-winning drink recipe, which tastes something like a Creamsicle, is from Linda Gassenheimer's book Keys Cuisine. *Her recipe serves 1, but I like to share it with a friend. Choose an unusually shaped glass for this dreamy cocktail. Rub the rim of the glass with some water, dip in a bowl of shredded coconut and garnish with a slice of lime. Or, for a fanciful yet functional touch, garnish with a strip of sugarcane as a stirrer. You can purchase fresh Key limes and fresh sliced sugarcane in farmers' markets in larger cities and some gourmet stores. If you live in an area that doesn't sell fresh Key limes, you can purchase the bottled juice or mail-order it (see Mail Order Sources).*

1 fl oz (30 ml) Nassau Royale, Cuarenta y Tres or other vanilla-flavored liqueur
1 fl oz (30 ml) Malibu coconut rum
⅓ cup (3 fl oz/80 ml) Coco Lopez cream of coconut
2 tablespoons Key lime juice
¼ cup (2 fl oz/60 ml) fresh orange juice
2 cups crushed ice

❋ In a blender, place all the ingredients and blend until thick and frothy. Serve at once.

SERVES 1 OR 2

Georgia

SUGARED PECANS

This recipe, provided by the Georgia Department of Agriculture, makes an addictive snack or a candylike finger food to serve at a cocktail party. Stored in pretty containers, they're also popular for gift-giving during the holidays.

1 cup (8 oz/250 g) sugar
⅓ cup (3 fl oz/80 ml) canned evaporated milk, undiluted
1 teaspoon ground cinnamon
1 tablespoon unsalted butter
1 teaspoon vanilla extract (essence)
dash of salt
3 cups (12 oz/375 g) pecan halves

❋ Lightly butter a baking sheet.
❋ In a medium saucepan over medium heat, combine the sugar, milk, cinnamon and butter. Bring to a boil, stirring occasionally, until the sugar has dissolved and the butter has melted, about 1 minute. Remove from the heat and stir in the vanilla, salt and pecans.
❋ Working quickly, spread the hot pecan mixture onto the prepared baking sheet. Let cool completely, then, using your fingers, separate the pecans. Serve at room temperature.

MAKES ABOUT 4 CUPS (16 OZ/500 G)

Clockwise from left: Kokomo, Sugared Pecans, Spicy Pecans, Benne Wafers

Clockwise from left: Fried Dill Pickles, Boiled Peanuts,
French-fried Peanuts

Mississippi

FRIED DILL PICKLES

This recipe has its roots deep in Mississippi. Some say Fried Dill Pickles were created at the Cock of the Walk, a popular catfish restaurant in Natchez and Jackson. Others say the pickles originated in Hollywood, Mississippi, at the local café. Fried Dill Pickles pair perfectly with fried catfish or with just an ice-cold mug of beer. Use the best dill pickles you can find—not those bland serrated hamburger pickles but good garlicky ones. Baby dill pickles work best, but you can use larger varieties. The pickles need a dunk in both wet and dry batters before being deep-fried. If you prefer a thicker coating, dip them twice.

1 egg
1 cup (8 fl oz/250 ml) milk
2 teaspoons Worcestershire sauce
¼ teaspoon hot pepper sauce
¼ teaspoon ground cayenne pepper
¼ teaspoon garlic powder
salt and fresh ground black pepper to taste
1½ cups (7½ oz/235 g) all-purpose (plain) flour
vegetable oil for frying
10 baby dill pickles, cut crosswise into slices
 ¼ in (6 mm) thick

❀ In a shallow bowl, beat together the egg and milk. Add the Worcestershire sauce, hot pepper sauce, cayenne, garlic powder and salt and pepper. Stir well and set aside. In a small bowl, place the flour and season it well with salt and pepper.
❀ Preheat an oven to 200°F (93°C).
❀ In a large, heavy saucepan over medium-high heat, pour the oil to a depth of 2 in (5 cm) and heat to 350°F (180°C) on a deep-fry thermometer. A few at a time, dip the pickle slices first in the egg mixture and then in the seasoned flour. Drop carefully into the hot oil and, using a slotted spoon, move the pickles around to brown evenly, about 1 minute. Remove with the slotted spoon to paper towels to drain. Repeat with the remaining pickles, keeping the fried pickles warm in the oven until all are ready to serve. Serve hot.

SERVES 4

Georgia

BOILED PEANUTS

The smoking black cauldron and homey hand-lettered sign of a boiled peanut stand are familiar sights along the country roads of Georgia, the nation's top peanut-producing state. Boiled peanuts surprise the uninitiated. After cooking in brine for all that time, the peanuts are less like nuts than soft, salty peas. The Georgia Peanut Commission suggests this recipe for making them at home. If green peanuts cannot be found, substitute mature ones.

1 lb (500 g) green (immature) peanuts or mature peanuts, in
 the shell
4 qt (4 l) water
3 tablespoons salt

❀ In a large colander, rinse the peanuts in their shells under cool, running water and gently rub them with your fingers to remove any soil or particles. Remove and discard any blemished peanuts. If using mature peanuts, place in a large bowl, add water to cover and soak for 8 hours.
❀ In a large pot over high heat, combine the peanuts, water and salt and bring to a boil. Reduce the heat to low, cover and simmer, stirring occasionally, about 50 minutes. If using mature peanuts, cook over medium heat, uncovered, about 4 hours. Test for doneness by breaking open a peanut shell; the nuts inside should be the texture of cooked peas or beans.
❀ Drain the peanuts. When cool enough to handle, remove the shells and serve warm.
❀ Alternatively, store the cooled boiled peanuts in their shells in an airtight container and freeze for up to 1 month. Reheat in a microwave oven.

MAKES ABOUT 2½ CUPS (1 LB/500 G)

Georgia

FRENCH-FRIED PEANUTS

In 1794 Thomas Jefferson recorded the cultivation of peanuts at Monticello. Since the Civil War, peanuts have found their way into a variety of cuisines. Here is an interesting and delicious way to serve and enjoy peanuts—courtesy of the Georgia Peanut Commission. It takes approximately 1⅓ pounds (about 21 oz/655 g) of unshelled peanuts to make 3 cups (18 oz/ 560 g) of shelled peanuts.

1½ cups (12 fl oz/375 ml) peanut oil
3 cups (18 oz/560 g) shelled, raw peanuts
salt to taste

❀ In a deep-fat fryer or electric frying pan, heat the oil to 350°F (180°C) on a deep-fry thermometer.
❀ Working in batches, submerge the peanuts 1 cup (6 oz/185 g) at a time into the oil for 2–4 minutes, or until the peanuts begin to turn a light golden color. Using a slotted spoon, remove the peanuts and transfer to a baking sheet lined with paper towels to drain.
❀ Sprinkle the peanuts with salt and serve warm.

MAKES 3 CUPS (18 OZ/560 G)

The South

SAUSAGE PINWHEELS

For these delightfully spicy rounds of biscuit dough and country pork sausage, be sure to use the best-quality bulk sausage (not links) that you can find. These pinwheels freeze and reheat beautifully.

2 cups (10 oz/315 g) all-purpose (plain) flour
2 tablespoons white cornmeal
2 teaspoons baking powder
½ teaspoon salt
¼ cup (2 oz/60 g) vegetable shortening
¾ cup (6 fl oz/180 ml) milk
3 tablespoons Dijon-style mustard
1 lb (500 g) spicy bulk pork sausage
paprika for garnish

❈ In a medium bowl, combine the flour, cornmeal, baking powder and salt. Add the shortening and, using a pastry blender, 2 knives or a fork, cut in until it resembles coarse crumbs. Gradually add the milk and combine with a fork until the dough just comes together.

❈ On a lightly floured work surface, knead the dough lightly with floured hands. Divide the dough in half, forming each part into a flat disk. Roll each disk into a square ¼ in (6 mm) thick. Neatly trim the edges to make a 9-in (23-cm) square. Lay a kitchen towel, with long side facing you, on a work surface. Carefully, so as not to tear the pastry, place one of the squares on top of the towel.

❈ Evenly spread half of the mustard on top of the pastry square all the way to the edges. Then spread half of the sausage, leaving a 1-in (2.5-cm) margin on all sides. Using the towel to help, roll up the pastry tightly lengthwise, enclosing the filling like a jelly-roll (Swiss roll). Repeat with the remaining pastry square, mustard and sausage. Wrap the logs in plastic wrap and refrigerate seam side down for 1 hour.

❈ Preheat an oven to 375°F (190°C).

❈ Unwrap and, using a heavy, straight-edged knife, slice the logs into pinwheels ⅔ in (18 mm) thick. Using a spatula, place the pinwheels ½ in (12 mm) apart on ungreased baking sheets. Bake on the middle oven rack until the pastry is crisp and golden brown and the pork is cooked throughout with no pink remaining, about 20 minutes. Lightly dust each pinwheel with paprika and serve at once.

SERVES 8–10

Lynchburg, Tennessee

LYNCHBURG LEMONADE

This lemonade, whose namesake is the home of Tennessee's famous sippin' whiskey, is strictly for adults. The libation comes from Jack Daniel's Spirit of Tennessee Cookbook *by The Jack Daniel Distillery. Great by the glass, or increase the recipe proportionately to make a pitcher. Fresh cherries may be substituted for maraschino.*

1 fl oz (30 ml) Jack Daniel's whiskey
1 fl oz (30 ml) Triple Sec
1 fl oz (30 ml) bottled sweet-and-sour mix
4 fl oz (125 ml) Sprite (lemon-lime soda)
crushed ice
lemon slices and maraschino or fresh cherries for garnish

In a tall glass, combine the Jack Daniel's whiskey, Triple Sec, sweet-and-sour mix and Sprite. Add ice and stir. Garnish with lemon slices and cherries.

SERVES 1

The South

FRONT PORCH LEMONADE

Nothing can quench thirst better than an ice-cold tumbler of lemonade, especially during a hot summer afternoon in the South. When children come to visit, greet them with a pitcher of "pink lemonade"—just tint this recipe with a few drops of red food coloring before serving.

zest strips from 1 lemon (see glossary)
1⅔ cups (13 oz/400 g) sugar
½ cup (4 fl oz/125 ml) cold water
1½ cups (12 fl oz/375 ml) fresh lemon juice,
    from about 12–13 small lemons
4½ cups (36 fl oz/1.1 l) ice water
finely crushed ice
lemon slices for garnish

❈ To make the lemon syrup, in a small saucepan over very low heat, combine the lemon zest, sugar and the ½ cup (4 fl oz/125 ml) cold water. Bring to a simmer, stirring until the sugar has dissolved, 3–4 minutes. Remove from the heat and let the syrup mixture cool completely in the saucepan. Then remove and discard the zest. The lemon syrup can be stored in an airtight container in the refrigerator for up to 1 month.

❈ To serve, in a large glass pitcher, combine the syrup, lemon juice and the 4½ cups (36 fl oz/1.15 l) ice water and stir until well blended. Serve in glass tumblers over crushed ice, garnished with lemon slices.

SERVES 6

Clockwise from top: Front Porch Lemonade, Lynchburg Lemonade, Sausage Pinwheels

Café Brûlot

Louisiana

CAFÉ BRÛLOT

In the theatrical experience of New Orleans dining, Café Brûlot is a rousing finale. Brûlot means "burned brandy" in French. The waiter who does the burning stands before the table like a Creole shaman and—poof!—makes fire. There's something thrillingly elemental about it. As the Federal Writers Project guide to New Orleans commented, "This can be very effective if the lights are turned out and the shadows allowed to play on the faces of the guests."

1 cinnamon stick, about 3 in (7.5 cm) long, broken into pieces
6 whole cloves
4 sugar cubes
2 orange zest strips, about 3 in (7.5 cm) long (see glossary)
1 lemon zest strip, about 3 in (7.5 cm) long (see glossary)
½ cup (4 fl oz/125 ml) brandy
2 cups (16 fl oz/500 ml) hot, double-strength coffee, made with 1½ cups (1½ oz/45 g) ground coffee

❀ In the blazer pan of a chafing dish, combine the cinnamon, cloves, 3 of the sugar cubes, orange and lemon zest and brandy.

❀ Place the blazer pan over the chafing dish burner. Heat the mixture, stirring occasionally, until it just comes to a simmer and the sugar has dissolved, about 5 minutes. Meanwhile, heat a long-handled metal ladle (preferably silver) in a small saucepan of hot water.

❀ Carefully remove the blazer pan from the heat and extinguish the burner. Using the warmed ladle, dip up some of the brandy mixture and place the remaining sugar cube in it. Very carefully, at arm's length, ignite the liquid in the ladle with a long-stemmed fireplace match. Cautiously lower the "flaming" ladle into the blazer pan to ignite all of the liquid. Working quickly, stir with the ladle, using a dipping and pouring back motion to release some of the flaming liquid, until the sugar cube has completely dissolved, about 3 minutes.

❀ While the mixture is still flaming, slowly add the hot coffee to the blazer pan, pouring it against the edge of the pan so as not to extinguish the flames. Using the ladle, stir to blend in the coffee. When the flames die out, ladle into café brûlot or demitasse cups and serve at once.

SERVES 4

Georgia

PECAN-SMOKED TROUT SPREAD

Ray L. Overton III, a culinary consultant, author and teacher, created this recipe, which reflects his relaxed approach to simple but stylish entertaining. He prefers this spread made with Georgia brook trout that has been smoked over applewood and cider-cooked pecan shells, but you don't need to be a fisherman to enjoy this—smoked trout is readily available in well-stocked supermarket delicatessens and fish markets. Smoked trout can be purchased in 1 pound quantities or more, so the large yield of this recipe makes great party fare for 10–15 people, when served with crackers or sliced French bread and a few other hors d'oeuvres. This spread can be made and refrigerated up to 3 days ahead. Leftover spread makes a delectable sandwich—just top with lettuce and tomato.

1 lb (500 g) smoked trout, deboned and skin removed
1 cup (4 oz/125 g) coarsely chopped pecans, lightly toasted
  (see glossary)
1 lb (16 oz/500 g) cream cheese, at room temperature
1 cup (8 oz/250 g) sour cream
½ cup (4 fl oz/125 ml) mayonnaise
¼ cup (2 fl oz/60 ml) pepper-flavored vodka
¼ cup (2 fl oz/60 ml) fresh lemon juice
2 tablespoons Dijon-style mustard
2 tablespoons prepared horseradish
1½ tablespoons finely chopped fresh dill
3 tablespoons capers, rinsed and drained
freshly ground pepper to taste
4 green (spring) onions, including tender green tops,
  thinly sliced
sprigs of fresh dill for garnish

❀ Pick through the smoked trout, removing and discarding any small bones, and then flake the trout. In a large bowl, combine the toasted pecans, cream cheese, sour cream, mayonnaise, vodka, lemon juice, mustard, horseradish, dill, capers and half of the smoked trout and stir until just lightly blended. Working in batches, place one-third of the trout mixture in the bowl of a food processor fitted with the metal blade or in a blender. Process until smooth, using a

rubber spatula to scrape down the sides. Transfer the mixture to a medium bowl. Repeat with the remaining 2 batches. Fold in the pepper, green onions and remaining flaked smoked trout.

❀ To serve, place the spread in a serving bowl, ramekin or crock and garnish with dill sprigs.

MAKES 4 CUPS (2 LB/1 KG)   *Photograph pages 30–31*

Donaldsonville, Louisiana

OYSTER AND ANDOUILLE PASTRIES

Louisiana chef and PBS cooking star John Folse is owner of two south Louisiana restaurants—Lafitte's Landing in Donaldsonville and White Oak Plantation in Baton Rouge. Folse calls this recipe an example of the evolution of Cajun and Creole cooking. Fresh oysters and spicy andouille sausage are added to a classic butter sauce and served on puff pastry squares.

1 package frozen puff pastry, thawed
1 egg, beaten

FOR THE SAUCE:

¼ cup (2 oz/60 g) unsalted butter, at room temperature
½ cup (4 oz/125 g) finely chopped andouille sausage
  (see glossary)
1 teaspoon minced garlic
½ cup (2 oz/60 g) sliced fresh mushrooms
¼ cup (1 oz/30 g) finely chopped green (spring) onion tops
¼ cup (2 oz/60 g) finely chopped tomatoes
¼ cup (1½ oz/45 g) finely chopped red bell
  pepper (capsicum)
2 dozen fresh shucked oysters, drained, reserving the liquid
¼ cup (2 fl oz/60 ml) Champagne
1 cup (8 fl oz/250 ml) heavy (double) cream
½ cup (4 oz/125 g) unsalted butter, chilled, cut into
  ¼-in (6 mm) pieces
salt and freshly ground pepper to taste

❀ Preheat an oven to 400°F (200°C). Lightly butter a baking sheet.

❀ Lay one sheet of puff pastry on top of the other and cut into six 3-in (7.5-cm) squares. Reserve the remaining pastry for another use. Place the puff pastry squares on the baking sheet and brush the tops with the beaten egg. Bake until golden brown, 10–12 minutes. Remove from the oven and keep warm.

❀ To make the sauce, in a large skillet over medium-high heat, melt the ¼ cup (2 oz/60 g) butter. Add the sausage, garlic, mushrooms, green onions, tomatoes and bell pepper. Sauté, stirring, until the vegetables are wilted, 3–5 minutes. Add the oysters, oyster liquid and Champagne, stirring to loosen any browned bits from the bottom and sides of the skillet. Cook, stirring, until the oysters are opaque and the edges begin to curl, about 2 minutes. Do not overcook. Remove the oysters with a slotted spoon and set aside.

❀ Add the cream to the skillet and bring to a boil over medium-high heat. Reduce the cream by half, about 20 minutes, lowering the heat to medium if it begins to boil over. When the cream has thickened to sauce consistency, gradually add the pieces of butter, swirling the pan until all the butter has been incorporated. Return the oysters to the skillet, add salt and pepper and stir to blend.

❀ To serve, split the warm pastry squares in half. Arrange the bottom halves on a plate and spoon the oyster sauce over them. Top with the pastry square tops and serve.

SERVES 6   *Photograph pages 30–31*

Tomato Aspic

The South

TOMATO ASPIC

Tangy, warmly spiced Tomato Aspic was once served throughout the South at elegant luncheons. It seems that aspic salads, in particular those with a vegetable foundation, are again gaining in popularity. This version uses fresh tarragon.

2½ cups (20 fl oz/625 ml) tomato juice
2 tablespoons (2 envelopes) unflavored gelatin powder
¼ cup (2 fl oz/60 ml) cold water
2 tablespoons fresh lemon juice
2 tablespoons sugar
½ teaspoon salt
¼ teaspoon ground cloves
¼ teaspoon ground allspice
½ teaspoon freshly ground pepper
1 tablespoon minced fresh tarragon
½ cup (2½ oz/75 g) finely chopped celery
3 tablespoons minced yellow onion
2 or 3 dashes hot pepper sauce, or to taste
Bibb lettuce leaves for serving
sprigs of fresh tarragon for garnish (optional)

❋ Lightly coat the interior and rim of an 8-in (20-cm) square glass baking dish or 2-qt (2-l) heatproof ring mold with vegetable cooking spray.
❋ In a large nonreactive saucepan over medium heat, bring the tomato juice to a boil, stirring occasionally. Remove from the heat and set aside.
❋ Sprinkle the gelatin over the cold water and let stand for 1 minute to soften. To the saucepan of hot tomato juice, add the gelatin, lemon juice, sugar, salt, cloves, allspice and pepper and stir until the gelatin and sugar have dissolved. Refrigerate, stirring occasionally, until the mixture begins to thicken, 30–40 minutes. Stir in the minced tarragon, celery, onion and hot pepper sauce.
❋ Working quickly, pour the mixture into the prepared dish. Cover with plastic wrap and refrigerate until set, about 1 hour.
❋ To serve, cut into 8 rectangles. Line individual salad plates with lettuce leaves and place one rectangle of aspic on each plate. Garnish with tarragon sprigs, if desired. Serve chilled.

SERVES 8

Kentucky

MINT JULEPS

There are many fervent opinions in Kentucky on how to make a proper mint julep. One school holds that juleps should be sipped without a straw so that the bourbon dilutes as it passes through the ice. Others insist on a short straw that allows the drinker to get a whiff of the mint sprigs. Then there's the faction that crushes the mint to release its flavor. Their opponents believe in being gentler with the mint. Whatever the technique, the goal is to make, as Kentucky statesman Henry Clay put it, "a silvery mixture as smooth as some rare Egyptian oil." While proportions and methods may differ (some even dispute whether or not the glass should be frosted) it is agreed that a well-constructed julep in a sterling-silver Julep cup (an item which has existed since at least the early 1800s) is essential for Derby Day—or just about any day.

Of all the methods of making mint juleps, the technique in this recipe for infusing a sugar syrup with mint draws the most flavor from this soothing herb. This recipe for mint syrup is enough for 10 Mint Juleps, 10 fluid ounces (310 ml) each. If you use smaller or larger glasses, simply adjust the amount of syrup and bourbon accordingly to taste, for a smooth but potent drink.

20 large sprigs fresh mint
2 cups (1 lb/500 g) sugar
2 cups (16 fl oz/500 ml) water
crushed ice
2½ cups (20 fl oz/625 ml) aged Kentucky bourbon

❦ Rinse the mint sprigs and pat completely dry. Select 10 of the sprigs for garnish and set aside. Place the remaining 10 mint sprigs between double layers of paper towels and, using a rolling pin, roll to bruise the mint.

❦ To make the mint syrup, in a medium saucepan over low heat, combine the sugar, water and bruised mint. Slowly bring to a boil, reduce the heat to very low and simmer, stirring, until the sugar has dissolved, about 5 minutes. Remove from the heat and let the syrup mixture cool completely in the saucepan. Then remove and discard the mint. The mint syrup can be stored in an airtight container in the refrigerator for up to 1 month.

❦ To serve, for each Mint Julep, pour ¼ cup (2 fl oz/60 ml) of the syrup into a silver cup or glass goblet. Fill the cup to the top with finely crushed ice. As soon as a frost forms on the outside of the cup, pour in ¼ cup (2 fl oz/60 ml) bourbon. Alternatively, briefly place the cup of syrup and ice in a freezer just long enough to form a frost; then add the bourbon. Using a long-handled bar spoon, with a chopping motion, stir together the syrup, bourbon and ice. Garnish with the reserved mint sprigs and serve at once.

SERVES 10

The South

BLACKBERRY CORDIAL

This cinnamon-and-clove-spiced potable has been made in American homes since colonial times. The use of wild berries is preferred, but the flavor resulting from fresh cultivated berries is also charming. This libation makes a stunning gift when packaged in a decorative bottle.

3 cups (12 oz/375 g) ripe blackberries
3 cups (1½ lb/750 g) sugar
3 cups (24 fl oz/750 ml) water
2 cinnamon sticks, each 3 in (7.5 cm) long and
    broken in half
4 whole cloves
¾ cup (6 fl oz/180 ml) premium French brandy

❦ In a food processor fitted with the metal blade or in a food mill fitted with the coarse disk, briefly purée the blackberries to a coarse consistency.

❦ Set a jelly bag or a fine-meshed sieve lined with 2 layers of dampened cheesecloth (muslin) over a large nonreactive bowl. Pour the purée into the jelly bag or sieve and let the juice drip through for about 3 minutes. When it slows to an occasional drip, press firmly on the purée with the back of a large spoon to yield more juice, being careful not to force any pulp through. The purée should yield 1½–1⅔ cups (12–13 fl oz/375–410 ml) of juice. Discard the pulp and set the juice aside.

❦ In a large, heavy nonreactive saucepan over medium heat, combine the sugar, water, cinnamon and cloves. Heat the mixture, stirring often, for about 4 minutes. When the sugar begins to dissolve, reduce the heat to low. Continue to heat, stirring constantly, until the sugar has completely dissolved and the mixture is clear, 4–6 minutes longer. Remove from the heat and transfer the sugar mixture to a medium nonreactive bowl. Let stand at room temperature to cool completely. Remove and discard the spices. Gently whisk the blackberry juice and brandy into the cooled sugar mixture until well blended.

❦ Using a funnel, pour the Blackberry Cordial into dry, sterilized bottles, leaving ½ in (12 mm) headspace. Cap or cork, using new corks, and store the bottles in the refrigerator. Let the cordial mellow in the refrigerator for 3 weeks. Store refrigerated for up to 6 months. Serve at room temperature.

MAKES 4 PINT-SIZE BOTTLES

Left to right: Blackberry Cordial, Mint Julep

Atlanta, Georgia

CHAMPAGNE PEACH CUP

A bubbly punch, usually made effervescent by the addition of Champagne, is often called a cup in the South. This Champagne Peach Cup is served with a lovely floating ice ring.

32 oz (1 kg) canned sliced peaches packed in fruit juice, undrained
⅓ cup (3 fl oz/80 ml) grenadine syrup
½ cup (4 oz/125 g) sugar
1 bottle (750 ml) dry white wine, chilled
1 bottle (750 ml) Champagne, chilled
sprigs of fresh mint for garnish

until the sugar has dissolved. Cover and refrigerate.

❋ Chill a 6–8-qt (6–8-l) punch bowl and punch cups in the refrigerator. Alternatively, fill the punch bowl with sealed plastic bags of ice for 30 minutes before serving.

❋ Just before serving, remove the ice ring from the mold by inverting the mold onto a plate and wrapping a hot, wet kitchen towel over the inverted mold for about 1 minute. Gently lift the mold to release the ice ring. If needed, repeat the hot towel process to release the ring completely.

❋ Working quickly, in the chilled punch bowl, combine the white wine mixture and Champagne until well blended. Carefully slide the ice ring, rounded side up, from the plate into the punch bowl and garnish with the mint sprigs. Serve the punch in chilled cups.

SERVES 10–12 *Photograph pages 30–31*

Yuletide Eggnog

Kentucky

YULETIDE EGGNOG

Over the years people have spiked their nog with everything from red wine and brandy to sherry and rum. But in the South, if it's spiked at all, it's almost always spiked with—what else?—bourbon. Serving eggnog during the holidays, from Christmas through New Year's, is a tradition for many. This recipe starts with a cooked-custard base (an idea suggested by a recipe in Eating Well *magazine), which eliminates any risk of salmonella poisoning.*

5 cups (40 fl oz/1.25 l) heavy (double) cream
3½ cups (28 fl oz/875 ml) milk
¼ cup (1 oz/30 g) cornstarch (corn flour)
½ cup (4 fl oz/125 ml) cold water
1¼ cups (10 oz/315 g) sugar
6 eggs, lightly beaten
3 teaspoons vanilla extract (essence)
1 cup (8 fl oz/250 ml) aged Kentucky bourbon
½ cup (4 fl oz/125 ml) Cognac
ice cubes
freshly grated nutmeg for garnish

❋ In a large, heavy nonreactive saucepan over medium-high heat, whisk together the cream and milk. Cook, whisking often, until scalded (when you can see steam rising and small bubbles appear around the edge, just below the boiling point), about 10 minutes. Transfer to a large, nonreactive heatproof bowl and set aside.

❋ In a small bowl, whisk together the cornstarch and cold water until well blended. In the same saucepan over medium heat, whisk together the sugar, cornstarch mixture and eggs. Gradually add the scalded milk mixture in a slow, steady stream while whisking continuously.

❋ Cook, whisking frequently, for about 15 minutes, until the custard is thick enough to coat the back of a spoon. Do not let the mixture boil or the eggs will curdle.

❋ Remove from the heat and whisk in the vanilla until blended. Strain through a fine-meshed sieve into the large, heatproof nonreactive bowl. Let the mixture cool completely, whisking often to speed cooling. Then cover tightly with plastic wrap and refrigerate for 4–6 hours or until completely chilled.

❋ Just before serving, whisk first the bourbon and then the Cognac into the chilled mixture until thoroughly blended.

❋ For each serving, in a blender, combine 1 cup (8 fl oz/ 250 ml) of the eggnog and 1 ice cube and blend on high until frothy, about 10 seconds. Pour into an eggnog cup, sprinkle with nutmeg and serve at once.

SERVES 10

❋ In a food processor fitted with a metal blade or in a blender, purée the peaches with their juice just long enough to leave a few medium pieces remaining.

❋ Transfer the purée to a 1–1½-qt (1–1.5-l) ring mold in an even layer. Cover tightly with plastic wrap and freeze overnight or until thoroughly frozen.

❋ In a large nonreactive bowl, whisk together the grenadine and sugar until well blended. Add the white wine and whisk

Georgia & the Piedmont

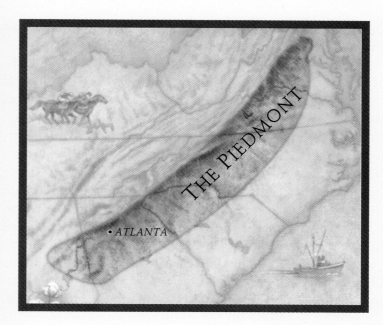

GEORGIA & THE PIEDMONT

"South of the North, yet north of the South, lies the City of Hundred Hills, peering out from the shadows of the past into the promise of the future." W. E. B. Du Bois was a professor at Atlanta University when he wrote those words about his new home at the dawn of the twentieth century. They still ring true. Atlanta, the closest thing the South has to a capital, has always been a cultural crossroads.

The city of the Centennial Olympics anchors the southern end of a region characterized by its in-between topography. The Piedmont curves 750 miles from the horse country of Virginia through the core of North Carolina to the up-country of South Carolina and the red clay hills of Georgia and western Alabama. It was all mountains once, and you can see a remnant here and there in outcrops like Stone Mountain, the granite leviathan east of Atlanta. Erosion reduced the rest to gently rolling hills, hence the word *piedmont,* from the foothills area of the same name in Italy. Hills—or the lack of them—define the Piedmont. The region is sandwiched between the blue-green uprising of the Appalachian Mountains to the north and the scrub-pine flatness of the coastal plain to the south. The lower boundary follows the Fall Line, the edge of an ancient sea, where rivers

Previous pages: A glow of hope emanates from the lights of the Martin Luther King, Jr. National Housing Project, framing this view of downtown Atlanta, Georgia. Left: Catfish fishermen launch their boat onto a lake outside Albany, Georgia. Fishing for the bottom feeders may become a lost art: Since 1960, hundreds of fields have been converted into commercial catfish farms to feed growing demand.

tumble over shoals—and a string of cities arose to exploit the ready water power.

The Creek and Cherokee peoples inhabited the southern reaches of the Piedmont until they were pushed off the land in the early 1800s. The first white settlements were little more than frontier outposts. George Washington visited one of them, Charlotte, North Carolina, during a presidential tour in the 1790s and dismissed it as a "trifling place." Had he lived to see it, he might also have said the same thing about early Atlanta. Today they are the two largest population centers of the Piedmont—Charlotte, more than one million; Atlanta, in excess of three million.

Founded in 1837, more than a century after James Oglethorpe landed in Savannah, Atlanta has never possessed the Old South charm of Georgia's first city. Indeed, *Gone With the Wind* (at least the film version) misleads people about antebellum days in the Georgia Piedmont. In her novel, Margaret Mitchell described the mansion Tara as an ugly, sprawling, columnless thing. "This section of north Georgia was new and crude compared with other sections of the South, and white columns are the exception rather than the rule," she wrote to a friend. Hollywood ignored her and made Tara look more like a Tidewater plantation.

Though the lower portion of the Piedmont did spawn cotton plantations, the generally thin topsoil was easily washed away. Underneath lies that famous red clay Scarlett O'Hara scratched through in her frantic hunt for food after the Yankees had laid waste to Atlanta and begun their march to the sea. As you'll recall, she shook a radish at the heavens and vowed never to go hungry again.

It took a while, but her patch of the South eventually made good on that promise. In the early 1900s the leaders of the Piedmont realized that their people would be better off spinning cotton in mills rather than trying to grow it. Henry Grady, an Atlanta newspaperman and silver-tongued orator, was the first to preach the gospel of industrialization in the 1880s. He called his vision the New South, and it took root like nowhere else in the difficult soil of the Piedmont.

By World World II, cheap, abundant labor had drawn much of the textile industry from New England and transformed the Piedmont—especially the Carolinas—into a landscape of mill towns. Textiles have been declining in recent years, but new enterprises such as auto-making and pharmaceuticals have more than replaced the lost jobs. Today, business magazines marvel at the growth along Interstate 85, the Piedmont's main

The thirteenth and last of the British colonies, Georgia was named after King George II by General James Oglethorpe in 1733.

Though burnt to the ground in 1864 by Union General William Tecumseh Sherman's troops,
Atlanta has since experienced an unrivaled comeback: Its cultural diversity, strong business
tradition and gracious hospitality have earned it a stellar reputation.

Two men stop to swap stories in Westville, Georgia, where locals have created a living history museum incorporating a working village of authentic homes and shops built before 1850.

street. From booming white-collar Atlanta to the banking center of Charlotte to the high-tech Research Triangle Park near Raleigh-Durham, this swath of the South attracts increasing numbers of newcomers from drawl-less climes. As a result, the suburbs of the Piedmont have become the South's latest cultural fault line. The culinary consequences are working themselves out, but it is worth noting that *National Geographic* magazine counted more sushi restaurants than barbecue joints within five miles of the Research Triangle Park.

The Piedmont's food heritage, like its topography, is for the most part a blending of other Southern regions. It does have its specialties, though. Coca-Cola, concocted by an Atlanta pharmacist in 1886, became the most famous product in the South, if not the world. Poultry is produced and consumed in great bulk throughout the Piedmont.

This also is peach country, as anyone knows who has driven I-85 past Gaffney, South Carolina, where the Big Peach water tower looms above the orchards. Georgia and South Carolina grow more peaches than any state outside of California, and local cooks use them in everything from pies to pizza.

Then there's barbecue, for which North Carolinians have a special flair. They typically smoke a whole hog, pull and chop the meat, and serve it with hush puppies, coleslaw and a thin vinegary sauce that contains a little tomato west of Raleigh and none at all east of there. In Lexington, a Piedmont town of 16,000, lacquer fumes from furniture factories mingle with smoke from an incredible sixteen barbecue restaurants. Like several other places in the South, Lexington claims to be *the* barbecue capital.

Atlanta reflects all these traditions and more. For years people from outside the South and from all over the South have moved to the swelling metropolitan area and brought their foodways with them. They have spurred a thriving and varied dining scene with representatives of almost every cuisine in the world; in fact, a 1995 study by the National Restaurant Association showed that Atlantans spend a higher percentage of their food budget eating out than residents in any other U.S. city.

It wasn't always that way. One 1940s guidebook placed Atlanta squarely in the hush-yo'-mouth school of cooking: "She is a hot-bread, boiled-greens, fried-chicken-and-cream-gravy town, where you are apt to get a dish of hot grits for breakfast, extra for free, whether you order it or not." Atlanta was sleepier and more stereotypically Southern then. Its best-known restaurants had names like Mammy's Shanty and Aunt Fanny's Cabin.

Ever striving, Atlanta yearned for a more sophisticated image as it grew during the 1960s and 1970s, billing itself as "The World's Next International City." In the process, many forward-looking Atlantans came to regard down-home Southern food as unsophisticated. Scott Peacock learned the hard way when he was executive chef at the Georgia governor's mansion. He planned an all-Southern dinner during the 1988 Democratic National Convention, but the menu did not pass muster. Couldn't he come up with something a little, well, classier? He ended up serving Maine lobster and chicken, a surf-and-scratch combo that could have come from Anywhere, U.S.A.

Peacock understood the psychology of this sort of thinking. It was a regional inferiority complex. He had once had it, too. As a boy in Alabama, he never gave a second thought to the classic Southern cooking going on in his family's kitchen. "I thought cooking was something you watched Julia Child do on TV," he says.

It was Edna Lewis, a venerable chef and cookbook author from the Virginia end of the Piedmont, who opened his eyes. Upon meeting her, the young Peacock announced his plans to go abroad and study Italian cuisine. *"What's wrong with Southern?"* she wanted to know.

Peacock and Lewis eventually cofounded the Society for the Preservation of Southern Food, an Atlanta-based group that would like to function as a sort of regional trust for culinary heritage. Peacock also put his convictions to work as chef at the Horseradish Grill, one of a class of new Atlanta restaurants that celebrates traditional Southern cooking and makes liberal use of local produce such as peaches, peanuts and sweet Vidalia onions from south Georgia. The *Atlanta Journal-Constitution* lists these restaurants under their own heading—Southern—as if they served Thai, Southwestern or some other cuisine. Not too many years ago, none of those categories would have been necessary; it was *all* Southern in Atlanta.

The New Southern restaurants don't bring grits without asking like the old ones did. But they do bring grits entrées with shrimp paste, smoked trout and a dozen other toppings. Atlanta chef Tim Patridge finds it all a little amusing. "These days," he says, "it's getting hard to find a regular old bowl of grits around here."

The sunset casts a glorious light over watermelon fields outside Cordele, Georgia.

SOUPS &
STEWS

A favorite ingredient in many traditional Southern dishes, okra was brought to the United States by slaves from West Africa.

SOUPS & STEWS

In all of Southern cooking, there's nothing as mysterious as stew. Whether it's burgoo, muddle, Frogmore or Brunswick stew, the menfolk generally make it, and they generally don't talk a lot about what's in it. Stew seems to have as much to do with sorcery as with cookery.

They haul out a big black washpot that has been in somebody's family since the movies were silent. They build a hardwood fire before dawn and throw large quantities of animal and plant life into the pot. They stir the brew for hours with an oar, adjusting flavors according to the taste buds of the most experienced stewmeister among them. Then, with bleary eyes, they ladle it out to family, church or some other large gathering. If someone asks for the recipe, they'll oblige, making sure to leave out something.

Centuries of ritual and folklore reside in the stews and soups of the South. Some are almost tourist attractions, so wrapped up in a place have they become. Visit Charleston and let your senses swim in the creamy tang of she-crab soup. Tour Kentucky in a bubbling pot of burgoo. Don't dare come back from New Orleans without some gumbo and jambalaya in your palate's souvenir scrapbook.

Being regional icons, such foods naturally provoke spirited discussion. Take Brunswick stew, the hearty, muddy stuff many Southerners eat with barbecue. Food historians agree that Native Americans and frontiersfolk made something like it using just about any critters they could catch, especially squirrels. But no one agrees where

the name Brunswick came from. Brunswick, Georgia; Brunswick County, Virginia; and Brunswick County, North Carolina, all claim to have originated the stew. (Virginia's claim wins the most votes.) Others say it was named for Caroline of Brunswick, wife of King George III.

But why fight over history when you can fight over recipes? Southerners have been known to lock horns over which vegetables are properly dumped into

Many Southerners take advantage of their favorable climate by growing their own vegetables in backyard gardens.

Previous pages: Left to right: Chicken Jambalaya (recipe page 72), She-Crab Soup (recipe page 70), Chilled Local Peach and Virginia Riesling Soup (recipe page 79)

A fresh crop of blue crab awaits packing at the Crab Connection of Chauvin, Louisiana.

Brunswick stew. Some add onions, potatoes and lima beans. "Why, that's vegetable soup!" purists scoff, giving their sanction only to corn and tomatoes.

Burgoo, a similar stew of uncertain parentage, plays the same role of barbecue sidekick in Kentucky. Lamb and a few vegetables usually find their way into a burgoo pot, but the governing principle varies little from Brunswick stew: if it can't crawl out, cook it.

As for the name, burgoo is even more obscure than Brunswick stew. In *The Dictionary of American Food and Drink,* John Mariani traces the word to eighteenth-century British sailors who used it to mean oatmeal pudding (one of the few additives *not* to turn up in a burgoo pot). There's also a story about a Civil War soldier with a speech impediment who cooked up some birds and called it burgoo when he meant to say bird stew.

In the Carolinas they cut through the etymological ambiguities and call their barbecue stew, simply, hash.

Unfortunately, hash suffers from a culinary ambiguity. At the North Carolina state barbecue cook-off one year, the hash competition brought out everything from a thin reddish gruel to a chunky yellow stew to a dish that looked like a Waldorf salad. Judging a hash cook-off is impossible because you don't know what you're looking for.

Carolinians must like blunt terminology. Another of their specialties (found also in Tidewater Virginia) is a thick fish stew whose very name implies that no mere cook could ruin its preparation: They call it muddle.

And then there is the most evocative name of all: Frogmore stew. This Low Country pot of boiled shrimp, crab and vegetables almost surely got its name from a town on St. Helena Island, South Carolina. South Carolinians delight in telling squeamish outsiders that the name came instead from one of the stew's main ingredients, frogs—but they're just pulling their legs. We think.

Muddle

MUDDLE

The word "muddle" is Southern for a mess of fish, otherwise known as fish stew. This version, which can use almost any white, firm, dry fish, such as grouper or red snapper, along with scallops and shrimp (prawns), was created by Carolina chef and cookbook author Bill Neal.

5 slices lean bacon, cut into ¼-in (6-mm) cubes
4 yellow onions, quartered and sliced
¾ cup (4 oz/125 g) finely chopped celery
1 teaspoon minced garlic
½ teaspoon finely grated orange zest (see glossary)
28 oz (875 g) canned tomatoes, drained and thinly sliced

1 lb (500 g) red waxy potatoes, peeled and cut into ½-in (12-mm) cubes
5 cups (40 fl oz/1.25 l) fish stock or shrimp stock (see glossary)
6 sprigs fresh thyme or ½ teaspoon dried thyme leaves
1 dried red chili pepper, about 3 in (7.5 cm) long
salt to taste
6 oz (185 g) skinless, boneless, white, non-oily fish, such as red snapper or grouper, cut into ¾-in (2-cm) pieces
6 oz (185 g) shrimp (prawns), peeled and deveined (see glossary)
6 oz (185 g) bay scallops, whole, or sea scallops, quartered
½ cup (1½ oz/45 g) finely chopped green (spring) onions, including tender green tops
1½ tablespoons finely chopped fresh basil
1½ tablespoons finely chopped fresh parsley

❋ In a large pot over medium-high heat, cook the bacon, stirring often, until crisp and rendered of fat. Remove the bacon to drain on paper towels and set aside.

❋ Add the onions, celery, garlic and orange zest to the bacon fat in the pot. Reduce the heat to low and simmer, stirring, 2 minutes. Add the tomatoes and cook 2 minutes longer. Add the potatoes, fish stock or shrimp stock, thyme, dried chili pepper and salt and stir well. Cover pot and simmer until the potatoes are just tender but not mushy, about 20 minutes. Add the fish and shrimp and simmer, uncovered, for 1 minute. Add the scallops, stir and cook 1 minute longer. Add more salt to taste and remove from the heat. Remove and discard the dried chili pepper.

❋ In a small bowl, combine the cooked bacon, green onions, basil and parsley.

❋ To serve, ladle the stew into individual bowls and garnish with the bacon mixture. Serve hot.

SERVES 4

Richmond, Virginia

Cream of Shiitake Soup with Virginia Ham

Jimmy Sneed, of the acclaimed Richmond restaurant The Frog and the Redneck, incorporates locally grown shiitakes and ham from Surry County into this delicious mushroom soup. If the cost of making the soup with all shiitakes is too prohibitive, use half button mushrooms and half shiitakes, saving some of the sliced shiitakes for garnish.

⅓ cup (3 fl oz/80 ml) extra-virgin olive oil plus 1 tablespoon olive oil
2 lb (1 kg) shiitake mushrooms, stemmed and sliced ¼ in (6 mm) thick
salt and freshly ground pepper to taste
2 teaspoons minced garlic
¾ cup (4 oz/125 g) finely chopped shallots
5 cups (40 fl oz/1.25 l) chicken stock, or as needed (see glossary)
1 cup (5 oz/155 g) chopped white onion
1 cup (8 fl oz/250 ml) dry white wine
2 cups (16 fl oz/500 ml) heavy (double) cream
3 oz (90 g) Virginia ham, julienned (see glossary)

❋ Place the ⅓ cup (3 fl oz/80 ml) olive oil in a large, heavy saucepan over medium heat. Add the sliced mushrooms and cook, stirring, for 15 seconds. Add the salt, pepper, garlic and ¼ cup (1½ oz/45 g) of the shallots and cook, stirring constantly so the mushrooms, garlic and shallots do not color or burn, 1 minute. Add 3 cups (24 fl oz/750 ml) of the stock and stir well. Reduce the heat to low and simmer until the mushrooms begin to soften, 4–5 minutes. Remove from the heat and let cool slightly. Purée the mixture in a food processor fitted with the metal blade or in a blender. Set aside.

❋ In a large saucepan over medium-high heat, combine the remaining shallots, onion and the 1 tablespoon olive oil and cook, stirring, until translucent, about 4 minutes. Add the wine and cook until it has reduced by two thirds, about 15 minutes. Add the remaining stock and cook until only ½ cup (4 fl oz/125 ml) remains in the pan, about 15 minutes. Add the cream, lower the heat to medium and cook, stirring, for 10 minutes. Remove the pan from the heat.

❋ Strain the mixture through a fine-meshed sieve and return to the pan. Add the shiitake purée, return the pan to medium-low heat and stir to combine. Add more salt and pepper, if desired. If the soup is too thin, add a little more chicken stock.

❋ Serve at once, garnished with the julienned Virginia ham.

SERVES 8

Melbourne, Arkansas

Watercress and Buttermilk Soup

This recipe hails from the Arkansas Ozarks region and spotlights watercress that grows wild in the spring. Adapted from Billy Joe Tatum's Wild Foods Field Guide and Cookbook, *this version blends buttermilk and sour cream with the watercress, making a refreshing soup for warm weather. Use fresh watercress, either wild or store-bought.*

3 cups (24 fl oz/750 ml) lowfat buttermilk, at room temperature
2 cups (3 oz/90 g) loosely packed watercress, coarsely chopped
2 or 3 drops hot pepper sauce
1 cup (8 oz/250 g) sour cream, at room temperature
salt to taste
sprigs of watercress for garnish

❋ In a food processor fitted with the metal blade or in a blender, combine the buttermilk and watercress. Process at low speed until smooth, 1 minute. Add the hot pepper sauce to taste, sour cream and salt. Process at medium speed until well combined. Refrigerate for 3 hours to chill.

❋ To serve, ladle into individual bowls and garnish with watercress sprigs.

SERVES 4

Top to bottom: Watercress and Buttermilk Soup, Cream of Shiitake Soup with Virginia Ham

Charleston, South Carolina

SHE-CRAB SOUP

A female blue crab has a reddish tip on her pincers, and her apron (on the belly) is broad and triangular, whereas the male's is T-shaped. The eggs of the "she-crab" add a subtle yet distinctive richness to this soup, a signature dish of Charleston, South Carolina. The crab roe will cook immediately upon stirring it into the hot soup, so delay this final step until just before serving. If your fishmonger is unable to sell you the crab roe (it is most plentiful in midwinter), you can substitute the crumbled yolks of 3 hard-cooked eggs, sprinkling them on the bottoms of the soup bowls before ladling in the soup.

1¼ cups (7½ oz/235 g) fresh, cooked blue crabmeat or other
    crabmeat such as Dungeness, picked over to remove
    cartilage and shell fragments
¼ cup (2 oz/60 g) unsalted butter
3 tablespoons all-purpose (plain) flour
4 cups (32 fl oz/1 l) milk, at room temperature
½ cup (4 fl oz/125 ml) heavy (double) cream, at
    room temperature
4 green (spring) onions, thinly sliced
½ teaspoon salt
½ teaspoon ground mace
½ teaspoon Worcestershire sauce
¼ teaspoon freshly ground white pepper
¼ cup (2 fl oz/60 ml) dry sherry
10 oz (315 g) crab roe (see note)
1 teaspoon paprika for garnish

❋ Place the crabmeat in a small bowl. Using a fork, fluff, but do not cut, the crabmeat to separate it into bite-sized pieces. Set aside.
❋ In a large, heavy nonreactive saucepan over medium heat, melt the butter. Whisk in the flour to form a roux. Cook, whisking constantly, for 3 minutes, but do not let brown. Gradually whisk in the milk and cream. Cook, whisking constantly, until the soup thickens, about 4 minutes.
❋ Reduce the heat to low, stir in the crabmeat, green onions, salt, mace, Worcestershire sauce and pepper until well blended. Cook, stirring often, just until the crabmeat is heated through, about 1 minute.
❋ Just before serving, stir in the sherry and crab roe until well blended. Ladle into individual shallow bowls, garnish with paprika and serve at once.

SERVES 4–6   *Photograph pages 64–65*

Louisiana

SEAFOOD GUMBO

How seriously do Louisiana cooks take their gumbo? The Picayune Creole Cookbook calls gumbo making an "occult science"—that's how seriously. A bowl full of this Seafood Gumbo is like a postcard from the bayou country, with its sweet crabmeat, rich shrimp and aromatic peppers, all thickened with fresh okra. Variations are legion, but cooks generally agree that the key to a successful gumbo is starting with a good roux.

1 lb (500 g) fresh, cooked blue crabmeat or other crabmeat
    such as Dungeness, picked over to remove cartilage and
    shell fragments
¾ cup (6 fl oz/180 ml) vegetable oil
1¼ lb (625 g) fresh okra, thinly sliced crosswise
1½ cups (6 oz/185 g) coarsely chopped onion
½ cup (2½ oz/75 g) coarsely chopped green bell
    pepper (capsicum)
½ cup (2½ oz/75 g) finely chopped celery
¼ cup (1½ oz/45 g) all-purpose (plain) flour
6 oz (185 g) canned tomato pàste
6 cups (48 fl oz/1.5 l) water

1 teaspoon red pepper flakes
½ teaspoon ground cayenne pepper
1 teaspoon paprika
3 cloves garlic, crushed through a garlic press
½ teaspoon dried thyme
1 tablespoon salt, or to taste
2 bay leaves
1 lb (500 g) medium shrimp (prawns), peeled and deveined
    (see glossary)
10 cups (3 lb/1.5 kg) hot cooked long-grain white rice
    for serving
10 fresh thyme sprigs for garnish (optional)

❋ Place the crabmeat in a bowl. Using a fork, gently fluff, but do not cut, the crabmeat to separate it into bite-sized pieces. Set aside.
❋ In a Dutch oven over high heat, heat ¼ cup (2 fl oz/60 ml) of the oil. Add the okra to the hot oil and sauté until tender, 8–10 minutes. Reduce the heat to low and add the onion, bell pepper and celery. Cook, stirring occasionally, until the vegetables are soft, 8–10 minutes. Remove the Dutch oven from the heat and set aside.
❋ To make the roux, in a large, heavy skillet over high heat, combine the remaining oil and the flour. Cook, stirring constantly, until chestnut brown, 4–6 minutes. Immediately transfer the roux to the vegetables in the Dutch oven.
❋ Add the tomato paste and water to the vegetables and stir until well blended. Stir in the red pepper flakes, cayenne, paprika, garlic, thyme, salt and bay leaves. Set the Dutch oven over medium heat, bring to a simmer and cook, stirring occasionally, for 10 minutes. Stir in the crabmeat and shrimp. Cook just until the crabmeat is heated through and the shrimp turn pink and the interiors are opaque throughout, 1–2 minutes. Remove and discard the bay leaves.
❋ To serve, fill individual soup bowls with the hot cooked rice and ladle the gumbo over. Garnish with thyme sprigs, if desired.

SERVES 10

Stuttgart, Arkansas

DUCK AND SAUSAGE GUMBO

Stuttgart, Arkansas, holds an annual duck gumbo cookoff. Out of respect for their tradition, here is a wonderful recipe for duck gumbo. It includes kielbasa sausage and uses filé powder (powdered sassafras leaves) as the thickening agent instead of okra.

2 tablespoons vegetable oil
1 duck, about 5 lb (2.5 kg), cut into 8 pieces
salt and freshly ground pepper
4½ cups (36 fl oz/1.15 l) chicken stock (see glossary)
8 oz (250 g) kielbasa sausage, cut into slices
    ¼ in (6 mm) thick
1 cup (5 oz/155 g) finely chopped celery
1 cup (4 oz/125 g) coarsely chopped onion
1 cup (5 oz/155 g) finely chopped green bell
    pepper (capsicum)
2 cloves garlic, minced
¼ cup (1½ oz/45 g) all-purpose (plain) flour
28 oz (875 g) canned whole plum tomatoes, puréed
1 bay leaf
½ teaspoon ground cayenne pepper
1 teaspoon filé powder
6 cups (30 oz/940 g) hot cooked long-grain white
    rice for serving

❋ In a large, heavy skillet over medium-high heat, heat the oil. Season the duck pieces with salt and pepper. Add duck to the hot oil, skin side down, in one layer. Cook until golden

Top to bottom: Duck and Sausage Gumbo, Seafood Gumbo

brown, 3 minutes on each side. Transfer the browned duck to a baking sheet and let cool 2–3 minutes. Drain the fat from the skillet, reserving 7 tablespoons (3½ fl oz/105 ml).

❋ Remove and discard the skin from the duck pieces. Place the duck in a large stockpot. Add the chicken stock and set the pot over high heat. Bring to a boil, then reduce the heat to medium and simmer, covered, for 1 hour.

❋ Meanwhile, return the skillet to medium-high heat and heat 2 tablespoons of the reserved duck fat. Add the kielbasa to the hot fat. Cook, turning occasionally, until light brown, about 1 minute. Transfer the cooked kielbasa to a large bowl. Return the skillet to high heat and heat 1 tablespoon more of duck fat. Add the celery, onion, bell pepper and garlic to the hot fat. Cook, stirring frequently, until the pepper is soft and the onion is translucent, about 3 minutes. Transfer the cooked vegetables to the bowl of kielbasa and set aside.

❋ To make the roux, heat the remaining duck fat in the skillet over medium-high heat. Add the flour all at once to the hot fat and cook, stirring constantly with a wooden spoon, until the roux is chestnut brown, about 4–6 minutes. Remove from the heat and set aside.

❋ When the duck is cooked, remove the duck pieces from the stock and set aside to cool, about 3 minutes. Skim as much fat as possible from the surface of the stock.

❋ Remove the duck meat from the bones and cut into medium dice. Add the duck meat, roux, kielbasa, cooked vegetables, tomatoes, bay leaf and cayenne to the saucepan and simmer over medium heat for 15 minutes. Remove the saucepan from the heat and discard the bay leaf. Sprinkle the gumbo with the filé powder and stir in gently with a wooden spoon.

❋ Fill individual shallow bowls with the cooked rice and ladle the gumbo over. Serve at once.

SERVES 6

Florida

CUBAN-STYLE GARBANZO SOUP

Hearty, rustic soups made of garbanzo beans are exclusive to Cuban communities such as those in south Florida. This recipe incorporates sausage, potatoes and ham and may be served as a main course.

2 tablespoons olive oil
1 lb (500 g) fresh chorizo, thinly sliced
   (see glossary)
1 large white onion, thinly sliced
5 cloves garlic, crushed through a garlic press
2 red or green bell peppers (capsicums), seeded and
   cut into small dice
1 lb (500 g) boiling potatoes, cut into large dice
8 oz (250 g) cooked lean country ham, cut into
   small dice (see glossary)
1 head green cabbage, about 1¾ lb (875 g), shredded
6 cups (48 fl oz/1.5 l) chicken stock (see glossary)
1 teaspoon ground turmeric
15 oz (470 g) canned chick-peas (garbanzo beans),
   drained and rinsed
salt and freshly ground pepper to taste

❀ In a large, heavy saucepan over high heat, heat the oil. Add the chorizo and fry until cooked through and no pink remains, about 3 minutes. Transfer the chorizo to a heatproof plate lined with paper towels to drain and set aside. Pour off the fat, reserving 1 tablespoon in the saucepan.
❀ Set the pan over medium heat and add the onion, garlic and bell peppers. Cook, stirring often, until soft but not browned, about 4 minutes. Add the potatoes, ham, cabbage and chicken stock and bring to a simmer. Cook, stirring often, until the potatoes are tender but not falling apart, about 20 minutes.
❀ Stir in the turmeric and chick-peas and cook, stirring often, for 5 minutes longer. Add salt and pepper to taste. Serve hot.

SERVES 6–8

Louisiana

CHICKEN JAMBALAYA

Like gumbo, jambalaya captures the multi-ethnic essence of Louisiana. Inspired by Spanish paella, the dish was transformed by Creole, Cajun and African cooks into perhaps the state's most famous culinary creation. A classic jambalaya contains rice, sausage, peppers and just about anything else that sounds good. Most contain shrimp or crawfish as well, although they certainly aren't necessary, as this seafood-less rendition proves.

¼ cup (2 fl oz/60 ml) olive oil
1 teaspoon ground cayenne pepper
1 tablespoon chili powder
2 teaspoons salt
1 frying chicken, 3½–4 lb (1.75–2 kg), cut into 8 pieces
8-oz (250-g) piece lean smoked ham, cut into
   small dice (see glossary)
8 oz (250 g) fresh andouille sausage, cut into slices ¼ in
   (6 mm) thick
1 white onion, cut into small dice
4 cloves garlic, minced
1 large red bell pepper (capsicum), cut into medium dice
1 large green bell pepper (capsicum), cut into medium dice

⅓ cup (3 fl oz/80 ml) dry white wine
1 teaspoon dried thyme
1 bay leaf
1 cup (7 oz/220 g) long-grain white rice
1 lb (500 g) tomatoes, cut into medium dice
1 cup (8 fl oz/250 ml) chicken stock (see glossary)
salt and freshly ground pepper to taste

❀ In a large, deep, heavy skillet over high heat, heat the oil. In a small bowl, combine the cayenne, chili powder and salt. Sprinkle this seasoning mixture on all sides of the chicken pieces. Add the chicken to the hot oil, skin side down, in one layer. Brown the chicken 1–2 minutes on each side, in 2 batches, if necessary. Transfer the chicken to a very large Dutch oven and set aside.
❀ Add the ham and andouille sausage to the skillet and reduce the heat to medium-high. Cook until the ham and sausage begin to brown, 1 minute. Using a slotted spoon, transfer the ham and sausage to the Dutch oven. Add the onion to the skillet and cook, stirring, until the onion is translucent, 1 minute. Add the garlic and cook, stirring, 30 seconds longer. Add the bell peppers and cook 1 minute longer. Add the wine, thyme and bay leaf. Remove from the heat and stir this mixture into the Dutch oven. Sprinkle the rice over all, add the tomatoes and chicken stock and toss until well combined.
❀ Set the Dutch oven over high heat and bring to a boil. Reduce the heat to low, cover and simmer, stirring occasionally, for 20 minutes. Uncover and continue to simmer 10 minutes longer, skimming the surface of any fat. Remove and discard the bay leaf. Season with salt and pepper and serve hot.

SERVES 6   *Photograph pages 64–65*

South Carolina

FROGMORE STEW

This "stew," which is more like a seafood boil, is named Frogmore after an old settlement on St. Helena Island (near Hilton Head). It's a taste of the African-American Gullah culture that once dominated the Carolina Sea Islands.

4 qt (4 l) water
2 teaspoons salt
4 tablespoons (1½ oz/45 g) Old Bay seasoning (see glossary)
1 teaspoon red pepper flakes
2 celery ribs, cut into pieces 2 in (5 cm) long
4 red-skinned potatoes, about 4 oz (125 g) each
4 ears of corn, husks and silks removed and ears cut in half
¾ lb (375 g) fresh chorizo or other spicy sausage, cut in half
   lengthwise and crosswise in quarters (see glossary)
2 lb (1 kg) medium shrimp (prawns), peeled and deveined
   (see glossary)

❀ In an extra-large stockpot over high heat, combine the water, salt, Old Bay seasoning, red pepper flakes and celery. Bring to a boil and cook for 5 minutes. Skim and discard any foam that rises to the top.
❀ Add the potatoes and cook until fork-tender, 20–25 minutes. Add the corn and chorizo and cook 3–5 minutes, depending on the age of the corn.
❀ Add the shrimp and cook until the shrimp just turn pink and the interiors are opaque throughout, 1–2 minutes. Do not overcook the shrimp. Drain and serve immediately.

SERVES 4

Top to bottom: Cuban-Style Garbanzo Soup, Frogmore Stew

CREAM OF FORDHOOK SOUP

Though the colorful, tropical Floridian ingredients usually get the most attention, there is a quieter, more subtle style of northern Florida cooking that begs to be explored. You can find it at The Yearling, a rustic fish and game restaurant in Cross Creek, where novelist Marjorie Kinnan Rawlings lived and worked while writing The Yearling *and* Cross Creek Cookery. *The following lima bean soup is adapted from the Cross Creek book and is based on the large Fordhook limas popular in the Florida backwoods. Onion juice can be found in the supermarket spice section. Or you can "squeeze" an onion as you would a lemon, with a hand-held reamer or juicer. Alternatively, you can substitute freshly grated onion if it's more convenient. Season, if desired, with a little grated nutmeg or paprika at the end for color.*

2 cups (14 oz/440 g) fresh or frozen Fordhooks
   (lima beans)
1 cup (8 fl oz/250 ml) water
½ teaspoon salt .
2 tablespoons unsalted butter
2 tablespoons all-purpose (plain) flour
1 cup (8 fl oz/250 ml) half & half, at
   room temperature
2 cups (16 fl oz/500 ml) chicken stock
   (see glossary)
½ teaspoon salt
¼ teaspoon ground white pepper
1 tablespoon fresh onion juice
⅛ teaspoon grated nutmeg or paprika for garnish (optional)

✻ Place the lima beans, water and salt in a small, heavy saucepan over high heat and bring to a boil. Reduce the heat to low, cover and simmer until tender, about 25–30 minutes. Drain and set aside.

✻ In a medium saucepan over medium heat, melt the butter. Add the flour, stir and cook until the flour just begins to color, about 1 minute. Whisk in the half & half and chicken stock. Increase the heat to medium-high and cook, stirring, until the mixture comes to a boil. Reduce the heat to low and simmer, uncovered, stirring occasionally, until the mixture thickens slightly and is smooth, about 10 minutes. Stir in the salt, white pepper and onion juice. Remove from the heat and set aside.

✻ In a food processor fitted with the metal blade or in a blender, purée the lima beans. Using the back of a wooden spoon, rub the puréed beans through a fine-meshed sieve to remove the hulls. Discard the hulls and stir the sieved beans into the half & half mixture. Return the pan to low heat and heat through but do not boil. Serve in individual bowls and garnish with a sprinkling of nutmeg or paprika, if desired.

SERVES 6

WHITE BEAN SOUP

Native Americans taught settlers how to dry beans and other vegetables. This preservation technique is still widely used in the Upper South and forms the basis for many tasty yet economical soups such as this one. A wedge of hot-from-the-skillet corn bread is all you need to complete the meal. Middle Tennesseans love this rustic soup, especially when it has been flavored with ham. If you'd prefer a vegetarian version, omit the ham.

1 lb (500 g) dried white kidney beans
2 qt (2 l) homemade vegetable stock (see glossary),
   canned vegetable broth or broth made with vegetable
   bouillon cubes
1 qt (1 l) water
2 lb (1 kg) lean ham neck bones with some meat attached
3 sprigs fresh parsley
2 white onions, coarsely chopped
5 carrots, cut crosswise into slices ¼ in (6 mm) thick
4 celery ribs, cut crosswise into slices ¼ in (6 mm) thick
3 cloves garlic, minced
1 teaspoon dried marjoram
1 teaspoon dried oregano
1 teaspoon dried thyme
2 bay leaves
¼ teaspoon freshly ground pepper
salt to taste
1 tablespoon minced fresh parsley or bay leaves for garnish

✻ Pick over the beans, removing and discarding any stones or blemished beans. Place the beans in a large bowl, add water to cover by 2 in (5 cm), cover with plastic wrap and soak overnight at room temperature. The next day, drain and rinse the beans. Alternatively, soak the beans the same day of cooking by placing them in a large, heavy saucepan over medium-high heat with water to cover by 2 in (5 cm). Bring to a boil. Remove the saucepan from the heat, cover and let stand for 1 hour. Drain the beans and rinse under cold running water.

✻ In a large, heavy pot over medium heat, combine the beans, vegetable stock or broth, the 1 qt (1 l) water, ham bones and parsley sprigs. Bring to a boil. Reduce the heat to medium-low and simmer, covered, for 1 hour, stirring occasionally and skimming and discarding any foam that rises to the top.

✻ Add the onions, carrots, celery, garlic, marjoram, oregano, thyme, bay leaves, pepper and salt and stir well. Cover and continue to simmer, stirring occasionally, until the beans are soft, 35–40 minutes longer.

✻ Remove the ham bones from the pot, cut off the meat, return the meat to the pot and discard the bones. Taste the soup and adjust the seasoning, if desired. Simmer for 10 minutes longer, stirring often.

✻ To serve, remove and discard the bay leaves and parsley sprigs. Transfer the soup to a large tureen or individual soup bowls and garnish with the minced parsley or bay leaves. Serve hot.

SERVES 10

KING'S ARMS TAVERN CREAM OF PEANUT SOUP

The peanut took a circuitous route to the South. A South American native, the peanut plant was taken to Africa by the Portuguese to feed slaves headed for America. Peanuts were planted and used for forage across the South. But it wasn't until after the Civil War that they gained national acceptance largely through the work of botanist George Washington Carver, of Alabama's Tuskegee Institute. In fact, peanut soup is sometimes called Tuskegee Soup. This recipe comes from the historic King's Arms Tavern in Colonial Williamsburg, where they make the surprisingly thin soup with peanut butter.

¼ cup (2 oz/60 g) salted butter
1 cup (5 oz/155 g) finely chopped white onion
2 celery ribs, finely chopped
1 tablespoon all-purpose (plain) flour
8 cups (64 fl oz/2 l) chicken stock (see glossary)

Top to bottom: White Bean Soup, King's Arms Tavern Cream of Peanut Soup, Cream of Fordhook Soup

1 cup (8 oz/250 g) smooth peanut butter
2 cups (16 fl oz/500 ml) light (single) cream, at
    room temperature
1 cup (6 oz/185 g) chopped roasted peanuts for garnish

❋ In a large, heavy saucepan over medium-high heat, melt the butter. When bubbling, add the onion and celery, reduce the heat to low and cook, stirring, until softened, about 4 minutes. Add the flour and stir to blend well. Add the chicken stock, increase the heat to medium-high and bring to a boil, stirring constantly. Reduce the heat to medium-low and simmer, uncovered, for 15 minutes. Remove from the heat.

❋ Strain the soup through a fine-meshed sieve into a large heatproof bowl, using the back of a wooden spoon to press the liquid from the solids. Discard the solids and return the sieved soup to the saucepan. Add the peanut butter and cream to the pan and stir.

❋ Return the pan to low heat and heat through but do not boil. Serve at once, garnished with chopped roasted peanuts.

SERVES 12

75

Ray's Old-fashioned Chicken 'n' Dumplings

RAY'S OLD-FASHIONED CHICKEN 'N' DUMPLINGS

To Ray L. Overton III, an Atlanta teacher and food writer, this recipe represents the Old South. "It has been in my family for generations, beginning with my Great-grandma Maude who learned to make it from her mother shortly before her wedding day," Overton says. "Especially popular during the Great Depression, it was a dish that could be stretched to serve a crowd after church meeting simply by adding a little more flour, lard or chicken fat, and water to the dumpling recipe. Over the years, it has been refined and adapted to suit the tastes of different family members."

FOR THE CHICKEN STOCK:

1 frying chicken, about 4 lb (2 kg), cut into 8 pieces
2–3 qt (2–3 l) water
1 onion, quartered
1 large carrot, cut into 4 pieces
1 celery rib, cut into 4 pieces

1 bay leaf
1 teaspoon whole peppercorns
1 teaspoon salt
1 sprig each of fresh parsley, sage, rosemary and thyme, tied together with kitchen twine

FOR THE DUMPLINGS:

3 cups (12 oz/375 g) sifted all-purpose (plain) Southern flour (see glossary)
½ teaspoon baking soda (bicarbonate of soda)
½ teaspoon salt
6 tablespoons (3 oz/90 g) vegetable shortening or lard, chilled
¼ cup (2 fl oz/60 ml) chicken stock (from recipe above)
⅔ cup (5 fl oz/160 ml) lowfat buttermilk
1 tablespoon minced fresh thyme or 2 teaspoons dried thyme

salt and freshly ground pepper to taste

❧ To make the stock, place the chicken pieces in a large, heavy stockpot with enough water to cover by 1 in (2.5 cm). Add the onion, carrot, celery, bay leaf, peppercorns, salt and

76

fresh herb bouquet. Bring to a boil over high heat. Reduce the heat to low and simmer for 1½–2 hours, stirring occasionally and skimming and discarding any foam that rises to the top.

❋ Remove the chicken from the pot and set aside to cool. When cool enough to handle, skin and bone the chicken, cut the meat into bite-sized pieces and set aside. Return the skin and bones to the pot and simmer for 1 hour longer. Strain the stock, discarding the solids, and return the stock to the pot. If desired, reserve the vegetables (omitting the bay leaf, peppercorns and fresh herb bouquet) to add back to the pot just before serving. Refrigerate the stock for at least 1 hour or overnight. Skim and discard any fat that has risen to the top.

❋ To make the dumplings, in a large bowl, sift together the flour, baking soda and salt. Add the shortening or lard and, using a pastry blender, 2 knives or a fork, cut into the flour mixture until it resembles coarse meal. Make a well in the center of the mixture and add the ¼ cup (2 fl oz/60 ml) chicken stock, buttermilk and thyme. Stir until well blended and a stiff dough forms. On a lightly floured work surface, knead the dough gently 8–10 times. Pat the dough into a flat disk, wrap tightly in plastic wrap and refrigerate for at least 1 hour or overnight.

❋ Bring the stock to a slow simmer over medium-low heat. On a lightly floured work surface, roll out the chilled dough about ⅛ in (3 mm) thick. Sprinkle the work surface with more flour if the dough begins to stick. Cut the dough into 1-in (2.5-cm) square dumplings. Drop the dumplings, one at a time, into the simmering stock. When all the dumplings have been added to the stock, stir gently and cook until the dumplings are tender but with a slight bite, 10–12 minutes. Add the reserved chicken meat, reserved vegetables, if desired, salt and pepper and stir gently. Serve at once.

SERVES 8

Mississippi

HAM, MUSTARD GREEN, RED BEAN AND SWEET POTATO SOUP

Lee Bailey, the New York designer and prolific cookbook author, grew up in Mississippi and Louisiana and often writes about his roots. The following soup, from his book Lee Bailey's Soup Meals, *is his vision of a classic, sturdy bean and green soup. Mustard greens are Bailey's green of choice, and here he joins them with red kidney beans, smoked ham hocks and sweet potatoes. Serve this soup with hot corn bread.*

1½ cups (10½ oz/330 g) dried red kidney beans, rinsed and
    picked over
1½ qt (1.5 l) water
4 lb (2 kg) smoked ham hocks, scrubbed
4 large garlic cloves, crushed through a garlic press
1½ teaspoons freshly ground pepper
1 teaspoon salt
4 large sprigs parsley
2 bay leaves
1½ teaspoons dried thyme
3 large leeks, white part only, thinly sliced (see glossary)
2 onions, coarsely chopped
1 lb (500 g) sweet potatoes, peeled and cut into ½-in
    (12-mm) cubes
1½ lb (750 g) mustard greens, stemmed and torn into
    large pieces
4 oz (125 g) cooked ham, cubed (optional)
1–2 cups (8–16 fl oz/250–500 ml) hot water, or as needed
sprigs of fresh thyme for garnish (optional)

❋ Rinse and pick over the beans, removing and discarding any stones or blemished beans. Place the beans in a medium saucepan, add 4 cups (32 fl oz/1 l) of the water and bring to a boil over medium-high heat. Reduce the heat to low and simmer for 2 minutes. Remove from the heat, cover and let soak for 1 hour. Alternatively, cover the uncooked beans with cold water and let soak overnight.

❋ Place the ham hocks in a large saucepan, add the remaining water and bring to a boil over medium-high heat. Reduce the heat to low and simmer, partially covered, about 2 hours. Skim occasionally and discard any foam that rises to the top. Remove the ham hocks from the water and set aside to cool.

❋ Degrease the cooking water by skimming the surface with a ladle. Drain the beans and add them to the saucepan of cooking water. Bring to a boil over medium-high heat, then reduce heat to low. Add the garlic, pepper, salt, parsley, bay leaves and thyme and simmer, covered, until the beans are just tender, about 1½ hours.

❋ Meanwhile, remove the meat from the ham hocks and discard the bones and skin. Chop the meat coarsely and add to the pan of beans.

❋ When beans are tender, add the leeks, onions and sweet potatoes. Continue cooking over low heat, covered, until the potatoes have cooked through, about 15 minutes. Add the greens and cook, covered, just until the greens have wilted, about 10 minutes. Add the cubed ham, if using. If the soup becomes too thick, add the hot water as needed.

❋ To serve, remove and discard the bay leaves. Ladle into individual bowls, garnish with thyme, if desired, and serve at once.

SERVES 8

Ham, Mustard Green, Red Bean and Sweet Potato Soup

Top to bottom: Kentucky Burgoo, Brunswick Stew

Kentucky

KENTUCKY BURGOO

In Owensboro, Kentucky, barbecued mutton has long been the major food attraction of political rallies and other outdoor gatherings. Often the leftovers go into a bubbling black pot of Burgoo, the Kentucky version of Brunswick Stew, which is typically served as a side dish to the barbecue. At home, it makes a hearty main dish that produces heavenly kitchen scents for hours as it simmers.

1 lb (500 g) lean beef chuck round, cut into 1-in (2.5-cm) cubes
8 oz (250 g) lean lamb, cut into 1-in (2.5-cm) cubes
1 lb (500 g) skinless, boneless chicken breasts, cut crosswise into strips ½ in (12 mm) wide
2 qt (2 l) vegetable stock or beef stock (see glossary)
1 cup (5 oz/155 g) large-diced boiling potatoes
1 cup (5 oz/155 g) finely chopped yellow onion
1 cup (6 oz/185 g) fresh or frozen lima beans
2 green bell peppers (capsicums), finely chopped
4 carrots, thinly sliced
1 cup (6 oz/185 g) fresh or frozen corn kernels
1 tablespoon salt, or to taste
1 teaspoon ground cayenne pepper, or to taste
½ teaspoon freshly ground pepper, or to taste
1 cup (4 oz/125 g) thinly sliced fresh okra
6 tomatoes, peeled, seeded and coarsely chopped
2 cloves garlic, crushed through a garlic press
2 tablespoons apple cider vinegar
sprigs of fresh parsley for garnish (optional)

❊ In a large, heavy nonreactive pot over high heat, combine the beef, lamb, chicken and vegetable stock and bring to a boil. Reduce the heat to low, cover and simmer, stirring occasionally, for 1½ hours.

❊ Add the potatoes, onion, lima beans, bell peppers, carrots and corn and stir until well blended. Stir in the salt, cayenne and pepper to taste. Cover and continue to simmer, stirring occasionally, for 3 hours longer.

❊ Add the okra, tomatoes, garlic and vinegar and stir until well blended. Cover and simmer, stirring occasionally, until the meat, poultry and vegetables are fork-tender and the flavors have melded, about 2 hours longer. If needed, add a little water while cooking if the stew is sticking or is thicker than desired.

❊ To serve, ladle the Burgoo into individual soup bowls and garnish with parsley, if desired. Serve hot.

SERVES 12–14

Virginia / North Carolina / Georgia

BRUNSWICK STEW

Southerners love to debate the origins of Brunswick Stew. Virginia, Georgia and North Carolina all claim to be its birthplace, but the truth most likely is that it originated with Native Americans. The first stews of early America contained all sorts of wild game. Some cooks still say it isn't Brunswick Stew unless it has squirrel. This tamer, more souplike version relies on chicken and a variety of vegetables some stew makers would find unnecessary. That's okay; it wouldn't be Brunswick Stew without a debate.

1 stewing hen, about 6 lb (3 kg)
4 qt (4 l) chicken stock (see glossary)
3 celery ribs
1 tablespoon sugar
2 lb (1 kg) boiling potatoes, cut into ½-in (12-mm) dice
1 lb (500 g) yellow onions, coarsely chopped
6 large ripe tomatoes, peeled, seeded and coarsely chopped
2½ cups (15 oz/470 g) fresh or frozen lima beans
2½ cups (15 oz/470 g) fresh or frozen corn kernels
2 green bell peppers (capsicums), finely chopped
2 tablespoons salt, or to taste
½ teaspoon freshly ground pepper, or to taste
thinly sliced green (spring) onions for garnish

❊ In a large, heavy nonreactive pot over medium heat, combine the hen, stock and celery. Cover and simmer until the meat pulls away from the bones, 2–3 hours. Remove from the heat. Transfer the chicken to a large heatproof plate and set aside until cool enough to handle. Remove the skin and meat from the bones. Discard the skin and bones and cut the meat into 1-in (2.5-cm) dice. Cover the meat and refrigerate until ready to use.

❊ Meanwhile, strain the stock through a medium-meshed sieve and skim off any foam or surface fat. Return the stock to the pot and set over medium-high heat. Add the sugar, potatoes, onions, tomatoes, lima beans, corn and bell peppers. Bring to a boil, then reduce the heat to medium-low. Cover and simmer, stirring occasionally, for 1 hour. Add the chicken, salt and pepper. Bring to a simmer. Cover and simmer, stirring occasionally, until the flavors have melded, 45 minutes. Adjust the seasoning with salt and pepper if needed.

❊ To serve, transfer the stew to a large soup tureen and garnish with green onions.

SERVES 12

Washington, Virginia

CHILLED LOCAL PEACH AND VIRGINIA RIESLING SOUP

Patrick O'Connell, chef at the Inn at Little Washington, is known for inspirational food based on Virginia ingredients. This refreshing chilled soup, published in Home Food, *begins with locally produced Riesling, but you can use any slightly dry Riesling wine. Use the most flavorful peaches you can find in your area at the peak of summertime.*

2 bottles (3 cups/24 fl oz/750 ml each) Virginia Riesling or other Riesling
8 whole cloves
1 cinnamon stick
¼ cup (2 oz/60 g) lightly packed light brown sugar
2 bay leaves
5 lb (2.5 kg) peaches, about 12, peeled, halved and pitted
1 orange, sliced
1 lemon, sliced
1½ cups (12 fl oz/375 ml) heavy (double) cream, or to taste
1 teaspoon fresh lemon juice
¼ cup (1 oz/30 g) sliced (flaked) almonds, toasted (see glossary; optional)

❊ In a large, nonreactive saucepan over medium-high heat, combine the Riesling, cloves, cinnamon stick, brown sugar and bay leaves and bring to a boil. Add the peaches, reduce the heat to medium and simmer, stirring occasionally, 20–25 minutes. Add the orange and lemon slices and simmer 5 minutes longer.

❊ Remove from the heat. Remove and discard the orange and lemon slices, cloves, cinnamon stick and bay leaves. Transfer the mixture to a food processor fitted with the metal blade or a blender and purée until smooth. Strain the mixture through a fine-meshed sieve into a bowl and refrigerate for 4 hours to chill.

❊ Just before serving, stir in as much cream as desired. Stir in the lemon juice. Ladle into individual bowls and sprinkle with toasted almonds, if desired.

SERVES 4   *Photograph pages 64–65*

Louisiana

LOUISIANA

Gulf of Mexico

NEW ORLEANS

LOUISIANA

Richard Simmons had ample reason to get into the exercise business. Long before he was sweating to the oldies, the diet maven was sweating over sugar and pecans at a praline shop in his native New Orleans. "For breakfast I had pralines, for lunch I had pralines, and for dinner I had pralines," he says. "I was 200 pounds in the eighth grade."

Louisiana will do that to you if you're not careful. It's the biggest banquet in the South—probably in all of the United States—with courses that run from breakfast beignets to lunchtime po' boys to dinnertime oysters with a few dashes of Tabasco to make them stand at attention.

The silt of half the continent washed down the Mississippi River to make the soupy land of southern Louisiana. The peoples of half the globe pushed up the river to make the gumbo that is southern Louisiana culture. Native Americans, Anglo-Americans, Spanish, French, French Canadians, Africans, Caribbeans, Italians—each brought new flavors that mingled with the others like the currents of the river. Together they formed a way of life that is quite different from anything else in the United States. They made Louisiana into something like the South's eccentric cousin.

There actually are two Louisianas. The northern half, an expanse of piney woods bisected by the Red River, was settled by Protestants from Alabama, Geor-

Previous pages: A bayou outside of Houma, Louisiana, is the result of an abandoned river channel. Spanish moss hangs from the cypress trees, dampening the cacophony of the owls' calls and bird-voiced tree frogs. Left: New Orleans is credited as the birthplace of jazz, a distinctly American art form combining African and European musical traditions.

83

gia and parts east—small farmers mostly, steeped in the customs and values of the Deep South. Northern Louisianans traditionally look askance at the southern portion of the state, most of which is a hot, moist tangle of moss-fringed swamps inhabited by Creoles, Cajuns and other Catholics of Latin extraction. In its middle sits lusty New Orleans, the city that care forgot. Each section has distinct foodways, and while they are not mutually exclusive, neither have they melded in any meaningful fashion. One native who straddled the two worlds of Louisiana was Huey Long, the state's unchallenged boss in the 1920s and 1930s.

The Kingfish didn't miss many meals. One time, to show his connection with the little people, he started talking up the health benefits of corn pone and pot likker, the humble dish of greens *au jus* he'd grown up with in northern Louisiana. He decreed that the proper way to eat it was to dunk the pone. Not so, the *Atlanta Constitution* editorialized, coming out in favor of crumbling the pone. Franklin D. Roosevelt jokingly promised to refer the matter to the Democratic platform committee. A few years later, Long took the floor of the U.S. Senate during a filibuster and killed time by describing in scrumptious detail his technique for frying southern Louisiana oysters. Whereas other senators may read aloud from telephone directories when they filibuster, only a Louisianan would recite a recipe.

Louisiana, more than perhaps any other state, regards food as art. Its most celebrated cuisines are, of course, Creole and Cajun. There are distinctions between the two, and they can be traced in the state's colorful history.

The explorer La Salle claimed Louisiana for France in the late 1600s, but colonization didn't begin in earnest until New Orleans was founded in 1717. The most welcome of the early settlers were *les filles à la cassette,* several shiploads of unmarried young Frenchwomen who were called "casket girls" because the government had granted each a chest full of clothing. Their new home certainly wasn't Paris. The frontier diet of unfamiliar Indian corn particularly galled them until they learned to

During Mardi Gras (French for Fat Tuesday), New Orleans overflows with carnival balls and ritualized costumed parades that celebrate the coming of the season of penance.

Mark Twain often wrote of this, his favorite river—"The great Mississippi, the majestic, the magnificent Mississippi, rolling its mile-wide tide along, shining in the sun"—that sidles through New Orleans before plunging into the Gulf of Mexico.

make corn bread and hominy from Choctaw women. The natives also introduced them to filé, a powder made from sassafras leaves and used to thicken stews.

As New Orleans grew over the next hundred years, one ethnic group after another descended the gangplank and added a pinch of this or a dash of that. Louisiana imported African slaves almost from the beginning, first to work in New Orleans (often as cooks), later to cultivate the vast sugarcane plantations that spread across the upriver parishes. Many of the slaves came via the West Indies, where they encountered new spices and seasonings to add to the ones they had known in Africa. They brought a number of foods with them, most notably okra—or gumbo, as they called it, from the Bantu *gombo*.

Both the vegetable and the name came to be used for Louisiana's signature dish, an anything-goes stew that has as many variations as jazz has riffs. African American cooks are also credited with red beans and rice. It was one of the favorite meals of Louisiana's greatest jazz musician, Louis Armstrong, who used to sign his letters "red beans and ricely yours." The Creole soul tradition is carried on admirably at Dooky Chase and dozens of less heralded New Orleans restaurants.

Another essential ingredient in Louisiana cooking came from a band of refugees. Exiled from Canada when the British took over in the 1760s, thousands of French-speaking Acadians resettled in the bayous and backwoods of southern Louisiana. These "Cajuns" found a

A deserted Creole outbuilding on the Laura Plantation in Vacherie, Louisiana, weathers the changing seasons.

world twitching with food—fish, waterfowl, crabs, shrimp, crawfish—which they put to good use in earthy gumbos, jambalayas and étouffées that echoed the heartiness of French country cooking.

The Spanish, too, had their fingers in the pot. France ceded Louisiana to Spain in 1762, and it ruled the colony for almost four decades before it was reclaimed by France. The Spanish rebuilt New Orleans twice after fires and in the process created the wrought-iron allure of the French Quarter. Their gastronomical influence is less obvious, but food historians do credit the Spanish with accelerating Louisiana's taste for spicy seasonings. Spanish paella clearly inspired the seafood-and-rice riot of jambalaya.

In time more immigrants added to the banquet. After the United States purchased Louisiana from France in 1803, Americans poured in with their English-derived cooking and riverboats full of foods from the nation's heartland. Germans, Irish and Italians came as well. Sicilians contributed a New Orleans classic, the salami-provolone-olive sandwich they call the muffuletta, after their word for a round loaf of bread.

With so many ethnic currents stirring, you begin to understand the Creole identity. The word means "native," more or less, and generations of Louisianans have used it to distinguish themselves from more recent immigrants. Strictly speaking, Creoles are descendants of the people who came to New Orleans in the 1700s, whether of French, Spanish or African origin or some café-au-lait combination. They are historically city people, as opposed to the country Cajuns, and their cooking reflects it.

It was the Creoles who established the restaurants that won New Orleans a reputation for exquisite dining. Visiting one such place in 1856, the English novelist William Makepeace Thackeray marveled that "We had a bouillibaisse than which a better was never eaten at Marseilles" [sic]. Antoine's, opened in 1840 in the French Quarter, set the tone for Creole dining with its dignified service and elegant dishes such as *huîtres en coquille à la Rockefeller*—better known as oysters Rockefeller. Arnaud's, Galatoire's, Brennan's, Commander's Palace and a host of celebrated restaurants sprang from the same tradition. Their menus sing with the Crescent City's greatest hits: shrimp remoulade, oysters Bienville, trout meunière, bananas Foster, bourbon bread pudding. Contemporary chefs like Emeril Lagasse and Susan Spicer have added nouvelle touches like Gulf fish beignets with tomato-corn tartar sauce and boudin-stuffed quail with fig sauce. No wonder Ella Brennan, the doyenne of Commander's Palace, likes to say, "Food in New Orleans is like sex. Everybody's interested."

There was a time when Creole cooking was considered distinct from Cajun. Creole was the richly sauced haute cuisine served in the better restaurants and homes of New Orleans. Cajun was the highly seasoned one-pot meal they made back in the bayou with whatever daddy and the boys were able to catch that day. Creole was jazz, Cajun was zydeco.

Actually the cuisines have overlapped all along. Both use the same seafoods and tropical flavors. And both use roux, a mixture of flour and fat that is browned to make a base for sauces and stews. There are endless roux variations, and Louisianans enjoy debating them as much as the French do wine. Creole and Cajun cooking have been merging more rapidly in recent years. The reason? Cajun has come to town.

Cajun, or at least a loud version of it, drew a large national audience in the 1980s thanks to promoters as different as Justin Wilson, the folksy television cook, and John Folse, another TV cook, who rose to prominence as chef at the Lafitte's Landing restaurant between New Orleans and Baton Rouge. But the major promoter has been chef Paul Prudhomme, who was raised in a large Cajun family (thirteen kids!) and loved to play in the kitchen. In his cookbooks and at his New Orleans restaurant, K-Paul's Louisiana Kitchen, Prudhomme popularized a spicy cuisine that he calls, not Cajun or Creole, but Louisianan. It's far hotter than the Cajun cooking that most people remember; he coats his best-known dish, blackened redfish, with incendiary ground peppers and then pan-sears it over high heat. It was so heavily copied that the government stepped in with new limitations to protect the species from overfishing.

There are no such concerns for the other creature most identified with Cajun cooking. Crawfish (only zoologists call them crayfish) are as ubiquitous in the wetlands as the mud they burrow into. Cajuns boiled and made gumbos with the tiny crustaceans for years, but few restaurants served them before the 1940s. They were swamp people's food—mudbugs.

Today crawfish turn up on half the menus in New Orleans. Souvenir shops sell almost as many of them in the form of ornaments and refrigerator magnets. You even see those crimson claws and creepy feelers blown up to science fiction proportions atop Mardi Gras floats.

One can imagine that Huey Long had a strong opinion on the proper way to eat boiled crawfish, but it is not known whether he ever officially addressed the public on the subject. Experts recommend ripping the head from the body, sucking out the spicy fat, then pinching the tail to release the morsel of white meat. Or, as the official T-shirt of the crawfish festival in Breaux Bridge, Louisiana, puts it, "Suck Me, Pinch Me, Eat Me."

That wouldn't make a bad state motto for Louisiana.

A fisherman mends his nets on Isle St. Charles in southern Louisiana.

With its endless Atlantic coastline, fresh seafood is one of the great raw materials of the South. This sign advertising the catch of the day is from the historic district of Savannah, Georgia.

FISH & SEAFOOD

As the Union Navy learned during the Civil War, the South has no shortage of coastline—three thousand miles in all, from the Chesapeake Bay south to the barrier islands of the Carolinas and Georgia around the Florida peninsula and west along the rim of the Gulf of Mexico to the Louisiana wetlands. That much shoreline may be bad for a naval blockade, but it's great if you love seafood. Southerners have from the beginning.

Hard-shell clams from the Eastern seaboard come in three sizes: The smallest are littleneck clams, the mid-sized are cherrystone clams, and the largest, chowder clams.

When the English colonized Virginia in 1607, Captain John Smith seemed to regard the Chesapeake as a sort of all-you-can-eat fish lodge. He described "an abundance of fish lying so thicke with their head above the water . . . we attempted to catch them with a frying pan." Too bad they didn't know about hush puppies and coleslaw.

The Native Americans knew exactly how to catch and cook almost every fish and shellfish eaten today in the South. The Powhatans introduced the English to crabs, still a Chesapeake delicacy boiled in pungent spices. The Seminoles of Florida were particularly skilled with seafood. Naturalist William Bartram ate with them in the late 1700s and gave a four-star review to their snapper steamed in oranges. Floridians still cook it that way. Like their native predecessors, they know seafood; Floridians eat shark, yellowtail, marlin, smoked mullet and a dozen other fish, as well as two shellfish that have become south Florida trademarks: conchs and stone crabs.

Until this century, probably the most widely eaten saltwater seafood in the South was the oyster. The succulent little mollusks sustained the poor in coastal cities even as they turned up on Gilded Age banquet tables. *The Picayune Creole Cook Book*, published in New Orleans in 1900, lists thirty-six oyster recipes, not including the most famous one, oysters Rockefeller, created the year before at Antoine's restaurant. Though still swallowed by the dozen at sawdust-floored oyster bars across the Gulf Coast, oysters are less important in the Southern diet today.

Previous pages: Left to right: Joe's Mustard Sauce for Stone Crabs (recipe page 103), Shrimp Creole (recipe page 100–101), Maryland Crab Cakes (recipe page 93)

Pollution concerns have made people queasy about eating them raw. As the humorist Roy Blount Jr. put it, "I prefer my oyster fried. Then I'm sure my oyster's died."

The reigning king of seafood is shrimp. Most of the U.S. harvest, the world's largest, comes from Southern waters. Virtually everyone eats shrimp these days, but before refrigeration became common in the early 1900s, only people near the coast could do so regularly. Low Country South Carolinians use the crustacean in one of their signature dishes, shrimp and grits. Once again, though, no Southerners have displayed more creativity with the shellfish than the cooks of Louisiana, who came up with shrimp creole, shrimp remoulade and barbecued shrimp (which is actually baked).

Louisiana cooks also made a star out of another crustacean, this one from fresh waters: the crawfish. The bright red mudbug resembles a tiny lobster and harbors a smidgeon of meat in its tail that makes some people wonder whether it's worth the trouble. Anyone who loves Cajun cooking thinks it is.

Although fish plays a smaller role in the kitchens of the inland South, there are notable exceptions. Mountain trout, bass, crappie and other lake fish are popular. But no creature with fins is as closely identified with Southern cooking as catfish.

Non-Southerners sometimes fail to understand the region's affinity for freshwater catfish. After all, it has a reputation as a bottom feeder, and it's plug-ugly to boot, with those bullwhip whiskers. Today's catfish is no scavenger, though; it's usually grain-fed and raised in a man-made pond in Mississippi or Arkansas. Its flaky white flesh is beginning to catch on with meat-wary consumers who've found that it grills or bakes as nicely as it fries. Southerners still tend to cook catfish the old-fashioned way: dredged in cornmeal and fried. It's usually eaten at a community fish fry or at one of the region's myriad catfish restaurants—typically rustic back country

Workers sort through blue crabs taken from a run in Dularge Bayou, Louisiana.

lodges where families retire to private dining cubicles and come out patting their stomachs and moaning about how much they ate.

William Least Heat Moon visited such a place near Athens, Georgia, during the wanderings that led to his book *Blue Highways*. The waitress pushed a cart full of fried catfish, fried perch, fried shrimp, hush puppies, coleslaw and who knows what else. "I had no moral right to eat so much. But I did," he wrote, imagining the headline in the next day's paper:

Stomach Pump Fails to Revive Traveler.

What one catches when fishing in rivers around Edisto Island, South Carolina, depends upon the season—channel bass and pompano in spring; Spanish mackerel, whiting, flounder and shrimp in summer; bluefish in fall; and dogfish in winter. Sea trout appear year-round.

New Orleans, Louisiana

FISH WITH PECAN BUTTER SAUCE AND MEUNIÈRE SAUCE

Perhaps no one has done more to inflame American palates than Paul Prudhomme, the jolly, bearded chef of K-Paul's Louisiana Kitchen in the French Quarter. His name and ever-smiling face have become synonymous with Cajun cooking, through cookbooks, television appearances and videos. His signature seasonings—now blended and bottled for sale in supermarkets and mail-order catalogs (see Mail Order Sources)—fire up both rustic Cajun dishes of his rural Louisiana upbringing, and the more refined, French-inspired fare typical of white-tablecloth New Orleans restaurants. Those spices, along with an ample handful of toasted pecans in both the sauce and breading, give any fish fillet a rich Louisiana flavor.

FOR THE PECAN BUTTER SAUCE:

¼ cup (2 oz/60 g) unsalted butter, at room temperature
½ cup (2 oz/60 g) coarsely chopped pecans, toasted
 (see glossary)
2 tablespoons finely chopped onion
1 teaspoon fresh lemon juice
½ teaspoon Chef Paul Prudhomme's Magic Pepper Sauce
¼ teaspoon minced garlic

FOR THE MEUNIÈRE SAUCE:

1 cup (8 fl oz/250 ml) seafood stock (see glossary)
¾ teaspoon minced garlic
1½ cups (12 oz/375 g) unsalted butter
2 tablespoons all-purpose (plain) flour
¼ cup (2 fl oz/60 ml) Worcestershire sauce
¼ teaspoon salt

FOR THE FISH:

½ cup (4 fl oz/125 ml) milk
1 egg, lightly beaten
1 cup (5 oz/155 g) all-purpose (plain) flour
2 tablespoons Chef Paul Prudhomme's Seafood Magic
6 trout or other firm-fleshed fish fillets, about 4 oz
 (125 g) each
vegetable oil for frying
6 tablespoons (1½ oz/45 g) coarsely chopped pecans,
 toasted (see glossary)

❈ To make the Pecan Butter Sauce, place all the ingredients in a food processor fitted with the metal blade or in a blender and process until creamy and smooth, 2–3 minutes, using a rubber spatula to scrape down the sides. Set aside.

❈ To make the Meunière Sauce, in a medium saucepan over high heat, combine the stock and garlic and bring to a boil. Reduce the heat to low and simmer for 2 minutes. Remove from the heat.

❈ In a small saucepan over high heat, melt ¼ cup (2 oz/60 g) of the butter. Add the flour and whisk until smooth, about 10 seconds. Remove from the heat.

❈ Return the stock saucepan to medium heat. Gradually add the butter mixture to the stock mixture, whisking constantly until smooth. Reduce the heat to very low. Add the remaining butter, about one third at a time, whisking constantly until the butter has melted.

❈ Gradually add the Worcestershire sauce, whisking constantly. Whisk in the salt. Continue to cook, whisking often, until the sauce thickens slightly, about 5 minutes. The sauce may be kept warm, or reheated, by setting the pan over another pan of hot, but not boiling, water.

❈ To prepare the fish, combine the milk and egg in a cake or pie pan until well blended. Place the flour in a separate pan, add 1 tablespoon of the Seafood Magic and mix well. Sprinkle

the remaining Seafood Magic lightly and evenly on both sides of the fish fillets, patting it in by hand.

❈ In a very large skillet over medium-high heat, pour the oil to a depth of ¼ in (6 mm) and heat to about 350°F (180°C) on a deep-fry thermometer. Meanwhile, dredge each fillet in the seasoned flour, shaking off the excess. Soak the fillets in the egg mixture. Just before frying, drain off the egg mixture and dredge the fillets again in the seasoned flour, shaking off the excess. Fry the fillets in the hot oil until golden brown, 2–3 minutes on each side. Increase the heat, if needed, to maintain the temperature at 350°F (180°C). Transfer to paper towels to drain and immediately spread the top of each hot fillet with a scant 2 tablespoons of the Pecan Butter Sauce.

❈ To serve, spoon ⅓ cup (3 fl oz/80 ml) of warm Meunière Sauce onto each dinner plate and place a fillet on top. Sprinkle each serving with 1 tablespoon pecans.

SERVES 6

Richmond, Virginia

GRILLED CATFISH WITH TWO SAUCES

Sarah Belk King, senior editor of Bon Appétit *magazine, was born in Richmond, Virginia, to parents from each of the Carolinas. This recipe, from her book* Around the Southern Table, *is a sophisticated, yet invitingly simple-to-make rendition of catfish, which in the Southern food lexicon is nearly always fried. Yet King demonstrates the catfish's chameleonlike versatility by grilling and then serving it with two sauces—an Herbed Tomato Salsa and a Celery Sauce—to delicious effect. She suggests that for easier handling you can use an oiled, hinged fish grill basket to hold the fish. The sauces can be made a day ahead.*

FOR THE HERBED TOMATO SALSA:

2 large, ripe tomatoes, diced
3 green (spring) onions, finely chopped
¼ cup (2 fl oz/60 ml) light olive oil
1 tablespoon red wine vinegar
1 large clove garlic, minced
1 tablespoon fresh thyme leaves or 1 teaspoon dried thyme
⅛ teaspoon salt
freshly ground pepper to taste

FOR THE CELERY SAUCE:

½ cup (2½ oz/75 g) finely minced celery
½ cup (4 oz/125 g) sour cream or plain yogurt
½ cup (4 fl oz/125 ml) mayonnaise
¼ cup (1½ oz/45 g) finely minced red onion
¼ cup (2 fl oz/60 ml) fresh lemon juice
1 heaping teaspoon celery seed

FOR THE FISH:

4–6 whole catfish (about 8–10 oz/250–315 g each),
 cleaned and skinned (see glossary)
olive oil or vegetable oil

❈ To make the 2 sauces, in a bowl, combine all the ingredients for the Herbed Tomato Salsa. In a separate bowl, combine all the ingredients for the Celery Sauce. Cover both bowls and let stand for 1 hour at room temperature to blend the flavors. Refrigerate for up to 24 hours.

❈ Prepare a medium-hot direct fire in a charcoal grill. Place the catfish in a lightly oiled hinged wire basket and brush the fish lightly with oil. Grill 4–6 in (10–15 cm) from coals for 4–5 minutes on each side, or until the fish flakes easily.

❈ To serve, place fillets on individual plates and spoon sauces on top. Serve hot.

SERVES 4–6

*Left to right: Fish with Pecan Butter Sauce and Meunière Sauce,
Grilled Catfish with Two Sauces*

Maryland

MARYLAND CRAB CAKES

*What the crawfish is to Louisiana, or the lobster to Maine, the blue
crab is to Maryland. The crustacean whose Latin name means
"beautiful swimmer" has become a symbol of the Chesapeake Bay.
Crab Cakes are a favorite way of enjoying rich, sweet crabmeat.
If you aren't cooking them right away, place the cakes on a baking
sheet lined with waxed paper, cover loosely with plastic wrap and
refrigerate up to 2 hours until ready to use.*

3 tablespoons lowfat mayonnaise
1 egg, lightly beaten
¾ cup (3 oz/90 g) unseasoned fine dried bread crumbs
½ cup (2½ oz/75 g) minced celery
½ cup (1½ oz/45 g) thinly sliced green (spring) onions,
    including tender green tops
1 tablespoon finely chopped fresh dill or 1 teaspoon dried
    dill, crumbled
1 tablespoon fresh lemon juice
2 teaspoons Dijon-style mustard
½ teaspoon salt
¼ teaspoon freshly ground pepper
3 dashes of hot pepper sauce
⅛ teaspoon ground nutmeg
1 lb (500 g) fresh cooked crabmeat, picked over to remove
    cartilage and shell fragments and flaked

1 tablespoon milk, or as needed (optional)
1 tablespoon vegetable oil
2 lemons, each cut into 4 wedges

❀ In a medium bowl, combine the mayonnaise, egg, bread
crumbs, celery, green onions and dill and stir until well blended.
Stir in the lemon juice, mustard, salt, pepper, hot pepper sauce
and nutmeg. Using a rubber spatula, fold in the flaked crabmeat
until well blended. The mixture should be moist enough to stick
together. If the mixture is not moist enough, add the milk, 1
teaspoon at a time, as needed. If it is too moist, refrigerate for 15
minutes before forming into cakes.
❀ Using a ¼ cup (2 oz/60 g) dry measuring cup, scoop up the
crab mixture, without packing it, and invert into your hand.
Using the back of the cup, gently flatten the mixture into a
cake against your palm. Repeat with the remaining mixture
for a total of 12 cakes. Do not overwork the mixture.
❀ Preheat an oven to 200°F (93°C).
❀ In a large nonstick skillet over medium-high heat, heat the
oil. Fry the cakes in 3 batches until browned, 3 minutes on each
side. Using a metal spatula, turn over carefully and flatten the
cakes again if needed. Drain briefly on paper towels. Repeat
with the remaining cakes, keeping the cooked cakes warm in
the oven until all are ready to serve.
❀ Serve hot, accompanied with the lemon wedges.

MAKES 12 CRAB CAKES, SERVES 4–6   *Photograph pages 88–89*

Top to bottom: Fried Catfish, Arkansas-style Frog Legs

FRIED CATFISH

Vertamae Smart-Grosvenor, the National Public Radio commentator, grew up in South Carolina. In her book Vibration Cooking, *she remembers the catfish back home: "Every Friday at Pee Wee's we had a fish fry. One of the favorites was fried croakers. I would buy small croakers and coat with cornmeal and fry in peanut oil. I got them every Friday and very fresh from Hessey on Avenue C. Sometime he would have catfish and that was the day you could tell who was above or below the Mason-Dixon line. When I would say we have fried catfish all the South Carolina and Georgia, 'Bama and 'Sippi folk would say, 'I'll have the fried catfish.' First off, you got to skin the catfish. To skin: draw a sharp knife around the fish in back of the gills and pull off the skin with the pliers. (You can use your hands.) Clean and cut up the catfish and salt and pepper, then pat with cornmeal. Fry in very hot grease in your heavy black cast-iron skillet."*

Fried catfish would typically be served with Hush Puppies (recipe on page 179). If you don't want to clean and skin the catfish yourself, ask your fishmonger or buy catfish fillets.

4 whole catfish, 8–10 oz (250–315 g) each, cleaned
    and skinned (see glossary)
1½ teaspoons salt, or to taste
½ teaspoon freshly ground pepper, or to taste
1 cup (5 oz/155 g) white cornmeal
4 cups (32 fl oz/1 l) vegetable oil
1 lemon, cut into 4 wedges
sprigs of fresh parsley for garnish (optional)

❀ Season both sides of the catfish with the salt and pepper. Place the cornmeal in a large, resealable plastic bag. One at a time, place the catfish in the bag, seal and shake the bag gently until the fish is thoroughly and evenly coated with cornmeal. Repeat with the remaining 3 fish.
❀ In a medium, deep, heavy cast-iron skillet over medium heat, heat the oil to 360°F (185°C) on a deep-fry thermometer. Add 2 of the catfish and increase the heat, if needed, to maintain the temperature at 360°F (185°C).
❀ Fry until the fish is opaque throughout and flakes easily with a fork, 4–6 minutes on each side. Check often for doneness to prevent overcooking. Drain on paper towels and keep warm. Repeat with the remaining 2 catfish.
❀ Serve with lemon wedges to squeeze over the hot fish. Garnish with parsley, if desired.

SERVES 4

ARKANSAS-STYLE FROG LEGS

The American commercial frog industry is primarily concentrated in the states along the Gulf Coast from Florida to Louisiana, but it is also prevalent in Arkansas. Succulent frog legs are an epicurean delicacy with a flavor and texture more subtle than that of chicken or rabbit, to which they are frequently compared. Though they can be served very elegantly—braised in dry white wine—they are equally tasty when prepared in this rustic manner.

8 pairs of frog legs, skin and feet removed, each pair tied
    together with kitchen twine at the first joint
vegetable oil for frying
½ cup (2½ oz/75 g) all-purpose (plain) flour
½ teaspoon salt
¼ teaspoon freshly ground pepper
1 cup (8 fl oz/250 ml) lowfat buttermilk
sprigs of fresh parsley for serving
2 green (spring) onions, thinly sliced, for garnish
lemon wedges

❀ Place the frog legs in a bowl and add salted water to cover. Refrigerate for 2 hours and drain. Rinse the frog legs thoroughly and pat dry with paper towels.
❀ In a large, heavy skillet over medium-high heat, pour in the oil to a depth of ¼ in (6 mm) and heat to 350°F (180°C) on a deep-fry thermometer.
❀ Meanwhile, in a large bowl, sift together the flour, salt and pepper. Pour the buttermilk into a shallow medium bowl. Dip the frog legs in the buttermilk and then dredge in the seasoned flour, turning to coat the legs on all sides and shaking off the excess flour.
❀ Fry the frog legs in 2 batches, 4 pairs at a time, 2–3 minutes on each side for small legs, 4–5 minutes on each side for large ones, until golden brown and opaque throughout. Do not overcook. Drain on paper towels. Remove and discard the kitchen twine. Cover the first cooked legs to keep warm until the second batch is done and ready to serve.
❀ Arrange the frog legs on a parsley-lined serving platter and garnish with green onions. Serve at once with lemon wedges.

SERVES 4 AS AN APPETIZER

MAY RIVER OYSTERS
WITH BRIOCHE TOAST

Elizabeth Terry was one of the first Southern chefs to produce what is called "new" Southern cooking, from her Savannah restaurant called Elizabeth on 37th, housed in a turn-of-the-century mansion built for a wealthy cotton broker. But Terry is careful not to take too many liberties with Southern fare. She wants it to be contemporary while maintaining its integrity. Her oyster recipe here is a good example. It incorporates only those flavors that meld well with oysters—good dry sherry, sweet leeks, country ham, rich cream and aromatic fresh thyme. While Terry uses the small local oysters from Savannah's waters, you can substitute almost any firm, fresh oysters.

3 tablespoons unsalted butter
4 oz (125 g) lean country ham, trimmed of fat and finely
    chopped (see glossary)
¼ cup (2 fl oz/60 ml) dry sherry
2 tablespoons all-purpose (plain) flour
1 cup (8 fl oz/250 ml) heavy (double) cream
1 tablespoon finely chopped fresh thyme
2 small leeks, white parts only, cleaned well and sliced into
    ¼-in (6-mm) rounds
2 dozen fresh shucked oysters, drained
12 slices (8 oz/250 g) fresh brioche or challah, toasted
1 tablespoon minced fresh tarragon

❀ In a large, heavy skillet over medium-high heat, melt 2 tablespoons of the butter. Add the ham and cook, stirring, until lightly browned, 3 minutes. Add the sherry, stir and cook until reduced by half, about 2 minutes. Lower the heat to medium and whisk in the flour. Cook, whisking, for 1 minute. Stir in the cream and thyme and simmer until thick, 3–4 minutes. Transfer the sauce to a nonreactive heatproof bowl and set aside at room temperature.
❀ Clean the skillet, return it to medium-high heat and melt the remaining 1 tablespoon butter. Add the leeks and oysters and cook, stirring, until the oyster edges begin to curl and they are opaque throughout, about 2 minutes. Do not overcook. Remove from the heat and set aside.
❀ To serve, arrange 2 toasted slices of brioche or challah on each of 6 individual plates. Reheat the sauce over medium heat and fold in the leeks and oysters. Very briefly heat through. Spoon the oyster mixture over the toasted bread and garnish with the minced fresh tarragon.

SERVES 6   *Photograph page 97*

New Orleans, Louisiana

GULF FISH BEIGNETS WITH TOMATO-CORN TARTAR SAUCE

Emeril Lagasse, award-winning chef of Emeril's and NOLA in New Orleans, has an inspired approach to Creole and Cajun cooking. Take his savory twist on that New Orleans staple, the beignet (recipe on page 175). The traditional sweet puffy variety is dredged in confectioners' (icing) sugar and dipped into café au lait. But in Lagasse's hands, beignets contain chunks of local Gulf fish, dipped into one of the best versions of tartar sauce around. This recipe is adapted from his cookbook Emeril's New New Orleans Cooking. *The recipe for the seasoning blend makes about ¾ cup.*

FOR EMERIL'S CREOLE SEASONING:

2½ tablespoons paprika
2 tablespoons salt
2 tablespoons garlic powder
1 tablespoon freshly ground pepper
1 tablespoon onion powder
1 tablespoon ground cayenne pepper
1 tablespoon dried oregano
1 tablespoon dried thyme

FOR THE TOMATO-CORN TARTAR SAUCE:

1 cup (8 fl oz/250 ml) mayonnaise
2 plum (Roma) tomatoes, peeled and finely chopped
1 ear of yellow or white corn, kernels removed and
    blanched in boiling water for 1 minute, then cooled
    in ice water for 1 minute
1 green (spring) onion, including tender green tops,
    finely chopped
1 teaspoon Emeril's Creole Seasoning
salt to taste
¼ teaspoon freshly ground pepper

FOR THE FISH BEIGNETS:

2 eggs
6 oz (185 g) drum, catfish, wahoo, scrod, bass or
    crawfish tails, cut into ½-in (12-mm) pieces
4 teaspoons plus ⅛ teaspoon Emeril's Creole Seasoning
¼ cup (1½ oz/45 g) finely chopped green bell
    pepper (capsicum)
¼ cup (1 oz/30 g) finely chopped green (spring) onions,
    including tender green tops
1 tablespoon minced garlic
1 teaspoon salt
1½ cups (7½ oz/235 g) all-purpose (plain) flour
1 teaspoon baking powder
½ cup (4 fl oz/125 ml) milk
vegetable oil for frying

❀ To make the Creole Seasoning, in an 8–fl oz (250-ml) jar with a lid, combine paprika, salt, garlic powder, pepper, onion powder, cayenne, oregano and thyme. Secure the lid and set aside.
❀ To make the tartar sauce, place the mayonnaise in a mixing bowl and fold in the tomatoes, corn, green onion, 1 teaspoon Creole Seasoning, salt and pepper. Set aside.
❀ Preheat an oven to 200°F (93°C).
❀ To make the fish beignets, place the eggs in a large mixing bowl and whisk until frothy. Add the fish, 3 teaspoons of the Creole Seasoning, bell pepper, green onion and garlic and stir to combine well. Fold in the salt, flour and baking powder. Add the milk and stir until just incorporated.
❀ In a large, heavy saucepan, pour the oil to a depth of 2 in (5 cm) and heat to 375°F (190°C) on a deep-fry thermometer. Working in batches, drop large spoonfuls of the beignet batter into the hot oil and fry until golden brown and crispy on both sides, about 3 minutes. As the beignets cook, use a slotted spoon to keep them submerged in the oil. Drain on paper towels. Repeat with remaining batter, keeping the beignets warm in the oven until all are ready to serve. Then sprinkle with 1 teaspoon Creole Seasoning.
❀ To serve, spoon ¾ cup (6 fl oz/180 ml) of the tartar sauce onto each of 4 individual plates. Place 5 or 6 beignets on top of the sauce and garnish with a sprinkling of the remaining ⅛ teaspoon Creole Seasoning. Serve hot.

SERVES 4

Charleston, South Carolina

CLASSIC CHARLESTON BREAKFAST SHRIMP WITH CREAMY GRITS

This Charlestonian version of a favorite Low Country dish is from Hoppin' John's Lowcountry Cooking *by John Martin Taylor. He writes that up until lately Low Country households ate this dish, often called "breakfast shrimp," every morning during shrimp season. This grits recipe yields enough for second helpings.*

FOR THE GRITS:

2 cups (16 fl oz/500 ml) water
2 tablespoons salted butter or 2 tablespoons unsalted butter
    plus ¼ teaspoon salt
½ cup (3 oz/90 g) stone- or water-ground whole-grain grits
1–2 cups (8–16 fl oz/250–500 ml) milk or half & half

FOR THE SHRIMP:

½ lb (250 g) shrimp (prawns), peeled and deveined
    (see glossary)
2 tablespoons fresh lemon juice
salt to taste
ground cayenne pepper to taste
3 tablespoons bacon drippings or unsalted butter
1 small onion, finely chopped
¼ cup (1½ oz/45 g) finely chopped green bell pepper (capsicum)
2 tablespoons unbleached all-purpose (plain) flour
¾–1 cup (6–8 fl oz/180–250 ml) hot water or stock (shrimp,
    chicken or vegetable; see glossary), or as needed

❀ To make the grits, place the water in a heavy-bottomed saucepan over medium heat, add the salted butter or the butter plus salt and bring to a boil. Stir in the grits and return to a boil. Reduce the heat to medium-low and cook at a low boil, stirring occasionally, until the grits are very thick and have absorbed most of the water, about 10 minutes.
❀ Add about ½ cup (4 fl oz/125 ml) of the milk or half & half, reduce the heat to low and simmer for about 10 minutes longer. As the liquid evaporates or is absorbed, add more milk or half & half, cooking the grits to the desired consistency, for a total cooking time of at least 1 hour. The grits should be slightly soupy but full-bodied enough that they do not run on the plate when served.
❀ To make the shrimp, place them in a bowl, sprinkle with the lemon juice, salt and cayenne and set aside.
❀ In a skillet over medium heat, heat the bacon drippings or melt the butter and sauté the onion and bell pepper until the onion begins to look translucent, about 10 minutes. Sprinkle the flour over the onion and bell pepper and cook, stirring constantly, until the flour begins to brown, about 2 minutes. Add the shrimp and about ¾ cup (6 fl oz/180 ml) of the hot water or stock. Cook 2–3 minutes, stirring constantly and turning the shrimp to cook evenly, until the shrimp are cooked through and the gravy is smooth, thinning with more hot water or stock if needed.
❀ Serve immediately over the hot grits.

SERVES 2; GRITS SERVE 2–4

Top to bottom: Classic Charleston Breakfast Shrimp with Creamy Grits, Gulf Fish Beignets with Tomato-Corn Tartar Sauce, May River Oysters with Brioche Toast (recipe page 95)

Crawfish Étouffée

CRAWFISH ÉTOUFFÉE

Crawfish tails are often sold precooked, peeled, cleaned and frozen, so all you have to do is thaw them and stir them into the stew at the end. But get them fresh if you can—your tastebuds will be richly rewarded. The shrimp-sized crustaceans are in season mid-March to mid-May and are commonly boiled in their shell for peeling and eating. Leftovers often end up in rich, spicy stews such as this one.

¼ cup (2 fl oz/60 ml) vegetable oil
3 tablespoons all-purpose (plain) flour
½ cup (2½ oz/75 g) finely chopped white onion
⅓ cup (2 oz/60 g) finely chopped celery
2 cloves garlic, crushed through a garlic press
1 cup (6 oz/185 g) coarsely chopped, peeled, seeded
   tomatoes (see glossary)
¼ cup (1½ oz/45 g) finely chopped green bell pepper (capsicum)
¼ cup (1½ oz/45 g) finely chopped red bell pepper (capsicum)
1⅓ cups (11 fl oz/330 ml) vegetable stock (see glossary)
⅓ cup (3 fl oz/80 ml) canned tomato sauce
½ teaspoon dried basil
¼ teaspoon dried thyme
¼ teaspoon ground cayenne pepper
¼ cup (¾ oz/20 g) thinly sliced green (spring) onions
1 lb (500 g) crawfish tails, cooked, peeled and cleaned
   (see glossary)
1 tablespoon minced fresh parsley
4 cups (1¼ lb/625 g) hot cooked white rice for serving
hot pepper sauce for serving

✤ In a large, heavy saucepan over high heat, heat the oil until it begins to smoke, about 4 minutes. Add the flour and whisk constantly until smooth. Cook, whisking constantly, until the roux is dark red-brown, 3–5 minutes. Do not let the roux burn.
✤ Remove the pan from the heat. Stir in the onion, celery, garlic, tomatoes and bell peppers until well blended.
✤ Return the pan to low heat, gradually pour in the vegetable stock and stir. Add the tomato sauce all at once, stirring until well blended. Stir in the basil, thyme and cayenne until well blended. Simmer, stirring often, until the vegetables are tender and the sauce has thickened, about 20 minutes. Stir in the green onions, crawfish tails and parsley until well blended, and simmer until the crawfish is just heated through, about 5 minutes longer.
✤ To serve, mound the rice in the center of a serving platter and ladle the crawfish mixture around the rice. Serve hot and pass with hot pepper sauce.

SERVES 4

YELLOWTAIL SNAPPER WITH RUM, BROWN BUTTER, MANGO, GINGER AND MINT

As chef/owner of Mark's Place in north Miami and Mark's Las Olas in Fort Lauderdale, Mark Militello creates his signature big, splashy flavors by weaving tropical ingredients with Californian and Mediterranean methods. In the following recipe, you may use almost any fresh, firm white fish. If the fillets exceed 1 inch (2.5 cm) thick, sauté as directed, then transfer to a baking pan and finish off the cooking in a

Yellowtail Snapper with Rum, Brown Butter, Mango, Ginger and Mint

preheated 350°F (180°C) oven for about 10 minutes while you proceed with the mango-rum sauce. If desired, serve with rice and black beans and, to sip, Steven Raichlen's Mojitos (recipe on page 36).

6 red snapper, yellow snapper or mutton snapper fillets, 6–8
   oz (185–250 g) each (see note)
salt and freshly ground pepper
1½ cups (7½ oz/235 g) all-purpose (plain) flour
½ cup (4 fl oz/125 ml) clarified butter (see glossary)
½ cup (4 oz/125 g) unsalted butter
½ cup (2½ oz/75 g) macadamia nuts
1 tablespoon peeled, julienned fresh ginger
1 cup (5 oz/155 g) finely chopped mango
¾ cup (1 oz/30 g) loosely packed fresh mint leaves
⅓ cup (3 fl oz/80 ml) dark rum

✤ Run your fingers across the fish fillets, feeling for pin bones, and remove any with pliers. Score the fillets three times on the diagonal with a sharp knife. Season on both sides with salt and pepper, then lightly dust with flour and shake off any excess.
✤ In a large skillet over medium-high heat, heat the clarified butter. Add the fish and sauté until golden brown and crispy, about 4 minutes on each side, or until opaque throughout but still springy to the touch. Transfer to a heatproof dish, cover to keep warm and set aside.
✤ Add the unsalted butter to the skillet and heat over medium until browned. Add the nuts, ginger, mango and mint. Stir and cook for 1 minute. Add the rum, stir and bring to a boil. Season with salt and pepper and remove from the heat. To serve, ladle the warm sauce over the fish.

SERVES 6

Wayland, Tennessee

CORNMEAL-BREADED TROUT WITH COUNTRY HAM AND HOMINY HASH

Nestled in the Great Smoky Mountains of Tennessee is a well-heeled yet cozy retreat known as The Inn at Blackberry Farm. It has attained Relais & Chateaux status, yet it hasn't lost touch with its roots. Chef John Fleer serves what he terms Foothills Cuisine, a style that wanders across the line between refined and rugged—this trout recipe, for example. The trout are locally farmed, dredged in a batter of cornmeal and buttermilk before frying and then served with a hash made of potatoes, onions, country ham and hominy. Typically, this dish would be served for brunch, accompanied by a poached egg and a light watercress salad.

FOR THE HOMINY HASH:

¼ cup (2 fl oz/60 ml) clarified butter (see glossary)
1 lb (500 g) potatoes, peeled, cut into 1-in (2.5-cm) dice
    and cooked until just tender
1 onion, finely chopped
¾ cup (4 oz/125 g) finely chopped red bell pepper (capsicum)
¾ cup (4 oz/125 g) finely chopped green bell
    pepper (capsicum)
4 oz (125 g) country ham, finely chopped (see glossary)
½ cup (2½ oz/75 g) finely chopped celery
2 cups (16 oz/500 g) canned hominy, drained
1 tablespoon finely chopped chives
1 tablespoon finely chopped parsley
1 teaspoon coarse salt
½ teaspoon freshly ground pepper
2 teaspoons finely chopped jalapeño pepper (optional;
    see glossary)

FOR THE TROUT:

1 cup (8 fl oz/250 ml) buttermilk
1 cup (4 oz/125 g) white cornmeal
1 cup (5 oz/155 g) all-purpose (plain) flour
1 tablespoon Old Bay seasoning (see glossary)
1 tablespoon onion powder
1 teaspoon celery salt
4 trout, about 8 oz (250 g) each, boned but heads and
    skin intact
¼ cup (2 fl oz/60 ml) clarified butter (see glossary)
sprigs of fresh flat-leaf (Italian) parsley for garnish

❋ To make the hash, in a large cast-iron skillet over medium-high heat, heat the clarified butter until almost smoking. Add the cooked potatoes and sauté, stirring, until brown and crisp, 4–5 minutes. Reduce the heat to medium-low and add the onion, bell peppers, ham and celery. Sauté, stirring, until the vegetables are soft, 3–4 minutes.
❋ Add the hominy, chives, parsley, salt and pepper and sauté, stirring, for 1 minute. Add the jalapeño pepper, if desired. Remove from the heat and set aside, keeping warm.
❋ To cook the trout, preheat an oven to 350°F (180°C).
❋ In a medium bowl, combine the buttermilk, cornmeal, flour, Old Bay seasoning, onion powder and celery salt and stir to blend well. Dip each trout into the batter and shake lightly to remove any excess.
❋ In a large cast-iron skillet over medium-high heat, heat the clarified butter. When hot, add the trout and brown for 1 minute on each side. Place the skillet of browned trout in the oven for 6 minutes or until opaque throughout but still springy to the touch.
❋ To serve, remove the trout from the oven, place on 4 individual plates and open up the cavities. Fill with the hominy hash and heap to overflow onto the plates. Garnish with the parsley sprigs.

SERVES 4

Louisiana

OYSTER-EGGPLANT GRATIN

A New Orleans–style vegetable and oyster casserole that features eggplant, a favorite staple of Louisianans. Serve hot as an appetizer or a side dish.

¼ cup (2 fl oz/60 ml) olive oil
1 eggplant (aubergine), about 1 lb (500 g), peeled and cut
    into ½-in (12-mm) cubes
2 white onions, finely chopped
2 red bell peppers (capsicums), seeded and finely chopped
8 oz (250 g) button mushrooms, thinly sliced
⅓ cup (½ oz/15 g) finely chopped fresh basil
2 tablespoons finely chopped fresh oregano
2 tablespoons finely chopped fresh parsley
2 lb (1 kg) fresh shucked oysters, drained, reserving the
    liquid, about ¼ cup (2 fl oz/60 ml)
4 cups (16 oz/500 g) dry herb-seasoned stuffing mix
3 cups (12 oz/375 g) shredded Gruyère cheese
1¼ cups (10 fl oz/310 ml) chicken stock (see glossary) or
    canned chicken broth, or as needed, to make 1½ cups
    (12 fl oz/375 ml) total liquid when combined with the
    oyster liquid
2 teaspoons hot pepper sauce
salt and freshly ground pepper to taste

❋ In a large skillet over medium heat, heat the olive oil. Add the eggplant, onions, peppers and mushrooms and cook until the vegetables are tender-crisp, 3–5 minutes. Remove the skillet from the heat. Add the basil, oregano, parsley and oysters, stir to mix well and set aside.
❋ Preheat an oven to 375°F (190°C). Lightly coat a shallow 3-qt (3-l) baking dish with vegetable cooking spray.
❋ Spread 1½ cups (3 oz/90 g) of the stuffing mix on the bottom of the prepared dish. Top with half of the vegetable mixture, followed by half of the Gruyère cheese. Repeat with another layer of 1½ cups (3 oz/90 g) stuffing mix, the remaining vegetables and remaining cheese.
❋ In a medium bowl, whisk together the chicken stock, oyster liquid, hot pepper sauce and salt and pepper until well blended. Pour over the layered gratin. Sprinkle with the remaining stuffing mix. Place on the middle oven rack and bake until the oysters are opaque throughout and cooked, the gratin is bubbling and the topping is light golden brown, 45–50 minutes. Do not overbake or the oysters will be tough.
❋ Serve hot directly from the baking dish.

SERVES 6–8

Louisiana

SHRIMP CREOLE

If New Orleans were to choose an official dish, Shrimp Creole would no doubt be a leading contender. Though it looks and tastes like gourmet fare that took hours of fussing over, it actually boils down to a simple skillet supper. Fresh cilantro, though not traditional, brightens the flavor. Filé, or powdered sassafras leaves, must only be added off the heat or the dish will turn stringy and unappetizing.

2 tablespoons olive oil
2 cups (7 oz/220 g) sliced white onion
4 cloves garlic, minced
2 celery ribs, cut into medium dice
2 medium green bell peppers (capsicums), seeded and cut
    into medium dice
1 teaspoon Old Bay seasoning (see glossary)
½ teaspoon ground cayenne pepper
2 cups (16 fl oz/500 ml) clam juice or fish stock (see glossary)

Top to bottom: Oyster-Eggplant Gratin, Cornmeal-Breaded Trout with Country Ham and Hominy Hash

28 oz (875 g) canned whole tomatoes in purée
1 teaspoon dried thyme
1 bay leaf
2 tablespoons tomato paste
2 lb (1 kg) medium shrimp (prawns), peeled and deveined (see glossary)
⅓ cup (½ oz/10 g) chopped fresh cilantro (fresh coriander) or fresh flat-leaf (Italian) parsley
2 teaspoons filé powder
6 cups (30 oz/940 g) hot cooked long-grain white rice for serving

❋ In a large, heavy pot over high heat, heat the oil. Add the onion to the hot oil and cook, stirring, 1 minute. Add the garlic and cook 30 seconds longer.

❋ Stir in the celery, bell pepper, Old Bay seasoning and cayenne. Reduce the heat to medium and cook, stirring occasionally, 2 minutes.

❋ Add the clam juice or fish stock, tomatoes, thyme and bay leaf. Cover and simmer 15 minutes. Stir in the tomato paste, cover and continue to simmer, 5 minutes longer. Stir in the shrimp and cook until the shrimp turn pink and the interiors are opaque throughout, 1–1½ minutes. Do not overcook.

❋ Remove from the heat. Remove and discard the bay leaf. Stir in the cilantro or flat-leaf parsley until well blended. Sprinkle the filé powder over the surface and stir in gently.

❋ To serve, fill individual bowls with the hot cooked rice and ladle the Shrimp Creole over. Serve hot.

SERVES 6   *Photograph pages 88–89*

Top to bottom: Acadian Peppered Shrimp, Pan-fried Soft-shell Crab

Louisiana

ACADIAN PEPPERED SHRIMP

Like boiled shrimp, this dish is a convivial, gather-round-the-table type of main course. French bread and a green salad round out the menu. Or serve these shrimp as an appetizer. This dish is flavored with a brown butter sauce along with a prodigal use of pepper, with almost fiery results. The flavor sensation to the palate can be addictive! However, if you are inclined to be fainthearted when it comes to spicy, hot foods, reduce the amount of black pepper by half.

4 lb (2 kg) medium shrimp (prawns), in the shell
1 cup (8 oz/250 g) unsalted butter
2 tablespoons fresh lemon juice
2 tablespoons Worcestershire sauce
4 cloves garlic, crushed through a garlic press
2 tablespoons black pepper, finely cracked in a mortar and pestle or an electric spice grinder
2 teaspoons dried basil
1 teaspoon dried oregano
1 bay leaf, broken in half
½ teaspoon salt
½ teaspoon ground cayenne pepper
dash of ground nutmeg
2 teaspoons minced fresh basil

❀ Rinse the shrimp and pat dry with paper towels.
❀ In a large, deep nonreactive skillet, preferably nonstick, over medium heat, melt the butter. Stir in the lemon juice, Worcestershire sauce, garlic, cracked pepper, basil, oregano, bay leaf, salt, cayenne and nutmeg. Cook, stirring often, until the butter turns almost chestnut brown, 10–15 minutes.
❀ Increase the heat to high, add the shrimp and sauté until the shrimp turn pink and the interiors are opaque throughout, 8–10 minutes. Remove from the heat. Remove and discard the bay leaf and stir in the fresh basil until well blended.
❀ Working quickly and using tongs, arrange the hot shrimp in a spiral pattern on a large round serving platter, leaving space in the center for a small ramekin. Drizzle some of the butter sauce over the shrimp and pour the remaining sauce in the ramekin. Serve hot.

SERVES 4

Charleston, South Carolina

PAN-FRIED SOFT-SHELL CRABS

Louis Osteen grew up on a South Carolina farm, and though he has trained in the kitchens of French chefs, he keeps coming back to his roots. At Louis's Charleston Grill in Charleston, South Carolina, he specializes in Low Country fare, making use of local farm produce and locally caught seafood. Osteen has a terrific method of breading and frying soft-shell crabs, as in this adaptation of his recipe in Home Food *by Debbie Shore and Catherine Townsend. The crabs are marinated in buttermilk and hot pepper sauce, then dredged in cornmeal and flour. Soft-shell crabs are blue crabs that have molted their small hard shell in order to grow a new larger shell. They are a springtime delicacy in the South—especially the Chesapeake Bay—whether deep-fried, grilled, sautéed or baked.*

3 cups (24 fl oz/750 ml) lowfat buttermilk
2 tablespoons hot pepper sauce
6 soft-shell crabs, cleaned
1 cup (5 oz/155 g) yellow cornmeal
1 cup (5 oz/155 g) all-purpose (plain) flour
1 teaspoon salt
1 teaspoon freshly ground pepper
½ teaspoon baking soda (bicarbonate of soda)
1½ cups (12 fl oz/375 ml) vegetable oil
1 tablespoon red wine vinegar
3 tablespoons fresh lemon juice
3 tablespoons water
1 cup (8 oz/250 g) unsalted butter, cut into 12 pieces
¼ cup (½ oz/15 g) finely chopped fresh parsley

❀ In a glass baking dish large enough to hold the crabs in a single layer, combine the buttermilk and hot pepper sauce. Add the crabs, turning them once to coat. Cover with plastic wrap and refrigerate for 1 hour.
❀ Meanwhile, combine the cornmeal, flour, salt, pepper and baking soda on a plate. Remove the chilled crabs from the buttermilk marinade, then dredge on all sides in the cornmeal mixture. Place the crabs on a baking sheet and refrigerate to allow the coating to dry, about 30 minutes.
❀ Preheat an oven to 200°F (93°C).
❀ In a large, heavy cast-iron skillet over medium-high heat, heat the oil to 350°F (180°C) on a deep-fry thermometer. Working in batches of 2 or 3 crabs at a time, carefully slide the crabs into the hot oil, bottom side down. Increase the heat if needed, to maintain the temperature at 350°F (180°C). When the crabs are golden brown on the bottom, after about 2 minutes, flip over and cook 2 minutes longer. Remove with a slotted spoon to paper towels to drain. Repeat with the remaining crabs, keeping the fried crabs warm in the oven for no longer than 10 minutes.
❀ In a small bowl, combine the vinegar, lemon juice and water. Carefully pour off and discard the oil from the skillet, leaving the browned bits. Place the skillet over medium heat, add the vinegar mixture and simmer, scraping up the browned bits with a wooden spoon, for 30 seconds. Add the butter and whisk into a sauce. Stir in the parsley.
❀ To serve, place the crabs on individual plates and pass the sauce.

SERVES 6

Miami, Florida

JOE'S MUSTARD SAUCE FOR STONE CRABS

In Miami Beach, you know stone crab season has begun when the lines start forming again at south Florida's most famous seafood institution, Joe's Stone Crab. Waits are often hours long, but customers don't seem to mind—that's just part of the ritual. The restaurant is only open from October to May, when the house specialty can be had fresh, though they're available in fish markets frozen throughout the year (to mail order from Joe's, see Mail Order Sources). The crabs are cooked just after harvesting, so all you need to do is crack and eat. At Joe's, the experience wouldn't be complete without dunking the sweet, tender meat in the creamy mustard sauce, which is almost as legendary as the crabs. Here is the recipe.

3½ teaspoons Colman's dry mustard, or to taste
1 cup (8 fl oz/250 ml) mayonnaise
2 tablespoons heavy (double) cream
2 tablespoons milk
2 teaspoons Worcestershire sauce
1 teaspoon A-1 Steak Sauce
pinch of salt

❀ Place 3 teaspoons of the dry mustard in a mixing bowl. Add the mayonnaise and, using an electric mixer on low speed, beat for 1 minute. Add the cream, milk, Worcestershire sauce, steak sauce and salt. Beat on low until creamy, about 2 minutes. Add the remaining ½ teaspoon dry mustard or more, if you desire more bite. Transfer the sauce to a small nonreactive bowl, cover with plastic wrap and refrigerate until serving. Serve with stone crabs.

MAKES 1¼ CUPS (10 FL OZ/310 ML);
SERVES 4–6

Photograph pages 88–89

Upper South

Kentucky

HORSE COUNTRY

Tennessee

UPPER SOUTH

The most striking monument in Kentucky is not one of those stone rebels who stands sentinel over so many courthouse squares across the South. The most striking monument in Kentucky doesn't even depict a human being. Man o' War, perhaps the greatest racehorse that ever lived, lies buried beneath a bed of marigolds in the pastel hills that roll out of Lexington at an easy gait. With its broad chest and finely muscled legs, the great bronze steed that marks the plot manages with no motion of its own to convey the power and grace of thoroughbred racing. In the land of bourbon and bluegrass, no figure looms larger.

The Upper South is horse country. Foals gambol and toss their tails like pom-poms behind the white plank fences that beribbon the pastures of central Kentucky. Tennessee walking horses march with high-hooved precision across the blue-green fields that spread out from Nashville like a rumpled quilt. Highborn thoroughbreds sail past the twin steeples of Churchill Downs as a hundred thousand sportingly attired spectators assemble in Louisville to wager, sip mint juleps and celebrate the other sacraments of the well-bred life.

The Kentucky Derby and the Bluegrass Country that supplies it with speed and romance are the most cherished tableaux of the Upper South. At Derby brunches and dinners every May, a who's who of Kentucky foods

Previous pages: Miles of wooden plank fences divide the legendary bluegrass of the central Kentucky hills. Left: From its world-famous Music Row to the Country Music Hall of Fame, Nashville, Tennessee, is the heart and soul of country music in the United States.

107

makes its ritual appearance: burgoo, cheese grits, asparagus vinaigrette, country ham.

But the foods and the horse culture are not exclusively the domain of Kentucky. Tennessee has a larger, if less storied, bluegrass region that actually produces a greater number of horses than that of Kentucky. The states share more than their three-hundred-mile border; they have a common geography, history and culture.

Kentucky and Tennessee stack together like long, flat fieldstones in a wall separating the Deep South from the North. The states divide neatly into three parts: the mountainous east, the river plain of the west and the rippled and rolling hill country in between. Much of this central section rests on limestone into which water leaches and forms labyrinthine passages, most spectacularly Kentucky's Mammoth Cave. The limestone soil supports hardwood forests and meadows blanketed in bluegrass. Whether it is really blue is a matter of debate. While the locals swear it takes on a purplish tint when it buds in the spring, many a tourist has squinted in vain. No one can doubt, however, that limestone water and grass build the strong, light bones a racehorse requires.

Horses have not been the only fleet animals to thrive here. Kentucky and Tennessee were the first frontier of the new United States, and pioneers in the late 1700s found buffalo roaming the land they called the Great Meadow. "So Rich a Soil, Covered in Clover in full Bloom, the Woods alive with wild game," one settler wrote. "Nature in the profusion of her Bounties had spread a feast for all that lives."

The large role game played in the early diet of the Upper South can still be seen in one of the most traditional Kentucky dishes: burgoo, a hearty hunter's stew that once contained squirrel and other assorted small mammals. Kentuckians today eat a less gamey version at barbecues, political rallies and other community gatherings. Naturally there is a Derby connection; the horse that won the 1932 race was Burgoo King.

Kentuckian style was set by Virginia. Kentucky was part of the Old Dominion before it became the nation's first inland state in 1792, and many of the early settlers were Virginians lured by land bounties the legislature offered to veterans of the Revolutionary War. They brought Virginian notions of the good life, as exemplified by the country squires of England, and in time expressed that ideal in the horsey culture of the bluegrass. Like Virginia, Kentucky isn't content to call itself a state; rather, they are commonwealths.

Tennessee, likewise, was a frontier offspring of North Carolina, and many of its pioneers were Carolina veterans due land for their war service. They pressed westward through the Appalachians and along the rivers, founding in 1780 the fort that became Nashville, the eventual capital of the state. Tennessee entered the Union four years after Kentucky. The ethnic ingredients in both states were English and Scots-Irish, seasoned with African slaves. The Latin influences that spiced the Deep South were nonexistent.

Two American folk heroes symbolize the frontier days in Kentucky and Tennessee. Daniel Boone in 1769

Backstage at the Grand Ole Opry in Nashville, Tennessee, a musician warms up before his performance.

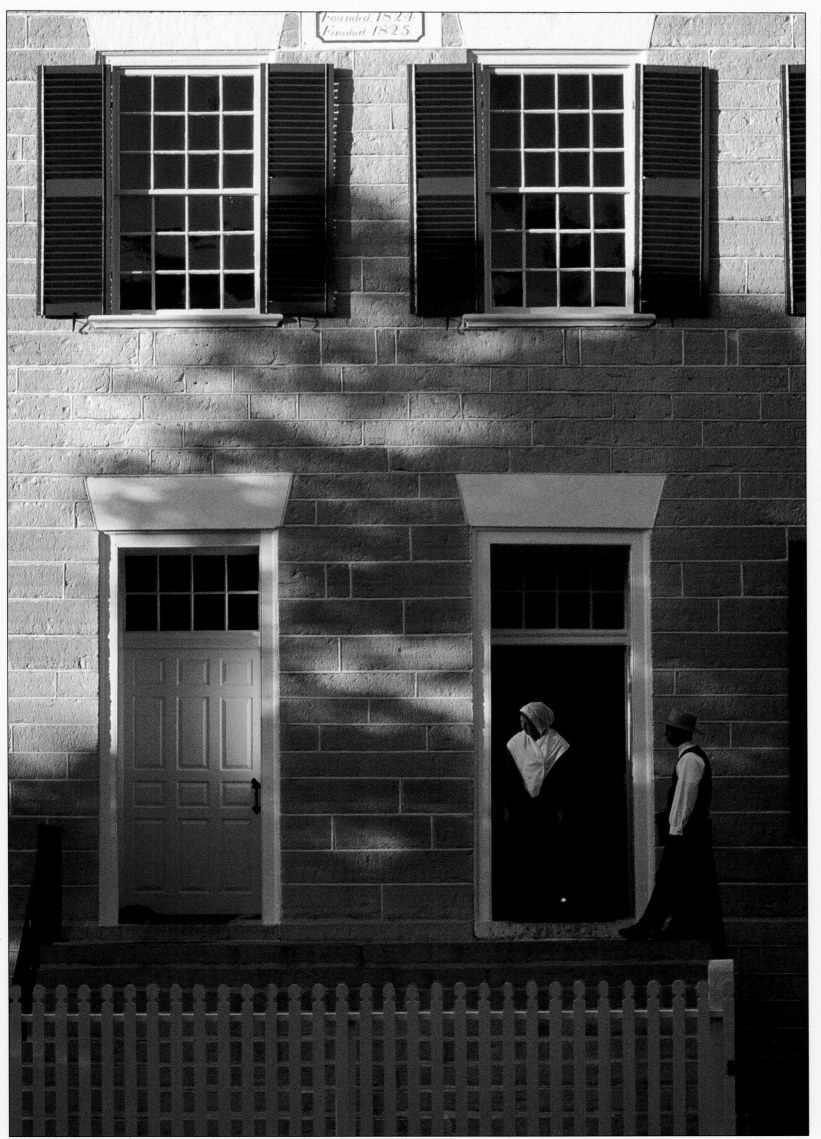

Known for their quest for simplicity and perfection in craftsmanship, the Shakers came to Kentucky in 1805.
Though the colony closed in 1910, Shaker Village of Pleasant Hill is presently a National Historic Landmark.

Followers have placed a commemorative wreath near the plaque that marks the site in Memphis, Tennessee, where Dr. Martin Luther King, Jr. was shot and killed on April 4, 1968.

led settlers through the Cumberland Gap into Kentucky, and six years later he established one of the territory's first settlements, Boonesboro, on the banks of the Kentucky River. Ever restless, he moved west and died in Missouri. His Tennessee counterpart in folklore, David Crockett, was a backwoods hunter and storyteller who rode his tall tales into a political career as a congressman in the 1820s. He, too, lit out for the west, dying at the Alamo "fightin' for li-ber-teee," as the Disney song has it.

The early years of both states resonate with other American legends: Andrew Jackson forging a new political party from his plantation outside Nashville; Henry Clay of Lexington trying to hold the slave and free states together as Speaker of the House; Abraham Lincoln, born in a log cabin in Kentucky, his family migrating north; Jefferson Davis, also born in a log cabin in Kentucky, his family migrating south.

Then, as now, politics was something of a contact sport in the Upper South. It was practiced, as elsewhere in the young republic, with liberal doses of distilled persuasion. George D. Prentiss, a Kentuckian, described it this way in an 1830 letter to a New England newspaper: "I have just witnessed a strange thing—a Kentucky election—and am disposed to give you an account of it. A Kentucky election lasts three days, and during that period whiskey and apple toddy flow through our cities and villages like the Euphrates through ancient Babylon."

The whiskey, of course, was bourbon. Americans had been making corn liquor since the natives had first introduced them to the grain. But according to tradition, it wasn't until 1789 that Elijah Craig, a Baptist minister in Bourbon County, Kentucky, hit upon the combination of corn, rye and barley that yields bourbon whiskey. No one knows who made the essential discovery—that it would taste better if aged in charred oak barrels. Food historian Eugene Walter offers an entertaining (if less than credible) explanation: lightning struck a barn in which a Kentucky farmer had buried several barrels of whiskey to age; finding the fire-scorched casks a few years later, he sampled the liquor and pronounced it good.

More than a century after Prentiss's observation, in 1964 Congress solemnized the ties between whiskey and politics by declaring bourbon the one true American spirit. By federal law, it must be distilled from mash that is more than half corn and must be aged at least four years in charred barrels that cannot be reused. By tradition, bourbon uses the same limestone water the thoroughbreds drink.

Nine distilleries make bourbon in Kentucky today. By law, they cannot sell whiskey on site. Thus visitors to landmarks such as the Jim Beam Distillery in Clermont, Kentucky, are both disappointed and amused to learn that while they can smell the whiskey and watch it being made they cannot sip it. The only taste of bourbon comes from the bourbon chocolate candy the company serves at the hospitality center.

The situation is nearly as bleak in Tennessee, where almost identical spirits known as Tennessee whiskey are made. The most famous label, Jack Daniel's, cannot be poured in public establishments in the distillery's own hometown of Lynchburg. In 1994 the county asked voters to let Jack Daniel's sell commemorative bottles. The people agreed, but then they would—half the residents of Moore County have appeared in the folksy black-and-white advertisements for which Jack Daniel's has become renowned.

Indeed, folksiness is a recurring theme in Upper South food. Many of the region's specialties—biscuits, sausage, country ham and redeye gravy, to name a few—have a just-folks feel to them. Two restaurant chains based in the Upper South play the down-home image to the hilt. Cracker Barrel, out of Lebanon, Tennessee, re-creates plank-floored country stores in its outlets. And the far-flung empire of Kentucky Fried Chicken was founded on the persona of a white-goateed colonel, Harland Sanders, who opened his first restaurant during the 1940s in the foothills town of Corbin. No one seemed to mind that the most familiar Kentucky colonel hailed from Indiana.

The best-known symbol of Kentucky hospitality might not be native either. Historians say the mint julep predates Kentucky and was probably created in Virginia. But Kentucky has elevated it to an art form. On the first Saturday in May for more than 120 years, horse lovers have raised their julep cups on Derby Day at Churchill Downs. They serve more than eighty thousand juleps at the race, some in plastic cups, some in frosty silver cups engraved with family names and handed down from generation to generation.

As with many iconic foods and drinks, there is spirited debate over the way to make a proper julep. Does one crush or merely bruise the mint? Do the sugar and water have to be heated to make a syrup? Is Kentucky bourbon the only liquor allowed, or will Tennessee whiskey suffice?

Henry Watterson, the turn-of-the-century editor of the *Louisville Courier-Journal,* showed what he thought of all the discussion when he published his personal recipe: "Pluck the mint gently from its bed, just as the dew of evening is about to form upon it. Select the choicer sprigs only, but do not rinse them. Prepare the simple syrup and measure out a half-tumbler of whiskey. Pour the whiskey into a well-frosted silver cup and throw the other ingredients away and drink the whiskey."

Spoken like a true Kentuckian.

From bluffs overlooking the Kentucky river, here the state Capitol building in Frankfort, Kentucky, stands amid autumn leaves.

Meat, Poultry & Game

As diners request healthier alternatives to red meat and pork, chicken, with its white meat, is more and more in demand.

MEAT, POULTRY & GAME

In the early 1990s, when Georgia and other states came under fire for flying reincarnations of the Confederate flag, a sociologist at the University of North Carolina suggested a less controversial symbol for the South: the dancing pig found on barbecue signs across the region. "A good barbecue joint," John Shelton Reed wrote, "may be the one place you'll find Southerners of all descriptions."

Rumor has it that the best place to partake in the revered tradition of Southern barbecue is at the roadside shacks featuring cords of hickory wood stacked up outside against the smokehouse.

Pork has always been the most Southern of meats. From bacon to barbecue, hocks to ham, chitlins to cracklin, it figures in many of the region's most characteristic foods.

Southerners eat plenty of other meats, of course. They enjoy beef, though they don't live off it like people do in Texas and the West. During hunting season Southerners will supplement the sideboard with venison, rabbit and game birds such as quail. And Lord knows they love poultry; fried chicken may be the most famous Dixie dish of all. But in historical significance each of these bows before the humble hog.

Like most Southerners, pigs are immigrants. The Spanish explorer Hernando de Soto is thought to have brought the first ones to America when he landed in Florida in 1539. The English introduced pigs to Virginia seventy years later. Colonists took to swine's flesh so readily that some of them, planter William Byrd quipped, "seem to grunt rather than speak."

Before refrigeration, salt pork was the most common way Southerners consumed hog meat. Slaves and poor whites made do with lower cuts like pig's feet and sow's belly, while the more fortunate savored bacon, ham and other cuts that come, literally, from high off the hog. At the top of this pork aristocracy sits the smoke-cured country ham, for which virtually every Southern state claims superiority. The most celebrated hams come from peanut-fed hogs in Smithfield, Virginia, and take almost as much time to turn out as a military academy cadet.

Previous pages: Left to right: Maude's Baked Ham (recipe page 120), Hot and Spicy Fried Chicken (recipe page 116), Deep-fried Whole Turkey (recipe page 119)

In the South, almost everyone has a personal recipe for barbecue sauce. Various varieties can be sampled at local farmers' markets.

ings and political rallies. In North Carolina, more than one journalist has observed, no one can be elected governor without eating more barbecue than is good for them.

The tradition continues today at hundreds of commercial pits and scores of barbecue contests across the region. Cook-off teams with pig-silly names like Swine Lake Ballet haul expensive smokers from fairground to fairground to show off their prowess and drink beer while they talk 'cue. One sure topic of debate is the bewildering variety of regional sauces and bastes. In the Carolinas alone there are pockets that swear allegiance to tomato-based sauces or mustard sauces or spiced vinegar sauces that contain no tomatoes at all. One devoted Carolinian hung a sign at his barbecue joint declaring his faith up front, like a member of a Pentecostal sect might: "We don't hold by tomatoes."

Southerners can be just as persnickety about their fried chicken. While increasing numbers of people buy it at fast-food chains these days, most families still keep an heirloom recipe stashed away. Some call for battering the chicken parts with flour and buttermilk, others call for cornmeal, a few even use ground pecans. Some cooks deep-fry their bird, most use a skillet; and some bake it, pour gravy over it and call it "oven-fried" chicken.

That last preparation, popular in Maryland and Virginia, plainly irritated Henrietta Stanley Dull, the Atlanta food editor whose 1928 collection, *Southern Cooking,* was a bible for two generations of home economists. Mrs. Dull was firm on the matter. "Never pour gravy over chicken if you wish Georgia fried chicken."

Yes, ma'am.

But the greatest expression of the Southern affection for pork is undoubtedly barbecue. To get a rise out of a true Southerner, just refer to a backyard wiener roast as a barbecue. *That* is a cookout. True barbecue means slow roasting pork, chicken or (in some places) beef or mutton over the smoke of hardwood embers. It's more than a cooking technique, though; it's a fond ritual as old as the South.

The earliest Spanish explorers found Caribbean natives smoking meat on a framework of green sticks they called a *barbacoa.* The word and the practice spread quickly to the mainland, where colonists became noted for whole-hog roasts, or pig-pickin's. In a 1769 diary entry George Washington mentions attending one such roast that lasted three days in Alexandria, Virginia. Barbecue became the centerpiece for enormous social gather-

With a hunting dog to retrieve his spoils, a hunter searches for game on a quail plantation in Albany, Georgia.

South

HOT AND SPICY FRIED CHICKEN

To many Americans, fried chicken is synonymous with Southern cooking. It comes as something of a surprise, then, that fried chicken wasn't such a universal dish until the turn of the twentieth century. Before then, Southerners were more likely to eat their chicken stewed or baked. There are hundreds of varieties of fried chicken, most calling for pan-frying instead of deep-frying. Whatever the cooking method, there's only one way to eat fried chicken: with your fingers.

1½ cups (7½ oz/235 g) all-purpose (plain) flour
2 teaspoons chili powder
1½ teaspoons paprika
1½ teaspoons salt
2 teaspoons freshly ground pepper
¾ teaspoon ground cayenne pepper
1 chicken, about 3 lb (1.5 kg), cut into 8 pieces
    and skin removed
1 cup (8 fl oz/250 ml) lowfat buttermilk
corn oil for frying
4 strips lean slab bacon

❀ In a large doubled brown paper bag, combine the flour, chili powder, paprika, salt, pepper and cayenne pepper and shake until well blended. Add the chicken pieces and shake gently until evenly coated, then gently shake off any excess.
❀ Pour the buttermilk into a large bowl. Dip each chicken piece briefly in the buttermilk until well coated, then gently shake off any excess. One by one, return each chicken piece to the bag of flour mixture and gently shake again until evenly coated. Place the chicken pieces, meat side up, on top of a large, flattened brown paper bag. Let stand for 10 minutes.
❀ Preheat an oven to 200°F (93°C).
❀ In a deep, heavy, large skillet, preferably cast-iron, over medium-high heat, pour enough oil to come halfway up the sides of the chicken and add the bacon. Heat the oil to 350°F (180°C) on a deep-fry thermometer.
❀ Working in batches, add 2 or 3 pieces of chicken, meat side up, to the skillet. Cover with a lid or aluminum foil and fry for 5 minutes. Remove the cover and reduce the heat to medium-low. Remove and discard the bacon and turn the chicken over. Fry, uncovered, until crisp and golden brown and the juices run clear when pierced at the thickest part, 10–15 minutes longer. Adjust the heat, if needed, to maintain the oil temperature at 350°F (180°C). Transfer each batch to paper towels to drain. Keep warm in the oven until ready to serve. Repeat until all the chicken pieces are cooked. Serve at once.

SERVES 4–6   *Photograph pages 112–113*

Georgia

GRILLED SWEET 'N' SPICY BEER-BASTED RIBS

A lot of people parboil ribs in the belief that they have to get rid of all that fat before the cooking even starts. They're mistaken. The whole idea of grilling or smoking ribs is to let the fat drip out slowly as the smoke filters into the meat. Besides, most pork is leaner these days. What you really have to be careful of is not to overcook it. There are myriad rubs, mops (or sops), marinades, finishing sauces, table sauces and dips (see glossary) used across the United States. This newfangled Sweet 'n' Spicy Beer Baste is quite delicious, with its sweet peach base and spicy Asian influence.

FOR THE RUB:

2 tablespoons dried minced garlic
2 tablespoons ground ginger
2 tablespoons firmly packed light brown sugar
1 teaspoon chili powder
½ teaspoon salt
¼ teaspoon ground cayenne pepper (optional)

3½–4 lb (1.75–2 kg) pork baby back ribs, spareribs or
    country-style ribs, in 2 or 3 pieces (see glossary)

FOR THE SWEET 'N' SPICY BEER BASTE:

2 cups (20 oz/625 g) Peach Preserves (recipe page 156)
⅓ cup (2½ oz/75 g) hot Chinese-style mustard
¼ cup (2 fl oz/60 ml) soy sauce
2 tablespoons peeled, finely chopped fresh ginger
4 cloves garlic, minced
1 teaspoon red pepper flakes
1 bottle (12 fl oz/375 ml) dark beer
4 green (spring) onions, thinly sliced

barbecue table sauce for serving

❀ To make the rub, in a small, nonreactive bowl, combine all the ingredients and stir until well blended.
❀ Coat the ribs evenly with the rub, wrap in plastic wrap and refrigerate for at least 8 hours or overnight.
❀ To make the finishing sauce, in a food processor fitted with the metal blade or in a blender, combine the Peach Preserves, mustard, soy sauce, ginger, garlic and red pepper flakes and process until well blended, 30 seconds. Transfer to a nonreactive bowl and stir in the beer and the green onions until well blended. Cover and refrigerate for 4–6 hours.
❀ Prepare a medium, indirect-heat fire in a charcoal grill and oil the grill rack. Grill the ribs, covered, for 30–40 minutes, turning every 10 minutes.
❀ During the last 15 minutes of cooking, using a pastry brush, brush both sides of the ribs with the finishing sauce. An instant-read thermometer should register 150°–155°F (65°–68°C) and the juices should run clear when the ribs are done.
❀ Wrap the cooked ribs tightly in aluminum foil, place in a large paper bag and seal to keep warm. Let stand at room temperature for about 10 minutes before serving.
❀ To serve, remove and discard the paper bag and foil. Using a meat cleaver or a heavy, sharp knife, separate into individual ribs. Serve hot and pass with the barbecue table sauce.

SERVES 4–6 AS A MAIN COURSE, 12 AS AN APPETIZER

Georgia

CLASSIC SMOKED BARBECUE RIBS WITH FINISHING SAUCE

If there's anything the various barbecue factions of the South can agree on it's ribs. They smoke them and savor them from the pork barbecue country of North Carolina to the beef barbecue plains of Texas. In this Georgia recipe, a dry rub is applied before smoking to seal in the juices and a finishing sauce is brushed on at the end to form a tangy glaze. For a slower, more flavorful smoke, soak the smoking chips in water before placing them in the aluminum foil. Alternatively, omit the aluminum foil altogether and simply throw the chips on the charcoal fire intermittently.

FOR THE RUB:

2 tablespoons chili powder
2 tablespoons ground cumin
2 tablespoons firmly packed dark brown sugar
2 teaspoons paprika
1 teaspoon freshly ground pepper

continues on page 118

Top to bottom: Classic Smoked Barbecue Ribs with Finishing Sauce, Grilled Sweet 'n' Spicy Beer-Basted Ribs

Top to bottom: Chicken Pot Pie with Tarragon,
Country Captain Chicken

continues from page 116

3½–4 lb (1.75–2 kg) pork baby back ribs, spareribs or
   country-style ribs, in 2 or 3 pieces (see glossary)

FOR THE FINISHING SAUCE:

2 cups (16 fl oz/500 ml) ketchup
½ cup (4 fl oz/125 ml) apple cider vinegar
¼ cup (2 fl oz/60 ml) Worcestershire sauce
1 tablespoon Dijon-style mustard
⅓ cup (2½ oz/75 g) firmly packed light brown sugar
¼–½ teaspoon red pepper flakes

barbecue table sauce for serving

❊ To make the rub, in a small, nonreactive bowl, combine all
the rub ingredients and stir until well blended.
❊ Coat the ribs evenly with the rub, wrap in plastic wrap and
refrigerate for at least 8 hours or overnight.
❊ To make the finishing sauce, in a heavy nonreactive saucepan over high heat, stir together all the finishing sauce ingredients until well blended. Bring to a boil, stirring constantly.
Then reduce the heat to very low and simmer, stirring occasionally, for 15 minutes. Transfer to a nonreactive bowl and let
stand to cool completely. Cover and refrigerate.

❊ Heat a smoker to its highest setting using charcoal. Wrap a
handful of hickory smoking chips in heavy-duty aluminum
foil and pierce holes all over the top of the foil packet. Bank the
ash-covered coals to one side in the smoker. Place the foil
packet, holes side up, on the mound of coals. Fill the water pan
and place in the smoker.
❊ Place the ribs on the grill rack in a single layer, meat side up,
on the side opposite the fire below the water tray. Cover and
smoke over indirect heat according to the manufacturer's directions for 4 hours, turning the ribs over after the first 2 hours.
❊ During the last 15 minutes of smoking, brush both sides of
the ribs with the finishing sauce. An instant-read thermometer should register 150°–155°F (65°–68°C) and the juices
should run clear when the ribs are done.
❊ Wrap the cooked ribs tightly in aluminum foil, place in a
large paper bag and seal to keep warm. Let stand at room
temperature for about 10 minutes before serving.
❊ To serve, remove and discard the paper bag and foil. Using
a meat cleaver or a heavy, sharp knife, separate into individual
ribs. Serve hot and pass with the barbecue table sauce.

SERVES 4–6 AS A MAIN COURSE, 12 AS AN APPETIZER

Mississippi

CHICKEN POT PIE WITH TARRAGON

A fine Chicken Pot Pie is a tradition in many Southern families, triggering memories of old-fashioned Sunday suppers. The following recipe makes excellent use of leftover chicken by cloaking it in a rich pie pastry. The filling is creamy but not high in fat, using evaporated skim milk and the additional fillip of white wine or vermouth and tarragon as aromatics.

1 unbaked single pie pastry round (see glossary; follow pie shell method up to rolling out dough to 10-in (2.5 cm) round)
1 teaspoon vegetable oil
8 oz (250 g) fresh mushrooms, stemmed and cut into quarters
2 cups (10 oz/315 g) finely chopped white onion
3 celery ribs, including leaves, thinly sliced
2 carrots, cut in half lengthwise and sliced 1/8 in (3 mm) thick
2 cups (16 fl oz/500 ml) chicken stock (see glossary)
5 teaspoons all-purpose (plain) flour
12 fl oz (375 ml) canned evaporated skim milk, undiluted
3/4 teaspoon dried tarragon
2 tablespoons dry white wine or dry vermouth
salt and freshly ground pepper to taste
3 cups (18 oz/560 g) coarsely chopped cooked chicken

❋ Prepare the pie pastry and set aside. Preheat an oven to 375°F (190°C).
❋ In a large, deep nonstick skillet over high heat, heat the oil. Add the mushrooms and sauté until lightly browned, about 3 minutes. Stir in the onion, celery and leaves, carrots and chicken stock until well blended. Bring to a boil. Reduce the heat to medium and gently boil, stirring occasionally, until the carrots are tender, 5 minutes. Strain the mixture through a medium-meshed sieve and set the vegetables aside. Reserve and set aside separately 1/2 cup (4 fl oz/125 ml) of the stock, adding water if there is not enough.
❋ In a small bowl, whisk together the flour and evaporated skim milk until well blended. Pour into the skillet and set over medium heat. Heat, whisking constantly, until the mixture just comes to a boil and is smooth, thickened and coats the back of a spoon, 4–5 minutes. Whisk in the reserved stock, tarragon and wine or vermouth until well blended. Season with salt and pepper to taste.
❋ In a 2-qt (2-l) round baking dish, 9 in (23 cm) in diameter, gently stir together the milk mixture, vegetables and cooked chicken until well blended. Lightly moisten the edges of the baking dish with water. Carefully place the pie pastry on top. Fold under the pastry overhang and crimp to seal onto the edge of the baking dish. Cut either 1 large steam vent with a cookie cutter or 3 parallel diagonal slits in the top of the crust.
❋ Bake on the middle oven rack until the crust is crisp and lightly browned, 30–40 minutes. If the crust browns too quickly, cover the edges loosely with aluminum foil.
❋ To serve, using a slotted spoon, serve hot directly from the dish, drizzling each serving with some of the sauce.

SERVES 6

Georgia

COUNTRY CAPTAIN CHICKEN

Story has it that a sea captain who had been stationed in India in the early 1800s brought this recipe—along with the essential flavorings—to Savannah, which was then a major shipping port for the spice trade. Since then it's been served to the likes of President Franklin Roosevelt and General George Patton, and it remains a Southern classic today.

8 skinless, boneless chicken breast halves, 6 oz (185 g) each
salt and freshly ground pepper to taste
3 tablespoons vegetable oil or olive oil

1 white onion, coarsely chopped
2 green bell peppers (capsicums), thinly sliced into rings 1/4 in (6 mm) wide
3 cloves garlic, crushed through a garlic press
1 cup (5 oz/155 g) minced celery
1 tablespoon curry powder or to taste
1/2 teaspoon salt
1/2 teaspoon dried thyme
1/4 teaspoon freshly ground pepper
28 oz (875 g) canned plum (Roma) tomatoes, crushed
8 cups (40 oz/1.25 kg) hot cooked long-grain white rice for serving
1/2 cup (3 oz/90 g) dried currants
1/2 cup (2 oz/60 g) sliced (flaked) almonds, toasted (see glossary)
mango chutney for serving (optional)

❋ Season the chicken with salt and pepper. In a large Dutch oven, preferably nonstick, over medium heat, heat the oil. Working in 2 batches, brown the chicken on both sides, then transfer to a platter and cover to keep warm.
❋ Reduce the heat to medium-low. Add the onion, bell pepper, garlic and celery to the Dutch oven and cook, stirring often, until soft, about 5 minutes.
❋ Reduce the heat to low and stir in the curry powder, salt, thyme and pepper until well blended. Simmer, stirring occasionally, for 10 minutes. Stir in the tomatoes. Add the browned chicken and cloak with sauce. Cover and simmer, stirring occasionally, until the chicken is tender and cooked throughout, about 30 minutes.
❋ To serve, using a slotted spoon, ladle the chicken over the top of the hot rice on a serving platter. Sprinkle with the currants and almonds and serve hot, with mango chutney, if desired.

SERVES 8

Louisiana

DEEP-FRIED WHOLE TURKEY

In recent decades, Cajuns have developed an unusual method for cooking turkey that's meltingly moist on the inside and crackly crisp on the outside. They deep-fry it, typically outdoors in a big black pot over a butane flame. You will want to watch for spattering of hot oil. Also, never leave a pan of oil unattended on a lit burner. Of course, you can't stuff this turkey, so be sure you make a nice rich stock with the neck and giblets to moisten an oven-baked stuffing. Use only peanut oil for this recipe—no substitutions.

1 turkey, 9–10 lb (4.5–5 kg), thawed completely if frozen
1/4 cup (1 1/4 oz/37 g) Cajun-style or Creole-style seasoning
8 qt (8 l) peanut oil, or as needed

❋ Remove the giblet bag and anything else tucked inside the turkey cavity and save for another use.
❋ Pierce the turkey all over with a fork. Season by sprinkling all surfaces, including inside cavity, with the Cajun seasoning.
❋ In an extra-large, heavy stockpot over medium-high heat, pour enough peanut oil to reach halfway up the sides of the pot. Heat the oil to 350°F (180°C) on a deep-fry thermometer.
❋ Using long-handled tongs to hold the turkey by one leg, slowly and carefully lower the turkey, breast side down, into the hot oil. The turkey should be completely submerged, but the oil level should be no higher than 7 in (18 cm) from the top of the pot.
❋ Fry breast side down about 20 minutes. Adjust the heat, if needed, to maintain the oil temperature at 350°F (180°C).
❋ Carefully turn the turkey over and fry breast side up until golden brown all over, 10–15 minutes longer. An instant-read thermometer inserted at the thickest part between breast and thigh should register 180°–185°F (82°–85°C).
❋ Using the tongs, carefully remove the turkey and transfer to a baking sheet lined with paper towels to drain. Let stand for 10–15 minutes before carving. Serve hot.

SERVES 6–8   *Photograph pages 112–113*

Georgia

MAUDE'S BAKED HAM

For as many people who feel that country ham is "not to their liking," there are twice as many who love its hardy, salty flavor and resilient texture. A nice sweet glaze balances the vigor of this tasty ham, which makes for a lovely presentation when "quilted" by scoring in a diamond pattern and studding with whole cloves. This recipe is adapted from a similar version in the book A Place Called Sweet Apple, a memoir by Celestine Sibley, longtime columnist with the Atlanta Journal-Constitution. The preparation of this ham is time consuming. You will need about 30 hours to prepare it, so begin the soaking process the morning of the day before serving. Before you can cook a country ham, it must first be scrubbed clean, trimmed and soaked. For mail-order sources for country hams, see Mail Order Sources.

1 dry-cured country ham, 12–14 lb (6–7 kg) (see glossary)
1 cup (8 fl oz/250 ml) dark molasses
2 cups (16 fl oz/500 ml) apple cider vinegar
1 cup (4 oz/125 g) unseasoned dried bread crumbs
¼ cup (½ oz/15 g) whole allspice or whole cloves
2 cups (16 fl oz/500 ml) Coca-Cola (optional)

❋ The morning of the day before serving, place the ham in an extra-large nonreactive pot with lukewarm water to cover by at least 1 inch (2.5 cm). Cover with a lid or plastic wrap and soak at room temperature for at least 12 hours but no longer than 24 hours. Change the water twice, every 6 or 10 hours.
❋ The following morning (the day of serving), remove the ham from the pot and discard the soaking water. Using a stiff bristle brush, scrub the ham vigorously under warm running water to remove any pepper or sign of mold.
❋ Return the ham to the pot. Add the molasses and vinegar and cold water to cover by 1 in (2.5 cm). Set over high heat and bring to a simmer. Reduce the heat to low and simmer, partially covered, for 4–6 hours (20–25 minutes to the pound) or until cooked, the skin soft and bubbled and an instant-read thermometer inserted into the interior of the ham at its thickest part away from the bone reads 160°F (71°C).
❋ Preheat an oven to 300°F (150°C).
❋ Remove the ham to a work surface to cool slightly. When cool enough to handle, using a small, sharp knife carefully remove the skin, leaving only an ⅛-in (3-mm) layer of fat. Sprinkle the bread crumbs evenly over the surface, and using your fingers, rub the crumbs in.
❋ Using the knife, score the ham into a "quilt" pattern. To do this, make crisscrossing cuts (diagonally in one direction, then diagonally in the other direction to form small diamond shapes) about 1 in (2.5 cm) apart on the fatty side of the ham, cutting through the fat just into the meat. Insert the allspice or cloves where the scoring lines intersect.
❋ Place the ham, scored side up, on a wire roasting rack set in a large shallow roasting pan. Bake on the middle rack of the oven for 20–30 minutes, basting occasionally with Coca-Cola if desired, until golden brown.
❋ Transfer the ham to a heatproof serving platter and let cool to room temperature. To serve, remove and discard the allspice cloves from the area you intend to carve. Cut a wedge-shaped piece out of the ham top about 6 in (15 cm) from the hock end. Carve the ham, starting from the wedge-shaped indent near the hock end, slicing on the diagonal and cutting into paper-thin slices. Make sure to carve around the ham as well, taking slices from the sides and top. Sliced ham will keep 2–3 weeks, well wrapped in the refrigerator.

SERVES 25–30   *Photograph pages 112–113*

The Carolinas

PULLED PORK BARBECUE SANDWICHES WITH CAROLINA PIG-PICKIN' SAUCE

When it comes to barbecue styles, Southerners are almost as tribal as they are about college football loyalties. Eastern Carolinians put vinegar on their pork, western Carolinians use tomato-based sauces and South Carolinians use mustard blends. History stands with the eastern Carolinians; their tomatoless spiced vinegar is America's oldest barbecue sauce and has been served at pig-pickin's—whole hog barbecues—since George Washington was in knee-highs. This recipe is from The Ultimate Barbecue Sauce Cookbook *by Jim Auchmutey and Susan Puckett.*

FOR THE SAUCE:

4 cups (32 fl oz/1 l) apple cider vinegar
¼ cup (2 oz/60 g) firmly packed dark
    brown sugar
1 tablespoon red pepper flakes
1½ teaspoons ground cayenne pepper
3 tablespoons salt, or to taste
1 teaspoon freshly ground pepper

FOR THE SOP:

2 cups (16 fl oz/500 ml) apple cider vinegar
1 teaspoon red pepper flakes
1 teaspoon salt

FOR THE PORK:

1 boneless, tied pork shoulder, 4–5 lb (2–2.5 kg)

8–10 hamburger buns

❋ Preheat an oven to 325°F (165°C).
❋ To make the sauce, in a nonreactive bowl, combine all the sauce ingredients and whisk until well blended. Let stand at room temperature for at least 4 hours.
❋ To make the sop, in a small nonreactive bowl, whisk together the vinegar, red pepper flakes and salt.
❋ Place the pork on a rack in a roasting pan. Pour 1½ cups (12 fl oz/375 ml) of the sop in the pan. Cook 1 hour per pound, basting every 30 minutes with the remaining sop, until the meat is tender, 4–5 hours. An instant-read thermometer should register at least 160°F (71°C) when inserted into the center of the roast.
❋ Alternatively, to cook in a smoker, heat the smoker to its highest setting using charcoal. Wrap 2 handfuls of hickory smoking chips in heavy-duty aluminum foil and pierce holes all over the top of the foil packet. Bank the ash-covered coals to one side in the smoker. Place the foil packet, holes side up, on the mound of the coals. Fill the water pan and place in the smoker. Cook the pork over medium heat, according to manufacturer's instructions, about 6 hours or until an instant-read thermometer registers 160°F (71°C). Baste with sop every 30 minutes.
❋ Remove the roast from the oven or smoker and let cool about 30 minutes. When cool enough to handle, shred or pull and chop the meat, discarding any fat. Pour 1 cup (8 fl oz/250 ml) of the sauce over the meat to moisten it.
❋ Make into sandwiches by piling the meat onto the buns, drizzling each with more of the sauce and capping with the bun tops. Store the unused sauce refrigerated in an airtight nonreactive container up to 3 months.

SERVES 8–10; MAKES 4 CUPS (32 FL OZ/1 L) SAUCE

*Top to bottom: Pulled Pork Barbecue Sandwich with Carolina Pig-Pickin'
Sauce, Country-fried Steak with Onion Gravy (recipe page 122)*

West Virginia

STUFFED QUAIL WITH ALLEGHENY CORN BREAD AND WILD MUSHROOMS SERVED ON A BED OF BRAISED GREENS

Hidden in the hills of West Virginia, the legendary Greenbrier is one of the country's oldest resorts. From Robert E. Lee to Lyndon B. Johnson, people have been taking the restorative waters of White Sulphur Springs since before the Civil War. Now they come for the food, too. Executive chef Robert Wong shows how elegance and Southern ingredients combine in the following recipe. The recipe for Allegheny Corn Bread will yield enough for the stuffing and then some—you'll find that the corn bread is quite delicious on its own.

FOR THE ALLEGHENY CORN BREAD:

1½ cups (7½ oz/235 g) all-purpose (plain) flour
1 cup (5 oz/155 g) white cornmeal
¼ cup (2 oz/60 g) sugar
1 tablespoon baking powder
1½ teaspoons salt
1½ cups (12 fl oz/375 ml) milk, at room temperature
2 egg yolks, at room temperature
¼ cup (2 oz/60 g) sour cream, at room temperature
2 tablespoons unsalted butter, melted
1 tablespoon vegetable oil
⅓ cup (2 oz/60 g) fresh corn kernels

FOR THE STUFFING:

½ lb (250 g) boneless, skinless chicken breasts, cut into
    2-in (5-cm) pieces
1 egg
½ cup (4 fl oz/125 ml) heavy (double) cream
1 tablespoon finely chopped fresh parsley
1 teaspoon finely chopped fresh sage or ½ teaspoon
    dried sage
1 teaspoon minced fresh thyme or ½ teaspoon
    dried thyme
1 cup (7 oz/220 g) sautéed thinly sliced wild mushrooms
    (such as shiitake), chilled
2–2½ cups (4–5 oz/120–150 g) crumbled, cooled
    Allegheny Corn Bread
salt and freshly ground pepper to taste

FOR THE BRAISED GREENS:

½ cup (2½ oz/75 g) finely chopped white onion
½ cup (3 oz/90 g) finely chopped bacon
1½ lb (750 g) mustard, turnip, beet, dandelion or collard
    greens, trimmed of tough stalks and rinsed well
2–3 cups (16–24 fl oz/500–750 ml) chicken stock (see
    glossary)
salt and freshly ground pepper to taste

FOR THE QUAIL:

6 partially boned quail, 4 oz (125 g) each, thawed if frozen
3 cups (24 oz/750 g) stuffing
2 tablespoons unsalted butter, melted
salt and freshly ground pepper to taste

❋ To make the corn bread, preheat an oven to 350°F (180°C). Lightly butter a 10-in (25-cm) cast-iron skillet or round layer cake pan.
❋ In a large mixing bowl, combine the flour, cornmeal, sugar, baking powder and salt. Make a well in the center and pour in the milk, egg yolks, sour cream, melted butter and vegetable oil. Using a fork, beat the egg yolks lightly with the wet ingredients to combine, then, using a wooden spoon,

gently fold together the wet and dry ingredients. Fold in the corn kernels and mix well. Spoon the batter into the prepared skillet or pan. Bake until lightly browned on top and a toothpick inserted in the center comes out clean, 35–40 minutes. Set the pan on a wire rack to cool for 10 minutes. Then remove the corn bread to cool completely.
❋ To make the stuffing, in a food processor fitted with the metal blade or in a blender, process the chicken pieces until smooth. Add the egg, cream, parsley, sage and thyme and process until smooth, 1 minute. Transfer the chicken mixture to a large mixing bowl. Fold in the chilled wild mushrooms and crumbled corn bread. Add salt and pepper and mix well. Cover the bowl with plastic wrap and refrigerate.
❋ To make the braised greens, in a large saucepan over medium-high heat, combine the onion and bacon. Cook, stirring, until the bacon begins to render its fat, then reduce the heat to medium and cook until soft, 4–5 minutes. Add the greens and 2 cups (16 fl oz/500 ml) of the chicken stock. Cover, reduce the heat to low and simmer until soft, 20–30 minutes. Stir the greens every 5 minutes while they cook to distribute them. Add more chicken stock as needed to keep from boiling dry. Add salt and pepper, set aside and keep warm.
❋ To prepare the quail, preheat an oven to 375°F (190°C).
❋ Fill each quail with about ½ cup (4 oz/125 g) stuffing. Truss or insert small metal skewers to close the cavities. In a 9-by-13-by-2-in (23-by-33-by-5-cm) baking pan, arrange the quail close together, breast side up, and brush with the melted butter. Season with salt and pepper. Bake until the legs jiggle easily, the quail are deep brown and the stuffing has cooked through, 25–30 minutes. An instant-read thermometer inserted at the thickest part, through the stuffing, should register 165°F (74°C).
❋ Remove the pan from oven and allow to rest 10 minutes, then remove the trussing or skewers. Arrange whole or sliced quail on a bed of braised greens with cooking juices poured over and serve.

SERVES 6   *Photograph pages 124–125*

Alabama

COUNTRY-FRIED STEAK WITH ONION GRAVY

To dress up less tender cuts of beef, Southern cooks bread and fry them in a preparation reminiscent of fried chicken. In fact, Texans and some Southerners know a version of this dish as chicken-fried steak. But most Southerners call it smothered steak or country-fried steak.

1 egg, lightly beaten
¼ cup (2 fl oz/60 ml) milk, at room temperature
1 cup (4 oz/125 g) plain dry bread crumbs
½ teaspoon ground cayenne pepper
½ teaspoon salt
4 beef cube steaks, 4 oz (125 g) each
¼ cup (2 fl oz/60 ml) bacon drippings

FOR THE GRAVY:

2 tablespoons bacon drippings
1 cup (5 oz/155 g) minced yellow onion
1 tablespoon all-purpose (plain) flour
1 cup (8 fl oz/250 ml) heavy (double) cream, at
    room temperature
1 cup (8 fl oz/250 ml) milk, at room temperature
salt and freshly ground pepper to taste
1 tablespoon minced fresh parsley

❀ Preheat an oven to 200°F (93°C).

❀ In a medium bowl, combine the egg and ¼ cup milk and whisk until well blended. In another medium bowl, combine the bread crumbs, cayenne and salt and stir with a fork until well blended. Transfer the crumb mixture to a large plate.

❀ One at a time, dip each steak into the egg-milk mixture, letting the excess drain back into the bowl. Then coat with the crumb mixture on both sides. Transfer the coated steaks to a piece of waxed paper.

❀ In a medium, heavy, deep skillet, nonstick or cast-iron, over medium-high heat, heat the ¼ cup (2 fl oz/60 ml) bacon drippings. Add the steaks to the hot drippings, 2 at a time. Cook until golden brown, about 2 minutes on each side. Transfer the cooked steaks to a baking sheet and keep warm in the oven while making the sauce. Reserve the drippings in the skillet and set aside.

❀ To make the gravy, add the 2 tablespoons bacon drippings to the skillet and set over high heat. Add the onion and cook, stirring constantly and scraping up any browned bits from the bottom and sides of the skillet, until the onion is translucent, 30–60 seconds. Sprinkle the onion with the flour and cook, stirring, for 30 seconds longer.

❀ Using a whisk, slowly whisk in the cream and 1 cup (8 oz/250 ml) milk and bring to a boil. Reduce the heat to medium and cook, whisking occasionally, until thickened, 5–8 minutes. Season generously with salt and pepper. Stir in the parsley.

❀ Place each steak on an individual dinner plate, ladle the gravy over and serve at once.

SERVES 4   *Photograph page 121*

Muffuletta

Louisiana

MUFFULETTA

This mammoth sandwich has been a French Quarter favorite ever since Salvatore Lupo created it in 1906 at the Central Grocery, where they still make it to order. Based on a Sicilian sandwich, the Muffuletta has knockout flavor: cheeses, meats and a piquant olive relish create a uniquely Louisianan foodstuff. If you can't find mortadella, use boiled ham instead.

Giardiniera is an Italian term for mixed pickled vegetables. The mixture usually includes an assortment packed in brine of these sliced vegetables: cauliflower, carrots, cucumbers, red bell peppers (capsicums), celery and peperoncini. You can find giardiniera in the condiment aisle of a well-stocked supermarket or gourmet shop or by mail-order (see Mail Order Sources).

FOR THE OLIVE RELISH:

2 tablespoons olive oil
3 tablespoons red wine vinegar
¼ teaspoon dried oregano
¼ teaspoon dried basil
¼ teaspoon minced garlic
⅓ cup (1½ oz/45 g) finely chopped, drained green olives with pimientos (sweet peppers)
⅓ cup (1½ oz/45 g) finely chopped, drained oil-cured black olives
2 tablespoons finely chopped fresh parsley
1 tablespoon finely chopped drained capers

FOR THE MUFFULETTA:

1 round loaf of crusty Italian-style white or wheat bread
4 oz (125 g) thinly sliced provolone cheese
4 oz (125 g) thinly sliced mozzarella cheese
5½ oz (170 g) thinly sliced mortadella or boiled ham
5½ oz (170 g) thinly sliced Genoa salami
6 Romaine lettuce leaves
2 ripe tomatoes, thinly sliced
8 oz (250 g) jarred *giardiniera,* drained (optional; see note)

❀ To make the Olive Relish, in a small nonreactive bowl, whisk together the olive oil, vinegar, oregano, basil and garlic until well blended. Stir in the olives, parsley and capers until well blended.

❀ To assemble the Muffuletta, using a serrated bread knife, slice the loaf in half horizontally and scoop out about half of the soft interior. Brush the insides of the loaf halves with some of the Olive Relish. On the bottom loaf half, layer on the cheeses and meats, followed by the lettuce and tomatoes. Using a slotted spoon, spread on as much of the remaining Olive Relish as possible, without allowing it to overflow the edges. Top with an even layer of the drained *giardiniera,* if desired. Cover with the top half of the loaf. Using the bread knife, slice the Muffuletta into 4 wedges.

SERVES 4

123

RAGOUT OF MISSISSIPPI RABBIT WITH WILD MUSHROOMS AND ORZO

At the Brick Oven Café in Ridgeland, Mississippi, outside Jackson, Grant Nooe has earned a national reputation for himself by experimenting with local and exotic ingredients in combination, such as rabbit and shiitake mushrooms.

2 rabbits, about 3 lb (1.5 g) each, cleaned, dressed and
   cut into foreleg, hindquarter and saddle portions
3 cups (15 oz/470 g) all-purpose (plain) flour
3 tablespoons clarified butter (see glossary)
1 cup (8 fl oz/250 ml) Cognac
1 lb (500 g) shiitake mushrooms, stemmed and sliced ½ in
   (12 mm) thick
1 lb (500 g) oyster mushrooms, sliced ½ in (12 mm) thick
½ cup (4 fl oz/125 ml) white wine
2 tablespoons minced garlic
1½ cups (7½ oz/235 g) finely chopped onion
2 tablespoons finely chopped fresh thyme
2½ qt (2.5 l) chicken stock (see glossary)
3 tablespoons Creole-style prepared mustard, or to taste
   (see glossary)
salt and freshly ground pepper to taste
1½ cups (7½ oz/235 g) coarsely chopped zucchini (courgettes)
1½ cups (7½ oz/235 g) finely chopped carrots
1½ cups (7½ oz/235 g) coarsely chopped yellow summer
   (crookneck) squash
8 cups (40 oz/1.25 kg) cooked orzo pasta
finely chopped fresh parsley for garnish

❋ Preheat an oven to 300°F (150°C).
❋ Dredge the rabbit pieces in the flour and set aside. In a nonreactive 5-qt (5-l) flameproof baking dish with a lid, over medium-high heat, heat 2 tablespoons of the clarified butter, uncovered. Add the rabbit pieces. Brown the legs and hindquarters on all sides and cook the saddles through, turning the pieces with tongs as they cook. Remove to a platter and set aside.
❋ Standing back a bit from the stove top, deglaze (see glossary) the dish with the Cognac. Using a wooden spoon, scrape up the browned bits on the bottom of the dish. Add the mushrooms, reduce the heat to medium-low and simmer, stirring, until softened, about 6 minutes. Remove the mushrooms with a slotted spoon and set aside.
❋ Add the white wine, garlic and onion to the dish and cook, stirring occasionally, until the wine has reduced by half, about 10 minutes. Add the thyme, rabbit legs and hindquarters, but not saddles, and chicken stock. Increase the heat to medium-high and bring to a boil, then reduce the heat to low and simmer, stirring occasionally, 10 minutes.
❋ Place the lid on the baking dish and set on the middle oven rack. Bake until the meat is tender, about 1½ hours. Remove the dish from the oven. Remove the meat from the bones and discard the bones. Set the meat aside and keep warm.
❋ Set the baking dish over low heat and stir in the Creole-style mustard and salt and pepper. Slice the rabbit saddles diagonally. Add all of the rabbit meat and mushrooms to the sauce. Reduce the heat to very low and cover to keep warm.
❋ In a heavy medium skillet over medium heat, heat the remaining clarified butter. Add the zucchini, carrots and squash and cook, stirring constantly, until cooked through but still crisp, about 5 minutes.
❋ To serve, place equal portions of the cooked orzo in the center of each individual plate. Spoon the stew around it, then top with the sautéed vegetables and garnish with parsley.

SERVES 8

BOUDIN-STUFFED QUAIL WITH FIG SAUCE

Chef Susan Spicer, who launched her cooking career in New Orleans in 1979, eagerly molds Louisiana's ingredients to her decidedly French style at her Bayona restaurant located in the French Quarter. Here she takes boudin blanc, *a spicy pork sausage with rice, and turns it into a stuffing for quail. (There is also a* boudin rouge, *a blood sausage.) If you can't locate* boudin blanc, *use the best quality, least fatty pork sausage you can find.*

FOR THE QUAIL:

1 tablespoon unsalted butter or olive oil
½ cup (2½ oz/75 g) finely chopped onion
½ cup (2½ oz/75 g) finely chopped celery
¼ cup (¾ oz/20 g) finely chopped green (spring) onion,
   including tender green tops
½ cup (2½ oz/75 g) cooked white rice
1 lb (500 g) *boudin blanc* sausages (see note)
1 teaspoon finely chopped fresh sage
1 teaspoon finely chopped fresh thyme
1 teaspoon finely chopped fresh parsley
salt and freshly ground pepper to taste

Clockwise from top: Boudin-Stuffed Quail with Fig Sauce, Ragout of Mississippi Rabbit with Wild Mushrooms and Orzo, Stuffed Quail with Allegheny Corn Bread and Wild Mushrooms Served on a Bed of Braised Greens (recipe page 122)

8 boneless or partially boned quail, 5–6 oz (155–185 g) each
1 tablespoon unsalted butter, at room temperature

FOR THE FIG SAUCE:

2 shallots, finely chopped
1 cup (8 fl oz/250 ml) white wine
4 cups (32 fl oz/1 l) chicken stock (see glossary)
2 tablespoons Fig Preserves (recipe on page 209)
1 teaspoon finely chopped fresh lemon thyme
½ cup (3 oz/90 g) finely chopped fresh figs
1 tablespoon apple cider vinegar
2–3 tablespoons unsalted butter
salt and freshly ground pepper to taste
2 teaspoons fresh lemon juice (optional)
sprigs of fresh lemon thyme for garnish

❋ To prepare the quail, in a small, heavy skillet over medium heat, melt the butter or heat the oil. Add the onion, celery and green onion and cook, stirring, 2–3 minutes. Remove from the heat and let cool.

❋ Transfer the cooled onion mixture to a bowl and combine with the rice. Remove the sausages from their casings and discard the casings. Crumble the sausage into the rice mixture. Add the sage, thyme, parsley and salt and pepper and blend well.

❋ Divide the stuffing mixture into 8 equal portions and stuff the cavities of the quail. Carefully truss or insert small metal skewers

to close the cavities. Arrange the quail close together, breast side up, in a roasting pan and rub with the room-temperature butter. Season with salt and pepper. Set aside.

❋ To make the Fig Sauce, in a nonreactive medium saucepan over medium-high heat, combine the shallots and wine. Bring to a boil, then reduce the heat to medium and simmer until the wine has reduced by half, about 12 minutes. Add the chicken stock, increase the heat to medium-high and bring back to a boil. Reduce the heat to medium and simmer until the stock has reduced to about 2 cups (16 fl oz/500 ml), about 25 minutes. Whisk in the Fig Preserves, chopped lemon thyme, fresh figs and vinegar. Simmer, stirring occasionally, 5 minutes longer. Whisk in the butter as desired. Season with salt and pepper. Adjust the flavor with the lemon juice if the sauce is too sweet for your taste.

❋ To finish the quail, preheat an oven to 400°F (200°C).

❋ Set the roasting pan of quail on the middle oven rack. Roast until the legs jiggle easily and the quail are golden brown and firm but the meat is not dry, about 15 minutes. An instant-read thermometer inserted at the thickest part, through the stuffing, should register 165°F (74°C).

❋ To serve, remove the trussing or skewers and place 2 quail on each individual plate. Ladle the fig sauce over the quail. Garnish with lemon thyme sprigs and serve.

SERVES 4

Roasted Pork Leg Sandwich with Crawfish Aioli

Birmingham, Alabama

ROASTED PORK LEG SANDWICH WITH CRAWFISH AIOLI

The Highlands Bar & Grill has put Birmingham on the culinary map thanks to the distinctive cooking style of Frank Stitt III, best known for his Provençal-style new Southern cuisine. Stitt grew up on traditional Southern fare in rural Alabama, studied classic French techniques in southern France and then learned California cuisine in Berkeley. This dish is the delicious result of all of those experiences. If you can't locate a whole fresh ham, use a 4-pound (2-kg) pork loin end roast and cook for 3–3¼ hours. Stitt makes his mayonnaise from scratch using commercially pasteurized egg yolks, but you may improvise by adding the seasonings and crawfish to store-bought mayonnaise. You will only need about half the amount of this spread. The mayonnaise will keep up to 3 days stored in the refrigerator.

FOR THE PORK:

2 tablespoons finely chopped garlic
1 tablespoon finely chopped fresh rosemary
1 tablespoon finely chopped fresh thyme
1 teaspoon whole black peppercorns, crushed
6 dried juniper berries
2 teaspoons sea salt
1 uncured, fresh whole ham (leg), 7–10 lb (3.5–5 kg), trimmed and boned (see note)
¼ cup (2 fl oz/60 ml) olive oil

FOR THE CRAWFISH AIOLI:

1 head garlic, roasted until tender and peeled (see glossary)
1 teaspoon finely chopped fresh parsley
1 teaspoon finely chopped fresh thyme leaves
¼ teaspoon sea salt
⅛ teaspoon ground cayenne pepper
2 cups (16 fl oz/500 ml) mayonnaise
3–4½ teaspoons sherry vinegar
freshly ground pepper to taste
8 oz (250 g) crawfish tails, cooked and shelled

10 thick slices sourdough bread, or more if needed, for serving
sprigs of watercress for garnish

❈ For the pork, in a small bowl, combine the chopped garlic, rosemary and thyme. In a mortar or in a clean coffee grinder, grind the peppercorns and juniper berries. Add this ground mixture to the garlic mixture. Add the sea salt and stir to combine. Generously rub this paste into the ham on all sides. Wrap in plastic wrap and refrigerate 12–24 hours.
❈ When the ham is chilled and ready to roast, preheat an oven to 325°F (165°C).
❈ Place the ham in a large roasting pan and drizzle with the olive oil. Roast until an instant-read thermometer inserted in the thickest part of the roast registers 170°F (75°C), 4 hours.
❈ Meanwhile, to make the Crawfish Aioli, in a mortar or in a blender, combine the garlic, parsley, thyme, salt and cayenne. Pound or blend until smooth. Set aside.
❈ In a medium nonreactive bowl, combine the mayonnaise and garlic mixture. Stir in the vinegar and pepper to taste. Fold in the crawfish. Cover with plastic wrap and refrigerate to chill for 3 hours.
❈ To serve, remove the roasted pork from the oven and let it rest 30 minutes in the pan. Then transfer the pork to a carving board and slice thinly. Arrange on slices of sourdough bread, top with crawfish aioli and garnish with watercress sprigs.

SERVES 10

Louisville, Kentucky

LOUISVILLE HOT BROWN

Created at the Brown Hotel in Louisville in the 1930s, the "Hot Brown" is the city's premier sandwich. A cross between a grown-up grilled cheese and a BLT, this sandwich makes a delightful dinner, lunch or brunch dish. Consider preparing it with leftover holiday turkey.

6 tablespoons (3 oz/90 g) unsalted butter
6 tablespoons (2 oz/60 g) all-purpose (plain) flour
3 cups (24 fl oz/750 ml) milk, at room temperature
¼ teaspoon freshly ground pepper
4 oz (125 g) medium-sharp yellow Cheddar cheese, shredded
6 slices white sandwich bread, toasted
6 medium-thin slices cooked lean turkey breast
6 slices lean, thick slab bacon, cooked until crisp
2 firm, ripe tomatoes, each cut into 6 thin slices
¼ cup (1 oz/30 g) freshly grated Parmesan cheese
½ teaspoon paprika for garnish

❈ Preheat an oven to 350°F (180°C).
❈ In a heavy medium saucepan over medium heat, melt the butter. Whisk in the flour until well blended and smooth. Cook, whisking constantly, for 2 minutes. Gradually pour in the milk in a slow, steady stream, whisking constantly until well blended. Bring to a boil, whisking often. Continue to cook, whisking often, until the sauce has thickened enough to coat the back of a spoon, 1–2 minutes. Remove from the heat and stir in the pepper and Cheddar cheese until the cheese has melted and the mixture is well blended.
❈ To assemble the sandwiches, ladle one-third of the sauce on the bottom of a 13-by-9-by-2-in (33-by-23-by-5-cm) baking dish. Arrange the slices of toasted bread in a single layer on top of the sauce. Top each piece of toast with a slice of turkey folded in half. Cover with an even layer of one-half of the remaining sauce, then top each sandwich with a slice of bacon and 2 overlapping tomato slices. Cover with an even layer of the remaining sauce. Sprinkle with the Parmesan cheese and dust with the paprika.
❈ Bake on the top oven rack until heated through, 15–20 minutes. Then broil 4 in (10 cm) from the heat source until the sauce bubbles and the Parmesan cheese is dappled golden brown, 1–2 minutes. Serve at once directly from the baking dish.

SERVES 6

Tennessee

COUNTRY HAM WITH REDEYE GRAVY

This is a classic Southern breakfast combination traditionally served with grits and biscuits alongside. There are many theories as to the meaning of "red eye," the most plausible of which is that when you pour the coffee into the gravy, a red eye appears in the center of the skillet. This richly flavored gravy is thinner than other styles of gravy, more like the consistency of the natural juices of meat. Traditionally, the fat from the ham would suffice to make the gravy base, but with the new, leaner hams on the market, you have the option of adding 2 rashers of bacon. If the ham you purchase includes at least a ½-inch (12-mm) rim of fat, omit the bacon.

3–4 slices (8–13 oz/250–410 g) packaged boneless country ham (see glossary)
2 slices lean, thick slab bacon (optional; see note)
1 teaspoon sugar
½ cup (4 fl oz/125 ml) lukewarm water
1 teaspoon instant coffee powder
2 teaspoons very hot water
Creamy Grits for serving (recipe page 96)
Touch of Grace Biscuits for serving (recipe page 178)

✤ Trim the fat from the ham and reserve the fat. Cut each ham slice into quarters, for a total of 12–16 pieces, each about 3 by 4 in (7.5 by 10 cm). Place the ham in a large bowl and add cold water to cover. Cover with plastic wrap and refrigerate overnight.
✤ The next day, drain, rinse and pat dry the ham with paper towels. In a large cast-iron skillet over medium heat, fry the reserved ham fat and bacon, if needed, until browned and crisp, about 5 minutes. Remove the skillet from the heat and, using a slotted spoon, transfer the browned pieces to paper towels to drain.
✤ In the same skillet over medium heat, place half of the ham in a single layer. Fry the ham until well browned, 4–5 minutes on each side. Do not let the drippings burn. Transfer the fried ham to paper towels to drain and cover with aluminum foil to keep warm. Repeat with the remaining ham.
✤ Remove the skillet from the heat and carefully pour off all but 1 tablespoon of the liquid fat. Return the skillet to medium heat and stir in the sugar. Cook, stirring constantly, until the sugar has dissolved and begins to caramelize, about 30 seconds.
✤ Immediately add the lukewarm water to the skillet and stir until well blended. Cook for 1 minute, stirring and scraping the bottom of the skillet to loosen any browned bits. Dissolve the instant coffee powder in the 2 teaspoons hot water. Add the coffee-water mixture to the skillet and stir until well blended.
✤ To serve, place equal amounts of ham on individual plates and ladle the hot gravy over. Serve at once, with grits and biscuits alongside.

SERVES 4

Left to right: Louisville Hot Brown, Country Ham with Redeye Gravy

Top to bottom: Blueberry Chutney–Glazed Game Hen, Grilled Duck Breast with Spicy Blackberry Glaze served on a bed of Arkansas Basmati and Wild Rice

Little Rock, Arkansas

GRILLED DUCK BREASTS WITH SPICY BLACKBERRY GLAZE SERVED ON A BED OF ARKANSAS BASMATI AND WILD RICE

Mark Abernathy, the chef at Juanita's restaurant in Little Rock, likes spicy flavors, barbecue sauces and local ingredients, such as wild duck and locally grown basmati rice. Abernathy acknowledges that most people don't have access to wild duck so he came up with this delicious glaze for more readily available domestic duck breasts. Prepare when fresh blackberries are in season or use good blackberry jam the rest of the year.

FOR THE SPICY BLACKBERRY GLAZE:

1½ cups (12 fl oz/375 ml) red wine vinegar
½ cup (4 oz/125 g) sugar
⅓ cup (3 fl oz/80 ml) fresh orange juice
1 tablespoon finely chopped jalapeño pepper
  (see glossary)
⅛ teaspoon ground nutmeg
1¼ cups (5 oz/155 g) fresh blackberries or ⅓ cup
  (3 oz/105 g) blackberry jam
salt and freshly ground pepper to taste

FOR THE RICE:

1 tablespoon unsalted butter
1 cup (5 oz/155 g) finely chopped yellow onion
1 teaspoon finely minced garlic
½ cup (3 oz/90 g) wild rice, rinsed and drained
1 cup (7 oz/220 g) basmati or long-grain white rice

128

2 cups (16 fl oz/500 ml) chicken stock (see glossary)
1 cup (8 fl oz/250 ml) water
½ cup (2½ oz/75 g) finely chopped red bell
    pepper (capsicum)
½ cup (2½ oz/75 g) finely chopped green bell
    pepper (capsicum)
1 tablespoon finely chopped fresh parsley

FOR THE DUCK:

4 boneless, skinless duck breasts, 6 oz (185 g) each, rinsed
    and patted dry
1 cup (8 fl oz/250 ml) barbecue sauce (see glossary)
1 teaspoon freshly ground pepper

❊ To make the glaze, in a heavy, medium nonreactive sauce-pan over medium-high heat, combine the vinegar, sugar, orange juice, jalapeño pepper and nutmeg. Bring to a boil, stirring until the sugar has dissolved, then reduce the heat to medium. Simmer until reduced by two-thirds and a foam begins to form, 40–45 minutes. The mixture will have dark-ened and slightly caramelized. Remove from the heat and keep warm.

❊ In a food processor fitted with the metal blade or in a blender, purée the fresh blackberries with 1 tablespoon water. Fold the blackberry purée, or blackberry jam, if using, into the warm vinegar mixture. Add salt and pepper and stir. Set aside and keep warm.

❊ To make the rice, in a medium saucepan over medium heat, melt the butter. Add the onion and garlic, stir and cook until soft, 3–4 minutes. Add the wild rice and basmati or long-grained rice, stir and cook until slightly browned, 2–3 minutes. Add the chicken stock, water, bell peppers and parsley. Bring to a boil, then reduce the heat to low, cover and simmer until puffed up and done, about 35 minutes. Uncover and let the rice rest 5 minutes before serving.

❊ To cook the duck, prepare a medium-heat, indirect fire in a charcoal grill and oil the grill rack. Brush the duck breasts on both sides with barbecue sauce and sprinkle well with pepper. Grill, covered, about 4 inches from the ash-covered coals until cooked but still springy to the touch, about 5 minutes on each side for medium-rare. You do want to sear the duck breasts but be careful not to burn the sauce; move the duck farther from the coals if necessary, then adjust the cooking time accordingly. Coat evenly with the blackberry glaze and return to the grill for 1 more minute on each side, to set the glaze.

❊ Remove the duck from the grill and let rest a few minutes for the juices to settle, then carve into lengthwise slices.

❊ To serve, mound the rice in the middle of a serving plate. Fan out the slices of duck on top of the rice and spoon some of the remaining glaze over the duck.

SERVES 4–6

Eureka Springs, Arkansas

BLUEBERRY CHUTNEY– GLAZED GAME HENS

Crescent Dragonwagon is known not only for the forty-some books she has authored and the splendid Ozark-style reception she staged at President Bill Clinton's inauguration. Along with her husband, Ned Shank, she also runs the acclaimed Dairy Hollow House in Eureka Springs, Arkansas, an Ozark resort town. During the summer months, blueberries grow wild in the Ozark Mountains and Dragonwagon turns them into chutney, which she uses as a glaze for game hens or with curries or just to perk up meat loaf. The hens can be marinated a day in advance. After baking, add those flavorful drippings to the sauce.

FOR THE BLUEBERRY CHUTNEY:

8 cups (2 lb/1 kg) fresh blueberries
2 cups (12 oz/375 g) raisins or dried blueberries
2¼ cups (11 oz/345 g) finely chopped yellow onion
1 green bell pepper (capsicum), finely chopped
2 jalapeño peppers, finely chopped (see glossary)
2 tablespoons peeled, finely chopped fresh ginger
1 tablespoon ground cinnamon
1 tablespoon salt
4 cloves garlic, crushed through a garlic press
1 teaspoon ground cloves
12 fl oz (375 ml) canned frozen unsweetened apple juice, thawed
2 cups (16 fl oz/500 ml) raspberry, blueberry or apple cider
    vinegar

FOR THE GAME HENS:

6 Cornish game hens, 1¼ lb (625 g) each, thawed if frozen
½ cup (4 fl oz/125 ml) raspberry, blueberry or apple cider vinegar
¼ cup (2 fl oz/60 ml) soy sauce
1 tablespoon finely chopped fresh rosemary
1 tablespoon finely chopped fresh thyme
¼ cup (2 fl oz/60 ml) peanut or corn oil
¼ cup (3 oz/90 g) honey
2 teaspoons paprika
6 green (spring) onions, roots and tough ends removed
6 unpeeled orange quarters, seeded
⅓ cup (3½ oz/105 g) Blueberry Chutney

FOR THE SAUCE:

reserved marinade
½ cup (4 fl oz/125 ml) chicken stock (see glossary)
2 cups (1¼ lb/625 g) Blueberry Chutney

❊ To make the chutney, in a large, heavy-bottomed, nonreactive saucepan, combine the blueberries, raisins or dried blueberries, onion, bell pepper, jalapeño peppers, ginger, cinnamon, salt, garlic and cloves. Add the apple juice and vinegar and stir. Set over medium-high heat and bring to a boil. Reduce the heat to low and simmer, uncovered, stirring often, until the mixture is thick and darkened, 1–1½ hours.

❊ Reserve 2⅓ cups (23½ oz/735 g) chutney for the recipe. Ladle the remaining chutney into hot, sterilized jars (see glossary). Secure lids on the jars and store refrigerated for up to 2 months.

❊ To prepare the hens, place them in a large, nonreactive bowl. In a large glass measuring cup, combine the vinegar, soy sauce, rosemary, thyme, oil, honey and paprika and pour over the hens. Cover the bowl with plastic wrap, refrigerate and let marinate at least 4 hours, preferably overnight.

❊ To bake the hens, about 2 hours before serving, preheat an oven to 350°F (180°C). Lift the hens from the marinade and reserve the marinade. Stuff each hen with a green onion folded over, an orange quarter and a heaping tablespoon of chutney. Tie the legs together with kitchen twine. Place the stuffed hens breast side down in a well-buttered 9-by-13-by-2-in (23-by-33-by-5-cm) baking pan. Bake 1 hour.

❊ Meanwhile, pour off and discard the oil from the marinade. In a small saucepan over medium-high heat, bring the mari-nade to a boil, then add the stock and the 2 cups (20 oz/625 g) chutney. Reduce the heat to low and simmer, uncovered, 10 minutes. Set aside and keep warm.

❊ After the hens have baked for 1 hour, turn them breast side up and brush with the pan drippings. Bake until golden brown and the legs jiggle easily, about 45 minutes longer. An instant-read thermometer inserted at the thickest part, through the stuffing, should register 170°F (75°C). Remove the hens from the oven. Pour off the pan drippings into a glass measuring cup and spoon off and discard as much fat as possible. Add the defatted drippings to the sauce and stir well.

❊ Place a spoonful of sauce atop each hen and return the hens to the oven until glazed, 2–4 minutes. Serve the hens at once and pass the remaining sauce.

SERVES 6

ROASTED SOUTH CAROLINA SQUAB ON SWEET POTATO SPOON BREAD WITH SOUR CHERRY COMPOTE

Chef Ben Barker of the Magnolia Grill in Durham, North Carolina, begins with local ingredients and creates dazzling spin-offs. The squab in his recipe is raised in South Carolina, but if you can't find fresh squab, use quail or chicken and adjust the cooking time accordingly. Or see Mail Order Sources. Barker likes a medley of flavors on the plate, and this recipe is a grand example. The sour cherries in the compote play off the sweetness of the potatoes and complement the roasted game. The sauce may be prepared up to 2 days ahead of serving; the compote up to 1 week ahead.

FOR THE SQUAB:

8 squab, about 1 lb (500 g) each (see glossary)
salt and freshly ground pepper
¼ cup (2 fl oz/60 ml) olive oil

FOR THE SAUCE:

¼ cup (2 fl oz/60 ml) olive oil
1 yellow onion, coarsely chopped
2 carrots, coarsely chopped
2 celery ribs, coarsely chopped
1 bay leaf
1 head garlic, cut in half
½ cup (4 fl oz/125 ml) red wine vinegar
¼ cup (2 fl oz/60 ml) dark blackstrap molasses
2 cups (16 fl oz/500 ml) fruity red wine such as Zinfandel
4 cups (32 fl oz/1 l) chicken stock (see glossary)
6 sprigs fresh thyme

FOR THE SOUR CHERRY COMPOTE:

3 whole cloves
1 cinnamon stick, whole
10 peppercorns
1 bay leaf
½ cup (4 fl oz/125 ml) Port
½ cup (4 fl oz/125 ml) fruity red wine such as Zinfandel
2 tablespoons dark blackstrap molasses
½ cup (2½ oz/75 g) dried cherries
2 cups (8 oz/250 g) fresh sour cherries, pitted

FOR THE SWEET POTATO SPOON BREAD:

2½ cups (20 fl oz/625 ml) milk
2 cups (16 fl oz/500 ml) half & half
1 tablespoon salt
1 tablespoon sugar
1 cup (5 oz/155 g) stone-ground white cornmeal
½ cup (2½ oz/75 g) all-purpose (plain) flour
½ cup (4 oz/125 g) unsalted butter, cut into ½-in (12-mm) pieces
6 eggs, separated
¼ cup (2 fl oz/60 ml) heavy (double) cream
¾ cup (6 oz/185 g) cooked puréed sweet potatoes
salt and freshly ground pepper to taste
sprigs of fresh thyme for garnish

❀ To prepare the squab, remove the giblets and reserve the livers for another use. Trim the wings at the first joint and reserve these wing tips. Cut off the legs, leaving enough skin to cover the breasts. Season the flesh side of the legs with salt and pepper. Cut the lower portion of the backbone from the squab, leaving the breast and first wing section attached to the rib cage. Reserve these backbones. Cover the legs and breasts with plastic wrap and refrigerate.

❀ To make the sauce, in a large, heavy nonreactive saucepan over medium heat, heat the olive oil. When the oil is shimmering, add the reserved wing tips and backs and cook, turning with tongs, until deep brown on all sides. Remove the wing tips and backs and set aside. Add the onion, carrots and celery to the pan and sauté until the onion is translucent, about 5 minutes. Add the bay leaf and garlic and cook, stirring, 1 minute longer. Add the vinegar and molasses and stir, scraping up the browned bits from the bottom of the pan. Add the red wine, increase the heat to medium-high and bring to a boil. Then lower the heat to medium and simmer until the wine has reduced by two-thirds, 18–20 minutes.

❀ Add the browned wing tips and backs and chicken stock to the pan, increase the heat to medium-high and bring to a boil. Reduce the heat to medium-low and simmer, skimming any foam off the top, until the liquid has reduced to about 1½ cups (12 fl oz/375 ml), about 25 minutes. Add the thyme sprigs to the pan and remove from the heat. Let the thyme infuse 10 minutes. Strain the sauce through a fine-meshed sieve, pressing on the solids with the back of a spoon. Discard the solids. Let the sauce cool at room temperature, then cover and refrigerate.

❀ To make the compote, place the cloves, cinnamon stick, peppercorns and bay leaf in a 6-in (15-cm) square of cheesecloth (muslin) and tie with kitchen twine. Place the spice bag in a medium saucepan and add the Port, red wine and molasses. Bring to a boil over medium-high heat. Add the dried cherries, bring back to a boil and remove from the heat. Stir in the fresh sour cherries and let the mixture cool. Remove the spice bag and cover and refrigerate the compote.

❀ To make the spoon bread, in a medium saucepan over medium heat, combine the milk, half & half, salt and sugar. When small bubbles appear around the edge, slowly whisk in the cornmeal and flour. Reduce the heat to medium-low and, stirring constantly with a wooden spoon, cook until the mixture thickens and is smooth and creamy. Remove from the heat and stir in the butter pieces until all the butter has been incorporated.

❀ In a small bowl, whisk together the egg yolks and cream. Gradually add the egg mixture to cornmeal mixture in the saucepan. Fold in the puréed sweet potatoes. Add salt and pepper and set aside.

❀ To bake the squab and spoon bread, preheat an oven to 350°F (180°C).

❀ Remove the squab breasts and legs from the refrigerator. In a large sauté pan over medium-high heat, heat the olive oil. Add the breasts and sauté on both sides until deep golden brown, turning once, about 3–4 minutes. Season with salt and pepper and place on a roasting rack set in a 13-by-9-by-2-in (33-by-23-by-5-cm) baking pan. In the same oil, over medium-high heat, sauté the legs on both sides, turning once, 3–4 minutes. Place the legs in a small sauté pan. Remove the sauce from the refrigerator and skim off and discard any congealed fat. Pour ½ cup (4 fl oz/125 ml) sauce over the legs. Reheat the remaining sauce, stirring over low heat, and keep warm.

❀ To finish the spoon bread, beat the egg whites until stiff peaks form. Fold the beaten whites into sweet potato mixture. Pour into a lightly buttered shallow 2-qt (2-l) casserole. Bake until golden brown, puffy and just set, about 30 minutes. Keep warm.

❀ Bake the squab breasts in the same oven about 10 minutes for medium-rare, 15 minutes for medium. Do not bake longer than 15 minutes or the squab will become dry and tough. Remove from the oven and keep warm.

❀ Place the sauté pan of legs over medium heat and cook until the sauce heats through and the legs cook to medium, about 8 minutes.

❀ To serve, cut the breasts off the rib cage and then cut each breast in half. Place a large spoonful of sweet potato spoon bread in the center of each of 8 individual warm plates. Arrange 2 squab breast halves and 1 pair of legs, intertwined. Pour the sauce over and top with the sour cherry compote. Garnish with a thyme sprig.

SERVES 8

Roasted South Carolina Squab on Sweet Potato Spoon
Bread with Sour Cherry Compote

TIDEWATER

TIDEWATER

Atlantic Ocean

TIDEWATER

Unlike the West Coast, where land plunges into sea like a cliff diver, the southern Atlantic shore wades into the surf as leisurely as an August sunbather. Part land, part sea, the Tidewater region of the South shimmers with the intricacies of bay and marsh, inlet and island, sound and sand spit. It is a wet womb of civilizations and of the fish and shellfish that nourished them. The place smells of birthing, novelist Pat Conroy wrote in *The Prince of Tides*—"the bold, fecund aroma of the tidal marsh, exquisite and sensual, the smell of the South in heat."

The American South was born here. The first colonies, the first plantations, the first stirrings of Southern hospitality happened in this strip of land close by the sea. It follows that the first American cookbooks appeared here as well.

Virginians commonly use the term Tidewater to refer to the Chesapeake Bay basin, but to other Southerners the word also denotes a far larger region. This greater Tidewater runs from Virginia, where the English established their first permanent colony, to the Outer Banks of North Carolina, where the earlier Roanoke settlement mysteriously vanished, to the Sea Islands of South Carolina and Georgia, where the Spanish and French tried but failed to gain a foothold. The region penetrates inland up to 125 miles, taking in swamps, sluggish rivers and flat

Previous pages: Whipped by wind, waves constantly lash Folly Beach, the land's end point of Folly Island off the South Carolina coast. Left: A local farmer relaxes after a day's work in Redlands, South Carolina.

On Wadmalaw Island in South Carolina, a worker picks tea leaves at the Charleston Tea Plantation, the only one of its kind in the United States.

expanses of pine barrens, before meeting the Fall Line and the hills of the Piedmont.

The first explorers of the Tidewater coast found dozens of small tribes cultivating maize, squash and other alien edibles. Their diet of vegetables, game and seafood lives on in words the English borrowed from the Powhatans of Virginia: hominy, pone, opossum, raccoon, terrapin. Their name for the many-fingered estuary they lived beside suggests their most reliable food source— Chesapeake means "great shellfish bay."

It was another Powhatan crop that allowed the British to flourish eventually in the Tidewater after colonists landed at Jamestown in 1607. The European yen for American tobacco turned the tiny village on the brink of starvation into a bustling colony by the end of the century. Most of the settlers had been middle-class merchants and craftspeople back home. Some had been Cavaliers, wellborn monarchists who fled England after Charles I was executed in the civil war of the 1640s. Whatever their backgrounds, the most prosperous of the colonists took the British country squire as their model and lived like landed gentry on the tobacco plantations they built along the tidal rivers.

Few Virginians actually entertained on the grand scale that visitors found at plantations such as the Byrd family's Westover or the Lee family's Stratford Hall. But there were enough such fiefdoms to conceive a legend. As a correspondent to *London Magazine* put it in 1746: "All over the Colony, a universal Hospitality reigns; full Tables and open Doors, the kind Salute, the generous Detention, speak somewhat like the old Roast-beef Ages of our Fore-

On the cusp of the Chowan River, in the quintessential small port town of Edenton, North Carolina, a local fisherman tries his luck.

Steering ships to shore in the town of Buxton, North Carolina, the Cape Hatteras Lighthouse is the tallest in the United States, standing at 208 feet.

fathers. . . . Strangers are sought after with Greediness, as they pass the Country, to be invited."

And what were these strangers offered? American and English foods usually prepared in the English manner by African slave cooks who often as not had spent some time in the pepper pot of the West Indies. Awestruck diarists tell of rich terrapin soup, roasted wild turkey, boiled blue crabs, oysters by the dozen, smoked Virginia hams from peanut-fed hogs, Jerusalem artichokes, field peas, sweet potato pudding, spoon bread made from corn, the English yeast bun called Sally Lunn, dark plum puddings, sweet Madeira wine.

Most Virginians didn't eat like this, of course; as elsewhere, the common folk subsisted on pone and pork and whatever else they could catch or cultivate. At its social pinnacle, though, the Old Dominion clearly knew how to throw a feast. Company was so routine at Mount Vernon, George Washington confided in a letter that he and Martha had not dined alone together in

twenty years. The First Lady took large-scale dining so much for granted that one of her cake recipes instructs, matter-of-factly, "Take 40 eggs."

Many of Martha Washington's recipes came directly from England. So did the first cookbook published in the colonies. *The Compleat Housewife,* published in Williamsburg, Virginia, in 1742, is in fact a reproduction of a 1727 English cookbook. Not until 1824 would a genuinely Southern cookbook appear. Mary Randolph was a daughter of the Virginian aristocracy who had to open a boardinghouse in Richmond after her husband's political career hit the skids. She poured her expertise into *The Virginia House-wife.* Its 225 pages include fried chicken, smoked hams, barbecue, catfish and dozens of other dishes that summarize a native cuisine any Southerner would recognize. "There are those who regard it as the finest book ever to come out of the American kitchen," food historian Karen Hess wrote in a 1984 facsimile edition.

Sea gulls and dolphins follow closely behind shrimp boats dragging their nets in the Savannah Arca-Tybee Islands.

Virginia wasn't the only culinary cradle in the Tidewater region. Southerners joke that North Carolina is a vale of humility between two mountains of conceit. The other mountain is South Carolina, which has contributed its considerable share of original cookery.

South Carolina was one of the more culturally diverse English provinces. Some of the earliest inhabitants of Charleston, where the colony began in 1670, were Englishmen from the West Indian island of Barbados. Other early immigrants included Sephardic Jews and French Huguenots fleeing religious persecution. The Huguenots especially influenced the residential architecture of the Battery, Charleston's charming harbor front, with its French-style balconies and hipped-roof houses. They were equally influential in cooking, bringing rich French desserts and probably creating the Low Country rice pilaf, or pilau, as Carolinians call it (usually pronounced PER-lo, to confuse matters further).

The largest group of newcomers, African slaves, began arriving after South Carolina discovered the crop that would make it rich: the marshy Low Country was perfectly suited to growing rice. The grain was so lucrative that people sometimes used it instead of money—Carolina Gold, they called it.

As tobacco had done in Virginia, rice begat a feudal society along the Carolina coast. But unlike Virginia, South Carolina developed more as a city-state, with plantations close enough to Charleston that planters usually spent their wealth on brightly hued townhouses and ornate gardens instead of lonely manors in the swampy countryside. That left the toilers in the rice fields more isolated. As a result, the slaves of the southern Tidewater retained more of their culture and foodways than perhaps any other group of slaves in America.

Consider their dialect, Gullah, a blending of West African and Caribbean tongues that has dwindled to small pockets along the coast today. The almost indecipherable patois has a grammar and vocabulary all its own. Gullah blacks brought African foods and the words for them such as okra, goober, benne (sesame) seeds. They also gave African names to the foods they found—cooter (turtle), cush (cornmeal cake) and buckra yams (Irish potatoes, from their word for white people).

Farther south, along the Georgia coast, Gullah blacks called themselves Geechees, probably after the Ogeechee River below Savannah. When the English philanthropist James Oglethorpe founded Savannah in 1733, he prohibited slavery in the new colony. Georgians envied the wealth of South Carolina, however, and within a few years human bondage was legalized, and rice plantations spread southward through the Sea Islands. With the new money from rice, and later indigo and cotton, lovely moss-draped Savannah joined Charleston as one of the cities that best exemplified the social graces of the Old South. From the vantage point of upstart Atlanta, *Gone With the Wind*'s Scarlett O'Hara thought the two cities were "like aged grandmothers fanning themselves placidly in the sun."

Even today, after thousands of Northerners have made resorts out of Hilton Head and half the islands of the Southern coast, Savannah and Charleston still taste of the old days. Here in the Tidewater, people still serve shrimp over grits at breakfast. They still indulge in she-crab soup. They still eat oyster pie on Thanksgiving. The best chefs—Savannah's Elizabeth Terry and Charleston's Louis Osteen, to name only two—are known for clever variations on traditional dishes.

And even today, years after it has ceased to be an important crop in South Carolina, rice remains the culinary gold standard. It turns up in everything from salads to barbecue hashes to dessert cakes and puddings. A Charleston dinner table is not complete without a long, broad-bladed rice spoon. As Vertamae Smart-Grosvenor put it in *Vibration Cooking,* her cookbook/memoir about growing up in the Low Country, "I was 16 years old before I knew that everyone didn't eat rice every day." To which a proper Charlestonian might reply, *"They don't?"*

Kids from McClellanville take shade in what is purported to be the oldest deerhead oak tree in South Carolina.

VEGETABLES,
RELISHES &
PRESERVES

In colonial times, every Southern household participated in preserving summer's bounty of fruits and vegetables for the long winter months.

VEGETABLES, RELISHES & PRESERVES

One of the quickest ways to wreck a car in the South is to tailgate during harvest season. Southerners are liable to slam on the brakes when they see a roadside stand with bushels of fresh produce and a hand-lettered sign—probably with a backward *s*—announcing "Vine-Ripe Tomatoes." Or it could be pole beans. Or Vidalia onions. Or sweet potatoes or Silver Queen corn or what the poet James Dickey called "the divine fact of okra." Because it is a natural fact: Southerners eat their vegetables.

This taste for good things from the earth reflects the South's rural heritage. Though the majority of the population now lives in or around cities, a lot of Southerners are no more than a generation or two removed from the farm. Country ways color even the largest urban areas. More than a few people tend miniature farms in their back yards, process and stock pantries full of canned 'maters and yellow squash, and spend hours putting up preserves and relishes to enter in fairs and give as gifts. In many Southern homes, Sunday still smells like a pot of green beans simmering with a chunk of ham hock.

Conventional wisdom has it that Southern cooks don't trust vegetables to speak for themselves. They fry them, candy them, soufflé them, boil them with pork fat. As historian Joe Gray Taylor recalled in his book *Eating, Drinking and Visiting in the South:* "My father objected to green beans that practically snapped in one's mouth instead of submitting quietly to mastication, and he insisted that a good pot of beans had to have enough grease in it to wink back when winked at."

Not as many people lard it up that much anymore. Many cooks have found that they can get deliciously old-fashioned results with less pork seasoning and shorter cooking times. No one complained when Mary Mac's Tea Room, an Atlanta landmark of traditional Southern dining, switched to boiling turnip greens with chicken stock instead of pork.

No other fruit signals the summer season more than tree-ripened juicy Georgia peaches.

Previous pages: Candied Sweet Potatoes (recipe page 150), Tomato Pudding (recipe page 150), Baked Whole Vidalia Onions (recipe page 161), Pickled Peaches (recipe page 152)

Long-necked gourds are on display during "Putting Up Day" at Governor Aycock Historic Site in Fremont, North Carolina, where nineteenth-century techniques of canning, drying and preserving food are demonstrated.

They may not know it, but in modernizing their recipes cooks are following some very old advice. Southern cookbooks of the 1800s specifically cautioned against overboiling vegetables. "They lose their good appearance and flavor if cooked too long," wrote Annabella P. Hill, a Georgian, in her widely read 1870 volume, *Mrs. Hill's New Cook Book.* The advent of the pressure cooker in the early 1900s worked to undo such wisdom.

There are certain vegetables whose very names seem to have a Southern drawl. Okra, brought to these shores by African slaves, is eaten fried, added to stews and even boiled (despite its sliminess). Black-eyed peas, another slave food, are part of the confusion of peas and beans enjoyed throughout the South. Whether crowders, cowpeas, purple-hulls, pole beans or string beans, they are usually cooked the same way: boiled with streak o' lean. The term *greens* covers another kettle of veggies. Southerners use the word to mean, not lettuce and salad greens, but turnips, collards, kale, mustard and a dozen other leafy things they eat boiled, along with their nutritious juice called pot likker. Taken with corn bread, greens make a much-loved meatless dinner, Southern style. "When we're talking about greens and pot likker," says Alabama food writer Eugene Walter, "we're not just talking about vegetables. We're talking table religion."

If so, the high priest—the most distinguished vegetable lover in Southern history—is undoubtedly Thomas Jefferson. From 1766 to 1824, the epicure of Monticello kept a diary recording all the plants he tried growing in the gardens and orchards of his Virginia estate. The 15 March 1774 entry shows his adventurous palate in fine form; on that day seeds of wild endive, Spanish onions, cabbage and lettuce were all sown. His curiosity was such that he experimented with thirty varieties of peas alone.

In his seventy-sixth year Jefferson attempted to explain the secret of his longevity in a letter to his doctor. His philosophy would have been at home in a healthy-heart cookbook a century and a half later. "I have lived temperately," he wrote, "eating little animal food, and that not as an aliment, so much as a condiment for the vegetables, which constitute my principal diet."

Jefferson must have cooked with only a moderate amount of fat as there is no record of his vegetables ever winking at him from the pot.

Top to bottom: Fried Okra, Black-eyed Peas

Georgia

FRIED OKRA

The trick to frying okra extra crisp is to soak it in ice water before cooking. Then fry in batches, just a little at a time, until evenly browned.

1 lb (500 g) fresh okra, cut crosswise into slices ½ in (12 mm) thick
2–3 qt (2–3 l) lightly salted ice water
2 cups (10 oz/315 g) yellow or white cornmeal
½ teaspoon salt
¼ teaspoon freshly ground pepper
vegetable oil for frying
salt and freshly ground pepper to taste

❀ Preheat an oven to 200°F (93°C).

❀ In a large bowl, place the sliced okra with enough lightly salted ice water to cover and soak for 15 minutes. Drain.

❀ In a medium bowl, combine the cornmeal, the ½ teaspoon salt and the ¼ teaspoon pepper. Using a fork, stir until well blended.

❀ In a heavy, medium saucepan over medium-high heat, pour the oil to a depth of ¾ in (2 cm) and heat to 350°F (180°C) on a deep-fry thermometer. Dip the okra into the seasoned cornmeal to coat evenly, shaking off any excess and wiping your hands frequently to avoid build-up.

❀ Fry the okra in 3 batches until crisp and light golden brown, about 8 minutes per batch. Working quickly with a slotted spoon, transfer the okra to a baking sheet lined with paper towels to drain. Then transfer the okra to a baking sheet lined with aluminum foil and place in the warm oven until all the batches are ready to serve. Sprinkle with salt and pepper and serve warm.

SERVES 6

BLACK-EYED PEAS

Black-eyed Peas, that good luck charm of the Southern pantry, have been gaining new respect from regional chefs for their versatility, as well as from nutritionists who applaud their virtues as a lowfat, high-fiber protein source. They turn up in soups, salads and meatless main courses. But their most traditional preparation as a spicy side dish is hard to beat.

2 strips thickly sliced hickory-smoked bacon,
   coarsely chopped
1 white onion, thinly sliced
2 celery ribs, thinly sliced on the diagonal
3 cloves garlic, minced
4 cups (1¼ lb/625 g) fresh black-eyed peas
5 cups (40 fl oz/1.25 l) chicken stock (see glossary)
3 small dried red chili peppers
salt and freshly ground pepper to taste
hot pepper sauce

❀ In a large, heavy saucepan over medium heat, cook the bacon to render some drippings. Add the onion, celery and garlic and cook, stirring occasionally, until soft, about 8–10 minutes.
❀ Add the peas, stock and dried chili peppers. Reduce the heat to medium-low. Cover and simmer until the peas are tender, 35–40 minutes. Remove and discard the chili peppers. Season with salt and pepper.
❀ Serve the peas hot in some of their juices and pass the hot pepper sauce.

SERVES 6

SPECKLED BUTTER BEAN SUCCOTASH

Virtually all the native people the colonists met in America made some version of succotash, a stew of corn and lima beans. The name itself comes from the Algonquin word for boiled corn kernels, msickquatash. *Today the dish appears widely in the South, often with speckled butter beans and intensified with a little cream.*

1½ cups (8 oz/250 g) fresh or frozen speckled butter beans
   or lima beans
1 oz (30 g) salt pork
1–1¼ cups (8–10 fl oz/250–310 ml) water, or as needed
½ teaspoon sugar
½ teaspoon salt
¼ teaspoon freshly ground pepper
1½ cups (9 oz/280 g) fresh or frozen corn kernels
2½ teaspoons all-purpose (plain) flour
¼ cup (2 fl oz/60 ml) light (single) cream, at
   room temperature

❀ In a large saucepan over medium-low heat, combine the beans, salt pork, 1 cup (8 fl oz/250 ml) of the water, sugar, salt and pepper. Stir until well blended and cover. Cook until the beans are just tender, about 15 minutes. Stir in the corn until well blended. Add up to ¼ cup (2 fl oz/60 ml) more water if needed just to cover the corn kernels. Cover and simmer until the corn is tender, about 5 minutes. Remove and discard the salt pork.
❀ In a small bowl, whisk together the flour and cream until well blended and smooth. Stir into the corn and bean mixture until well blended. Cook, uncovered, stirring constantly, until the mixture has thickened, 3–4 minutes longer. Serve at once.

SERVES 4–6

BRAISED CABBAGE WITH COUNTRY HAM

Southerners don't season their vegetables with pork products as freely as they did in the old days, but many still keep a can of collected bacon drippings in the refrigerator for that occasional cholesterol splurge. In this recipe, just enough bacon grease and country ham are added to impart that much-loved smoky flavor (though you can substitute butter for the drippings if you insist).

1 large head green cabbage, about 3 lb (1.5 kg), trimmed of
   outer leaves, cored and quartered
¼ cup (2 fl oz/60 ml) bacon drippings or unsalted butter
8 oz (250 g) cooked lean country ham, coarsely chopped
   (see glossary)
4 yellow onions, coarsely chopped
2 celery ribs, coarsely chopped
1 green bell pepper (capsicum), seeded and coarsely chopped
4 cloves garlic, crushed through a garlic press
4 green (spring) onions, including tender green tops,
   thinly sliced
1½ cups (12 fl oz/375 ml) chicken stock (see glossary) or
   canned chicken broth
salt and freshly ground pepper to taste
Pepper Vinegar for serving (see glossary)

❀ Chop each cabbage quarter into 8–10 pieces and separate the leaves.
❀ In a large pot over medium heat, heat the bacon drippings or melt the butter. Add the ham, onions, celery, bell pepper, garlic and green onions and stir until well blended. Raise the heat to medium-high and cook 6–8 minutes, stirring often. Add the cabbage pieces and stir well. Cook until the cabbage leaves are wilted, about 5 minutes. Add the chicken stock or broth and stir. Cover, reduce the heat to low and simmer, stirring occasionally, for 45 minutes.
❀ To serve, add the salt and pepper and serve hot or at room temperature. Pass a bottle of pepper vinegar.

SERVES 8–10

*Top to bottom: Braised Cabbage with Country Ham,
Speckled Butter Bean Succotash*

145

The South

GREEN TOMATO CHUTNEY

Enjoy this savory, sweet-and-sour chutney, punctuated with pieces of apples, as an accompaniment to beef, pork or game.

1 lb (500 g) green tomatoes, peeled and coarsely chopped
    (see glossary)
1 lb (500 g) Granny Smith apples or other slightly tart
    apples, peeled and cut into 1-in (2.5-cm) dice
2 white onions, thinly sliced
2½ cups (20 fl oz/625 ml) white wine vinegar
2 cups (16 fl oz/500 ml) water
2 cups (12 oz/375 g) golden raisins (sultanas)
2 cups (14 oz/440 g) firmly packed light brown sugar
1 teaspoon ground ginger
1 teaspoon ground allspice
1 teaspoon crushed peppercorns
1 tablespoon salt
4 garlic cloves, minced

❀ In a large, heavy nonreactive saucepan over high heat, combine all the ingredients and stir until well blended. Bring to a boil, stirring occasionally. Reduce the heat to low and simmer, stirring often, until the chutney has thickened to a jamlike consistency and most of the liquid has evaporated, leaving just enough to coat the chutney.

❀ Working quickly, pack the chutney into hot, sterilized half-pint (8 fl oz/ 250 ml) jars, leaving ½ in (12 mm) headspace. Wipe the jar rims and seal. Process for 15 minutes in a hot-water bath (see glossary). Store in a cool, dark place for up to 12 months. Refrigerate after opening.

MAKES 4 HALF-PINTS (2½ LB/1.25 KG)

The South

SHOEPEG CORN RELISH

White Shoepeg corn is a very sweet, older corn variety with tiny kernels. Silver Queen is another sweet white corn that can be substituted in this recipe, or use your favorite yellow corn variety.

2 tablespoons salt
2 cups (1 lb/500 g) sugar
2 tablespoons dry mustard
2 teaspoons ground turmeric
1¼ teaspoons celery seeds
3 cups (24 fl oz/750 ml) distilled white vinegar
7 cups (42 oz/1.3 kg) kernels from 10–12 ears of white
    Shoepeg corn (see note)
3 cups (15 oz/470 g) finely diced red bell pepper (capsicum)
5 cups (25 oz/780 g) finely chopped white onion

❀ In a large, heavy nonreactive saucepan over medium heat, combine the salt, sugar, mustard, turmeric, celery seeds and vinegar and stir until well blended. Bring to a boil, stirring frequently. Stir in the corn, bell pepper and onion until well blended. Reduce the heat to low and simmer, stirring often, until the mixture has thickened and most of the liquid has evaporated, leaving just enough to coat the corn, 45 minutes.

❀ Working quickly, pack the relish into hot, sterilized half-pint (8 fl oz/ 250 ml) jars, leaving ½ in (12 mm) headspace. Wipe the jar rims and seal. Process for 15 minutes in a hot-water bath (see glossary). Store in a cool, dark place for up to 12 months. Refrigerate after opening.

MAKES 12 HALF-PINTS (7½ LB/3.75 KG)

Left to right: Shoepeg Corn Relish, Green Tomato Chutney

Fried Green Tomatoes

Georgia

FRIED GREEN TOMATOES

Ever since their starring role in the feature film of the same name, the popularity of fried green tomatoes has grown. It is no longer necessary to grow your own tomatoes or drive to a roadside stand—they can be found at many farmers' markets and even some supermarkets. Crunchy on the outside and lemony-tart on the inside, Fried Green Tomatoes are easy to make and a great way to use up the last of the season's harvest, those that just won't ripen. If you want an extra boost of flavor, heat the oil with a few strips of bacon and when the oil is ready, remove and discard the bacon. Serve with grilled meats or Pan-fried Soft-shell Crabs (recipe on page 103) or for breakfast with eggs.

1 egg
2 tablespoons milk
½ teaspoon salt
¼ teaspoon freshly ground pepper
½ cup (2 oz/60 g) sifted all-purpose (plain) flour
¾ cup (4 oz/125 g) yellow cornmeal
vegetable oil for frying

3 firm green (unripe) tomatoes, cored and cut into 12 slices
salt and freshly ground black pepper to taste
sprigs of fresh thyme for garnish (optional)

❋ Preheat an oven to 200°F (93°C).
❋ In a medium bowl, combine the egg, milk, the ½ teaspoon salt and the ¼ teaspoon pepper and beat until well blended. In another medium bowl, combine the flour and cornmeal.
❋ In a heavy, deep skillet over medium-high heat, pour the oil to a depth of ½ in (12 mm) and heat to 350°F (180°C) on a deep-fry thermometer. Dip the tomato slices in the egg mixture to coat evenly. Then dip in the cornmeal mixture, shaking off any excess and wiping your hands to avoid build-up. Fry the tomatoes in 3 batches, turning once, until the coating is crisp and light golden brown on both sides, a total of 3–5 minutes per batch.
❋ Working quickly with a slotted spatula, transfer the tomatoes to a baking sheet lined with paper towels to drain. Then transfer the tomatoes to a baking sheet lined with aluminum foil and place in the warm oven until all the batches are ready to serve. Sprinkle with salt and pepper and serve warm. Garnish with thyme sprigs, if desired.

SERVES 4

Left to right: Creole-Style Okra with Tomatoes, Pole Beans with Streak o' Lean and New Potatoes

The South

SWEET POTATO– ORANGE CASSEROLE

Southern cooks have traditionally had a hard time resisting the temptation to smother sweet potato casseroles with enough butter, sugar and miniature marshmallows to match the caloric value of the richest pie. Lately, though, it seems that the vegetable's natural flavor is gaining a new appreciation. This casserole contains no butter (except for greasing the pans) and a minimum of sugar, with orange juice and spices giving it an extra flavor boost.

2½ lb (1.25 kg) sweet potatoes, cooked, cooled, peeled and halved lengthwise
3 eggs
½ cup (4 oz/125 g) sugar
⅓ cup (3 fl oz/80 ml) frozen orange juice concentrate, thawed
½ teaspoon ground allspice
½ teaspoon freshly grated nutmeg
¼ teaspoon ground ginger

❀ Preheat an oven to 300°F (150°C). Lightly butter a 2-qt (2-l) round casserole or baking dish.
❀ Arrange the cooked sweet potatoes, cut side down, in the dish.
❀ In a medium bowl, combine the eggs, sugar, orange juice concentrate, allspice, nutmeg and ginger and whisk until well blended. Pour over the sweet potatoes. Bake on the middle oven rack until the top is puffy and the edges lightly browned and the mixture has set, about 50 minutes.
❀ Serve hot directly from the dish.

SERVES 6–8

Louisiana

STUFFED MIRLITONS

Pale-green mirlitons, known elsewhere as chayote squash or vegetable pear, were brought to Louisiana by South Americans in the mid-1700s. They have been a favorite vegetable among Cajuns and Creoles ever since, for pickling, sautéing and especially for stuffing with a savory mixture such as this one.

2 mirlitons (chayotes), 8 oz (250 g) each
1 small yellow onion, minced
3 cloves garlic, crushed through a garlic press
½ cup (2 oz/60 g) seasoned fine dried bread crumbs
½ cup (¾ oz/20 g) finely chopped fresh parsley
¼ cup (2 fl oz/60 ml) water
6 oz (185 g) cooked smoked lean ham, very finely chopped (see glossary)
salt and freshly ground pepper to taste
1 tablespoon unsalted butter, cut into ½-in (12-mm) dice

❀ Preheat an oven to 350°F (180°C). Lightly coat a 2-qt (2-l) square baking dish with vegetable cooking spray. The dish should be large enough to hold the mirlitons snugly in one layer.
❀ Cut each mirliton in half and remove and discard the seeds. Place the mirliton halves in a vegetable steamer basket set over boiling water and cover. Steam the mirliton halves until tender when pierced with a small sharp knife, about 10 minutes.
❀ Drain the mirlitons and scoop out the flesh, leaving the shells ¼ in (6 mm) thick. Cut the flesh into small pieces and place in a medium bowl. Using a potato masher or the back of a fork, mash the flesh. Stir in the onion, garlic, bread crumbs, parsley, water and ham until well blended. Season with salt and pepper. Set aside to let stuffing cool completely.
❀ Spoon the cooled stuffing into the reserved mirliton shells and firmly pack the stuffing, mounding the top slightly. Arrange the mirlitons in the prepared baking dish and sprinkle the diced butter over the stuffing. Bake on the middle oven rack until the tops are golden brown, about 30 minutes. Serve at once.

SERVES 4

Louisiana

CREOLE-STYLE OKRA WITH TOMATOES

As in gumbo, the okra in this spicy side dish acts as a thickener. It is a salubrious and tasty addition to almost any repast. Serve it alongside fried or grilled chicken, or any simple roast meat. Though an untraditional idea, I have even used leftovers as a quick pasta sauce.

2 tablespoons vegetable oil
1 yellow onion, cut into medium dice
2 cloves garlic, crushed through a garlic press
1 lb (500 g) fresh or frozen okra, cut crosswise into slices ½ in (12 mm) thick
1 green bell pepper (capsicum), seeded and cut into medium dice
2 lb (1 kg) tomatoes, coarsely chopped
1 teaspoon salt
¼ teaspoon freshly ground pepper
⅛ teaspoon ground cayenne pepper
2 tablespoons minced fresh parsley

❀ In a large, heavy skillet over medium-high heat, heat the oil. Add the onion and garlic and cook, stirring often, for 2 minutes. Add the okra and bell pepper and cook, stirring constantly, for 2 minutes. Stir in the tomatoes, salt, pepper and cayenne. Cover and simmer, stirring occasionally, until the okra is tender, about 20 minutes. Stir in the parsley until well blended. Transfer to a heated serving dish and serve hot.

SERVES 6

The South

POLE BEANS WITH STREAK O' LEAN AND NEW POTATOES

Southerners have long been accused of cooking their green beans to near mush. With pole beans, that's not such a bad idea. The opposite of young, tender haricots verts, pole beans are long, flat and tough—but loaded with flavor if cooked with an extra helping of patience. Streak o' lean—salt pork with a lean line of meat showing—gives the beans a creamy quality.

3 cups (24 fl oz/750 ml) water
2 cups (16 fl oz/500 ml) vegetable stock (see glossary)
1 lb (500 g) pole beans, ends snapped, stringed and broken
  into pieces 1 in (2.5 cm) long

1 oz (30 g) streak o' lean, finely diced (see glossary)
1 large white onion, finely chopped
8 oz (250 g) new potatoes
salt and freshly ground pepper to taste
2 tablespoons minced fresh parsley

❈ In a large nonreactive saucepan over medium heat, combine the water and vegetable stock and bring to a boil. Add the beans and streak o' lean. Reduce the heat to low, cover and simmer for 45 minutes. Add the onion and potatoes. Simmer uncovered, stirring occasionally, until the beans are tender and the potatoes are tender when pierced with a toothpick but not falling apart, 15–20 minutes. Season with salt and pepper.
❈ To serve, ladle with the broth into individual shallow bowls and sprinkle with the parsley. Serve hot.

SERVES 4

Top to bottom: Stuffed Mirlitons, Sweet Potato–Orange Casserole

The South

CANDIED SWEET POTATOES

Versions of this beloved recipe turn up at almost every traditional Southern holiday feast—often smothered with marshmallows, nuts or a streusel topping. This recipe is plenty sweet, but still allows the taste of the tuber to shine through. A thinner, more refined syrup than the thick, cloyingly sweet canned version blankets the sweet potatoes.

2½ lb (1.25 kg) thin-skinned red sweet potatoes, unpeeled
¾ cup (6 oz/185 g) firmly packed light brown sugar
¾ teaspoon ground cinnamon
¼ cup (2 oz/60 g) unsalted butter, cut into small pieces
1 teaspoon vanilla extract (essence)
¼ cup (2 fl oz/60 ml) hot water

❧ In a large pot, place the sweet potatoes and add water to cover by 1 in (2.5 cm). Bring to a boil over medium heat and cook until barely tender, about 30 minutes. Drain and set aside to cool. When cool enough to handle, peel the sweet potatoes and cut crosswise into rounds ½ in (12 mm) thick.
❧ Preheat an oven to 350°F (180°C).
❧ Lightly butter a shallow 1½-qt (1.5-l) casserole or baking dish. Arrange the sweet potatoes in the dish, slightly overlapping them in layers. Sprinkle evenly with the brown sugar and cinnamon. Dot with the butter. Stir the vanilla extract into the hot water and drizzle over the top.
❧ Cover tightly with aluminum foil and bake on the middle oven rack for 20 minutes. Uncover and continue to bake until the sweet potatoes are very tender, 10–20 minutes longer, basting the sweet potatoes once with their juices.
❧ Serve hot directly from the baking dish.

SERVES 8   *Photograph pages 140–141*

Kentucky

TOMATO PUDDING

Alongside roasted meat, fish or fowl, this sweet and spicy Tomato Pudding plays the same role as candied sweet potatoes. It is almost as rich, too, which makes sense, considering that tomatoes are fruits not vegetables, and some horticulturists even consider them a berry. This recipe is adapted from Cooking in the New South *by Anne Byrn, former food editor of the* Atlanta Journal-Constitution. *You can also vary it by substituting different fresh herbs. Though canned crushed tomatoes are preferable, you can replace them with fresh summer tomatoes, when available.*

28 oz (875 g) canned crushed tomatoes (see note)
¾ teaspoon salt
1 cup (7 oz/220 g) firmly packed light brown sugar
¾ cup (6 fl oz/180 ml) boiling water
8 slices white bread, toasted and cut into 1-in
   (2.5-cm) cubes
¼ cup (2 oz/60 g) unsalted butter, melted
¼ cup (½ oz/15 g) minced fresh chives for garnish (optional)

❧ Preheat an oven to 350°F (180°C).
❧ In a nonreactive medium bowl, combine the tomatoes, salt, brown sugar and boiling water and stir until well blended. Place the toast cubes in the bottom of a shallow 2-qt (2-l) casserole dish. Pour the tomato mixture over the toast cubes and drizzle with the melted butter. Bake until heated throughout and the exposed bread cubes are golden brown, about 40 minutes.
❧ Garnish with chives, if desired, and serve hot directly from the dish.

SERVES 6–8   *Photograph pages 140–141*

Atlanta, Georgia

YELLOW SQUASH SOUFFLÉ

When Mary Mac's Tea Room opened in Atlanta in 1945, the "meat-and-three" blue plate was standard lunch fare. For many patrons, the combination wouldn't have been complete without this squash casserole. Though technically not a soufflé (egg whites aren't beaten and incorporated), this version by longtime owner Margaret Lupo is just as light and fluffy. It comes from her book Southern Cooking from Mary Mac's Tea Room.

½ cup (4 fl oz/125 ml) water
¼ cup (2 oz/60 g) unsalted butter, at room temperature
1 teaspoon salt, or to taste
2 lb (1 kg) yellow (crookneck) squash, sliced ½ in
   (12 mm) thick
2 eggs, at room temperature
1 cup (8 fl oz/250 ml) milk, at room temperature
1 tablespoon melted butter or bacon drippings, at
   room temperature
½ teaspoon freshly ground white pepper
½ cup (2 oz/60 g) unsalted soda cracker crumbs, crushed
   with a rolling pin until fine

❧ In a heavy medium saucepan over medium-high heat, combine the water, unsalted butter and ½ teaspoon of the salt and bring to a boil. Add squash, reduce the heat to low, cover and simmer until the squash is soft, about 15 minutes. Using a potato masher or fork, mash the squash in the pan, strain to remove excess liquid and set aside.
❧ Preheat an oven to 350°F (180°C). Lightly butter a 2-qt (2-l) baking dish.
❧ In a large bowl, beat the eggs. Add the squash and stir to combine. Add the milk, melted butter or bacon drippings, the remaining ½ teaspoon salt, if desired, and white pepper and stir to combine. Pour into the prepared pan. Top with the crushed soda cracker crumbs.
❧ Bake until set, about 35 minutes. If desired, garnish with chives to serve.

SERVES 8

Kentucky

DERBY DAY ASPARAGUS

Derby Day gives Kentuckians a good excuse to indulge in a lavish spring menu that typically includes an asparagus side dish. Choose only tender, thin, lavender-tipped green asparagus for this dish.

1 lb (500 g) cooked thin asparagus spears, cooled

FOR THE MARINADE:

¼ cup (2 fl oz/60 ml) white wine vinegar
¼ cup (2 fl oz/60 ml) extra-virgin olive oil
2 cloves garlic, crushed through a garlic press
1 tablespoon minced fresh dill or 2 teaspoons dried dill
½ teaspoon grated orange zest (see glossary)
½ teaspoon salt
¼ teaspoon freshly ground pepper
2 orange slices, halved, for garnish
sprig of fresh dill for garnish

❧ The day before serving, arrange the cooked asparagus spears on a serving dish, with all the tips pointing in one direction.
❧ In a medium nonreactive bowl, combine all the marinade ingredients and whisk until well blended. Pour the marinade over the asparagus, coating them well. Cover and refrigerate overnight.
❧ The next day, garnish with the orange slice halves arranged in a fan shape on top of the asparagus. Top with the dill sprig. Serve at room temperature.

SERVES 4

Top to bottom: Yellow Squash Soufflé,
Derby Day Asparagus

The South

PICKLED PEACHES

Southerners love to pickle fruit and Pickled Peaches are a very popular condiment. They make a wonderful accompaniment to ham and a lovely, aromatic garnish for poultry. Use peaches that are ripe, but not too soft.

2 tablespoons whole cloves
3 cinnamon sticks, 3 in (7.5 cm) long, broken in half
1 tablespoon peeled, coarsely chopped fresh ginger
2 lb (1 kg) sugar
2 cups (16 fl oz/500 ml) apple cider vinegar
3 cups (24 fl oz/750 ml) water
4 lb (2 kg) firm, ripe peaches

❈ Tie the cloves, cinnamon sticks and ginger together in a piece of cheesecloth (muslin). Place the spice bag, sugar, vinegar and water in a large, heavy nonreactive saucepan over medium heat. Bring to a boil, stirring frequently. Boil, stirring often, until the sugar has dissolved into a syrup, 15 minutes. Remove the pan from the heat and set aside.
❈ Fill a large pot three fourths full of water and bring to a boil. Using a slotted spoon, gently lower the peaches a few at a time into the boiling water and parboil for 30 seconds. Using the slotted spoon, transfer each batch to a colander and drain under cold running water. When cool enough to handle, gently remove and discard the skins. Repeat until all the peaches have been blanched and peeled.
❈ Add the peaches to the sugar-spice mixture and return the saucepan to low heat. Cover and simmer until the peaches are heated through and just tender when pierced with a fork, about 10 minutes. Remove from the heat, uncover and let the peaches cool in the pan to room temperature. Remove and discard the spice bag. Cover the pan and refrigerate overnight.
❈ The next day, set the pan, uncovered, over medium heat. Heat until the peaches are heated throughout and the syrup has come to a boil, about 10 minutes.
❈ Working quickly, using a slotted spoon, pack the peaches into hot, sterilized half-pint (8 fl oz/250 ml) jars, leaving ¾ in (2 cm) headspace. Pour the boiling syrup into the jars, covering the peaches by ¼ in (6 mm) and leaving ½ in (12 mm) headspace. Slide a clean, new plastic chopstick or wooden skewer along the inside of each jar to release any air bubbles. Wipe the jar rims and seal. Process for 20 minutes in a hot-water bath (see glossary).
❈ Store in a cool, dark place up to 12 months. Refrigerate after opening.

MAKES 7 HALF-PINTS (4½ LB/2.25 KG) *Photograph pages 140–141*

Georgia

VIDALIA ONION RELISH

Vidalia onions are renowned for being so sweet and mild, you can eat them like an apple without shedding a tear. Wonderful as they are raw, they are also highly versatile and make excellent relishes such as this one. It is a delightful condiment for a homey all-vegetable dinner or grilled hamburgers, as well as for a sophisticated entrée, such as filet mignon.

10 lb (5 kg) Vidalia onions
¼ cup (2 oz/60 g) salt
4 cups (32 fl oz/1 l) apple cider vinegar
1 teaspoon ground turmeric
2 teaspoons pickling spice
1½ teaspoons minced red bell pepper (capsicum)
4½ cups (2¼ lb/1.1 kg) sugar

❈ Peel and trim the onions. In a food processor fitted with the large-holed shredding disk, grate the onions in batches and transfer to a large bowl. Alternatively, use the coarse side of a metal box grater. Stir in the salt until well blended. Cover and let stand for 30 minutes at room temperature.
❈ Using your hands, squeeze out as much juice as possible from the onions, discarding the juice and transferring the onions to a large, heavy nonreactive pot. Stir in the vinegar, turmeric, pickling spice, bell pepper and sugar until well blended. Set the pot over medium-high heat and bring to a boil, stirring often. Reduce the heat to low and simmer, stirring often, until the mixture has thickened and most of the liquid has evaporated, leaving just enough to coat the onions, about 30 minutes.
❈ Working quickly, pack the relish into hot, sterilized pint (16 fl oz/500 ml) jars, leaving ½ in (12 mm) headspace. Wipe the jar rims and seal. Process for 10 minutes in a hot-water bath (see glossary). Store in a cool, dark place for up to 12 months. Refrigerate after opening.

MAKES 8 PINTS (10 LB/5 KG)

Tennessee

CHOWCHOW

Americans have been pickling their summer bounty for year-round use for more than 200 years. Chowchow, a spicy pickled relish, has been cherished throughout the United States—but especially in the South—since the mid-1800s. Though ingredients vary somewhat from one recipe to the next, most contain cabbage, onions, bell peppers, cucumbers, green tomatoes and whatever else there is an excess supply of in the garden.

2 qt (2 l) cold water
½ cup (4 oz/125 g) kosher salt
2 cups (6 oz/185 g) shredded green cabbage
2 cups (10 oz/315 g) finely diced cucumber
2 cups (10 oz/315 g) coarsely chopped green bell pepper (capsicum)
2 cups (10 oz/315 g) finely chopped yellow onion
2 cups (12 oz/375 g) finely chopped green tomatoes
2 cups (12 oz/375 g) small butter beans (lima beans)
2 cups (8 oz/250 g) coarsely chopped green beans
2 cups (10 oz/315 g) finely chopped carrots
2–2½ qt (2–2.5 l) boiling water, or as needed
4 cups (2 lb/1 kg) sugar
4 cups (32 fl oz/1 l) distilled white vinegar
¼ cup (¾ oz/20 g) yellow mustard seeds
2 tablespoons celery seeds
1 tablespoon ground turmeric

❈ Place the cold water in a large nonreactive bowl and stir in the salt until dissolved. Stir in the cabbage, cucumber, bell pepper, onion and green tomatoes until well blended. Cover and let soak overnight in the refrigerator.
❈ The next day, in a large, heavy nonreactive pot, combine the butter beans, green beans and carrots. Add enough boiling water to cover the mixture by ¼ in (6 mm). Cook over medium heat, stirring occasionally, until just tender, about 3 minutes. Drain and transfer back into the pot. Then drain the vegetables that have been soaking overnight and stir into the pot of beans and carrots.
❈ Set the pot over medium heat. Stir in the sugar, vinegar, mustard seeds, celery seeds and turmeric until well blended. Bring to a boil. Then reduce the heat to medium-low and simmer, stirring occasionally, for 10 minutes.
❈ Working quickly, pack the relish into hot, sterilized pint (16 fl oz/500 ml) jars, leaving ½ in (12 mm) headspace. Wipe the jar rims and seal. Process for 15 minutes in a hot-water bath (see glossary). Store in a cool, dark place for up to 12 months. Refrigerate after opening.

MAKES 8 PINTS (10 LB/5 KG)

Left to right: Pickled Whole Okra, Chowchow, Vidalia Onion Relish

PICKLED WHOLE OKRA

Even if you have sampled cooked okra, which can have a slightly gelatinous texture, it is an eye-opener to taste pickled okra. Pickling brings out the sprightly character of okra and the texture is crisp but tender. Pickled okra is a delightful addition to a crudité platter, and also goes well with cooked beans, greens, chicken or turkey. Choose small, tender okra pods for the best results.

3 lb (1.5 kg) small, young, tender okra
sprigs of fresh dill
3 cups (24 fl oz/750 ml) distilled white vinegar
3 cups (24 fl oz/750 ml) water
6 tablespoons (3 oz/90 g) kosher salt
½ teaspoon red pepper flakes

❀ Trim the okra pods to remove any darkened stem tips, but do not remove caps entirely, and leave each pod intact with a stem stub. Rinse the okra well and drain. Using a small, sharp knife, prick each pod twice in two different places.
❀ Working quickly, pack the okra into hot, sterilized pint (16 fl oz/500 ml) jars, placing the pods vertically side by side, alternating the direction of the caps. Pack just tight enough to keep the pods standing upright. Insert 2 dill sprigs into each jar with the okra, leaving ¾ in (2 cm) headspace.
❀ In a large, heavy nonreactive pot over medium heat, combine the vinegar, water, salt and red pepper flakes and bring to a boil. Pour the boiling liquid into the jars, covering the okra by ¼ in (6 mm) and leaving ½ in (12 mm) headspace. Slide a clean, new plastic chopstick or wooden skewer along the inside of each jar to release any air bubbles. Wipe the jar rims and seal. Process for 15 minutes in a hot-water bath (see glossary). Store in a cool, dark place to let the pickles mellow for 8 weeks before serving. Store up to 12 months. Refrigerate after opening.

MAKES 6 PINTS (3¾ LB/1.9 KG)

Finger Pepper, Squash and Corn Pudding

The South

FINGER PEPPER, SQUASH AND CORN PUDDING

This creamy country-style custard is composed of straight-from-the-garden summer ingredients: Finger-shaped peppers, tender squash and nuggets of corn create a custard dish with a creamy fresh flavor.

FOR THE VEGETABLES:

2 tablespoons olive oil
4 yellow wax or sweet Italian peppers (capsicums),
   halved, seeded and thinly sliced
1 yellow onion, thinly sliced
1 red bell pepper (capsicum), seeded and chopped
4 cloves garlic, minced
2 lb (1 kg) yellow (crookneck) squash, coarsely chopped
kernels from 4 ears of yellow corn or 1 lb (500 g) frozen
   corn kernels

FOR THE CUSTARD:

1 cup (8 fl oz/250 ml) milk, at room temperature
1 cup (8 oz/250 g) lowfat sour cream, at room temperature
3 eggs, at room temperature
3 egg yolks, at room temperature
1 tablespoon minced fresh thyme leaves
1 teaspoon salt
¼ teaspoon freshly ground pepper
pinch of ground nutmeg
10 oz (315 g) sharp yellow Cheddar cheese, shredded

❉ Preheat an oven to 375°F (190°C). Lightly coat a 3-qt (3-l) baking dish with vegetable cooking spray.
❉ To prepare the vegetables, in a large skillet over high heat, heat the oil until sizzling. Add the finger peppers, onion, bell pepper and garlic. Sauté until soft, about 5 minutes. Add the squash and corn. Sauté until the squash is tender and most of the juices have evaporated, about 10 minutes.
❉ To make the custard, in a large bowl, combine the milk,

154

sour cream, eggs, egg yolks, thyme, salt, pepper and nutmeg. Whisk until smooth. Stir in the shredded cheese until well blended. Pour over the vegetables in the baking dish.

❉ Bake on the middle oven rack until the custard is set, but still slightly soft in the center, 45–50 minutes. Let the custard cool for 10 minutes before serving. Serve hot.

SERVES 8

Vidalia, Georgia

BUTTERMILK-BATTERED VIDALIA ONION RINGS

Buttermilk does double-duty in this recipe. It is used in both the marinade and the batter as a flavoring agent. These onion rings are nice and crunchy, and the rich and slightly sweet-tart buttermilk adds a snappy contrast to the sweet Vidalia onions.

2 Vidalia onions, 12 oz (375 g) each, cut into slices ½ in (12 mm) wide
4 cups (32 fl oz/1 l) lowfat buttermilk
2 cups (10 oz/315 g) sifted all-purpose (plain) flour
1 teaspoon salt
½ teaspoon ground cayenne pepper
3 eggs, lightly beaten
2 tablespoons vegetable oil
peanut oil for deep frying
salt and freshly ground pepper to taste

❉ Separate the onion slices into rings. In a large nonreactive bowl, combine the onion rings and buttermilk. Cover and refrigerate for 1 hour. Drain the onion rings, reserving ¾ cup (6 fl oz/180 ml) of the buttermilk marinade. Pat the onion rings dry on paper towels.

❉ To make the batter, in a medium bowl, stir together the flour, salt and cayenne. Whisk in the beaten eggs, the reserved buttermilk marinade and vegetable oil until smooth.

❉ In a heavy, deep skillet over medium heat, pour in enough peanut oil to come halfway up the sides of the skillet. Heat the oil to 375°F (190°C) on a deep-fry thermometer.

❉ Preheat an oven to 200°F (93°C).

❉ Working in 3 batches, dip the rings into the batter and then drop them into the hot oil. Fry, turning the rings with tongs, until golden brown on both sides, 3–4 minutes cooking time. Drain on paper towels. Repeat with the remaining batter and onion rings, keeping the fried rings warm in the oven.

❉ To serve, lightly season the onion rings with salt and pepper to taste. Serve at once.

SERVES 4–6

The South

MACARONI AND CHEESE

Newcomers to the South often are amused to find that macaroni and cheese is considered a vegetable at most cafés and restaurants. This version has slightly more nutmeg than others, for a very pleasing result. For a subtler nutmeg flavor, reduce the amount by half, or omit altogether if you prefer. Lightly salting the water for the macaroni brings out the flavor of the pasta. Many food historians claim that Mary Randolph, in The Virginia House-wife *(1831), printed what might be the first recipe for a macaroni and cheese dish in the United States. However, her recipe was just cooked macaroni layered with butter and cheese and baked, while modern versions add a white sauce to the dish.*

1 lb (500 g) elbow macaroni
3 tablespoons unsalted butter
3 tablespoons all-purpose (plain) flour

2½ cups (20 fl oz/625 ml) milk, at room temperature
4 cups (1 lb/500 g) shredded sharp yellow Cheddar cheese
½ teaspoon ground nutmeg
⅛ teaspoon ground cayenne pepper
salt and freshly ground pepper to taste

❉ Fill a large pot three fourths full of water and bring to a boil. Add salt, if desired (see note). Add the elbow macaroni to the boiling water and stir. Return to a boil and boil, stirring occasionally, until al dente, about 5 minutes or according to package directions. Drain and transfer to a lightly buttered shallow 3-qt (3-l) casserole or baking dish and set aside at room temperature.

❉ Preheat an oven to 350°F (180°C).

❉ In a heavy medium saucepan over medium heat, melt the butter. Add the flour and whisk until large bubbles appear, about 2 minutes. Cook 2 minutes longer, whisking constantly; do not let brown. Remove the pan from the heat. Gradually pour in the milk, whisking constantly across the bottom and around the sides of the pan until blended and smooth. Return the pan to medium heat and cook, whisking constantly, until thickened, about 10 minutes.

❉ Remove the saucepan from the heat. Whisk in 3 cups (12 oz/375 g) of the Cheddar cheese until just melted and smooth and creamy. Whisk in the nutmeg and cayenne pepper until well blended. Add salt and pepper to taste.

❉ Pour the cheese sauce over the macaroni in the baking dish and gently stir until the macaroni is well coated and evenly spread. The dish will appear soupy, but when baked the macaroni will absorb most of the sauce and become thickened. Sprinkle the remaining 1 cup (4 oz/125 g) Cheddar cheese evenly over the top.

❉ Bake on the middle oven rack until bubbly and the edges are golden brown, about 30 minutes. Adjust seasoning with more salt and pepper, and serve hot directly from the baking dish.

SERVES 8–10

Top to Bottom: Macaroni and Cheese, Buttermilk-Battered Vidalia Onion Rings

155

Clockwise from top left: Appalachian Apple Butter, Peach Preserves, Blueberry Jam

Appalachia

APPALACHIAN APPLE BUTTER

Margaret Agnew writes that Appalachians from West Virginia to Alabama would traditionally cook apple butter outside in a black kettle over a campfire. This recipe, which appears in her book Southern Traditions, *is a great fall favorite. Make it a family affair to pick apples in the morning at a pick-your-own farm, then prepare the apple butter later that day. Children can give a jar of this apple butter to their schoolteacher for a memorable Christmas gift, as a variation on giving "an apple to the teacher."*

12 cooking apples, peeled, cored and coarsely chopped
6 cups (1.5 l) apple cider
⅓ cup (2½ oz/75 g) red cinnamon candies
1⅓ cups (11 oz/345 g) sugar
1 tablespoon apple cider vinegar
1½ teaspoons ground cinnamon
½ teaspoon ground cloves

❊ In a large Dutch oven over medium heat, combine the apples, cider and candies. Bring to a boil, then cover, reduce the heat to low and simmer until the apples are tender, about 1 hour. Drain the apples and transfer to a food processor fitted with the metal blade. Process until just smooth. Alternatively, transfer the drained apples to a large bowl and, using a potato masher, mash thoroughly. Return the mashed apples to the Dutch oven over medium heat and add the sugar, vinegar, cinnamon and cloves. Cook, uncovered, stirring often, until thickened, 45–50 minutes.
❊ Remove from the heat. Ladle the apple butter into hot, sterilized half-pint (8 fl oz/ 250 ml) jars, leaving ¼ in (6 mm) headspace. Wipe the jar rims and seal. Process in a hot-water bath for 10 minutes (see glossary). Store in a cool, dark place for up to 12 months. Refrigerate after opening.
MAKES 5–6 HALF-PINTS (3–3¾ LB/1.5–1.9 KG)

The Ozarks

BLUEBERRY JAM

Blueberry fields are abundant in the South and summertime finds many people out picking their supply to put up in jam. Enjoy this recipe spooned over pound cake or slathered on toast. If fresh blueberries are unavailable you may use frozen ones, but the taste will not be as flavorful.

16 cups (4 lb/2 kg) fresh blueberries
6 cups (3 lb/1.5 kg) sugar
2 teaspoons fresh lemon juice

❊ In a large, heavy nonreactive saucepan over medium heat, combine the blueberries, sugar and lemon juice and bring to a boil, stirring often. Reduce the heat to medium-low. Gently boil until the mixture has thickened, 60–70 minutes. During cooking, stir occasionally, skimming and discarding any foam from the surface. During the last 30 minutes, stir often to prevent sticking.
❊ Working quickly, pack the jam into hot, sterilized half-pint (8 fl oz/ 250 ml) jars, leaving ¼ in (6 mm) headspace. Wipe the jar rims and seal. Process for 10 minutes in a hot-water bath (see glossary). Store in a cool, dark place for up to 12 months. Refrigerate after opening.
MAKES 10 HALF-PINTS (6¼ LB/3.15 KG)

Alabama

PEACH PRESERVES

The best kind of peaches for preserving are those that are ripe and flavorful but still a little firm to the touch. These preserves are scrumptious when spread on toast or spooned over waffles—what better breakfast to wake up to!

5¾ lb (2.9 kg) firm, ripe peaches, peeled and thinly sliced
6 cups (3 lb/1.5 kg) sugar

❊ In a large bowl, stir together the sliced peaches and sugar. Cover and refrigerate overnight.
❊ The next day, transfer the peach-sugar mixture to a large, heavy nonreactive pot over medium heat. Bring to a boil, stirring often. Reduce the heat to medium-low. Gently boil until the mixture has thickened, 45–55 minutes. During cooking, stir occasionally, skimming and discarding any foam from the surface. During the last 15 minutes, stir often to prevent sticking.
❊ Working quickly, pack the preserves into hot, sterilized half-pint (8 fl oz/250 ml) jars, leaving ¼ in (6 mm) headspace. Wipe the jar rims and seal. Process for 10 minutes in a hot-water bath (see glossary). Store in a cool, dark place up to 12 months. Refrigerate after opening.
MAKES 7 HALF-PINTS (4½ LB/2.25 KG)

Virginia

DAMSON PLUM PRESERVES

Edna Lewis is not impressed that it's now possible to eat fresh cherries in the dead of winter or acorn squash in the heat of summer. The granddaughter of a freed slave, Lewis grew up in the Virginia countryside where seasonal cooking is a way of life. She's expressed her purist philosophy in cookbooks, cooking classes and savvy New York restaurants where she has been a chef. This recipe demonstrates her fresh, basic approach to maximizing the flavor of Damson plums, small, dark-skinned fruits in season in the South in late summer. She preserves them by using a three-day process that allows them to set gradually. Lewis leaves the pan on the kitchen counter, but you may prefer to refrigerate. The plum seeds and skins are retained for their color, flavor and thickening qualities. This recipe is adapted from Lewis's third cookbook, In Pursuit of Flavor.

3 lb (1.5 kg) firm Damson plums
4½ cups (2¼ lb/1.1 kg) sugar

❋ Pierce each plum a few times with a cake tester or bamboo skewer and place in a large, heavy nonreactive saucepan. Sprinkle the sugar over the plums, cover and refrigerate overnight.

❋ The next morning, set the pan over medium-low heat and bring to a simmer. Cook, covered, until the plums are tender and the syrup is thick, stirring often so the sugar does not stick and burn, 1½–2 hours. Halfway through the simmering process, uncover the pan and continue cooking. When the syrup runs off a spoon in a single drop, remove the pan from the heat. Set aside to cool, then cover and refrigerate overnight.

❋ The next morning, set the pan over medium-high heat, uncovered. Bring to a boil, then reduce the heat to low and simmer 5 minutes.

❋ Ladle the preserves into hot, sterilized half-pint (8 fl oz/ 250 ml) jars, leaving ¼ in (6 mm) headspace. Wipe the jar rims and seal. Process in a hot-water bath for 10 minutes (see glossary). Store in a cool, dark place for up to 12 months. Refrigerate after opening. Alternatively, do not process, but store the sealed jars in the refrigerator for up to 6 months.

MAKES 6 HALF-PINTS (3 LB/1.5 KG)

Damson Plum Preserves

Top to bottom: Hot Pepper Jelly, Watermelon Rind Pickles

Virginia

WATERMELON RIND PICKLES

Southern cooks have been frugal gourmets all along. In a region that has seen more than its share of poverty, homemakers hate to throw anything out—not even watermelon rind. This recipe, using the whole portion of the rind, is thought to have originated in colonial Virginia.

1 watermelon, about 18½ lb (9.25 kg), sliced in quarters
2 qt (2 l) cold water
¼ cup (2 oz/60 g) kosher salt
4 cups (2 lb/1 kg) sugar
4 cups (32 fl oz/1 l) distilled white vinegar
1 cup (8 fl oz/250 ml) water
1 lemon, thinly sliced
1 cup (4 oz/125 g) peeled, thinly sliced fresh ginger
1 tablespoon whole allspice
2 teaspoons whole cloves
2 cinnamon sticks, 3 in (7.5 cm) long

❋ Using a vegetable peeler, peel away and discard the green outer skin of the watermelon slices. Then scoop away all the pink flesh and reserve for another use. Cut the white rind into 1-in (2.5-cm) pieces.

❋ In a large, heavy nonreactive pot, combine the 2 qt (2 l) cold water and salt and stir in the rind. Cover the pot and refrigerate overnight.

❋ The next day, drain in batches in a colander and rinse under cold running water. Return the rind to the pot and add enough cold water to cover. Set over medium heat and bring to a boil. Reduce the heat to low and simmer, stirring occasionally, until the rind is fork-tender, about 10 minutes. Drain, transfer the rind to a large bowl and set aside.

❋ In the same pot over medium heat, combine the sugar, vinegar and the 1 cup (8 fl oz/250 ml) water. Bring to a boil and boil, stirring often, until the sugar has dissolved, about 5 minutes. Add the rind, lemon slices, ginger, allspice, cloves and cinnamon and boil, stirring occasionally, until the rind is translucent, about 30 minutes.

❋ Working quickly, pack the watermelon rind into hot, sterilized pint (16 fl oz/500 ml) jars, leaving ¾ in (2 cm) headspace. Pour the boiling liquid into the jars, covering the rind by ¼ in (6 mm) and leaving ½ in (12 mm) headspace. Slide a clean plastic chopstick or wooden skewer along the inside of each jar to release any air bubbles. Wipe the jar rims and seal. Process for 15 minutes in a hot-water bath (see glossary). Store in a cool, dark place for up to 12 months. Refrigerate after opening.

MAKES 5 PINTS (6¼ LB/3.15 KG)

The South

HOT PEPPER JELLY

This sweet-hot jelly is very pretty with its flecks of green jalapeño peppers and red bell peppers—a winsome color combination that makes jars of this jelly ideal for stocking stuffers during Christmas time. It is delicious when spooned over cream cheese and spread on crackers for an instant hors d'oeuvre. Try it as a glaze for chicken breasts or alongside smoked ham. It makes a chic addition to a breakfast of biscuits and cheese omelettes or scrambled eggs.

5 or 6 (4 oz/125 g) jalapeño peppers (see glossary)
2 tablespoons apple cider vinegar
⅔ cup (3½ oz/105 g) minced red bell pepper (capsicum)
5½ cups (2¾ lb/1.4 kg) sugar
1⅓ cups (11 fl oz/345 ml) apple juice
¾ cup (6 fl oz/180 ml) liquid fruit pectin

❋ Wearing rubber gloves, prepare the jalapeño peppers by washing, seeding, stemming and removing membranes. In a food processor fitted with the metal blade or in a blender, process the jalapeños briefly until just evenly chopped but not

Crowder Peas with green beans

puréed, 5 seconds. Add up to 1 tablespoon of the vinegar, if needed, to facilitate the processing.

❋ Transfer the chopped jalapeños to a medium, heavy saucepan over medium-high heat. Add the vinegar, bell pepper, sugar and apple juice and bring to a boil, stirring often. Reduce the heat to medium and gently boil, stirring constantly, for 5 minutes. Stir in the pectin until well blended. Increase the heat to medium-high and bring to a full rolling boil, stirring constantly. Boil for 1 minute, stirring constantly. Remove from the heat and stir briefly, skimming and discarding any foam from the surface.

❋ Working quickly, pack the jelly into hot, sterilized half-pint (8 fl oz/250 ml) jars, leaving ½ in (12 mm) headspace. Wipe the jar rims and seal. Process for 10 minutes in a hot-water bath (see glossary). Let the jars cool completely, turning them over several times while cooling, to keep the pepper pieces evenly distributed until the mixture gels. Store in a cool, dark place for up to 12 months. Refrigerate after opening.

MAKES 5 HALF-PINTS (3 LB/1.5 KG)

Alabama

CROWDER PEAS AND BEANS

The crowder pea is a cousin of the black-eyed pea but a little smaller. A traditional way to cook it is with some of the fresh tender green pods, or "snaps," of the peas. If snaps are unavailable use green beans which are also delicious.

4 cups (20 oz/625 g) shelled fresh crowder peas
    or lady peas (see glossary)
½ cup (2½ oz/75 g) green beans cut into pieces
2 oz (60 g) salt pork, thinly sliced (see glossary)
½ teaspoon salt, or to taste

❋ Pick over the fresh peas, removing and discarding any particles or blemished peas. Rinse well and drain.

❋ In a heavy, medium saucepan over high heat, place the salt pork with water to cover and bring to a boil. Reduce the heat to medium-low and simmer, 10 minutes.

❋ Add the peas and salt. Add more water, if needed, to cover. Increase the heat to high and bring to a boil. Reduce the heat to low and simmer, covered, stirring occasionally for 10 minutes. Add the beans and continue simmering until the peas are soft but not mushy, 10–20 minutes. Drain and serve hot.

SERVES 8

Nashville, Tennessee

WILTED DANDELION GREENS WITH HOT BACON DRESSING

Wild greens have been part of the Southern table since the colonial era. Appalachians and African Americans, in particular, boiled them or used them in salads to add vitamins to their sometimes-meager diets. Jessica B. Harris, a New York food writer with Southern roots, included this recipe in her book, The Welcome Table. *Her father's family—which was "poorer than poor" during the Great Depression—used to pick dandelion greens on the lawn of Fisk College in Nashville.*

1 lb (500 g) fresh dandelion greens
1 small red onion, sliced
4 strips sliced slab bacon, cut into 1-in (2.5-cm) pieces
2 teaspoons dark brown sugar
2 tablespoons apple cider vinegar
salt and freshly ground pepper to taste

❧ Wash the dandelion greens thoroughly, spin them dry and place them in a salad bowl. Separate the onion slices into rings and scatter over the greens.
❧ In a heavy skillet over medium-high heat, cook the bacon pieces until crisp. When they have rendered all of their drippings, pour off all but 1 tablespoon of drippings, leaving the bacon pieces in the skillet. Return the skillet to medium heat and rapidly stir in the brown sugar and vinegar.
❧ Pour the hot bacon dressing over the greens and onion. Add salt and pepper and serve at once.

SERVES 4

Tennessee

TURNIP GREENS WITH CORNMEAL DUMPLINGS

In the Upper South, the green of choice comes from the turnip—a slightly peppery, leafier green than the collards of the Deep South. Greens are believed to bring monetary gain if eaten on New Year's Day, when they are customarily served with black-eyed peas, which are also said to bring good luck. Old-timers serve sliced hard-boiled eggs along with cooked turnip greens instead of dumplings.

FOR THE GREENS:

3 lb (1.5 kg) fresh turnip greens
4 oz (125 g) salt pork, finely chopped (see glossary)
6 cups (48 fl oz/1.5 l) water, plus 2–3 cups (16–24 fl oz/ 500–750 ml) more water, if needed
2 teaspoons salt
1 teaspoon freshly ground pepper

FOR THE DUMPLINGS:

1 cup (5 oz/155 g) all-purpose (plain) flour
¾ cup (4 oz/125 g) yellow cornmeal
1 teaspoon baking powder
½ teaspoon baking soda (bicarbonate of soda)
¼ teaspoon salt
1 egg white, lightly beaten
¾ cup (6 fl oz/185 ml) milk

boiling water, as needed
pinch of sugar (optional)
Pepper Vinegar for serving (see glossary)

❧ To prepare the turnip greens, remove any large, tough stems. Pick through the greens, discarding any brown or yellow leaves. Wash thoroughly to remove all grit. Coarsely chop the leaves.
❧ In a large, heavy stockpot or Dutch oven over medium heat, cook the salt pork, stirring often, for 10 minutes. Add the 6 cups (48 fl oz/1.5 l) water and bring to a simmer. Simmer, stirring occasionally, for 5 minutes.
❧ Add the greens in 3 batches, stirring each batch down until wilted and submerged in the liquid. If needed, add more water to cover the greens by 1 in (2.5 cm). Stir in the salt and pepper. Bring back to a simmer and simmer, stirring occasionally, until the greens are tender, 45–60 minutes. The length of cooking time depends on the age of the greens; the older the greens, the longer it takes to tenderize them. The liquid (called pot likker, see below) should be reduced by one-third.
❧ Meanwhile, to make the dumplings, combine all the dumpling ingredients in a medium bowl and stir until well blended. Cover and refrigerate until ready to use.
❧ When the greens are tender, if needed, add some boiling water to have enough liquid to cook the dumplings, and bring back to a simmer. Drop the dumpling batter by heaping rounded tablespoonfuls into the simmering liquid in the pot. You should have about 16 irregularly shaped dumplings.
❧ Cover the pot tightly and let the dumplings gently simmer undisturbed for 15–20 minutes, until a toothpick inserted in the center of a dumpling comes out clean. Taste and correct the seasoning. If desired, add a pinch of sugar or several dashes of Pepper Vinegar.
❧ Serve the greens, pot likker and dumplings in a large serving bowl and pass with the Pepper Vinegar. Serve hot.

SERVES 4

The South

COLLARD GREENS WITH HAM HOCK AND POT LIKKER

Pot likker is an invigorating, concentrated broth that is created in the pot when greens have been cooked for a long time. Younger, smaller collard greens are preferable to older, larger ones, which can become bitter as they mature. This side dish leaves you warm from head to toe and wanting more. Serve with corn bread and crumble it into the pot likker to sop up the emerald juice.

4 lb (2 kg) fresh collard greens
½ lb (250 g) smoked ham hock (see glossary)
8 cups (64 fl oz/2 l) water, plus 2–3 cups (16–24 fl oz/ 500–750 ml) more water, if needed
Pepper Vinegar for serving (see glossary)

❧ To prepare the collard greens, pick through the greens, discarding any large stems and brown or yellow leaves. Wash thoroughly to remove all grit. Tear the greens into bite-sized pieces.
❧ Place the ham hock in a large pot over medium-high heat and add enough water to cover by 2 in (5 cm). Bring to a boil. Then reduce the heat to medium-low, cover and simmer for 45 minutes.
❧ Add the greens in 4 batches, stirring each batch down until wilted and submerged in the liquid. If needed, add more water to cover the greens by 1 in (2.5 cm). Increase the heat to medium and simmer uncovered, stirring occasionally, until the greens are tender, 30–60 minutes. The length of cooking time depends on the age of the greens; the older the greens, the longer it takes to tenderize them. The liquid (pot likker) should be reduced by one half. Remove the ham hock.
❧ To serve, spoon the greens into individual shallow bowls, drizzling some of the pot likker over all. Pass the Pepper Vinegar and serve hot.

SERVES 8

Georgia

BAKED WHOLE VIDALIA ONIONS

Though Vidalia onions are delicious raw, they're better baked. Vidalias rose to cultlike status during Jimmy Carter's presidency and grew so popular nationwide that the name has become almost synonymous for any sweet onion. Georgia farmers have fended off counterfeit onions for years. The only true Vidalia, they insist, springs from the sandy loam around Vidalia, Georgia. See Mail Order Sources. These baked onions are delicious with roasted game or chicken. They are even good served cold. Leftovers can be chopped and put to excellent use in sauces or as a topping for pizza.

4 Vidalia onions, about 3 in (7.5 cm) in diameter and about
    8 oz (250 g) each (see glossary)
1½ cups (12 fl oz/375 ml) tomato juice
½ cup (4 fl oz/125 ml) plus 2 tablespoons hot water
2 tablespoons unsalted butter, melted
2 tablespoons honey
½ teaspoon salt

❀ Preheat an oven to 350°F (180°C).
❀ Lightly coat a shallow 2-qt (2-l) baking dish or casserole with vegetable cooking spray.
❀ Peel the onions and cut a thin slice off the top and bottom so they can stand upright. Place the onions stem end up in the baking dish.
❀ In a small bowl, whisk together the tomato juice, the ½ cup (4 fl oz/125 ml) hot water, butter, honey and salt and pour over the onions. Bake, covered, on the middle oven rack for 45 minutes. Turn the onions over—stem end down—and add the 2 tablespoons hot water to the bottom of the baking dish, if needed, to prevent the sauce from sticking or burning. Continue baking uncovered until the onions are soft when pierced with a fork, 15–30 minutes longer. Cooking time may vary depending on the size of the onions. Serve hot as a side dish, spooning some of the sauce over the onions.

SERVES 4   *Photograph pages 140–141*

Clockwise from top: Collard Greens with Ham Hock and Pot Likker, Wilted Dandelion Greens with Hot Bacon Dressing, Turnip Greens with Cornmeal Dumplings

Highlands

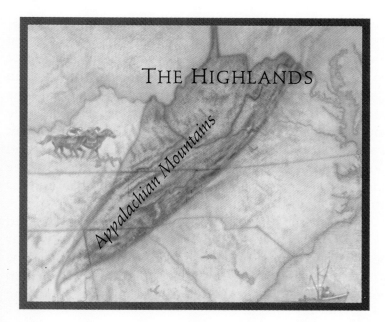

HIGHLANDS

In the mountains of the South—the mother lode of country music—you are what you sing. The pickers and fiddlers who fashioned the music early this century left the hills with a wealth of songs that stretched clear back to the glens of Scotland. Their jigs, hymns and ballads foreshadowed modern country music's preoccupation with hard times, cheatin' hearts and dear old mama. Judging from song titles, those pioneer musicians had another preoccupation as well: food. A full day's menu could be drawn from a list of early country tunes. "Polly Put the Kettle On" before breakfast. "Chicken in the Bread Tray" and "Guinea in the Pea Patch" at midday. "Bacon and Collards" and "Turkey in the Straw" for supper, with a little "June Apple" topping it off for dessert. With all that singing about food, it's no wonder that one of the first fiddle bands to hit it big on records in the 1920s was Gid Tanner and the Skillet Lickers.

There's nothing pretentious about the mountain culture of the South. Simplicity and directness characterize everything from clothes and cooking to music and speech (less a drawl than a twang). If the plantation belt and the Mississippi Delta blues represent one pole of Southern identity, the highlands and the keening sound of country represent the other.

The mountain South covers an enormous territory that touches nine of the twelve states included in this

Previous pages: Fog rises and casts a purple haze across the Blue Ridge Mountain range. Left: White Mill is a working grist mill in the Walker Mountains near Abingdon, Virginia.

book. To the west lie the Ozarks, the continent's oldest mountains, an emerald island of low, rounded peaks that traverse the northwestern third of Arkansas. To the east lie the Appalachians, the 1,500-mile spine that rises in Canada and soars to its greatest heights in North Carolina before reaching its tailbone in northeastern Alabama. The southern Appalachians take in the pastoral Shenandoah Valley of Virginia, the coal fields of eastern Kentucky and West Virginia, the Great Smoky Mountains of Tennessee and North Carolina and the Blue Ridge that crowns northern Georgia.

Though the Ozarks and Appalachians are separated by hundreds of miles, they were settled by similar people with similar histories and folkways. The regions somewhat resemble each other in their misty green beauty. And there's one other thing that links them: the Cherokee.

When the first European explorers penetrated the upland, Cherokees had been dwelling there for hundreds of years. They inhabited most of the southern Appalachians and much of the Piedmont, living off deer and game, berries and nuts, beans and maize. Like countless Southerners to come, they made corn bread and boiled vegetables with meat (using bear fat instead of pork). They also dried many foods to preserve them, still a trait of Appalachian cooking. In *The Southeastern Indians,* historian Charles Hudson credits the Cherokee with drying beans in the pod, a tasty soup starter mountain folk call "Leather Britches" (which also happens to be the name of a fiddle tune).

The fate of the Cherokee people is a familiar and tragic chapter of American history. After fighting the Europeans on and off for two hundred years, the Cherokee started to accommodate the white man in the late 1700s. They gave up their Piedmont lands and retreated to the Georgia mountains, where they created an alphabet and established a government modeled after the one in Washington. The discovery of gold in Cherokee country in the 1820s set off an invasion of squatters. President Andrew Jackson ordered the removal of the Cherokee people, and in 1838 the first of fifteen thousand were rounded up and marched eight

Canoers wade in the placid stream of Steel Creek before they launch into the rapid waters of the Buffalo River, Arkansas.

A transient carnival provides diversion to a rural mountain community in West Virginia.

hundred miles west to the far reaches of the Ozarks beyond the Arkansas border. Disease and the elements claimed four thousand lives along the Trail of Tears. Today's Cherokee live on either end of that trail in Oklahoma and North Carolina.

The white settlers who replaced them in Appalachia were for the most part British, Irish and Scottish. They began streaming south during the mid-1700s, some coming from the lowlands but most migrating from Pennsylvania along the wagon road of the Great Valley, a crease in the mountains that runs hundreds of miles diagonally from Virginia through Tennessee. The new mountain folk found the rugged terrain unsuited for large-scale agriculture. What corn they grew was easier to get to market as distilled whiskey. What cotton they produced went for clothes. Slavery was irrelevant in the highlands, and that put the region at odds with the plantation lowlands.

The mountain South wanted no part of the Civil War. Appalachian counties from Virginia to Alabama opposed secession and saw no reason to fight to save the "peculiar institution." West Virginia was born when the western part of the Old Dominion split with Richmond over the issue. Other areas showed their loyalty long after the war by voting for the party of Lincoln; not too many years ago, the only Republican enclaves in the Solid South were in the mountains.

In the late 1800s the outside world discovered Appalachia when absentee companies bought rights to extract timber and coal. The boom-and-bust cycle of mining transformed the highlands, particularly the ridges and hollows of southwestern Virginia, eastern Kentucky and West Virginia. After World War II, as other energy sources reduced the demand for coal, Appalachia's chief export became its people. The sons and daughters of the highlands—like the sons and daughters of the Deep South—flocked to factories in Detroit, Cleveland and other Northern cities. But unlike the black migrants, they also moved in large numbers to Southern textile centers. Many cities had a mill village full of mountain folk in their midst. Atlanta's was called

167

Inside the antique-laden Gilbert General Store in Gilbert, Arkansas, locals enjoy ice cream amid the relics of days gone by.

Cabbagetown, because the smell of boiling cabbage seemed to drift from every kitchen window (another early fiddle tune: "Boil Them Cabbage Down").

The Southern mountains have always been known for their beauty and their distinctive folkways. In the early 1960s they also became known for something else: poverty. John F. Kennedy was appalled by the deprivation he saw in West Virginia during the 1960 presidential campaign. When Lyndon B. Johnson declared his War on Poverty four years later, he designated Appalachia as the first battleground, flying to eastern Kentucky to tour the region and visit with an unemployed father on the porch of his run-down shack.

Despite such images, it would be a mistake to regard the cooking of the highland South as nothing but poor people's food. The mountains have long harbored resort villages and hotels that serve exquisitely well-prepared dishes. There's nothing peasant about the Greenbrier, the grand hotel in White Sulphur Springs, West Virginia, where members of Congress have hobnobbed for more than a century. The Biltmore House, the Vanderbilt estate near Asheville, North Carolina, makes some of the finest wines in the East. On the other side of the Smokies, chef John Fleer of the Blackberry Farm resort in Walland, Tennessee, is using local ingredients to create something he calls "foothills cuisine." Across the region in Arkansas, a children's book author named Crescent Dragonwagon has won acclaim for updating Ozarks cookery at a Eureka Springs inn, the Dairy Hollow House. Dragonwagon certainly has a knack for names; she calls it "Nouveau'Zarks Cuisine."

Most mountain cooking needs no such slogans. It is as straightforward and plentiful as the heaping portions people help themselves to at the family-style boarding-houses that dot the region. The leaders of Foxfire, the educational program documenting folklife in the Georgia mountains, put it this way in the introduction to *The Foxfire Book of Appalachian Cookery:* "You'll find no slivered sautéed mushrooms in these pages, or stir-fried bean sprouts or soft-shell crabs or delicate pastries or casseroles with enough ingredients to fill a shopping bag. You'll just find normal food rooted in, and infused by, an age when what was consumed was what one raised."

Traditional mountain cooking is about apples grown in the crisp high country air from Winchester, Virginia, to Ellijay, Georgia. It's about wild greens—dandelion, mustard, poke sallet—gathered in the woods and boiled like collards. It's about ramps, smelly wild onions that people either love or hate because of their devastating effect on the breath. Above all, it's about corn grown in hollows and bottoms throughout the mountains, eaten fried, roasted or in dishes made from meal ground in one of the picturesque grist mills that still hug the banks of white-water streams here and there.

"Corn bread is the holy grail of the mountains, and it's never puffed up and self-important with sugar or flour," says Ronni Lundy, a Louisville music and food writer with roots in the Kentucky Cumberlands. She figures the only reason country luminaries like Chet Atkins return her calls is that they've tasted her corn bread and know she understands. Could be. Corn in all its forms has inspired many a musician. One of the performers at the 1920 Old-Time Fiddlers' Convention in Atlanta said it well. Up in Rabun Gap, Uncle Bud Littlefield told a reporter, "We raise corn, hell and fiddlers, and we had a pretty good crop this year, all around."

Arkansas' Hot Springs National Park is a magnet for tourists who wish to "take the waters" from one of the valley's forty-seven thermal springs; here, the side of an old cigar store in downtown Hot Springs.

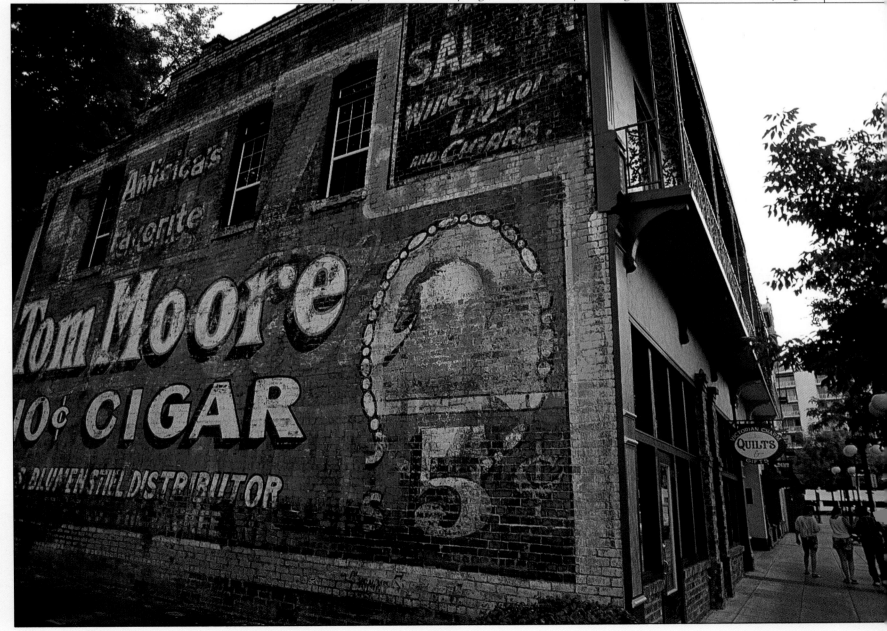

BREADS & GRAINS

The ninety-three-year-old Dutch Maid Bakery in Tracy City, Tennessee, still uses its original bread-slicing machine.

BREADS & GRAINS

During an extended tour of Europe in 1879, Mark Twain complained that the local bread was "cold and tough and unsympathetic." He vented his gastronomical homesickness by listing the American foods he craved, including six hot breads—all "Southern style." Born of Southern parents and raised on Southern cooking, the great American novelist never lost his taste for corn bread and biscuits.

From corn pudding, dumplings, bread and biscuits to hush puppies, hominy and spoon bread, corn is a staple in the Southern diet.

Nor has the South. Until recent years, it was hard to find loaves of crusty French or Italian bread outside of Louisiana and a few cosmopolitan enclaves. Even today, as other cuisines flourish, Southerners prefer their breads hot and soft. Split open for butter, they exhale a puff of steam and soak up the yellow nectar like thirsty little sponges.

The original Southern bread comes from the original grain. Native Americans made corn bread for eons and freely shared their expertise when Europeans arrived in large numbers during the 1600s. The newcomers, who preferred their wheat and rye breads, had to learn to appreciate maize or starve. By the time wheat flour became widely available in the South in the 1800s, corn bread had become so entrenched that one name no longer sufficed. There were pones, dodgers, dumplings, fritters, spoon bread, ashcakes, johnnycakes, hoecakes, hush puppies—each name an essay on the bread's origins. Hoecakes? Slaves baked them on the blades of their hoes. Hush puppies? Supposedly they were created at outdoor fish fries as a way of silencing insistent canines.

Though Southerners no longer rely as heavily on corn bread, they still love it. The top cornmeal miller, Martha White Foods of Nashville, estimates that four fifths of the corn bread made in the United States is made in the South (including Texas). Some cooks use yellow cornmeal, the predominant variety in the North, but most Southerners prefer white cornmeal, which they believe has a sweeter taste and requires little or no added sugar. Authentic

Previous pages: Clockwise from left: Rice Quick Bread Muffins (recipe page 184), Sally Lunn Bread (recipe page 176), Miniature Sweet Potato Dinner Scones (recipe page 183)

Southern corn bread has a grittier consistency than the floured and cakey Midwestern version, which Southerners dismiss as "Yankee corn bread."

Wheat breads have been made in the South since the colonial era, but they didn't take their place in the region's culinary pantheon until commercial baking powder spread after the Civil War. Southerners have always baked yeast and other wheat breads, which they called lightbread to distinguish them from corn.

Of all the wheaten baked goods available, biscuits are particularly prized. Paired with sausage or country ham, hot biscuits are traditional breakfast fare in the South. Angel biscuits, beaten biscuits, cathead biscuits—whatever the name, they share one important ingredient: Southern flour made from soft winter wheat. It makes a fluffier biscuit.

Breads aren't the only way Southerners take their grain (and we don't mean corn whiskey). Rice, one of the region's great staples, turns up in kitchens across the South, especially in South Carolina, where the crop started in the New World, and Louisiana. Two traditional dishes symbolize the rice culture. South Carolina's Hoppin' John, a mixture of rice, black-eyed peas and ham hock, has ushered in the New Year for generations of Southerners. And Louisiana's red beans and rice, usually spiced with sausage, has ridden the Cajun wave to become a regionwide favorite.

There is one other grain dish worth noting because it is central to Southern identity: grits. Some people make fun of grits. Maybe for the unappetizing name, which suggests a mouthful of sand. Or maybe for the consistency; when grits cool and congeal, there's no

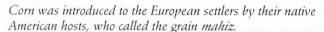

Corn was introduced to the European settlers by their native American hosts, who called the grain mahiz.

In Westville Historic Village, Georgia, a baker displays her biscuits in a cast-iron skillet.

getting around the fact that you've got a bowl of spackling paste on your hands.

Yet Southerners defend grits like they would a bullied sibling. Cooking authorities like Nathalie Dupree of Atlanta champion the dish, pointing out that essentially it's polenta with a drawl. Growing numbers of chefs serve grits with shrimp and sausage and anything else that needs a good bed to sop up flavors. The citizens of St. George, South Carolina, celebrate the staple with the World Grits Festival in which contestants show their devotion by diving into a trough of hominy.

Grits gets under your skin, as the novelist and Civil War historian Shelby Foote knows. Once, staying in a Texas hotel, he hung his breakfast order on the doorknob specifying grits instead of potatoes. Alas, room service brought potatoes. That night the Mississippi native again ordered grits and appended a note in which he spoke for Southern patriots everywhere: "This morning you brought me potatoes. Do not commit this outrage again."

Angel Biscuits, Beaten Biscuits (with pricked surface)

Virginia

BEATEN BISCUITS

In the Upper South, especially in Virginia and Maryland, beaten biscuits are an institution. Once made by beating the dough with a stick or rolling pin until it crackled, nowadays the dough is pounded by a special machine called a brake. These biscuits are baked longer than other types of biscuits, resulting in a texture and flavor similar to that of a soda cracker. In addition, they are shorter and have a pricked surface. These biscuits will keep much longer, too—about a month in an airtight container at room temperature. Serve alongside thin slices of country ham, or be true to Southern custom and tuck the ham inside the biscuits.

2 cups (8 oz/250 g) all-purpose (plain) Southern flour
  (see glossary)
1 tablespoon sugar
1 teaspoon baking powder
¼ teaspoon salt
¼ cup (2 oz/60 g) vegetable shortening
⅓ cup (3 fl oz/80 ml) milk, plus 2 tablespoons milk as
  needed

❈ In a medium bowl, sift together the flour, sugar, baking powder and salt three times. Using a pastry blender, 2 knives or a fork, cut in the shortening until it resembles coarse crumbs. Gradually pour in the milk in a slow, steady stream while stirring until the dough begins to come together in a ball but is not too moist, adding up to 2 more tablespoons of milk if needed.

❈ Break apart the ball of dough, place the pieces in a food processor fitted with the metal blade and process 2 minutes. Remove dough and, on a lightly floured work surface, knead with your hands for 2 minutes.

❈ Roll out the dough into a tall rectangle ¼ in (6 mm) thick. Fold into a smaller rectangle by folding the top of the dough down and the bottom up to meet it, edges touching in the middle without overlapping. Then fold the left half over the right and gently pound with the rolling pin to flatten and seal to a ¼-in (6-mm) thickness. Turn the dough over so the folded edge is on your right. Repeat the process, rolling out and folding the dough as before, three more times, using a little more flour as needed to prevent sticking, or until the dough is smooth and glossy.

❈ Preheat an oven to 325°F (165°C).

❈ Roll out the dough to a ½ in (12 mm) thickness. Using a 1½-in (4-cm) round biscuit cutter, cut out biscuits and place no closer than ½ in (12 mm) apart on an ungreased baking sheet. Using a fork, pierce each biscuit all the way to the bottom, making 3 evenly spaced parallel rows across the top.

❈ Bake on the middle oven rack until slightly browned on the bottom and very lightly golden on top, 30–35 minutes. Turn off the heat and leave the biscuits in the oven for 5 minutes longer. Transfer the baking sheets to a wire rack to cool for 5 minutes before serving.

MAKES 1 DOZEN BISCUITS

Nashville, Tennessee

ANGEL BISCUITS

Award-winning author and Southern food historian John Egerton not only knows how Southern food evolved, but he actually cooks the cherished recipes that are the mainstay of Southern cuisine. Adapted from his book, Southern Food, *this is one of the South's best-loved breads, a biscuit that contains yeast. It rises up nice and light, thus the name Angel Biscuit. Egerton bakes these biscuits in the lower third of the oven for the first few minutes, then moves them up to the middle rack for even browning from top to bottom. Roll out as many biscuits as you can eat at one time, then return the dough to the refrigerator, where it will keep for 2 days.*

5½ cups (27 oz/860 g) all-purpose (plain) flour
¼ cup (2 oz/60 g) sugar
1 tablespoon baking powder
1 teaspoon baking soda (bicarbonate of soda)
1 teaspoon salt
1 cup (8 oz/250 g) vegetable shortening
1 package (¼ oz/7 g) active dry yeast
2 tablespoons warm water
1½–2 cups (12–16 fl oz/375–500 ml) lowfat buttermilk,
  or as needed
¼ cup (2 oz/60 g) salted butter, melted

✳ In a large bowl, sift together the flour, sugar, baking powder, baking soda and salt. Using a pastry cutter, 2 knives or a fork, cut in the shortening until it resembles coarse crumbs.

✳ Dissolve the yeast in the warm water. Add the dissolved yeast and the 1½ cups (12 fl oz/375 ml) buttermilk to the flour mixture. Stir with a fork and add enough of the remaining buttermilk to form a cohesive dough. Turn the dough out onto a floured work surface and knead a few minutes with floured hands. Add more flour if needed to work the dough more easily.

✳ On a lightly floured surface, roll out the dough about ½ in (12 mm) thick. Using a 2-in (5-cm) round biscuit cutter, cut out biscuits and place close together on a baking sheet. Brush with the melted butter. Cover with a kitchen towel and let rise 30 minutes in a warm place.

✳ Preheat an oven to 400°F (200°C). Bake the biscuits on a rack set in the lower third of the oven for 3 minutes, then move to the middle oven rack and bake until browned on top, 9–12 minutes longer, for a total of 12–15 minutes. Serve hot.

MAKES ABOUT 4 DOZEN BISCUITS

New Orleans, Louisiana

FRENCH QUARTER BEIGNETS

It is easy to find the Café du Monde in the French Market of New Orleans: just follow the powdered-sugar footprints. For more than one hundred years, tourists and New Orleanians alike have beat a path to the café for steaming cups of chicory-laced café au lait and plates of beignets—puffy jewels of deep-fried dough dusted with snowy confectioners' sugar. The tourists are the ones who inhale before biting and fall into coughing fits. The beignet (French for fritter) is traditionally square, but in this recipe it's cut into a diamond shape so you can get more in a mouthful.

3½–4 cups (14–16 oz/440–500 g) sifted all-purpose (plain)
  flour, or as needed
1 package (¼ oz/7 g) active dry yeast
¼ teaspoon salt
¼ cup (2 oz/60 g) granulated sugar
⅔ cup (5 fl oz/160 ml) hot water (120°F/50°C)
1 egg, lightly beaten
⅓ cup (3 fl oz/80 ml) light (single) cream, at room temperature
peanut oil for frying
confectioners' (icing) sugar for dusting

✳ In a food processor fitted with the dough blade or a mixer, combine the 3½ cups (14 oz/440 g) of flour, the yeast, salt and granulated sugar. With the processor set on process or the mixer on low speed, gradually add the hot water until well blended. Add the egg and cream. Process or beat on high to make a soft dough, adding a little more flour, as needed, to prevent sticking. Use a rubber spatula to scrape down the sides of the bowl as necessary. Knead for 1 minute in a food processor or for 5 minutes in a mixer fitted with the dough hook. Place the dough in a lightly oiled large bowl, turn to coat with oil, cover with plastic wrap and refrigerate overnight.

✳ The next day, on a lightly floured work surface, punch down the dough. Knead for about 2 minutes to soften. Roll the dough out ½ in (12 mm) thick. Cut the dough into diamond shapes 2 by 3 in (5 by 7.5 cm), rerolling the dough scraps until you have about 24 diamonds. Let rest on a lightly floured baking sheet for 30 minutes.

✳ Preheat an oven to 200°F (93°C).

✳ In a large, heavy saucepan over medium-high heat, an electric skillet or a deep-fat fryer, pour the oil to a depth of 2 in (5 cm) and heat to 375°F (190°C) on a deep-fry thermometer, or until a small cube of bread dropped in the hot oil browns in about 30 seconds.

✳ Working in batches, deep-fry the beignets, 2 or 3 at a time, turning in the oil as needed, until they are light golden brown on both sides, about 45 seconds total. Using a large slotted spoon, transfer the beignets to a baking sheet lined with paper towels to drain. Then transfer them to a baking sheet lined with aluminum foil and place in the warm oven until all the beignets are ready to serve. Dust with confectioners' sugar just before serving. These are at their best served at once, and do not store well.

MAKES ABOUT 2 DOZEN BEIGNETS

French Quarter Beignets

Georgia

GRANDMA'S CATHEAD BISCUITS

Tim Patridge, an Atlanta-based chef, teacher, food writer and lecturer, contributed this recipe for Cathead Biscuits, so called because they are about the size of a cat's head. "When I think about my grandmother, I always remember arriving at her house and going to the food chest and getting a biscuit. Her biscuits were good even cold. She made them by hand and I remember seeing her knead the dough in this big wooden bread bowl (which I now have). Her hands always shaped the biscuits perfectly round. Then she put them in the oven of a wood-burning stove. When we were lucky enough to be there when they came out of the oven, we broke them open and spread fresh churned butter on each side with homemade peach or fig preserves or cane or sorghum syrup."

3 cups (9 oz/280 g) sifted all-purpose (plain) Southern
    flour (see glossary)
⅔ cup (5 oz/155 g) unsalted butter or lard, or
    as needed
2 pinches of salt
4½ teaspoons baking powder
¼–½ cup (2–4 fl oz/60–125 ml) lowfat buttermilk,
    as needed

❀ Preheat an oven to 400°F (200°C).
❀ In a large bowl, combine the flour, butter or lard, salt and baking powder by hand, squeezing between your fingers until well mixed and crumbly. Add enough buttermilk until the dough comes together in a soft ball. On a lightly floured work surface, knead until just smooth. Do not overknead. Shape by hand into biscuits about 1 in (2.5 cm) high and 3½ in (9 cm) across.
❀ Place in an ungreased baking pan or on a baking sheet. For soft sides, let the biscuits touch; for crisp sides, set them apart. Bake on the middle oven rack until golden brown, 15–20 minutes.

MAKES 3–4 BISCUITS

Georgia

CORN STICKS

To many a Southern cook even today, there is no more valuable kitchen utensil than a cast-iron skillet, which gives corn bread its crisp crust and moist interior. A well-seasoned corn stick pan for making fanciful shapes is a bonus. For a source to mail-order cast-iron corn stick pans and other cast-iron cookware, see Mail Order Sources. Most corn stick pans hold 7 sticks—this recipe yields 2 pans' worth, or 14 sticks. Serve as an accompaniment to main dishes, soups, stews or vegetable plates.

1 cup (4 oz/125 g) sifted all-purpose (plain) flour
1 cup (4 oz/125 g) sifted yellow or white cornmeal
1½ teaspoons baking powder
¾ teaspoon salt
1 tablespoon sugar
1 egg, at room temperature
1 cup (8 fl oz/250 ml) milk, at room temperature
¼ cup (2 fl oz/60 ml) vegetable oil or bacon drippings

❀ Preheat an oven to 425°F (220°C).
❀ Generously coat 2 cast-iron corn stick pans with vegetable cooking spray. Place the pans in the oven to heat while preparing the batter.
❀ In a medium bowl, combine the flour, cornmeal, baking powder, salt and sugar. In a small bowl, beat together the egg, milk and oil or bacon drippings. Make a well in the center of the dry ingredients and pour in the egg mixture. Stir until well blended but do not overmix. (Mixture will be slightly lumpy.)
❀ Carefully pour a scant ¼ cup (2 fl oz/60 ml) of batter into each corn stick well of the hot pans, filling each until almost level with the rim. Bake on the middle oven rack until the sticks are browned and spring back when pressed lightly in the center, 15–20 minutes. Let cool in the pans for 10 minutes, then remove by loosening with a spatula and inverting the pans. Serve hot. These do not store well, and are best when served the day they are made.

MAKES 14 CORN STICKS

Virginia

SALLY LUNN BREAD

Who was Sally Lunn? Some say she was a woman who sold this buttery, yeasty bread on the streets of Bath, England, in the 1700s. Others believe the name comes from the French words soleil *and* lune, *because the top of the bread was as golden as the sun and the bottom as pale as the moon. However the name came about, loaves like this—with a texture halfway between bread and cake—provided a taste of the old country to Virginia's first English colonists.*

1 cup (8 fl oz/250 ml) milk, at room temperature
1 package (¼ oz/7 g) active dry yeast
½ cup (4 oz/125 g) unsalted butter, at room temperature
½ cup (4 oz/125 g) sugar
3 eggs, at room temperature
4 cups (16 oz/500 g) sifted all-purpose (plain) flour
1 teaspoon salt

❀ Generously coat a 10-in (25-cm) tube or Bundt pan with vegetable cooking spray.
❀ In a heavy, medium saucepan over medium heat, scald the milk until bubbles form around the edge, about 3 minutes. Remove from the heat and let cool to 105°–115°F (40°–42°C), about 15 minutes. Add the yeast and stir until dissolved.
❀ In a large mixing bowl, combine the butter and sugar and, using an electric mixer, beat on medium speed until creamy. Add the eggs, one at a time, beating well after each addition, until well blended.
❀ In another large bowl, sift together the flour and salt. Alternately add the flour mixture and milk mixture to the butter mixture, beginning and ending with flour and beating well after each addition. On a floured surface, turn out the dough and knead briefly. Place in a large bowl, cover with a kitchen towel and let rise in a warm place until almost doubled in bulk, about 1 hour.
❀ Punch down the dough using a wooden spoon, beat it for 1 minute, and spread evenly in the prepared pan. Cover with a kitchen towel and let rise in a warm place until doubled in bulk, about 1½ hours.
❀ Preheat an oven to 350°F (180°C), 10 minutes before the end of the rising time.
❀ Bake on the bottom oven rack until the bread is browned on top and pulls away from the sides of the pan, 40–45 minutes. Cool in the pan on a wire rack for 30 minutes, then turn out.
❀ To serve, slice with a serrated knife and serve warm.

SERVES 10–12   *Photograph pages 172–173*

Left to right: Grandma's Cathead Biscuits, Corn Sticks

Atlanta, Georgia

TOUCH OF GRACE BISCUITS

Shirley Corriher, an Atlanta author, teacher and food consultant, also holds a degree in chemistry. She learned an early lesson in the chemistry of biscuits from her grandmother. "As a little girl, I followed her around the kitchen. She made the lightest, most wonderful biscuits in the world. I used her bread bowl, her flour, her buttermilk—I did everything the same—but mine always turned out a dry, mealy mess. I would cry and say, 'Nanny, what did I do wrong?' She would give me a big hug and say, 'Honey, I guess you forgot to add a touch of grace.'" It took Corriher years to figure out her grandmother's secret: She made a very wet dough. These biscuits are marvelous alone or slathered with Peach Preserves (recipe on page 156).

1½ cups (6 oz/185 g) self-rising Southern flour (see glossary) or 1 cup (5 oz/155 g) self-rising all-purpose (plain) flour, ½ cup (2 oz/60 g) unleavened cake flour and ½ teaspoon baking powder (if self-rising flour is not available, use 1½ teaspoons baking powder)
⅛ teaspoon baking soda (bicarbonate of soda)
½ teaspoon salt
1 tablespoon sugar
3 tablespoons vegetable shortening
1–1¼ cups (8–10 fl oz/250–310 ml) lowfat buttermilk or cream or a mixture of the two
1 cup (5 oz/155 g) all-purpose (plain) flour
2 tablespoons unsalted butter, melted
butter or preserves for serving

Touch of Grace Biscuits

❋ Preheat an oven to 475°–500°F (246°–260°C). Lightly coat an 8-in (20-cm) round cake pan with vegetable cooking spray.
❋ In a medium mixing bowl, combine the 1½ cups (6 oz/185 g) self-rising Southern flour, baking soda, salt and sugar. Using your fingers or a pastry blender, work the shortening into the flour mixture until the shortening lumps are pea-sized or smaller. Stir in the buttermilk or cream and let stand 2–3 minutes.
❋ This dough is so wet that you cannot shape it in the usual manner. Pour the 1 cup (5 oz/155 g) all-purpose flour onto a plate. Flour your hands well. Spoon a biscuit-sized lump of wet dough into the flour and sprinkle with flour to coat the exterior lightly. Pick up the biscuit and shape into a soft round, while shaking off any excess flour, though the dough is so soft that it will not hold its shape. As you shape each biscuit, place it in the prepared pan, pushing the biscuits tightly together so they will rise up and not spread out. Continue shaping biscuits in this manner until all the dough is used.
❋ Brush the biscuits with the melted butter and bake just above the oven center until lightly browned, 15–20 minutes. Cool a minute or two in the pan. Split the biscuits in half, spread with butter or preserves and serve at once.

MAKES ABOUT 10 BISCUITS

Louisiana

DIRTY RICE

This bayou peasant dish owes its name to its light and dark speckled colors—rice intermingled with finely minced chicken livers and gizzards. Sausage, pork or some other meat is often included as well. Though often served as a side dish, it also makes a rich and hearty main course. Here, we eliminated the gizzards; if you don't like liver or want to cut some of the cholesterol, you could replace it with lean ground beef. But it won't have the same distinctively rich, earthy flavor that only the livers can provide.

3 cups (24 fl oz/750 ml) chicken broth (see glossary) or water
1 small bay leaf
1 1/2 cups (10½ oz/330 g) long-grain white rice
½ lb (250 g) hot Cajun or Italian sausage, casings removed
½ lb (250 g) chicken livers, rinsed
1 tablespoon unsalted butter
1 large onion, finely chopped
1 celery rib with leaves, finely chopped
1 large green bell pepper (capsicum), stemmed, seeded and cut in small dice
2 large cloves garlic, minced
4 green (spring) onions, thinly sliced
salt, freshly ground pepper and hot pepper sauce to taste

❋ In a medium saucepan, bring the chicken broth or water to a boil with the bay leaf. Add the rice, cover and reduce heat to low. Cook 15–18 minutes, or until rice is tender. Remove the bay leaf.
❋ Meanwhile, in a deep, heavy nonstick skillet over medium heat, cook the sausage until lightly browned and no longer pink, about 10 minutes.
❋ With a slotted spoon, transfer the sausage to a plate lined with paper towel and set aside; drain off all but 1 tablespoon of fat in the skillet. Add livers to the hot fat and cook, stirring, until just cooked through, about 10 minutes.
❋ With a slotted spoon, remove livers to a chopping board. Finely chop the livers and set aside.
❋ Add the butter to the skillet. When melted, add the chopped onion, celery, bell pepper and garlic and sauté until tender, about 10 minutes.
❋ Return the sausage and livers to the skillet. Add the rice and green onions and gently toss with the meat mixture until combined. Cook, tossing constantly, until the rice is heated through, 1–3 minutes. Season to taste with salt, pepper and hot pepper sauce.

SERVES 8–10

Top to bottom: Dirty Rice, Hush Puppies

North Carolina

HUSH PUPPIES

Just about all Southerners eat hush puppies with fried catfish. But only Carolinians love them enough to eat them with barbecue, too. James Villas, cookbook author and food editor of Town & Country *magazine, searched the Carolina coast for fifteen years with his mother, Martha Pearl Villas, looking for the perfect hush puppy. They found it at the Center Pier restaurant in Carolina Beach, North Carolina, and scribbled the recipe on paper napkins as they ate. This recipe is inspired by a similiar one that appeared in their book,* My Mother's Southern Kitchen.

2 cups (10 oz/315 g) all-purpose (plain) flour
1½ cups (7½ oz/235 g) white cornmeal
2 tablespoons sugar
1 teaspoon baking powder
1 teaspoon salt
¾ cup (4 oz/125 g) finely chopped white onion
1⅓ cups (11 fl oz/345 ml) milk, or as needed
⅓ cup (3 fl oz/80 ml) vegetable oil, plus 8 cups (64 fl oz/2 l) vegetable oil for frying
1 egg, beaten

❋ In a large bowl, combine the flour, cornmeal, sugar, baking powder and salt. Fold in the onion. Add the milk, the ⅓ cup (3 fl oz/80 ml) oil and the beaten egg and stir lightly, to just incorporate. Add more milk if needed to make the batter soft and slightly sticky.
❋ In a large saucepan over medium-high heat, heat the 8 cups (64 fl oz/2 l) oil to 375°F (190°C) on a deep-fry thermometer. Working in batches, scoop up rounded half-tablespoons of the dough, smooth the rough edges, then drop into the hot oil. Fry until golden brown, about 2 minutes. Remove them with a slotted spoon, drain on paper towels and keep warm in a warm oven until all are ready to serve.

MAKES 3 DOZEN HUSH PUPPIES

New Orleans, Louisiana

PAIN PERDU

Pain perdu *(translation "lost bread")* is a Creole pun for "saved bread," since this is a way of redeeming stale day-old bread that might otherwise be discarded. Pain Perdu is basically Creole-style French toast, and it can be served for breakfast or dessert.

1½ cups (12 fl oz/375 ml) milk
3 eggs, lightly beaten
⅓ cup (3 oz/90 g) granulated sugar
2 tablespoons brandy
1 teaspoon vanilla extract (essence)
1 teaspoon grated lemon zest (see glossary)
pinch of salt
8 slices day-old French bread, 1½ in (4 cm) thick, with crusts
6 tablespoons (3 oz/90 g) unsalted butter
2 tablespoons confectioners' (icing) sugar
1 teaspoon freshly grated nutmeg
fresh raspberries for garnish (optional)
cane syrup for serving (optional)

❋ Preheat an oven to 200°F (93°C).
❋ In a medium bowl, combine the milk, eggs, sugar, brandy, vanilla, lemon zest and salt and whisk until well blended. Lay the bread slices on a jelly-roll (Swiss roll) pan and pour the egg mixture over all. Let the bread soak at room temperature until moistened evenly, about 5 minutes.
❋ In a large, heavy nonstick skillet over medium heat, melt the butter until it is very hot but not smoking. Fry the bread, 3 or 4 slices at a time, for 2 minutes on each side; turn the slices carefully and regulate the heat so that they brown evenly without burning. Transfer the browned bread slices to a baking sheet and place in the warm oven until all are ready to serve.
❋ Sprinkle with the confectioners' sugar and nutmeg and garnish with raspberries, if desired. Serve at once. If you like, accompany it with a pitcher of pure cane syrup.

SERVES 4

Atlanta, Georgia

SWEET POTATO FRITTERS

The Ritz-Carlton Buckhead's executive chef, Mauro Canaglia, devised this dessert when a convention of food writers descended on his Atlanta hotel in 1994. Cooked sweet potato cubes are folded into a batter lightened with egg whites, then dropped by teaspoonfuls into hot oil. As a final touch, he rolls the crispy fritters in honey and dredges them in ground pecans, confectioners' sugar and cocoa.

FOR THE FRITTERS:

1 cup (5 oz/155 g) all-purpose (plain) flour
½ cup (4 oz/125 g) granulated sugar
1 tablespoon ground cinnamon
2 teaspoons baking powder
½ teaspoon ground nutmeg
¼ teaspoon salt
2 eggs, separated
⅔ cup (5 fl oz/160 ml) milk
1 tablespoon unsalted butter, melted and cooled
3 sweet potatoes, baked, cooled, peeled and cut into 1-in (2.5-cm) cubes
1 cup (4 oz/125 g) confectioners' (icing) sugar, or as needed
vegetable oil for frying

FOR THE COATING:

¼ cup (3 oz/90 g) honey
½ cup (2 oz/60 g) pecan halves, finely ground
¼ cup (1 oz/30 g) confectioners' (icing) sugar
1 teaspoon unsweetened cocoa powder

❋ Preheat an oven to 200°F (93°C).
❋ For the fritters, in a large bowl, combine flour, granulated sugar, cinnamon, baking powder, nutmeg and salt. In a smaller bowl, whisk together the egg yolks, milk and melted butter. Add half of this liquid mixture to the dry ingredients and mix to form a smooth batter. Stir in remaining liquid but do not beat. Let the batter rest at room temperature for 30 minutes.
❋ After the batter has rested, beat the egg whites until stiff peaks form. Fold the beaten egg whites into the batter. Dredge the sweet potato cubes in confectioners' sugar and fold them into the batter.
❋ In a large, heavy saucepan over medium-high heat, pour in the oil to a depth of 2 in (5 cm) and heat to 325°F (165°C) on a deep-fry thermometer. Working in batches, drop the batter by tablespoonfuls into the hot oil and fry until golden, about 3–4 minutes. Remove the fritters with a slotted spoon, drain on paper towels and place in the warm oven until all the fritters are fried.
❋ Drizzle the honey over the hot fritters. In a small bowl, combine the pecans, confectioners' sugar and cocoa powder. Dredge the honey-coated fritters in the mixture and serve hot.

SERVES 8–12

Kentucky

SPOON BREAD

This soufflé-like corn bread is soft and custardy enough to eat with a spoon. It's a frequent accompaniment to ham or other brunch entrées.

5 eggs, separated, at room temperature
1 cup (5 oz/155 g) yellow cornmeal
2 cups (16 fl oz/500 ml) evaporated skim milk, undiluted
½ cup (4 fl oz/125 ml) cold water
2 tablespoons unsalted butter
1 tablespoon sugar
1 teaspoon salt

❋ Preheat an oven to 375°F (190°C). Lightly coat a 2-qt (2-l) soufflé dish with vegetable cooking spray.
❋ In a large heatproof bowl, whisk the egg yolks until lightly beaten and set aside.
❋ In a large measuring cup, whisk the cornmeal into ½ cup (4 fl oz/125 ml) of the milk and the water until well blended.
❋ In a large, heavy saucepan over medium-low heat, bring the remaining milk to a boil, whisking occasionally. Reduce the heat to low and gradually pour in the cornmeal mixture in a slow, steady stream while whisking vigorously and constantly to blend well. Continue to whisk just until mixture becomes smooth, stiff and thick and begins to pull away from the sides of the pan, about 30 seconds to 3 minutes. The mixture will be very thick and somewhat strenuous to whisk.
❋ Remove the saucepan from the heat and whisk in the butter, sugar and salt until the butter has melted and blended.
❋ Add one fourth of the hot cornmeal mixture to the bowl of egg yolks, whisking constantly until well blended. Then whisk the remaining cornmeal mixture into the egg yolks until well blended and reserve.
❋ In a large bowl, using an electric mixer on high speed, beat the egg whites until glossy, stiff but not dry peaks form and, when the beaters are raised upside down, the peaks hold their shape, about 3 minutes.
❋ Working quickly, stir one fourth of the beaten egg whites into the cornmeal mixture until well blended. Using a rubber spatula, gently fold the remaining egg whites into the cornmeal mixture until just blended.
❋ Pour the batter into the prepared dish and bake on the middle oven rack until puffed and golden brown on top, 30–45 minutes. The interior of the spoon bread will be soft and fluffy, while the surface and sides will be crispy. Serve at once from the soufflé dish.

SERVES 6

Clockwise from top: Spoon Bread, Sweet Potato Fritters, Pain Perdu

Top to bottom: Joel Chandler Harris's Cast-iron Skillet Corn Bread, Hoppin' John

Coastal South Carolina

HOPPIN' JOHN

Hoppin' John is the traditional New Year's dish in the South. Legend claims that if you eat this dish with a platter of collard greens on New Year's Day you will have financial success in the coming year. When cooked with a dime, it assures the lucky finder good fortune. Hoppin' John pairs peas with rice, *which is the premier crop of South Carolina's Low Country. To save cooking time, this version uses frozen black-eyed peas rather than dried—the results are just as good. Because legumes and rice constitute a complete protein, this dish has good nutritional value. For a vegetarian version, omit the bacon and replace the bacon drippings with vegetable oil.*

182

4 oz (125 g) lean bacon
3 cups (20 oz/625 g) frozen black-eyed peas
3 cups (24 fl oz/750 ml) boiling water
2 tablespoons bacon drippings or vegetable oil
1 large white onion, coarsely chopped
1 red bell pepper (capsicum), seeded and coarsely chopped
1 green bell pepper (capsicum), seeded and coarsely chopped
½ teaspoon dried thyme
3 cups (15 oz/470 g) hot cooked white rice
2 teaspoons salt, or to taste
⅛ teaspoon freshly ground pepper
½ teaspoon hot pepper sauce, or to taste

✿ In a large, heavy skillet over medium heat, cook the bacon to render fat. Remove the bacon, reserve the drippings in the skillet and set aside.

✿ In a large, heavy saucepan over medium heat, place the bacon, peas and water and bring to a boil. Reduce the heat to low, cover and simmer, stirring occasionally, until tender, about 30 minutes.

✿ Meanwhile, place the skillet with the bacon drippings over medium heat. Add the onion and red and green bell peppers and cook, stirring occasionally, for 2 minutes. Add the thyme, stir, and transfer the mixture to the peas in the saucepan. Continue to cook the peas until they are soft, but not mushy. Then remove and discard the bacon.

✿ On a large serving platter, toss together the pea mixture, hot rice, salt, pepper and hot pepper sauce. Serve hot and pass with more hot pepper sauce, if desired.

SERVES 6

Atlanta, Georgia

JOEL CHANDLER HARRIS'S CAST-IRON SKILLET CORN BREAD, WITH VARIATIONS

Joel Chandler Harris is best known as the author who popularized Brer Rabbit, Brer Fox and other African American folklore characters in the Uncle Remus stories. But he was also an Atlanta newspaperman, and in that capacity he often wrote about the Southern foods he loved, such as corn bread. "Real democracy and real republicanism, and the aspirations to which they give rise, are among the most potent results of cornmeal," he once editorialized. Being a Georgian, he took his corn bread in the traditional way: white cornmeal batter poured into a sizzling cast-iron skillet coated with bacon drippings, creating a crunchy crust touched with pork flavor. A variation with the same taste is Cracklin' Corn Bread, using crisp bits of rendered pork fat. In the past, when people drew their lard supply from fresh pork fat, cracklings were in ready supply. But nowadays, many people fry diced salt pork instead. These crispy morsels are wonderful when added to salads and soups, too. You can use 2 tablespoons of the drippings for the corn bread recipe.

3 cups (15 oz/470 g) white cornmeal
2½ teaspoons baking powder
1 teaspoon salt
1½ cups (12 fl oz/375 ml) milk, at room temperature
2 eggs, at room temperature
2 tablespoons bacon drippings or vegetable shortening

FOR THE TRADITIONAL SOUTHERN VARIATION:

1½ cups (12 fl oz/375 ml) lowfat buttermilk, at room temperature
1 teaspoon baking powder
1 teaspoon baking soda (bicarbonate of soda)

FOR THE CRACKLIN' VARIATION:

8 oz (250 g) salt pork, cut into ¼-in (6-mm) dice (see glossary)

✿ Preheat an oven to 450°F (230°C).

✿ In a large bowl, sift together the cornmeal, baking powder and salt. Measure the milk in a 2-cup (16–fl oz/500-ml) glass measuring cup and lightly beat in the eggs. Pour into the dry ingredients, stirring until just blended. The batter should be slightly lumpy. Do not overmix.

✿ In a large cast-iron skillet over medium-high heat, heat the bacon drippings or vegetable shortening until it just begins to smoke. Spoon the batter into the hot skillet (the batter will make a sizzling sound) and smooth the surface. Using oven mitts, set the skillet on the middle oven rack. Bake until golden brown, 18–20 minutes. Invert the bread on to a plate and serve warm.

✿ To make Traditional Southern Corn Bread, use lowfat buttermilk instead of milk and replace the 2½ teaspoons baking powder with the 1 teaspoon baking powder and the 1 teaspoon baking soda. Follow the recipe as directed from the point at which you make the batter.

✿ To make Cracklin' Corn Bread, in a large cast-iron skillet over medium heat, fry the diced salt pork, stirring frequently until almost all the fat has been rendered, 20–30 minutes. Reduce the heat to medium-low and continue to cook, stirring occasionally until the fat in the skillet barely moves and the cracklings are crisp and well browned, 10–15 minutes longer. Using a slotted spoon, transfer the cracklings to paper towels to drain thoroughly. Carefully pour off the fat from the skillet, reserving for another use if desired. Then prepare the corn bread batter, following the recipe. Stir the cracklings into the batter until well blended and evenly distributed, then spoon the batter into the skillet. Continue to follow the recipe as directed.

SERVES 8

South

MINIATURE SWEET POTATO DINNER SCONES

These old-fashioned sweet potato biscuits, baked in the charming form of miniature scones, are studded with currants.

1¼ cups (6 oz/185 g) all-purpose (plain) flour
2 teaspoons baking powder
½ teaspoon salt
¼ teaspoon freshly ground pepper
¼ cup unsalted butter, diced and chilled
1 egg, lightly beaten
¼ cup (2 fl oz/60 ml) milk
⅓ cup (2 oz/60 g) dried currants
1 cup (6 oz/185 g) diced (¼-in/6-mm), cooled, cooked sweet potato

✿ Preheat an oven to 450°F (230°C).

✿ In a medium bowl, sift together the flour, baking powder, salt and pepper. Using a pastry blender, 2 knives or a fork, cut in the butter until it resembles coarse crumbs. Stir in the egg, milk and currants until the mixture just forms a soft dough. Fold in the diced cooked sweet potato until just well blended.

✿ Drop by well-rounded tablespoonfuls, about 1 in (2.5 cm) apart, onto an ungreased baking sheet. Bake on the middle oven rack until the exteriors are crisp and lightly golden, 15–20 minutes. Serve at once.

MAKES 12 SCONES   *Photograph pages 172–173*

The Carolinas

RICE QUICK BREAD MUFFINS

Sarah Rutledge's recipe for rice bread in her 1847 book, The Carolina Housewife, *inspired these muffins. They can be enjoyed as a portable breakfast on the way to work or as a dinner bread, to accompany a marvelous roast beef. They're a great way to use leftover rice.*

1 egg, at room temperature
¾ cup (6 fl oz/180 ml) milk
⅓ cup (3 fl oz/80 ml) vegetable oil
1¾ cups (7 oz/220 g) sifted all-purpose (plain) flour
¼ cup (2 oz/60 g) sugar
1½ teaspoons baking powder
½ teaspoon salt
½ teaspoon ground nutmeg
1 cup (5 oz/155 g) firmly packed, cooked long-grain white rice, cooled to room temperature

❀ Preheat an oven to 400°F (200°C). Lightly coat 12 standard muffin cups with vegetable cooking spray or line them with paper muffin liners.
❀ In a small bowl, whisk together the egg, milk and vegetable oil until well blended. In a large bowl, combine the flour, sugar, baking powder, salt, nutmeg and cooked rice. Using a fork, stir until well blended. Make a well in the center of the rice mixture and pour in egg mixture. Stir until just moistened. The batter should be slightly lumpy.
❀ Divide the mixture among the prepared muffin cups. Bake on the middle oven rack until the edges are golden brown, 20–25 minutes. Serve at once.

MAKES 12 MUFFINS   *Photograph pages 172–173*

The South

THREE-CORN BREAD

This cakelike creation is made with not just one form of corn but three: meal, grits and whole kernels. The additon of grits makes this bread so moist it doesn't even need butter—just slice and drizzle it with a little honey.

2 cups (10 oz/315 g) yellow cornmeal
2 cups (8 oz/250 g) sifted all-purpose (plain) flour
1 tablespoon baking powder
1 teaspoon baking soda (bicarbonate of soda)
½ teaspoon salt
½ cup (4 oz/125 g) sugar
10 oz (315 g) frozen corn kernels, thawed and squeezed dry
½ cup (4 oz/125 g) firmly packed cooked grits, cooled to room temperature
2 cups (16 fl oz/500 ml) lowfat buttermilk
⅔ cup (5 oz/155 g) unsalted butter, melted and cooled to room temperature
4 eggs

❀ Preheat an oven to 400°F (200°C). Lightly coat a 9-in (23-cm) round cake pan with vegetable cooking spray and dust with flour.
❀ In a large bowl, combine the cornmeal, flour, baking powder, baking soda, salt, sugar and corn kernels. Using a fork, stir until well blended. In a medium bowl, combine the grits, buttermilk, butter and eggs and whisk until well blended and smooth.
❀ Make a well in the center of the cornmeal mixture and pour in the buttermilk mixture. Stir until well blended. The batter should be slightly lumpy. Do not overmix.

❀ Spoon the batter into the prepared pan. Bake on the middle oven rack on an aluminum-foil lined baking sheet until golden brown and a toothpick inserted in the center comes out clean with just a few crumbs adhering, 50–70 minutes. About 15 minutes before the end of baking, remove the bread from the oven and, using a knife, slash an X across the top of the bread about ¼ in (6 mm) deep. Return the bread to the oven to finish baking. If the bread browns too quickly, cover the top with aluminum foil. Set on a wire rack to cool in the pan for 15 minutes. Serve warm or at room temperature.

SERVES 8

Alabama

CHEESE GRITS SOUFFLÉ

Enriched with eggs and cheese, an everyday Southern side dish becomes elegant company fare. Serve it for brunch or alongside grilled quail and wild mushrooms.

¼ cup (1½ oz/45 g) regular grits
½ cup (4 fl oz/125 ml) milk
½ cup (4 fl oz/125 ml) water
¼ teaspoon salt
1 cup (4 oz/125 g) shredded sharp white Cheddar cheese
3 egg yolks
4 egg whites, at room temperature
¼ teaspoon cream of tartar
1 tablespoon minced fresh chives for garnish

❀ Preheat an oven to 350°F (180°C).
❀ In a large saucepan over high heat, combine the grits, milk, water and salt and stir until well blended. Bring to a boil, stirring constantly. Reduce the heat to low, cover and simmer, stirring occasionally, until the grits are soft and thickened, 15–20 minutes. Add the cheese and continue to cook, stirring constantly until melted. Remove the saucepan from the heat and set aside.
❀ Place the yolks in a small bowl and whisk lightly. Gradually whisk 3 tablespoons of the warm grits into the yolks until well blended. Then whisk this mixture into the saucepan of grits until well blended.
❀ In a medium bowl, using an electric mixer on high speed, beat the egg whites with the cream of tartar until stiff but not dry peaks form, about 1 minute. Working quickly, stir one-third of the beaten egg whites into the grits mixture in the saucepan until well blended. Then pour the grits mixture over the remaining egg whites and fold in just until combined.
❀ Pour into an ungreased 1-qt (1-l) soufflé dish. Bake on the middle oven rack until puffy, golden brown and a knife inserted 1 in (2.5 cm) from the center comes out clean, about 40 minutes. Garnish with the chives and serve at once.

SERVES 4

Low Country

RED RICE

Spanish rice, Creole rice, tomato pilaf—by any name, this simple, spicy dish has long been a favorite in the old rice country of coastal Georgia and South Carolina. Louisianians like it too and often serve it with shrimp.

6 strips lean hickory-smoked bacon, cut into ½-in (12-mm) pieces
1 cup (5 oz/155 g) finely chopped white onion
1 green bell pepper (capsicum), seeded and coarsely chopped

Top to bottom: Three-Corn Bread, Cheese Grits Soufflé, Red Rice

1 cup (7 oz/220 g) long-grain white rice
16 oz (500 g) canned crushed tomatoes
1–1¼ cups (8–10 fl oz/250–310 ml) cold water
¾ teaspoon salt
2 or 3 dashes of hot pepper sauce

❀ In a heavy medium saucepan over medium heat, cook the bacon until crisp. Remove the bacon to drain on paper towels and set aside. Pour off the bacon drippings, reserving 1 tablespoon in the pan.

❀ Add the onion and bell pepper to the pan. Increase the heat to medium-high and cook, stirring occasionally, until tender but not browned, about 3 minutes. Reduce the heat to low, add the rice and cook, stirring often, for 2 minutes.

❀ Stir in the tomatoes, 1 cup (8 fl oz/250 ml) of the water, salt and hot pepper sauce to taste. Bring to a boil, then cover and simmer, without stirring, until the rice is tender and the liquid has been absorbed, 25–30 minutes. After the first 15 minutes, check the rice and, if needed, add ¼ cup (2 fl oz/60 ml) water to prevent the rice from sticking.

❀ To serve, transfer the rice mixture to a serving dish, crumble the bacon on top and let stand for 5 minutes. Serve warm.

SERVES 4

Grits and Vegetable Cakes with Dipping Sauce

Nashville, Tennessee

GRITS AND VEGETABLE CAKES WITH DIPPING SAUCE

Debra Paquette and Michael Cribb, chefs of the Bound'ry restaurant in Nashville, have built close to an entire menu from appetizers. One of their creations transforms classic Southern flavors—black-eyed peas, grits and cabbage—into deliciously intriguing cakes, especially when dipped into soy sauce and savored with a bit of pickled ginger and a dab of Japanese wasabi. The grits are added uncooked; when fried they give a pleasantly crunchy crumblike coating to the vegetables. For a mouth-watering appetizer, serve these crispy fried cakes on a pretty tray alongside bowls of the accompaniments.

1 cup (6 oz/185 g) cooked black-eyed peas, cooled
1 cup (5 oz/155 g) cooked basmati rice, cooled
1 cup (3 oz/90 g) shredded green cabbage
1 cup (3 oz/90 g) shredded carrots
½ cup (2½ oz/75 g) grated onion
½ cup (3 oz/90 g) quick-cooking grits
1 tablespoon finely chopped fresh thyme
1 tablespoon finely chopped garlic
1½ teaspoons seasoning salt or celery salt, or to taste
1 teaspoon ground white pepper, or to taste
2 eggs, lightly beaten
1 cup (4 oz/125 g) unseasoned dried bread crumbs,
   or as needed
vegetable oil for frying

FOR SERVING:

½ cup (4 fl oz/125 ml) soy sauce
2 tablespoons pickled ginger
2 teaspoons wasabi

❀ In a large bowl, combine the black-eyed peas, rice, cabbage, carrots, onion, grits, thyme, garlic, seasoning or celery salt and white pepper and stir until well blended. Add the beaten eggs and enough bread crumbs to bind the mixture together. Firmly pack a dry, ¼-cup, measuring cup with the mixture and using your hands flatten mixture to form into a 2-oz (60-g) cake approximately 3-in (7.5-cm) in diameter and set aside. Repeat this process until you have a total of approximately 15 cakes.

❋ Preheat an oven to 200°F (95°C).

❋ In a large, heavy skillet over medium-high heat, pour the oil to a depth of ¼ in (6 mm) and heat until a small amount of the mixture dropped into the oil sizzles, rises and begins to cook. Working in batches, fry the cakes until golden brown and crispy on both sides, 4–5 minutes total.

❋ Using a slotted spoon or spatula, remove the cakes to paper towels to drain. Then transfer to a heatproof serving platter and keep warm in the preheated oven. Repeat until all the cakes are done, adding more oil to the pan as needed.

❋ To serve, arrange a dish of soy sauce, a small mound of pickled ginger and a dab of wasabi on the serving platter with the cakes and serve warm.

SERVES 10–12

Louisiana

RED BEANS AND RICE

This is a traditional Monday dinner in New Orleans. Not only does it use Sunday's leftover ham, but it can be made ahead and left to simmer—an important consideration back when Monday was wash day. Red kidney beans are used in most versions of this dish, but many Louisianans prefer the smaller beans known in local stores as "round red beans" or just "red beans." They take less time to cook up creamy.

1 lb (500 g) dried red beans
2 qt (2 l) water plus 1 cup (8 fl oz/250 ml) water
2 cups (10 oz/315 g) finely chopped white onion
¼ cup (2 fl oz/60 ml) vegetable oil
1 lb (500 g) lean smoked ham, cut into ½-in (12-mm) dice
1 lb (500 g) smoked pork sausage, cut into slices ½ in (12 mm) thick
2 tablespoons minced garlic
1 bay leaf
1 tablespoon freshly ground pepper
3 tablespoons minced fresh parsley
1 teaspoon dried thyme
¼ teaspoon ground cayenne pepper
salt to taste
4 cups (20 oz/625 g) hot cooked white rice for serving
hot pepper sauce for serving

❋ Pick over the beans, removing and discarding any stones or blemished beans. Rinse and drain.

❋ Place the beans in a large pot and add the 2 qt (2 l) water and onion. Set over medium-high heat and bring to a boil. Reduce the heat to low, cover and simmer, stirring occasionally, until the beans are tender but not mushy, about 1 hour. Remove from the heat and stir well, mashing some beans against the side of the pot. Set aside.

❋ In a large skillet over high heat, heat the oil. Add the ham and sausage. Sauté until cooked through and browned, about 5 minutes. Transfer to the beans in the pot. Return the skillet to high heat, add the 1 cup (8 fl oz/250 ml) water and, using a wooden spoon, stir to dislodge any browned bits from the bottom. Pour this liquid into the beans and add the garlic, bay leaf, pepper, parsley, thyme, cayenne and salt.

❋ Return the pot to medium-high heat and bring to a boil. Reduce the heat to low and simmer, uncovered, stirring occasionally, until the beans are soft and creamy, 30–60 minutes. Remove and discard the bay leaf.

❋ Ladle over the hot rice and pass the hot pepper sauce.

SERVES 8

Tennessee

CORN LIGHT BREAD

This is what happens when corn bread goes to town and gets sophisticated. Unlike the common Southern corn bread, which comes out of the skillet dense and crispy crusted, Corn Light Bread has a supple crust and delicate, cake-like texture. In the past, its "lightness" was not due to color or texture, but was born from the yeast fermentation process. Here is a more modern version.

1 cup (5 oz/155 g) yellow cornmeal
1 cup (4 oz/125 g) sifted all-purpose (plain) flour
1 teaspoon baking powder
1 teaspoon baking soda (bicarbonate of soda)
¾ teaspoon salt
½ cup (4 oz/125 g) sugar
1¼ cups (10 fl oz/310 ml) lowfat buttermilk
½ cup (4 fl oz/125 ml) unsalted butter, melted and cooled to room temperature
2 eggs

❋ Preheat an oven to 400°F (200°C). Lightly coat a 9-by-5-in (23-by-13-cm) loaf pan with vegetable cooking spray and dust with flour.

❋ In a large bowl, combine the cornmeal, flour, baking powder, baking soda, salt and sugar. Using a fork, stir until well blended. In a medium bowl, combine the buttermilk, butter and eggs and whisk until well blended.

❋ Make a well in the center of the cornmeal mixture and pour in the buttermilk mixture. Stir until well blended. The batter should be slightly lumpy. Do not overmix.

❋ Spoon the batter into the prepared pan. Bake on the middle oven rack until golden brown and a toothpick inserted in the center comes out clean, 30–35 minutes. About 10 minutes before the end of the baking, remove the bread from the oven and, using a knife, slash the bread lengthwise down the middle, about ¼ in (6 mm) deep. Return the bread to the oven to finish baking. Set on a wire rack to cool in the pan for 15 minutes.

❋ Serve warm or at room temperature.

SERVES 8

Left to right: Red Beans and Rice, Corn Light Bread

FLORIDA

FLORIDA

Gulf of Mexico

MIAMI

FLORIDA

To comprehend Florida, consider the parable of the stone crab. Fishermen used to discard the large-clawed crustacean because it didn't have much meat, and what it did have tasted faintly medicinal. Then, in 1923, a Harvard professor visiting Miami noticed that the crab resembled a delicious variety he had eaten in Cuba. Word of this reached Joseph Weiss, who ran a seafood joint on Miami Beach. He boiled a pot of the crabs and tried the claw meat chilled. It *was* delicious; the chilling seemed to get rid of the medicinal taste. Not long after Weiss started serving stone crabs, newspaper columnist Damon Runyon dropped by and touted the new delicacy, which had, he cracked, "a shell harder than a landlord's heart." Today Floridians eagerly await stone crab season each fall, and that seafood joint has become perhaps the state's most famous restaurant, Joe's Stone Crab.

That's Florida in a nutshell. Something unvalued was discovered by an outsider, and with the help of a little refrigeration and press agentry, it made it big.

Southerners like to grouse that Florida doesn't feel very Southern. They're right; much of it doesn't. The state's population has more than doubled since 1970, the great majority coming from other regions and other nations where people aren't expected to know the difference between pot likker and corn liquor. More than any other Southern state, Florida has been shaped by transplants—

Previous pages: A bather demonstrates his umbrella-opening technique at Barefoot Beach in Bonita Springs, Florida. If one were to stretch the Sunshine State's coast into a straight line, it would extend for over 1,800 miles. Left: The Art Deco architecture in South Miami Beach was created during the 1930s and continues to reflect the gloss and glamour of the Moderne movement.

191

Alligators thrive in the dense swamplands of northern Florida. The name of the American alligator,
Alligator mississippiensis, *came from Spanish sailors who called it* el largota *(the lizard).*

Miami Beach is a hot spot at night: the sounds of jazz, blues and reggae spill out into the streets and swarms of entertainment seekers frequent the discos and clubs.

Midwesterners on the Gulf Coast, Northeasterners on the Atlantic coast, Latin Americans on the southeastern tip, amusement park mice in the middle. Every year the line seems to creep northward, the line dividing that newer version of Florida from the older Florida where a Southern accent seems as natural as a breeze rustling through a live oak. And yet there's a Southern spine to Florida culture and cooking, even if it's not as conspicuous as all those cars tooling south with Ohio tags.

Like any good theme park, Florida has several motifs. The most obviously Southern part of the state, the northern third, stretches from the old Spanish port of Pensacola on the Gulf to the industrial port of Jacksonville on the Atlantic. Some Floridians refer to this portion of the state as south Georgia. Georgians call it the Redneck Riviera.

Below Jacksonville, the Florida peninsula juts 350 miles into the sea like God's own fishing pier. The interior begins with rolling horse farms around Ocala, levels out as it moves south into the lake distict of Orlando and Disney World, then bursts into citrus-quilted hills that produce most of the nation's orange juice concentrate. Farther south, the peninsula becomes one vast waterworks, as the shallow inland sea of Lake Okeechobee drains into the Everglades, that ceaseless river of grass, and on into mangrove thickets at the ocean's edge. Along the margins, where the wetlands have been drained, migrant laborers harvest much of America's sugarcane and winter vegetables on fields as flat as those of the Mississippi Delta.

To the east of this hardworking land lies the glitter of the Gold Coast, a seventy-five-mile barrier reef of condominiums culminating in the northernmost outpost of the Caribbean, Miami. To the west lies the Sun Coast and the twin cities of Tampa Bay trailing along the shore in one retirement mecca after another. To the south lie the Florida Keys, the archipelago that punctuates the state with an exclamation point at Margaritaville itself, Key West.

Florida's original tourists spoke Spanish. After Ponce de León landed at St. Augustine in 1513, the Spanish built a string of forts and missions across the northern half of the state. The Timucua and Apalachee peoples they encountered introduced them to maize. The Spanish introduced the natives to cattle, hogs, peaches and oranges. Citrus fruit took to the subtropical climate so well that by the beginning of the 1600s, travelers noted thick stands of wild oranges growing along the St. Johns River. Another group of Spanish immigrants, from the Mediterranean island of Minorca, brought a supremely hot pepper called the datil that is still used in spicy seafood pilaus around St. Augustine.

Except for one twenty-year interval, Spain ruled Florida until 1819, when it ceded the colony to the United States. Not everyone valued the new territory. It was too wild, too wet, too hot, too remote. Runaway slaves found sanctuary in it. A band of renegade Creeks from Alabama and Georgia fled to it, regrouping as Seminoles and fighting three guerrilla wars against the United States. One soldier who journeyed south to pursue them in the

A tourist swings out over the shimmering sea in the Florida Keys—a string of thirty-one islands linked together by the forty-two bridges of the Overseas Highway.

1840s was future general William T. Sherman. "This country," he wrote, "is not worth a damn."

While the plantation culture of the Deep South spread to northern Florida, most of the state remained primitive and sparsely settled throughout the 1800s. It was Cracker country. The word, now used to mean any rural native Floridian, derived from the sound of cattlemen cracking their bullwhips as they drove livestock across the prairies of central Florida. The cooking of backcountry laborers— cattle drivers, turpentine workers, fruit pickers, white and black—was a campfire version of Southern with the addition of Florida foods such as gator, cooter (freshwater turtles), mangoes, citrus fruits and swamp cabbage (hearts of palm, the core of a young palm tree).

No one captured this wild-haired cousin of Southern cuisine better than Marjorie Kinnan Rawlings, the novelist who wrote about her home in the swampy backwoods south of Gainesville. Rawlings lavished so much atten-

tion on food in her 1942 book, *Cross Creek,* that she followed it with a cookbook *Cross Creek Cookery.* It is so full of cooter and corn bread and Utterly Deadly Southern Pecan Pie that you'd never know the author was a born and bred Northerner. "Enchantment lies in different things for each of us," she wrote. "For me, it is in this: to step out of the bright sunlight into the shade of orange trees; to walk under the arched canopy of their jadelike leaves; to see the long aisles of lichened trunks set ahead in a geometric rhythm; to feel the mystery of a seclusion that yet has shafts of light striking through it."

Far to the south, a different sort of native cooking was taking shape on the Florida Keys. Like the Crackers, the people of Key West—the old pirate haunt at the end of the line—made do with local foods. Key limes, sour and lemon-looking, were combined with evaporated milk (the only kind available on the islands) to make Key lime pie. Conchs, the tough little morsels in the big beautiful shells, were pounded into tenderness and used in fritters, salads and chowders. The Keys became so identified with conchs, in fact, that longtime residents—Bahamians and Brits, mostly—called themselves Conchs. When U.S. immigration policy angered Key West in the 1980s, the city threatened to secede and declare itself the Conch Republic.

It was a full century before that, in the 1880s, that modern Florida began to emerge. The entire state then had a population of 260,000, about the size of Tallahassee today. Things started changing with a couple of real estate sharps named Henry.

Before Henry M. Flagler and Henry B. Plant, two tycoons from the North, took an interest in Florida, the southern half of the state was as untamed as the Amazon. Flagler, who controlled the Atlantic Coast railroad, built the state's first grand resort hotel in St. Augustine in 1885. Plant, who ran the Gulf Coast line, countered with the Tampa Bay Hotel. Flagler retaliated by running his railroad south to Palm Beach and opening the Breakers, an even more magnificent hotel. When a hard freeze destroyed most of the state's citrus crop in 1894, a real estate investor in the scruffy town of Miami sent Flagler some orange blossoms to show that southern Florida was below the frost line. Flagler extended his railroad to Miami and eventually all the way to Key West.

Florida hasn't been the same since. With each wave of migrants, new flavors and foodways have been stirred into the local culture. The Cubans who came to Tampa to make cigars in the late 1800s brought a refined old Spanish cuisine. The Greek sponge fishers who settled around Tarpon Springs brought their seafood soups and grilled fish dishes. The Jews from the Northeast who populated Miami brought their bagels and delicatessen foods. The refugees who fled Fidel Castro brought their black beans, *arroz con pollo* and Cuban sandwiches. More recent arrivals from Haiti, Nicaragua and all over Latin America have added their seasonings; Miami, after all, is as close to Kingston, Jamaica, as it is to Atlanta, Georgia.

As a result of all this fresh blood, Florida probably has the most varied cuisine of any Southern state, and Miami has developed one of the nation's most innovative dining scenes. Chefs such as Mark Militello, Norman Van Aiken and Allen Susser combine Southern, Caribbean and California cooking to create a sort of calypso cuisine that makes liberal use of native seafoods, hot peppers and tropical fruits like mangoes, guavas and the star-shaped carambola. Susser calls it New World cuisine. Others call it "Floribbean."

Whatever its name, this new fusion cuisine should sound familiar to any lover of Southern food. What they're doing in Florida today is what Creole cooks were doing in Louisiana decades ago. If the results are anywhere close to comparable, the South will be a very tasty place for generations to come.

The flavor of traditional Cuban culture can be experienced in the Miami neighborhood of Little Havana. Here lovers stay out all night in this popular Cuban restaurant where a customer hears only rapid-fire Spanish. The strong Latin influence in the city adds to its cosmopolitan character.

Desserts
& Candies

Due to their favorable climate, Southern cooks have an abundance of fresh native fruits available to them, from oranges and peaches to the tropical papaya and star fruits (carambolas).

DESSERTS & CANDIES

One of the first fund-raising events of Jimmy Carter's campaign for the presidency in 1976 was a dinner hosted by his mother in their hometown of Plains, Georgia. Miss Lillian really laid out a spread. Reporters counted an incredible fifty-five dishes. But the thing that floored them was that fifteen of the offerings—more than a fourth—were desserts.

Like Lillian Carter's dinner, the dessert chapter you are beginning is by far the largest portion of the feast set out in this book. It has to be. In a nation known for its sugar fixation, Southerners surely have the biggest sweet tooth of all.

Go to any family reunion and you'll see kinfolk clucking over the expansive tablescape of cakes, puddings and pies. Go to any church or school gathering and you'll find at least one lady known for her prizewinning cake or cobbler. Go to any cafeteria and notice the backward order in which the foods are presented, desserts and salads almost always coming first. *Southern Living* magazine certainly recognizes the importance of sweets. One of its food stylists frosted cakes so artistically that the staff nicknamed her Queen Swirl.

The root of this sweet tooth is clearly European. The native peoples of the South didn't get carried away with sweets. It wasn't until the English arrived with their fondness for puddings and pies that the institution of dessert took hold. Apple pie, the most American of desserts, fell out of the British family tree.

Virtually every other European group that touched Southern shores also contributed to the sweet tooth, from the French who inspired Louisiana's sugar-and-pecan confection, the praline, to the Moravians who brought their Eastern European Christmas cookies to Winston-Salem, North Carolina. African foods figured as well. Benne seeds, as slaves called sesame seeds, were used in dessert wafers

Line after line of cookies pour from the ovens at the Bird Cookie Company in Savannah, Georgia.

Previous pages: Left to right: Mississippi Christmas Cake (recipe page 209), Rum-Soaked Dried Peach Fruitcake (recipe page 227), Moravian Cookies (recipe page 215), Persimmon Pudding (recipe page 212)

Deemed America's favorite dessert, ice cream is a popular treat in the South, especially when temperatures soar in the summer months.

that are still beloved in the South Carolina Low Country. And peanuts, which originated in South America but were introduced to North America by way of Africa, turn up in numerous candies and pies.

Southerners found dessert makings everywhere around them. The region burst with sweet fruits—peaches, blackberries, strawberries, oranges—which naturally landed in desserts. Nuts did too; pecans probably show up in more desserts and candies than any other Southern food.

The South has never lacked for sweetening agents either; since the early 1800s, the region has grown most of the nation's sugarcane. It has been supplemented by local sweeteners such as tupelo honey, taken from the nectar of tupelo gum tree blossoms in the Florida Panhandle, and sorghum syrup, from sorghum grass grown in pockets around the South. One of them, Cairo, Georgia, nicknamed its high school football team the Syrupmakers.

Despite the abundance of raw materials, antebellum Southerners were not obsessed with sweets, to judge from early cookbooks. Recipes for pies, puddings and cakes appear, but not nearly as frequently as today. Food historians trace the rise of sweets to the late 1800s and early 1900s when easy-to-use granulated sugar became widely available. About the same time packaged treats appeared. Two from Tennessee, Moon Pies and Goo

Goo Clusters, assumed the status of regional symbols.

While sweets dominate Southern cookbooks and reunion spreads, the impression of a people who live for chess pie may be a little deceptive. Southerners don't indulge in these rich foods at every meal. Elaborate desserts are a special event, an excuse for cooks to strut their stuff and frost their reputations. They're a sweet sacrament of celebration in a region that hasn't always had a lot to celebrate.

Truman Capote described this ritual aspect of Southern sweets in "A Christmas Memory," his short story about finding holiday joy in the midst of the Depression-era Alabama he knew as a child. Every November, he wrote, his elderly cousin pressed her face against the windowpane and exclaimed, "It's fruitcake weather!" And off they went to the pecan groves and the market and the bootlegger to buy whiskey, because, despite their poverty, they had thirty fruitcakes to bake and send to friends and to people who felt like friends, such as President Roosevelt.

Capote's story wasn't the first time a Southern woman has been remembered for her cake. Preachers have been praising the desserts of the departed for years in their eulogies; they probably figure it'll help open the Pearly Gates. Anyone who has ever dug into a Southern dessert knows that they might be on to something.

Left to right: Banana Pudding with Meringue, Brennan's Bananas Foster

Kentucky

BANANA PUDDING WITH MERINGUE

No one seems to know the origin of banana pudding, but it's been a Southern favorite for decades. Elvis Presley is said to have requested it at least once a week. The epicenter of the banana pudding universe must be Fulton, Kentucky, and South Fulton, Tennessee. In the 1880s, when railroads started shipping bananas north, trains stopped in these twin towns on the state border to re-ice the fruit. Fultonians celebrate those days with a banana festival and the making of a one-ton banana pudding. Elvis would be pleased. For best results, use very ripe bananas, whose peels are speckled brown. Wait to slice the bananas until needed, since they quickly discolor.

FOR THE PUDDING:

⅔ cup (5 oz/155 g) sugar
⅓ cup (½ oz/45 g) cornstarch
¼ teaspoon salt
4 cups (32 fl oz/1 l) milk
4 egg yolks
2 tablespoons unsalted butter, at room temperature
1 teaspoon vanilla extract (essence)
5 fully ripe bananas, about 1½–2 lb (750 g–1 kg)
52 vanilla wafers, about 6 oz (185 g) (reserve 10 of the wafers)

FOR THE MERINGUE:

4 egg whites, at room temperature
¼ teaspoon cream of tartar
¼ cup (2 oz/60 g) sugar

❋ To make the pudding, in a large, heavy saucepan over medium heat, combine the sugar, cornstarch, salt and milk and stir until well blended. Cook the mixture, stirring constantly, until it begins to thicken and just comes to a boil, 8–10 minutes. Boil for 1 minute, stirring constantly, until thick enough to coat the back of a spoon. Remove the saucepan from the heat.

❋ In a medium bowl, using a whisk, lightly beat the egg yolks. Slowly whisk ½ cup (4 fl oz/125 ml) of the pudding mixture into the egg yolks, then transfer this mixture to the saucepan and stir until well blended. Return the saucepan to medium heat. Cook, stirring, just until it bubbles, about 2 minutes. Do not overcook. Remove from the heat and stir in the butter and vanilla until the butter has melted and blended. Strain through a fine-meshed sieve into a medium heatproof bowl, discarding any solid particles left in the sieve. Set aside.

❋ Preheat an oven to 425°F (220°C).

❋ Peel and cut the bananas into thin slices. In the bottom of a round 1½-quart (1.5-l), 8-in diameter (20-cm) casserole or baking dish, arrange one third of the vanilla wafers. Cover evenly with one third of the sliced bananas, followed by an even layer of one third of the pudding. Repeat to make two more layers, ending with the pudding on top. Ring the edge with the reserved 10 wafers inserted vertically (this helps anchor the meringue so it won't shrink from the sides of the baking dish when baked).

❀ To make the meringue, in a medium bowl, using an electric mixer on high speed, beat the egg whites with cream of tartar until frothy, about 2 minutes. Gradually beat in the sugar, a tablespoon at a time, until all the sugar is incorporated and continue to beat until glossy, stiff but not dry peaks form and, when the beaters are raised upside down, the peaks hold their shape, about 1 minute.

❀ Working quickly, using a rubber spatula spread the meringue to cover the top of the pudding completely, starting from the edge and moving toward the center (to keep from sinking into filling). Spread meringue to the edges, using a spoon to swirl and peak the meringue for a decorative touch.

❀ Bake on the middle oven rack until the meringue is golden brown, about 5 minutes. Set the baking dish on a wire rack to cool for 30 minutes. Serve warm. Alternatively, let cool completely, cover and refrigerate for 4 hours and serve chilled.

SERVES 8

South

THREE-BERRY SOUTHERN SHORTCAKES WITH CHANTILLY

Southern shortcakes are made of rich, sweetened biscuit dough formed a little larger than your average biscuit and served hot, split, topped with lush berries and crowned with mounds of whipped cream. When it's strawberry season, you can replace the entire quantity of mixed berries with strawberries.

FOR THE BERRY TOPPING:

1 cup (4 oz/125 g) fresh strawberries, trimmed and halved
½ cup (2 oz/60 g) fresh blueberries
½ cup (2 oz/60 g) fresh blackberries
½ cup (2 oz/60 g) confectioners' (icing) sugar

FOR THE CHANTILLY:

1 cup (8 fl oz/250 ml) heavy (double) cream, chilled
1 teaspoon vanilla extract (essence)
2 tablespoons confectioners' (icing) sugar

FOR THE SHORTCAKES:

Touch of Grace Biscuits, recipe on page 178

❀ To make the berry topping, in a medium bowl, combine the strawberries, blueberries, blackberries and confectioners' sugar. Stir until well blended, cover and set aside at room temperature until ready to use.

❀ To make the Chantilly, whip the cream and vanilla at high speed with clean, chilled beaters until soft peaks form. Add the confectioners' sugar and continue beating until stiff peaks form. Transfer the whipped cream to a sieve set over a bowl, cover tightly with plastic wrap and refrigerate up to 2 hours.

❀ To make the shortcakes, follow biscuit recipe directions with these changes: Add 1 tablespoon sugar, for 2 tablespoons total. Use light cream instead of buttermilk. Decrease the amount of all-purpose (plain) flour for coating and shaping the dough to ½ cup (2½ oz/75 g). Divide the dough in quarters and shape each into a round approximately 3 in (7.5 cm) in diameter. Decrease the amount of melted butter for brushing the biscuit tops to 1 tablespoon.

❀ To serve, using a serrated knife, split the shortcakes. Arrange the bottom halves cut side up on a serving platter or individual dessert plates. Top with berries and a dollop of Chantilly. Crown with the biscuit tops, a few more berries and Chantilly.

SERVES 4

New Orleans, Louisiana

BRENNAN'S BANANAS FOSTER

As the South's leading port, New Orleans has long been the place where bananas from Central and South America were unloaded for the journey inland. In 1951 one of the city's most famous restaurants put the fruit to work when restaurateur Edward Brennan asked chef Paul Blange to prepare a little something sweet for breakfast. Now a dessert spooned over ice cream, Blange named his creation for businessman Richard Foster, a devoted patron, and it remains the most requested dish at Brennan's. For more detailed flambé instructions, see the recipe for Café Brûlot on page 50.

¼ cup (2 oz/60 g) unsalted butter
1 cup (7 oz/220 g) lightly packed light brown sugar
½ teaspoon ground cinnamon
¼ cup (2 fl oz/60 ml) banana liqueur
4 bananas, cut in half lengthwise and then crosswise
¼ cup (2 fl oz/60 ml) dark rum
1 qt (1 l) vanilla ice cream

❀ In a 10-in (25-cm) flambé or sauté pan over low heat either on an alcohol burner or on top of a gas stove, combine the butter, brown sugar and cinnamon. Cook, stirring, until the sugar has dissolved and the butter has melted. Stir in the banana liqueur, then place the banana pieces in the pan. Cook until banana sections soften and begin to brown, turning with tongs to brown on both sides, about 6 minutes. Carefully pour in the rum and cook until the rum is hot, about 1 minute. Then carefully tip the pan very slightly to the side just to catch a tiny bit of the burner flame in the pan, to ignite the rum. Immediately straighten the pan upright. Do not move the pan; let it stand until the flames die out.

❀ Scoop the vanilla ice cream into 4 individual dishes. Place 4 pieces of banana atop the ice cream. Spoon the warm sauce over the top and serve at once.

SERVES 4

Three-Berry Southern Shortcakes with Chantilly

Alabama

DEEP-DISH BLACKBERRY LATTICE PIE WITH CLASSIC SOUTHERN PIE PASTRY

In days gone by, the milder, unadulterated "leaf lard" with genuine, pure pork-fat flavor was widely available, but now it can be found only in some butcher shops and select supermarkets. The more flavorful commercial lard available in today's supermarkets tends to contain preservatives and has usually been hydrogenated, which can make it difficult to dissolve. Nevertheless, it makes a distinctive and, many feel, superlative pie crust. Lard crusts tend to be crispier and flakier than other types of pie crust. Its flavor complements rich berry pies, and when you have a juicy fruit filling, a crisper crust is preferable to help hold in those yummy juices.

FOR THE PIE PASTRY:

2½ cups (10 oz/315 g) sifted all-purpose (plain) flour
¾ teaspoon salt
½ cup (4 oz/125 g) lard, cut into ¼-in (6-mm) dice, chilled
2–4 tablespoons ice water

FOR THE FILLING:

½ cup (4 oz/125 g) sugar
2 tablespoons cornstarch (corn flour)
¼ teaspoon ground nutmeg
8 cups (2 lb/1 kg) fresh blackberries
5 tablespoons (3 fl oz/80 ml) fresh lemon juice

❋ To make the pastry, in a bowl, stir together the flour and salt. Using a pastry blender, 2 knives or a fork, cut in the lard until the mixture resembles coarse crumbs. Sprinkle the ice water over the mixture, 1 tablespoon at a time, as needed, stirring with a fork until the dough begins to come

together but is not sticky. Divide the dough in half and shape each half into a flat disk. Wrap one of the disks in waxed paper and refrigerate.

❋ Meanwhile, on a lightly floured work surface, roll out the other dough disk into a round 10¼ in (26 cm) in diameter. Gently lift the dough frequently as you roll it and lightly reflour the surface to prevent sticking. Lightly moisten the edges of a deep 9-in (23-cm) pie pan with water. Carefully transfer the pastry to the pie pan. Fit the pastry into the pan and refrigerate.

❋ Remove the other dough disk from the refrigerator. On a lightly floured work surface, roll out the dough into a round ⅛ in (3 mm) thick and at least 10 in (25 cm) in diameter. Gently lift the dough frequently as you roll it and lightly reflour the surface to prevent sticking. Using a fluted pastry wheel, cut the dough into strips 1 in (2.5 cm) wide.

❋ Preheat an oven to 425°F (220°C).

❋ To make the filling, in a large bowl, sift together the sugar, cornstarch and nutmeg. Using a rubber spatula, gently fold in the blackberries and lemon juice until well blended.

❋ Pour the filling into the pie shell. Carefully lay half of the dough strips across the pie, spacing evenly apart and letting any extra hang over the sides. Weave in the remaining dough strips to create a lattice top. Using a small, sharp knife, trim the overhanging pastry flush with the edge. Set the pie pan on a baking sheet. Bake on the bottom oven rack for 30 minutes. Then reduce the heat to 350°F (180°C) and bake until the crust is light golden brown and crispy and the filling is bubbling, 10–15 minutes longer. If the pie crust browns too quickly, cover loosely with aluminum foil. Do not overbake.

❋ Let the pie cool in the pan on a wire rack at least 20 minutes before slicing. Serve warm or at room temperature, if you want the juices to thicken before slicing.

SERVES 8

Deep-dish Blackberry Lattice Pie with Classic Southern Pie Pastry

Louisville, Kentucky

KENTUCKY BOURBON BALLS

Kentuckians are funny about bourbon. They talk like it's sacrilegious to drink it with anything but ice and water and then they turn around and use it in enough dishes to fill a cookbook. Louisville caterer, chef and restaurateur Kathy Cary makes thousands of these decadent little confections around Christmastime, a tradition that began with her family more than thirty years ago. A couple days are set aside to prepare, roll, dip and package these sweet treats for an ever-growing list of friends and relatives. No wonder—they are filled with pecans that have soaked overnight in good Kentucky bourbon. The trick to an even cloak of chocolate is to pour it hot over the chilled fillings. Do this on a rack over waxed paper to speed cleanup. These Kentucky Bourbon Balls will keep for 2–3 weeks in the refrigerator.

1¾ cups (7 oz/220 g) very finely chopped (but not
    pulverized) pecans
¾ cup (6 fl oz/180 ml) aged Kentucky bourbon
1 cup (8 oz/250 g) salted butter, at room temperature
3 cups (12 oz/375 g) confectioners' (icing) sugar
2 lb (1 kg) semisweet chocolate chips

❋ In a glass bowl, place the chopped pecans and pour the bourbon over them. Cover with plastic wrap, refrigerate and let soak overnight.

❋ The next day, in a large mixing bowl, using an electric mixer on medium-low speed, beat together the butter and confectioners' sugar until fluffy, 3–4 minutes. Drain the pecans and discard any remaining bourbon. Add the pecans to the butter-sugar mixture and, using a rubber spatula, fold until well blended. Cover the bowl with plastic wrap and refrigerate at least 4 hours or, preferably, overnight.

❀ Working quickly, shape the chilled mixture into 1-in (2.5-cm) balls using a teaspoon and your fingers. Place the balls on baking sheets lined with waxed paper, loosely cover with plastic and refrigerate for 2 hours. Refrigerate mixture briefly and periodically during the shaping process if needed to facilitate forming into balls.

❀ Melt the chocolate chips in the top of a double boiler over barely simmering water on low heat, stirring constantly. Place the chilled balls on wire racks with closely spaced bars set over waxed paper. Use a candy dipping fork to coat the balls. Or, using a small ladle, pour a little of the melted chocolate over each ball, allowing it to cloak the ball and drip down the sides. If the chocolate becomes too thick during the coating process, return to the double boiler and heat as before. Transfer the racks of bourbon balls to baking sheets and let them set 1 hour in the refrigerator uncovered, then place in individual fluted paper candy cups. Store refrigerated between sheets of waxed paper in an airtight container.

MAKES ABOUT 6 DOZEN 1-IN (2.5-CM) BALLS

Top to bottom: Brown Sugar Short'nin' Bread, Pecan-Orange Pralines, Kentucky Bourbon Balls

Louisiana

PECAN-ORANGE PRALINES

This incredibly rich, sweet and delicious confection has been part of Louisiana cuisine since as early as 1762, though its origins are French. The praline was named after a seventeenth-century French diplomat, César du Plessis-Praslin. During Christmastime in Louisiana, pink pralines were a tradition. Originally, they were colored with cochineal (a red dye made from the dried bodies of scale insects). This adaptation uses orange zest, which makes for extraordinary pralines, fairly soft to the bite, not brittle.

3 cups (1½ lb/750 g) sugar
3 cups (12 oz/375 g) pecan halves
1⅓ cups (11 fl oz/345 ml) lowfat buttermilk
6 tablespoons (3 oz/90 g) unsalted butter
¼ teaspoon salt
1½ teaspoons baking soda (bicarbonate of soda)
1 teaspoon vanilla extract (essence)
2 tablespoons grated orange zest (see glossary)

❀ In a large, heavy saucepan over very low heat, combine the sugar, pecans, buttermilk, butter, salt and baking soda and stir. Cook, stirring, until the sugar dissolves completely, brushing down the sides of the pan with a pastry brush that has been dipped in warm water. When the sugar has dissolved, slowly bring to a boil, cooking to the soft ball stage, 236°–239°F (113°–115°C) on a candy thermometer. Avoid stirring mixture, stirring only to prevent sticking. Do not scrape down the sides to prevent sugar from crystallizing.

❀ Working quickly, remove from the heat and stir in the vanilla and orange zest. Beat rapidly with a wooden spoon until the mixture begins to cool, thicken, and the color turns opaque and lusterless. Be careful not to scrape the hard crystals from the sides of the pan. Working very quickly, drop the candy by heaping tablespoons, using a second spoon to scoop the batter off the first, onto lightly buttered parchment paper. Each praline will be about 2-in (5-cm) in diameter. Let stand at room temperature until firm. Wrap individually in waxed paper sealed closed with tape. Store in an airtight container for up to 10 days at room temperature. Do not refrigerate.

MAKES ABOUT 3 DOZEN PRALINES

The South

BROWN SUGAR SHORT'NIN' BREAD

This is the Southern version of shortbread—the traditional Scottish accompaniment to a cup of tea. In the South, shortbread is called Short'nin' Bread, and it characteristically includes brown sugar and "short'nin'" (in this case, butter), for a quick-and-easy melt-in-the-mouth cookie. This recipe is best when made a day ahead of serving.

1 cup (8 oz/250 g) salted butter, at room temperature
½ cup (3½ oz/105 g) firmly packed light brown sugar
2½ cups (10 oz/315 g) sifted all-purpose (plain) flour
¼ teaspoon salt

❀ Preheat an oven to 325°F (165°C). Lightly butter a 9-in (23-cm) springform pan.

❀ In a large mixing bowl, using an electric mixer on high speed, beat the butter for 1 minute or until creamy. Add the brown sugar and beat until light and fluffy, not grainy, about 3 minutes.

❀ On a piece of waxed paper, sift together the flour and salt, then add to the butter mixture and beat on low speed until just combined. Do not overbeat. Spread the dough smoothly and evenly into the prepared pan.

❀ Using the tines of a fork, pierce the dough surface at ½-in (12-mm) intervals, going all the way through to the bottom of the pan. Bake until golden brown and the bread pulls away from the sides of the pan, 35–40 minutes.

❀ While hot, cut into 16 triangular-shaped wedges (as you would cut a pie). Let cool completely in the pan on a wire rack before removing and serving. Store in an airtight container at room temperature for up to 4 days.

MAKES 16 WEDGES

Florida

SORGHUM TEA COOKIES

During the Civil War, when sugar was scarce, sorghum became a common substitute. Sorghum grows in stalks that, like sugarcane, yield a juice when pressed. The juice is boiled down to make sorghum syrup. Nowadays, you can find sorghum syrup in most well-stocked supermarkets, gourmet shops and health food stores or by mail-order (see Mail Order Sources). These cookies, from Margaret Agnew's Southern Traditions, *are small and dainty with a light caramel color. I like to cut them out using cookie cutters with a playing card motif; then after they cool, I sift them lightly with a dusting of confectioners' sugar. They are the perfect ending to a luncheon or bridge club social. If you don't want to bake them all at once, you can wrap the dough tightly in plastic wrap and refrigerate for up to 2 days.*

1 cup (8 oz/250 g) unsalted butter, at room temperature
¼ cup (2 oz/60 g) granulated sugar
3 eggs, at room temperature
1 cup (8 fl oz/250 ml) sorghum syrup
2 tablespoons lowfat buttermilk, at room temperature
6¾ cups (27 oz/845 g) sifted all-purpose (plain) flour
1 teaspoon baking soda (bicarbonate of soda)
2 teaspoons ground cinnamon
granulated sugar or confectioners' (icing) sugar for dusting

❊ Place the butter in a large bowl and, using an electric mixer on low speed, cream the butter. Gradually add the granulated sugar, beating on medium speed until light and fluffy. Add the eggs, one at a time, beating well after each addition. Add the sorghum syrup and buttermilk. Mix well.
❊ In a separate bowl, sift together the flour, baking soda and cinnamon. Gradually add the flour mixture to the butter mixture and stir until well blended. The dough will be sticky and elastic, similar to the texture of bread dough. Tightly wrap the dough with plastic wrap and refrigerate overnight.
❊ The next day, preheat an oven to 375°F (190°C). Lightly coat a baking sheet with vegetable cooking spray.
❊ On a generously floured work surface, roll out the dough to ¼ in (6 mm) thick. The dough will be very sticky; sprinkle lightly with flour, as needed, to prevent sticking. Using a 1½-in (4-cm) round cookie cutter, cut out the cookies, flouring the cutter between cuts. Place the cookies ¼ in (6 mm) apart on the baking sheet.
❊ Sprinkle lightly with granulated sugar. Alternatively, after the cookies are baked and cooled, using a fine-meshed sieve, dust with confectioners' sugar.
❊ Bake on the middle oven rack until crisp and golden brown, 8–10 minutes. Cool on wire racks. Store in an airtight container for up to 2 weeks.

MAKES ABOUT 9 DOZEN COOKIES

The South

PECAN TASSIES

"Tassies" are lilliputian tartlets with a cream cheese crust. Southerners fill these two-bite–sized morsels with a mixture much like that for pecan pie. According to Nathalie Dupree in her book New Southern Cooking, *tassies are "frequently served at weddings and special occasions which may require a finger-food dessert treat."*

FOR THE PASTRY:

1 package (3 oz/90 g) cream cheese, at room temperature
½ cup (4 oz/125 g) unsalted butter, at room temperature
1 cup (4 oz/125 g) sifted all-purpose (plain) flour

FOR THE FILLING:

1 egg, at room temperature
⅔ cup (4½ oz/140 g) firmly packed dark brown sugar
2 tablespoons unsalted butter, melted
1 teaspoon vanilla extract (essence)
½ teaspoon salt
¾ cup (3 oz/90 g) coarsely chopped pecans

❊ Lightly coat 2 miniature muffin pans with vegetable cooking spray, each pan having 12 muffin cups that hold 2 tablespoons each.
❊ To make the pastry, in a food processor fitted with the dough blade, combine the cream cheese and butter. Add the flour and pulse until well blended and a soft dough forms. Wrap the dough tightly in plastic wrap and refrigerate for at least 1½ hours or until ready to use.
❊ Shape the dough into 24 balls, using about 2 teaspoons of the dough for each. Wrap the balls individually in plastic wrap and refrigerate for 30 minutes.
❊ Preheat an oven to 350°F (180°C).
❊ Unwrap the dough balls, place in the prepared muffin cups and press with floured fingertips against the bottom and sides to form shells. Place the pans of pastry shells in a freezer while you prepare the filling. This helps prevent dough shrinkage while baking—the shells will not freeze during this time.
❊ To make the filling, in a medium bowl, combine the egg, brown sugar, butter, vanilla and salt and stir until well blended and smooth. Stir in the pecans. The filling will be thick.
❊ Fill each shell with 2 teaspoons of filling. Bake on the middle oven rack until a toothpick inserted in the center comes out clean and the crusts are golden brown, 20–25 minutes. Set the pans on a wire rack to cool for 5 minutes, then remove the tartlets from the pans to cool completely. Serve at room temperature. Store wrapped tightly in plastic wrap and refrigerate for up to 4 days, or wrap in freezer paper and freeze for up to 1 month.

MAKES 2 DOZEN TASSIES

South Carolina

SOUTH CAROLINA LACE COOKIES

These thin, ethereal cookies have a texture that resembles lace, with the extra Southern touch of pecans. Some recipes include oatmeal for a coarser texture. But this version is more refined and dainty—and extremely delicious.

1 cup (4 oz/125 g) pecan halves, toasted and cooled
   (see glossary)
1 cup (4 oz/125 g) sifted all-purpose (plain) flour
¼ cup (2 oz/60 g) granulated sugar
¼ cup (2 oz/60 g) firmly packed light brown sugar
½ teaspoon salt
¼ cup (2 fl oz/60 ml) light corn syrup
½ cup (4 oz/125 g) unsalted butter
½ teaspoon vanilla extract (essence)

❊ Preheat an oven to 350°F (180°C). Line 2 baking sheets with aluminum foil, placing the shiny side of the foil face down, and butter lightly.
❊ In a food processor fitted with the metal blade or in a blender, finely chop the pecans for 10–20 seconds, being careful not to pulverize. In a large bowl, combine the pecans and flour and set aside.
❊ In a large, heavy saucepan over medium-low heat, combine the granulated sugar, brown sugar, salt, corn syrup and butter. Cook, stirring constantly, until the butter has melted and both sugars have dissolved, about 5 minutes.

Clockwise from left: Sorghum Tea Cookies, Pecan Tassies, South Carolina Lace Cookies

❋ Remove the saucepan from the heat. Gradually add the flour-pecan mixture, stirring until well blended. Stir in the vanilla extract.

❋ Drop the batter by tablespoons onto the lined baking sheets, allowing only 6 cookies per baking sheet and leaving at least 3 in (7.5 cm) between the cookies to allow room to spread as they bake. Using buttered fingertips, press each cookie flat and even, to a diameter of about 3 in (7.5 cm).

❋ Bake until golden brown and bubbly, 8–10 minutes. Keeping the cookies on the aluminum foil, transfer the foil from the baking sheets to wire racks to cool for 2–3 minutes. When the cookies are firm but still warm, quickly but carefully peel the foil from the cookies and transfer them back to the wire racks to cool completely. If the cookies become too firm to remove from the foil, return them to the oven briefly to soften.

❋ Store the cookies in an airtight container between layers of waxed paper, at room temperature, for up to 4 days, or wrap in freezer paper and freeze for up to 1 month.

MAKES ABOUT 2 DOZEN COOKIES

North Carolina

GRANNY LOU'S COCONUT CAKE WITH LEMON CURD FILLING

Coconut cake is a favorite Southern dessert, often filled with lemon curd. Ray L. Overton III, an Atlanta food consultant, has many memories associated with his Granny Lou's recipe. "I remember this as a special holiday cake at my grandmother's farmhouse, a lovely Victorian homestead built in the early 1900s in North Carolina. From Thanksgiving to New Year's, the pantry, refrigerator and freezer were filled with holiday offerings." Lemon curd is a tart, yellow, chiffonlike custard that is sometimes used in place of jam in England, and is readily available at most well-stocked supermarkets or gourmet shops or by mail-order (see Mail Order Sources).

FOR THE CAKE:

½ cup (4 oz/125 g) unsalted butter, at room temperature
1¼ cups (10 oz/315 g) sugar
3 egg yolks, at room temperature
3 cups (12 oz/375 g) sifted all-purpose (plain) Southern flour (see glossary) or sifted unleavened cake flour
1 tablespoon baking powder
½ teaspoon salt
1⅓ cups (11 fl oz/345 ml) milk, at room temperature
1 tablespoon vanilla extract (essence)
½ teaspoon coconut extract (essence)
3 egg whites, at room temperature

FOR THE ICING:

1⅓ cups (11 oz/345 g) sugar
⅛ teaspoon salt
⅔ cup (5 fl oz/160 ml) water
4 egg whites, at room temperature
1 teaspoon vanilla extract (essence)
¼ teaspoon coconut extract (essence)

1 cup (10 oz/315 g) prepared lemon curd or seedless raspberry preserves
3 cups (12 oz/375 g) sweetened, shredded coconut, toasted in a preheated oven at 400°F (200°C) for 5–7 minutes, stirring often

❀ Preheat an oven to 350°F (180°C). Lightly coat two 9-in (23-cm) round cake pans with vegetable cooking spray and flour.

❀ In a large bowl, using an electric mixer on medium-high speed, beat together the butter and 1 cup (8 oz/250 g) of the sugar until light and fluffy, about 3 minutes. Add the egg yolks, one at a time, beating 20 seconds after each addition and scraping down the sides of the bowl as needed.

❀ On a piece of waxed paper, sift together the flour, baking powder and salt. Add the flour mixture to the butter-sugar mixture alternately with the milk, beginning and ending with the flour. Beat in the vanilla and coconut extracts.

❀ In another large bowl, using clean beaters, beat the egg whites until they form soft peaks. Gradually add the remaining ¼ cup (2 oz/65 g) sugar while beating until glossy stiff but not dry peaks form. Stir one third of the beaten egg whites into the batter. Then, using a rubber spatula, fold the remaining beaten egg whites into the batter.

Granny Lou's Coconut Cake with Lemon Curd Filling

❈ Pour the batter into the prepared pans and bake until a wooden skewer inserted in the center comes out clean, 25–35 minutes. Set the pans on a wire rack to cool for 5 minutes, then remove from the pans and cool completely on the wire rack.

❈ To make the icing, in a small, heavy saucepan over low heat, combine the sugar, salt and water. Stir slowly until the sugar dissolves. Increase the heat to medium-high and bring to a rolling boil. With a candy thermometer in place, cook the syrup to 230°F (110°C). At this point, in a large bowl, beat the egg whites on high speed until they form soft peaks. When the sugar syrup reaches 240°F (115°C), carefully pour it into the egg whites in a slow, steady stream while beating on high speed. Continue beating until cool, thick and glossy, about 7 minutes. Beat in the vanilla and coconut extracts.

❈ To assemble, place one of the cake layers on a serving plate. Spread the top with lemon curd to within ½ in (12 mm) from the edge. Top with the second layer. Spread the top and the sides with a thick layer of icing. Carefully press the toasted coconut onto the top and sides of the cake. Store refrigerated until ready to slice and serve.

SERVES 12–16

Top to bottom: Coca-Cola Cake, Goober Clusters

Georgia

COCA-COLA CAKE

According to Phillip Stephen Schulz in his book As American as Apple Pie, *an Indianapolis homemaker first had the inspiration for this recipe. But with the Coca-Cola Company located in Atlanta, this cake has been eagerly adopted across the South. Though there are many variations of the original recipe, almost all include this soft drink in the cake, and many of them include it in the icing. When the cake is baked, the marshmallows inside vanish, leaving only a sweet, gooey trace running throughout.*

FOR THE CAKE:

2 cups (8 oz/250 g) sifted all-purpose (plain) flour
1 cup (7 oz/220 g) firmly packed light brown sugar
½ cup (4 oz/125 g) granulated sugar
1 cup (8 oz/250 g) unsalted butter, at room temperature
1 cup (8 fl oz/250 ml) Coca-Cola
¼ cup (¾ oz/20 g) Dutch-processed cocoa powder
  (European style)
½ cup (4 fl oz/125 ml) lowfat buttermilk, at room temperature
2 eggs, lightly beaten
1 teaspoon baking soda (bicarbonate of soda)
1 teaspoon vanilla extract (essence)
2 cups (3½ oz/105 g) miniature marshmallows

FOR THE ICING:

9 oz (280 g) semisweet chocolate, coarsely chopped
½ cup (4 oz/125 g) unsalted butter
⅓ cup (3 fl oz/80 ml) Coca-Cola
⅓ cup (3 fl oz/80 ml) light corn syrup
½ cup (½ oz/15 g) miniature marshmallows for garnish

❈ To make the cake, preheat an oven to 350°F (180°C). Lightly coat a 9-by-13-in (23-by-33-cm) baking pan with vegetable cooking spray and dust with flour.

❈ In a large bowl, combine the flour, brown sugar and granulated sugar. In a heavy, medium saucepan over low heat, combine the butter, Coca-Cola and cocoa and heat until the butter has melted, stirring often. Increase the heat to medium-high and bring just to a boil, stirring often. Remove from the heat and pour over the flour mixture in the bowl, whisking constantly until well blended and smooth. Whisk in the buttermilk, eggs, baking soda and vanilla until well blended. Stir in the marshmallows.

❈ Pour the batter into the prepared pan. Bake until a toothpick inserted in the center comes out clean with just a few crumbs adhering to it, 30–35 minutes. When baked, the cake top will have a craterlike surface where the marshmallows have melted. Let the cake cool completely in the pan on a wire rack.

❈ To make the icing, in the top of a double boiler set over simmering, not boiling, water over low heat, melt the chocolate and butter, stirring constantly. Remove from the heat and whisk in the Coca-Cola and corn syrup until well blended. Set aside to cool to room temperature. Then spread the cooled icing in an even layer over the top of the cake. Sprinkle with the marshmallows. To serve, cut into squares and serve directly from the baking pan.

SERVES 12

Georgia

GOOBER CLUSTERS

In the South, kids sing about "goober peas"—a slang term derived from a West African word for "peanuts." Here the goobers provide the crunch factor in a fun and easy-to-make candy. "Eating goober peas" was a ditty that was popular among Civil War soldiers.

8 oz (250 g) semisweet chocolate chips
½ cup (3 oz/90 g) salted, roasted peanuts
½ cup (3 oz/90 g) seedless raisins

❈ Line 2 baking sheets with waxed paper and tape down the edges.

❈ In the top of a double boiler set over hot, not boiling, water over low heat, melt the chocolate, stirring continuously with a wooden spoon, until smooth, about 2 minutes.

❈ Remove from the heat, keeping the double boiler assembled to keep the chocolate liquefied. Stir in the peanuts and raisins, thoroughly coating them with chocolate.

❈ Working quickly, drop tablespoonfuls of the mixture onto the waxed paper, spacing them about 1 in (2.5 cm) apart. Let the clusters stand at room temperature until firm, about 5 hours. Store between layers of waxed paper in an airtight container at room temperature for up to 2 weeks.

MAKES ABOUT 16 CLUSTERS

Left to right: Marinated Figs with Buttermilk-Honey Sorbet, Grits Pudding with Peaches and Honey Sauce

Memphis, Tennessee

GRITS PUDDING WITH PEACHES AND HONEY SAUCE

What better place to eat grits than at the Peabody Hotel, a Memphis, Tennessee, landmark and symbol of Southern hospitality. This recipe originated in the hotel's fine dining restaurant, Chez Philippe. It is a wonderful, aromatic way to cook grits—scented with cinnamon, vanilla and lemon, spooned into bowls of sautéed peaches and cloaked with a citrus-honey sauce.

FOR THE PUDDING:

3 cups (24 fl oz/750 ml) milk, at room temperature
4 strips lemon zest, ½-by-2-in (12-mm-by-5-cm) long
   (see glossary)
1 cinnamon stick
1 cup (6 oz/185 g) quick-cooking grits
4 egg yolks, at room temperature
½ cup (4 oz/125 g) sugar
½ teaspoon vanilla extract (essence)

FOR THE PEACHES AND SAUCE:

2 large peaches
1½ teaspoons unsalted butter
½ cup (6 oz/185 g) honey
1 tablespoon grated lemon zest (see glossary)
1 tablespoon grated orange zest (see glossary)
¼ cup (2 fl oz/60 ml) water

sprigs of fresh mint for garnish

❀ To make the pudding, preheat an oven to 400°F (200°C). Lightly butter a shallow 2-qt (2-l) casserole or baking dish.
❀ Pour the milk into a heavy medium saucepan over medium-high heat. Add the lemon strips and cinnamon stick and bring to a boil. Reduce the heat to low and gradually stir in the grits. Let simmer, uncovered, stirring constantly, until the grits thicken, 4–5 minutes. Remove from the heat.
❀ In a small bowl, beat together the egg yolks, sugar and vanilla. Pour into the grits mixture and stir to combine well. Pour this mixture into the prepared dish and place on the middle oven rack. Bake until most of the liquid has evaporated, 13–14 minutes.

❦ Remove from the oven and remove and discard the lemon zest and cinnamon stick.

❦ To make the peaches and the honey sauce, peel and slice each peach into 12 slices for a total of 24 slices. In a small saucepan over medium heat, melt the butter. Add the peach slices and cook until lightly browned, 3–4 minutes. Remove the peaches from the pan and set aside. Add the honey to the pan, reduce the heat to medium-low and cook, stirring, for 4 minutes. Add the lemon and orange zests and water and cook, stirring, until slightly thickened, about 4 minutes.

❦ To serve, place 4 peach slices in each of 6 individual dishes or soup plates and spoon the grits pudding over. Cover with honey sauce and garnish with a sprig of mint.

SERVES 6

Atlanta, Georgia

MARINATED FIGS WITH BUTTERMILK-HONEY SORBET

Guenter Seeger, the German-born, Swiss-trained, Michelin-starred chef of the Ritz-Carlton Buckhead in Atlanta, developed his love of fresh, local ingredients at a young age from his parents, who were in the produce business. Today he bases his classic, yet whimsical, Euro-American regional creations on what is in season. In this recipe, Seeger creates a buttermilk, honey and citrus sorbet to showcase fresh figs, which have first been marinated in crème de cassis and then baked in buttered parchment paper.

FOR THE SORBET:

4 cups (32 fl oz/1 l) lowfat buttermilk
1 cup (8 fl oz/250 ml) heavy (double) cream
⅔ cup (8 oz/250 g) honey
juice and grated zest of 1 lemon
  (see glossary)
juice and grated zest of 1 orange
  (see glossary)

FOR THE FIGS:

¾ cup (6 fl oz/180 ml) clarified butter (see glossary)
2 lb (1 kg) fresh figs, cut in half and marinated in 1 cup
  (8 fl oz/250 ml) crème de cassis for 2 hours
1 stalk lemongrass, cut into 6 equal pieces
6 vanilla beans

❦ To make the sorbet, in a large mixing bowl, blend the buttermilk, cream, honey and the citrus juices and zests. Pour the mixture into an ice-cream freezer and freeze according to manufacturer's directions, to make a somewhat loose, creamy sorbet (not as stiff as ice cream). Keep frozen.

❦ To bake the figs, preheat an oven to 425°F (220°C). Brush six 12-in (30-cm) square pieces of parchment paper with the clarified butter. Fold the parchment sheets in half and place equal portions of the figs on one half of each sheet. Top figs with a piece of lemongrass and 1 vanilla bean. Fold the other half of the parchment over the fig mixture. Then fold the edges over together or pleat and twist the corners to seal tightly.

❦ Place the parchment parcels on a baking sheet. Bake until the figs are heated through, 6–9 minutes. Remove the figs from the oven. When cool enough to handle, cut open the parchment and remove and discard the lemongrass and vanilla beans. Carefully transfer the figs to 6 individual goblets or bowls. Top with sorbet.

SERVES 6

Mississippi

MISSISSIPPI CHRISTMAS CAKE

One of Craig Claiborne's holiday recipes is a bourbon-scented, pecan-packed cake from his cookbook Craig Claiborne's Southern Cooking. *It contains fig preserves—make your own or use a good commercial brand. This cake slices more easily after it has rested a day or has been chilled. Offer just a small slice of this very rich, festive cake with eggnog during the Christmas season.*

FOR THE FIG PRESERVES:

7 cups (3½ lb/1.75 kg) sugar
¼ cup (2 fl oz/60 ml) fresh lemon juice
6 cups (48 fl oz/1.5 l) water
4½ lb (2.25 kg) ripe, firm figs
2 lemons, coarsely chopped and seeds removed
1 cup (8 fl oz/250 ml) boiling water, or as needed

FOR THE CAKE:

1½ cups (12 oz/375 g) unsalted butter, at room temperature
2 cups (1 lb/500 g) sugar
6 eggs, at room temperature
4 cups (20 oz/625 g) all-purpose (plain) flour
1 cup (8 fl oz/250 ml) bourbon, brandy or dark rum
½ cup (4 fl oz/125 ml) dark corn syrup
1 cup (10 oz/315 g) Fig Preserves
6 cups (36 oz/1.15 kg) seedless raisins
8 cups (32 oz/1 kg) pecans, broken into pieces
2 teaspoons ground cinnamon
1 teaspoon ground nutmeg
1 teaspoon ground cloves

❦ To make the Fig Preserves, in a large, nonreactive saucepan over medium-high heat, combine the sugar, lemon juice and water and bring to a boil. Reduce the heat to medium-low and stir until the sugar has dissolved, 10 minutes. Add the figs to the syrup and cook, stirring occasionally to prevent sticking, for 10 minutes. Add the chopped lemons and continue cooking until the figs are almost translucent, about 10–15 minutes. If the syrup becomes too thick, add boiling water as needed, about ¼ cup (2 fl oz/60 ml) at a time.

❦ Remove the preserves from the heat. Reserve 1 cup (10 oz/315 g) for the cake. Let the pan of remaining preserves stand in a cool place, covered, overnight or for up to 24 hours. When ready to put into jars, bring the preserves back to a boil, then ladle into hot, sterilized half-pint (8 fl oz/250 ml) jars, leaving ¼ in (6 mm) headspace. Wipe the jar rims and seal. Process in a hot-water bath for 10 minutes (see glossary). Store in a cool, dark place for up to 12 months. Refrigerate after opening.

❦ To make the cake, preheat an oven to 275°F (135°C). Generously butter a 10-by-4-in (25-by-10-cm) tube pan.

❦ In a large bowl, using an electric mixer on medium speed, beat the butter and sugar until light and fluffy, about 5 minutes. Using a rubber spatula, scrape down the sides of the bowl. Add the eggs one at a time, beating only long enough after each addition to incorporate the yolk. Using the rubber spatula, fold in the flour. Using the electric mixer on low speed, beat until incorporated, 1 minute. Add the bourbon, brandy or rum. Add the corn syrup and preserves and beat on low until well combined, 1 minute. Fold in the raisins, pecans, cinnamon, nutmeg and cloves. Pour the batter into the prepared tube pan and smooth the top.

❦ Set the pan on the middle oven rack. Bake until golden brown on top and the cake is just set, 2½–2¾ hours. Set on a wire rack to cool for 1 hour in the pan. Unmold the cake, then wrap well in plastic wrap and store in a cool, dark place for up to 6 weeks.

SERVES 16; MAKES 9 HALF-PINTS (90 OZ/2.8 KG) PRESERVES
Photograph pages 196–197

The South

BLACK BOTTOM PIE

This beautiful pie, whose origin goes back to at least the turn of the century, is traditionally made with a gingersnap or graham cracker–crumb crust, filled with a chocolate-flavored custard, followed by a second custard layer lightened with egg whites or whipped cream and sometimes flavored with rum, and then topped with meringue. Nowadays the custard is more often topped with whipped cream.

FOR THE CRUST:

24 gingersnaps
¼ cup (2 oz/60 g) unsalted butter, melted

FOR THE FILLING:

¼ cup (2 fl oz/60 ml) cold water
1 tablespoon (1 envelope) unflavored gelatin powder
1¾ cups (14 fl oz/440 ml) milk, at room temperature
4 egg yolks, at room temperature
½ cup (4 oz/125 g) granulated sugar
1 tablespoon cornstarch (cornflour)
pinch of salt
4 oz (125 g) semisweet chocolate
1 teaspoon vanilla extract (essence)
1 cup (8 fl oz/250 ml) heavy (double) cream, chilled
⅓ cup (1½ oz/45 g) confectioners' (icing) sugar
1 tablespoon white rum

FOR THE TOPPING:

1 cup (8 fl oz/250 ml) heavy (double) cream, chilled
3 tablespoons confectioners' (icing) sugar
chocolate curls for garnish (see glossary)

✳ Preheat an oven to 375°F (190°C).
✳ To make the crust, in a food processor fitted with a metal blade, in a blender or using a rolling pin, pulverize the gingersnaps. In a deep, well-buttered 9-in (23-cm) pie pan, combine the gingersnap crumbs and melted butter. Stir until all the crumbs are moistened. Using a narrow spatula dipped in water or your fingers, press the crumb mixture firmly and evenly onto the bottom and sides of the pan. Bake on the middle oven rack until dark golden brown, 8–10 minutes. Set on a wire rack to cool completely.
✳ To make the filling, pour the cold water into a small heatproof bowl and sprinkle the gelatin over it. When the gelatin has softened for 2–3 minutes, transfer the mixture to the top of a double boiler set over simmering water over low heat. Whisking constantly, cook until the gelatin has completely dissolved. Remove from the heat, keeping the double boiler assembled to keep the gelatin liquefied.
✳ In a heavy medium saucepan over low heat, heat the milk until small bubbles begin to form around the edges. Remove from the heat and cover to keep warm.
✳ In a medium bowl, whisk together the egg yolks, granulated sugar, cornstarch and salt until the yolks are light-colored and slightly thickened, 3–4 minutes. While whisking constantly, pour in the hot milk in a thin stream, then pour the mixture back into the saucepan. Set over low heat and, stirring constantly with a wooden spoon, bring to a simmer. Simmer, stirring constantly, until the custard is steaming and thick enough to lightly coat the back of the spoon, 10–12 minutes. Do not let the mixture boil.
✳ Remove from the heat and, working quickly, strain through a fine-meshed sieve into a medium heatproof bowl. Stir the dissolved gelatin into the custard. Transfer 1 cup (8 fl oz/250 ml) of the custard mixture to a small heatproof bowl. Reserve the remaining custard for the rum layer.
✳ To make the chocolate layer, in a small, heavy saucepan over low heat, melt the chocolate, stirring constantly to prevent burning.

✳ While stirring the 1 cup (8 fl oz/250 ml) custard constantly, slowly pour in the melted chocolate until well blended. Stir in the vanilla. Gently pour the chocolate mixture into the cooled pie shell and smooth with a rubber spatula. Cover and refrigerate for at least 1 hour until set.
✳ To make the rum layer, in a medium bowl, using an electric mixer with chilled beaters on high speed, beat the cream until soft peaks form. Add the confectioners' sugar and continue to beat until stiff peaks form. Whisk in the reserved custard. Working quickly, using a rubber spatula, stir in the rum and one fourth of the whipped cream. Fold in the remaining whipped cream gently but thoroughly. Ladle the mixture into the pie and smooth with the spatula. Cover and refrigerate for 3 hours until set.
✳ Just before serving, to make the topping, in a medium bowl using an electric mixer with chilled beaters on high speed, beat the cream until soft peaks form. Add the confectioners' sugar and continue to beat until stiff peaks form. Using a rubber spatula, spread the topping evenly over the surface of the pie. Then, using a spoon, swirl and peak the whipped cream for a decorative touch. Top with the chocolate curls and serve at once.

SERVES 8

Charleston, South Carolina

HUGUENOT TORTE

Some of the earliest inhabitants of Charleston were Huguenots, French Protestants looking for religious freedom in the New World. Charlestonians for years assumed that this three-layered apple-pecan torte descended from earlier Huguenot kitchens. Then in the 1980s, John Martin Taylor, a local food writer who goes by the name "Hoppin' John," broke the scandalous news that the recipe didn't even appear until 1942 and seems to have been based on an Arkansas dessert called Ozark Pudding.

FOR THE TORTE:

⅓ cup (2 oz/60 g) all-purpose (plain) flour
1 teaspoon baking powder
2 cups (8 oz/250 g) pecan halves, toasted (see glossary)
3 eggs, at room temperature
¾ cup (6 oz/185 g) granulated sugar
2 large Granny Smith or other tart apples, unpeeled, finely chopped

FOR THE FILLING AND TOPPING:

1½ cups (12 fl oz/375 ml) heavy (double) cream, chilled
2 tablespoons confectioners' (icing) sugar
2 tablespoons Calvados
1 small Granny Smith or other tart apple, unpeeled
8 pecan halves for garnish

✳ Preheat an oven to 350°F (180°C). Lightly coat three 8-in (20-cm) round cake pans with vegetable cooking spray and dust with flour.
✳ In a large bowl, sift together the flour and baking powder and set aside. In a food processor fitted with the metal blade or in a blender, process the toasted pecans in 2 batches until finely chopped but not pulverized. Set aside.
✳ In a large bowl, using an electric mixer on high speed, beat the eggs and granulated sugar until very thick and pale, 8–10 minutes. Using a fork, stir the chopped pecans and apples into the flour mixture until well combined. Then, using a rubber spatula, fold the pecan-apple mixture into the egg mixture until well blended.
✳ Divide the batter among the cake pans and smooth the surfaces. Bake on the middle oven rack until lightly browned and just beginning to pull away from the sides of each pan, about 25 minutes. Transfer the torte layers to a wire rack and

Top to bottom: Huguenot Torte, Black Bottom Pie

let cool completely in the pans before carefully unmolding.
❋ To make the filling and topping, just before serving, pour the cream into a large bowl. Using an electric mixer with clean, chilled beaters on high speed, beat the cream until soft peaks form. Add the confectioners' sugar and Calvados and continue to beat until stiff peaks form.
❋ To assemble the cake, place 1 cooled torte layer on a cake pedestal or serving platter. Spread the top evenly with one third of the cream mixture. Repeat with the remaining two layers, leaving the sides exposed.
❋ To garnish the torte, thinly slice the apple and arrange overlapping slices in a spiral pattern on top of the cake. Arrange the pecans in the center of the spiral. Slice and serve.

SERVES 8

The Carolinas

PERSIMMON PUDDING

Bill Neal pioneered new Southern cooking in the 1980s at Crook's Corner, his restaurant in Chapel Hill, North Carolina. The recipe for this traditional holiday dessert appears in his book Biscuits, Spoonbread and Sweet Potato Pie. *For a spicier flavor, add ½ teaspoon ground ginger. Serve it warm with vanilla ice cream or, in the holiday spirit, eggnog ice cream.*

½ cup (4 oz/125 g) plus 2 tablespoons unsalted butter, at room temperature
1½ cups (12 oz/375 g) granulated sugar
3 eggs, at room temperature
2 cups (8 oz/250 g) persimmon pulp, from about 5 ripe persimmons (about 25 oz/780 g total), peeled and forced through a fine-meshed sieve with the back of a wooden spoon, and seeds discarded
1¼ cups (5 oz/155 g) sifted all-purpose (plain) flour
½ teaspoon ground nutmeg
1 teaspoon ground cinnamon
½ teaspoon salt
¾ cup (6 fl oz/180 ml) milk, at room temperature
grated zest of 1 orange (see glossary)
¼ cup (2 fl oz/60 ml) fresh orange juice
¼ cup (2 fl oz/60 ml) plus 2–3 tablespoons dark rum
2 tablespoons confectioners' (icing) sugar

❊ Preheat an oven to 325°F (165°C). Lightly coat a 9-by-12-in (23-by-30-cm) baking dish with vegetable cooking spray.
❊ In a medium bowl, using an electric mixer on low speed, beat the ½ cup (4 oz/125 g) butter and granulated sugar until creamy. Add the eggs one at a time, beating well after each addition. Add the persimmon pulp and stir until well blended.
❊ In a large bowl, sift together the flour, nutmeg, cinnamon and salt. Add the persimmon mixture, alternating with the milk and stirring after each addition. Add the orange zest and juice and the ¼ cup (2 fl oz/60 ml) rum and stir. Pour into the prepared baking dish.
❊ Bake on the middle oven rack until lightly browned and set, about 1 hour. Remove from the oven to a wire rack to cool for 10 minutes.
❊ In a small bowl, using a spoon, blend the 2 tablespoons butter, confectioners' sugar and the remaining dark rum to taste. Prick the top of the pudding all over with the tines of a fork. Spread the butter mixture evenly over the top to be absorbed by the warm pudding. Serve warm.
SERVES 16   *Photograph pages 196–197*

New Orleans, Louisiana

WHITE CHOCOLATE BREAD PUDDING

Jamie Shannon, executive chef of Commander's Palace in New Orleans, has concocted the most delicious bread pudding there is. It has been featured at various tastings and included in Lee Bailey's New Orleans, *co-authored with Commander's proprietor Ella Brennan. For a fancy presentation, serve on black dessert plates.*

FOR THE PUDDING:

4 oz (125 g) French bread, crusts removed and cut into slices ¼ in (6 mm) thick
1½ cups (12 fl oz/375 ml) half & half, at room temperature
½ cup (4 fl oz/125 ml) heavy (double) cream, at room temperature
1 egg, at room temperature
4 egg yolks, at room temperature

¼ cup (2 oz/60 g) sugar
1½ teaspoons vanilla extract (essence)
4 oz (125 g) white chocolate, melted

FOR THE WHITE CHOCOLATE SAUCE:

¾ cup (6 fl oz/180 ml) heavy (double) cream, at room temperature
4 oz (125 g) white chocolate, melted

shavings of white and dark chocolate for garnish (see glossary; optional)

❊ To make the pudding, preheat an oven to 350°F (180°C). Generously butter six ½-cup (4–fl oz/125-ml) custard cups.
❊ Cut the bread slices into strips slightly narrower than the depth of the custard cups. Place the strips on a baking sheet and bake on the middle oven rack until golden, about 10 minutes. Remove from the oven and set aside.
❊ In a small, heavy saucepan over low heat, heat the half & half and cream until hot but not boiling. Remove from the heat. In a small mixing bowl, whisk together the egg, egg yolks and sugar. Whisk 2 tablespoons of the cream into the egg mixture. Then, while whisking constantly, slowly add the egg mixture to the saucepan of cream. Stir in the vanilla.
❊ Pour the melted white chocolate into a large mixing bowl and slowly whisk in the cream mixture. Line the sides of the custard cups with the toasted bread strips, breaking the bread as necessary to fit. Strain the pudding through a fine-meshed sieve into the cups and let the bread absorb it for 10 minutes.
❊ Meanwhile, fill a medium saucepan three fourths full of water and bring to a boil. Place the cups into a 9-by-13-by-2-in (23-by-33-by-5-cm) baking pan. Add more pudding if the bread has absorbed it all. Pour enough boiling water into the pan to come halfway up the sides of the cups. Carefully place the pan on the middle oven rack. Bake until a knife inserted in the centers comes out clean, 35–45 minutes. Carefully remove the custard cups from the pan to cool completely on a wire rack. Then cover and refrigerate for 1 hour.
❊ Just before serving, make the sauce. In a small saucepan over medium-high heat, heat the cream until almost boiling. Pour the melted white chocolate into a small mixing bowl and whisk in the hot cream. Using a rubber spatula, blend until smooth.
❊ To serve, unmold the puddings by running a sharp knife around the edges of the cups and inverting onto individual plates. Serve on a pool of white chocolate sauce and garnish with shavings of white and dark chocolate, if desired.
SERVES 6

Mississippi

MISSISSIPPI MUD CAKE

There are umpteen versions of this chocolate cake, so named because its color resembles that of the deep brown-black mud of the Mississippi River. Perhaps the best known is a dense, ultrasweet chocolate sheet cake studded with pecans and marshmallows and covered in a rich chocolate icing. But earlier versions were actually lighter, more delicate cakes featuring a slight mocha flavor and no nuts. This one is baked in a Bundt pan, infused with coffee liqueur and glazed with both dark and white chocolate for an elegant, contemporary look. No one will miss the nuts and marshmallows.

2–3 tablespoons unsweetened Dutch-processed cocoa powder (European style)
2¼ cups (9 oz/280 g) sifted all-purpose (plain) flour
1 teaspoon baking soda (bicarbonate of soda)
¼ teaspoon salt
2 tablespoons instant coffee
¾ cup (6 fl oz/180 ml) boiling water
¼ cup (2 fl oz/60 ml) coffee liqueur
5 oz (155 g) unsweetened chocolate

Top to bottom: Mississippi Mud Cake, White Chocolate Bread Pudding

1 cup (8 oz/250 g) unsalted butter, cut into quarters, at
   room temperature
2 cups (1 lb/500 g) sugar
3 eggs, at room temperature

FOR THE SEMISWEET CHOCOLATE GLAZE:

4 oz (125 g) semisweet chocolate
2 tablespoons unsalted butter
½ cup (4 fl oz/125 ml) heavy (double) cream

FOR THE WHITE CHOCOLATE GLAZE:

3 oz (90 g) "confectionary coating" white chocolate
   (see glossary)
1 tablespoon unsalted butter
¼ cup (2 fl oz/60 ml) heavy (double) cream

❋ Preheat an oven to 325°F (165°C). Lightly butter a 2-qt
(2-l), 10-in (25-cm) Bundt pan, preferably nonstick, and dust
with the cocoa powder.
❋ In a medium bowl, sift together the flour, baking soda and
salt and set aside. In a small bowl, dissolve the instant coffee
in the boiling water.
❋ In a medium saucepan over medium-low heat, combine the
coffee mixture and coffee liqueur and stir until well blended.
Bring to a simmer, then reduce the heat to low. Stir in the
unsweetened chocolate and butter and cook, stirring constantly, until melted and smooth. Remove from the heat and stir
in the sugar until well blended. Transfer to a large heatproof
bowl and let cool to room temperature, about 40 minutes. Using

an electric mixer on low speed, beat the eggs into the cooled
chocolate-coffee mixture one at a time, beating well after each
addition. Beat in the flour mixture in 4 additions until just
blended and smooth, using a rubber spatula to scrape down the
sides of the bowl as needed. The batter will be very thin.
❋ Pour the batter into the Bundt pan and smooth the surface.
Bake on the middle oven rack until a toothpick inserted near
the center hole comes out clean with just a few crumbs
clinging to it, 60–70 minutes. Set on a wire rack to cool in the
pan for 15 minutes. Then invert the cake onto the rack, remove
the pan and let cool completely.
❋ To make the semisweet glaze, in a small, heavy saucepan
over low heat, combine the semisweet chocolate, butter and
cream, whisking constantly until the chocolate has melted and
the mixture is well blended. Remove from the heat and let the
mixture cool about 15 minutes until thick but still pourable.
❋ To make the White Chocolate Glaze, in a separate pan over
low heat, combine the white chocolate, butter and cream and
repeat the process as for the semisweet glaze. If either mixture
becomes too thick to pour, return to low heat for 1 minute,
whisking constantly.
❋ Pour the semisweet glaze over the cake, working from the
inside edge to the outside. Let the glaze drip down the sides.
Using a ladle, gradually drizzle in a slow, steady stream one-
half of the White Chocolate Glaze over the cake in a zigzag
pattern. Repeat with the remaining White Chocolate Glaze,
crisscrossing the first pattern. Slice and serve.

SERVES 10–12

213

Top to bottom: Minnie Pearl's Chess Cake, Lemon Buttermilk Chess Pie

Nashville, Tennessee

MINNIE PEARL'S CHESS CAKE

For more than a half century, Minnie Pearl has walked onto the stage of the Grand Ole Opry with her flowered straw hat, price tag dangling, and bellowed, "How-DEEE!" Many fans

don't know that behind their beloved comedienne is a refined woman named Sarah Cannon—and boy, can she cook. This cake, a bar cookie really, is inspired by one prepared by her household. It bakes into a moist puddinglike consistency, much like chess pie. Don't be surprised when the cake rises and then falls—it's supposed to.

1 cup (8 oz/250 g) unsalted butter or margarine, at
    room temperature
2 cups (14 oz/420 g) lightly packed light brown sugar
¾ cup (6 oz/185 g) granulated sugar
4 egg yolks, lightly beaten
1 teaspoon vanilla extract (essence)
2 cups (10 oz/315 g) all-purpose (plain) flour
2 teaspoons baking powder
¼ teaspoon salt
1 cup (4 oz/125 g) finely chopped pecans
4 egg whites

❊ Preheat an oven to 350°F (180°C). Lightly butter and flour a 9-by-13-in (23-by-33-cm) baking pan.

❊ In a medium saucepan over low heat, melt the butter. Remove from the heat and stir in the sugars, egg yolks and vanilla. In a small bowl, sift together the flour, baking powder and salt. Using a wooden spoon, fold the flour mixture into the butter-sugar mixture until well blended. Fold in the pecans.

❊ In a medium bowl, using an electric mixer on high speed, beat the egg whites until stiff peaks form. Using a rubber spatula, gently fold the beaten egg whites into the saucepan of batter. Turn the batter into the prepared pan.

❊ Bake on the middle oven rack until the cake begins to shrink away from the sides of the pan but the center is still slightly wet, 35–40 minutes. Set on a wire rack to cool for 30 minutes in the pan. Cut into bars and serve.

SERVES 18

Atlanta, Georgia

LEMON BUTTERMILK CHESS PIE

No one loves Southern classics more than Atlanta's Scott Peacock, who cooked at the Georgia Governor's Mansion with mentor Edna Lewis before becoming chef at the Horseradish Grill. Here he serves updated Southern favorites, notably this true-to-the-South Lemon Buttermilk Chess Pie, made with buttermilk and lemon juice and zest, traditional enough to serve your Southern grandmother, yet fresh and unusual enough for your West Coast dinner guests.

FOR THE PIE PASTRY:

1½ cups (7½ oz/235 g) all-purpose (plain) flour
pinch of salt
pinch of sugar
½ cup (4 oz/125 g) vegetable shortening or lard, chilled and
    cut into small pieces
3 tablespoons ice water

FOR THE FILLING:

1½ cups (12 oz/375 g) granulated sugar
1 tablespoon yellow cornmeal
1 tablespoon all-purpose (plain) flour
¼ teaspoon salt
4 eggs, at room temperature
⅓ cup (3 oz/90 g) unsalted butter, melted and cooled to
    room temperature
1 tablespoon finely grated lemon zest (see glossary)
⅓ cup (3 fl oz/80 ml) fresh lemon juice
½ cup (4 fl oz/125 ml) lowfat buttermilk, at room temperature
1 teaspoon vanilla extract (essence)

lemon slices for garnish (optional)
1 tablespoon confectioners' (icing) sugar, sifted, for garnish

❊ To make the pastry, in a large mixing bowl combine the flour, salt and sugar. Using a pastry blender, 2 knives or a fork, cut in the shortening until the mixture resembles coarse crumbs. Add the ice water and stir with a fork until blended and the dough begins to come together in a rough mass. Form into a flattened disk. On a lightly floured work surface, roll out the pastry to ¼ in (6 mm) thick, large enough to fit into a 9-in (23-cm) pie pan. Crimp the edges of the crust and prick the interior a few times with a fork. Place in the refrigerator to chill for 1 hour.

❊ Preheat an oven to 350°F (180°C).

❊ To make the filling, in a small bowl, combine the granulated sugar, cornmeal, flour and salt. In a larger bowl, beat the eggs until lemon-colored. Add the dry ingredients to the eggs, mixing well. Add the melted butter, lemon zest, lemon juice, buttermilk and vanilla and stir until well blended.

❊ Pour the mixture into the chilled crust and carefully place on the middle oven rack. Bake until the top is golden brown, the filling has set and the crust is deep brown, 35–40 minutes. Remove from the oven to a wire rack to cool. When completely cool and just before serving, garnish with lemon slices and a sprinkling of sifted confectioners' sugar.

SERVES 8

North Carolina

MORAVIAN COOKIES

The Moravians, a devout group of Protestants from Germany, have settlements in Pennsylvania, Florida, and North Carolina. Their simple, crisp, paper-thin, spicy cookies are still prepared in the restored village of Old Salem, North Carolina. You can make them easily in your own home, with this recipe adapted from John Egerton's book Southern Food. *The yield will vary, depending on the sizes and shapes of your cookie cutters. You can also order different types of Moravian cookies by mail order (see Mail Order Sources).*

½ cup (3½ oz/105 g) firmly packed light brown sugar
½ cup (4 oz/125 g) vegetable shortening
1 cup (8 fl oz/250 ml) sorghum or cane syrup (see glossary)
4 cups (16 oz/500 g) all-purpose (plain) flour
1 teaspoon ground cinnamon
1 teaspoon ground cloves
½ teaspoon ground ginger
½ teaspoon ground mace
½ teaspoon ground allspice
1 teaspoon baking soda (bicarbonate of soda)
1 teaspoon grated lemon zest (see glossary)
1 tablespoon brandy

❊ In a large mixing bowl, combine the brown sugar and shortening and, using an electric mixer on medium speed, beat until creamy. Stir in the syrup. In a separate bowl, sift together the flour, cinnamon, cloves, ginger, mace, allspice and baking soda. Gradually add the flour mixture to the brown sugar mixture and stir until well blended. Stir in the lemon zest and brandy. The dough will be very stiff. Divide the dough into equal thirds and form each into a flat disk. Wrap tightly in plastic wrap and refrigerate until thoroughly chilled, about 4 hours.

❊ Preheat an oven to 350°F (180°C). Lightly coat 2 baking sheets with vegetable cooking spray.

❊ Work with one third of the dough at a time, keeping the remaining dough in the refrigerator. On a lightly floured surface, roll out the dough ⅛ in (3 mm) thick. Using various cookie cutters, cut out the cookies, flouring the cutters frequently to prevent sticking. Place the cookies 1 in (2.5 cm) apart on the prepared baking sheets. Bake on the middle oven rack until lightly browned, 8–10 minutes. Do not overbake. Store in an airtight container for up to 3 weeks.

MAKES 2–4 DOZEN COOKIES   *Photograph pages 196–197*

Appalachia

DEEP-FRIED APPLE-PEAR PIES

In Appalachia, fried fruit pies are a traditional treat. Cookbook author Hillary Davis-Tonken lives in New York City but fell in love with Highland cuisine while visiting her parents in North Carolina. She created this recipe, a combination of Northeastern ingredients and the crescent-shaped, deep-fried fruit pies of the South. The flaky cream cheese–crust pockets hold an apple-pear filling studded with cranberries or currants and fragrant with cinnamon and a splash of orange brandy.

FOR THE PIE PASTRY:

1½ cups (7½ oz/235 g) all-purpose (plain) flour
½ cup (2 oz/60 g) unleavened cake flour
1 teaspoon salt
2 tablespoons granulated sugar
½ cup (4 oz/125 g) cream cheese, at room temperature
6–10 tablespoons (3–5 fl oz/90–160 ml) ice water

FOR THE FILLING:

¼ cup (1 oz/30 g) dried cranberries or currants
2 tablespoons Grand Marnier
2 tablespoons unsalted butter
2 small Granny Smith apples, peeled and cut into small dice
2 small Anjou or Bartlett pears, peeled and cut into small dice
⅓ cup (3 oz/90 g) granulated sugar
¼ teaspoon ground cinnamon
2 teaspoons cornstarch (corn flour)
2 tablespoons fresh lemon juice
vegetable oil for frying
2 tablespoons confectioners' (icing) sugar, sifted, for garnish

❋ To make the pastry, in a large bowl sift together the flours, salt and granulated sugar. Using a pastry blender, 2 knives or a fork, cut in the cream cheese until the mixture resembles coarse crumbs. Sprinkle the ice water over the mixture, 1 tablespoon at a time, as needed, and stir with a fork until the dough comes together easily in a ball but is not sticky. Do not overwork the dough. Wrap in plastic wrap and refrigerate for 1 hour.

❋ Meanwhile, to make the filling, in a small bowl, combine the cranberries or currants and Grand Marnier and set aside to macerate.

❋ In a large, heavy skillet over medium-high heat, melt the butter. When the foam subsides and the butter begins to brown, add apples and pears and stir well to coat. Sauté, stirring occasionally with a wooden spoon, until the fruit has softened and begins to brown, 10–15 minutes. Sprinkle in the granulated sugar and continue to cook, stirring often, until the sugar melts and begins to caramelize, about 5 minutes longer.

❋ Remove from the heat. Stir in the cinnamon. In a small cup, dissolve the cornstarch in the lemon juice and stir into the fruit mixture. Drain the cranberries or currants. Stir into the mixture in the skillet until well blended. Set aside to cool for about 10 minutes.

❋ Remove the chilled dough from the refrigerator and let sit at room temperature for 5 minutes. On a lightly floured work surface, roll out the dough ⅛ in (3 mm) thick. Using a 6-in (15-cm) diameter bowl as a guide, cut out 6 rounds, rerolling the dough scraps, if needed.

❋ Place about ¼ cup (2½ oz/75 g) filling on one half of each round about 1 inch from the edge. One at at time, use a pastry brush to wet the edges of the rounds with water. Fold the other half over the filling, pressing the edges together with the tines of a fork to seal.

❋ In a very large, heavy pot over medium-high heat, pour the oil to a depth of 4 in (10 cm) and heat to 360°F (182°C) on a deep-fry thermometer. Fry the pastries one at a time until golden brown, 2–3 minutes on each side, adjusting the heat to maintain the temperature. Remove with tongs and drain on paper towels. Cover and keep warm until all are ready to serve.

❋ While still warm, sprinkle with confectioners' sugar and serve at once.

SERVES 6

Georgia

BRANDIED SWEET POTATO PIE

A classic Southern dessert resembling pumpkin pie, this Brandied Sweet Potato Pie is moister and has a more subtle flavor. This richly aromatic version is spiked with brandy and keeps well. Use either mashed or cooked fresh sweet potatoes or canned sweet potatoes (which are sometimes labeled "yams"). This pastry recipe makes a single crust for a 9-in (23-cm) pie. If you want, substitute the Classic Southern Pie Pastry (recipe on page 202). In either case, for an evenly baked pastry, set the pie pan on a heavy-duty baking sheet (a thinner sheet might buckle) covered with aluminum foil for easy cleanup. Top with dollops of Cinnamon-scented Whipped Cream or Brandied Whipped Cream (follow directions for Chantilly, recipe page 201, adding 1 teaspoon cinnamon or 1 tablespoon brandy with the confectioners' sugar). Garnish with a cinnamon stick.

FOR THE PIE PASTRY :

1 cup (4 oz/125 g) sifted all-purpose (plain) flour
½ teaspoon salt
⅓ cup (3 oz/90 g) vegetable shortening
2½–3 tablespoons ice water

FOR THE FILLING:

1½ cups (15½ oz/485 g) firmly packed mashed cooked fresh sweet potatoes, cooled to room temperature, or canned mashed sweet potatoes or canned whole sweet potatoes (not in heavy syrup), drained and mashed
3 eggs, at room temperature
½ cup (4 oz/125 g) sugar
⅓ cup (3 fl oz/80 ml) milk, at room temperature
1 teaspoon vanilla extract (essence)
½ teaspoon ground cinnamon
½ teaspoon ground ginger
¼ teaspoon ground nutmeg
½ teaspoon salt
2 tablespoons brandy

❋ To make the pastry, in a medium mixing bowl combine the flour and salt. Add the shortening and, using a pastry blender, 2 knives or a fork, cut in until the mixture resembles coarse crumbs. Sprinkle the ice water over the mixture, 1 tablespoon at a time, as needed, stirring with a fork until the dough just begins to come together and leaves the sides of the bowl but is not sticky.

❋ Preheat an oven to 350°F (180°C).

❋ Shape the dough into a flat disk. On a lightly floured work surface, roll out the dough into a 10-in (25-cm) circle. Lightly moisten the edges of a 9-in (23-cm) pie pan with water. Transfer the pastry to the pan, being careful not to stretch it or it will shrink when baked. Fit the pastry into the pan, folding under the pastry overhang to build up the rim and crimping to form a decorative edge.

❋ Reroll the scraps of dough and, using a cookie cutter, cut out a decorative shape no larger than 3½ in (9 cm) in diameter, or several smaller ones, to garnish the top of the pie. Transfer the cutout(s) to a baking sheet lined with waxed paper and refrigerate along with the pastry-lined pie pan until ready to use.

❋ To make the filling, in a large bowl, place the sweet potatoes. Using an electric mixer on low speed, add the eggs one at a time, beating well after each addition. Add the sugar, milk, vanilla, cinnamon, ginger, nutmeg and salt and beat until well blended. Gradually pour in the brandy in a slow, steady stream, while beating until incorporated. Pour the filling into the pie shell and arrange the pastry cutout(s) on top. Set the pan on a baking sheet.

❋ Bake on the bottom oven rack until a knife inserted 1 in (2.5 cm) from the center comes out clean, 50–60 minutes. If the pie crust or filling browns too quickly, loosely drape some aluminum foil around it. Do not overbake. Serve warm or at room temperature.

SERVES 8

Appalachia

APPLE STACK CAKE

Stack cake is a traditional dessert in the east Tennessee mountains. Appalachian cooks prepare a thick jam of fresh or dried apples (depending on the season) and sandwich it between thin layers of spicy cake. Left to rest a day or two, the flavors meld and the cake becomes even more delicious. During pioneer times, the stack cake was a traditional wedding cake: Each guest would bring a cake layer to be "stacked" at the reception.

FOR THE FILLING:

1 lb (500 g) Golden Delicious apples,
   peeled, cored and thinly sliced
½ cup (4 fl oz/125 ml) water
1 cup (8 oz/250 g) sugar
¼ teaspoon ground cinnamon
⅛ teaspoon ground allspice

FOR THE CAKE:

1 cup (8 oz/250 g) unsalted butter,
   at room temperature
½ cup (4 fl oz/125 ml) molasses or
   sorghum syrup
1 cup (8 oz/250 g) sugar
2 eggs, at room temperature
¼ cup (2 fl oz/60 ml) lowfat buttermilk,
   or as needed, at room temperature
6 cups (30 oz/950 g) all-purpose (plain) flour
1 teaspoon baking soda (bicarbonate of soda)
1 teaspoon ground cinnamon

❋ To make the filling, in a nonreactive medium saucepan over medium-high heat, combine the sliced apples and water and bring to a boil. Reduce the heat to low, cover and simmer until the apples are soft and the water has evaporated, about 25 minutes. Remove from the heat. Mash the apples with the back of a fork and fold in the sugar, cinnamon and allspice. Return the pan to medium-low heat and simmer, stirring occasionally, until the sugar has dissolved and the mixture is thick, about 20 minutes. Set aside to cool.

❋ Preheat an oven to 350°F (180°C).

❋ To make the cake, in a large bowl, combine the butter, molasses or sorghum, sugar and eggs. Using an electric mixer on medium speed, beat until light and fluffy, about 4 minutes. Add the buttermilk and blend well. In a separate

Top to bottom: Apple Stack Cake, Deep-fried Apple-Pear Pies, Brandied Sweet Potato Pie

bowl, sift together the flour, baking soda and cinnamon. Using a wooden spoon, fold the flour mixture into the creamed mixture until well blended.

❋ Turn the dough out onto a lightly floured work surface. Divide dough into 10 equal portions. Using the outline of an 8-in (20-cm) round baking pan, draw a circle on waxed paper. Roll out 1 portion of the dough to fit the circle, then slide the dough circle and waxed paper onto a baking sheet and bake on the middle oven rack until golden brown, 12–14 minutes. Slide the round off the baking sheet onto a wire rack to cool, removing the waxed paper while still warm. Repeat with the remaining dough for a total of 10 baked rounds.

❋ To assemble the cake, place 1 cooled round layer onto a serving plate and spread with 1–2 tablespoons of cooled apple filling. Top with another cake layer, spread with filling and repeat, alternating cake layers with filling and ending with cake. Do not spread filling over the top cake layer. Cover tightly with plastic wrap and store at room temperature for up to two days before serving.

SERVES 15

217

Clockwise from left: Lane Cake with Brown Sugar Frosting,
Peanut Brittle, Peanut Pie

Virginia

PEANUT PIE

This pie, the ultimate ode to the peanut, was inspired by the Virginia Diner in Wakefield, Virginia. The friendly, folksy restaurant is well-known for its down-home cooking—in particular the array of menu items featuring fat Virginia peanuts. The first bite of this Peanut Pie reveals beneath its crunchy top layer of peanuts—almost like a brittle—a shimmering, sticky-sweet pecan pie–style filling, but with a more assertive flavor. If you don't have time to make a pie crust, you may use a prepackaged, store-bought shell.

4 eggs, at room temperature
1 cup (8 oz/250 g) sugar
1 cup (8 fl oz/250 ml) dark corn syrup
½ cup (4 oz/125 ml) unsalted butter, melted and cooled
1 teaspoon vanilla extract (essence)
¼ teaspoon ground cinnamon
3 cups (18 oz/560 g) lightly salted, roasted peanuts, coarsely chopped
1 deep, unbaked 9-in (23-cm) pie shell (see glossary)

❋ Preheat an oven to 350°F (180°C).
❋ In a large bowl, using an electric mixer on medium speed, lightly beat the eggs. Add the sugar, corn syrup, butter, vanilla and cinnamon and beat until well blended and thickened, about 1 minute. Stir in the peanuts until well blended.
❋ Pour the filling into the pie shell and set the pie pan on a baking sheet. Bake on the bottom oven rack until golden brown and a knife inserted 1 in (2.5 cm) from the center comes out clean, 50–70 minutes. If the pie crust or filling browns too quickly, cover loosely with aluminum foil. The very center of the pie should be slightly soft, whereas the edges and near center should be set. Do not overbake.
❋ Let the pie cool in the pan on a wire rack for 15 minutes before slicing. Serve warm or at room temperature.

SERVES 8

218

LANE CAKE WITH BROWN SUGAR FROSTING

Emma Rylander Lane of Clayton, Alabama, publishd the recipe for this famous Southern cake in her 1898 book Some Good Things to Eat. *It's usually made as a white layer cake full of coconut, raisins and nuts crowned by a fluffy frosting. Unlike the original, this version has a brown sugar frosting, flavored like penuche—a brown sugar, nut fudge.*

FOR THE CAKE:

3½ cups (10½ oz/330 g) sifted unleavened cake flour
1 tablespoon baking powder
¼ teaspoon salt
1¼ cups (10 oz/315 g) unsalted butter, at
    room temperature
2½ cups (1¼ lb/625 g) granulated sugar
1½ cups (12 fl oz/375 ml) milk, at room temperature
1½ teaspoons vanilla extract (essence)
8 egg whites, at room temperature

FOR THE FILLING:

8 egg yolks, at room temperature
1 cup (8 oz/250 g) granulated sugar
½ cup (4 oz/125 g) butter, at room temperature
1 teaspoon vanilla extract (essence)
½ teaspoon ground mace
½ cup (4 fl oz/125 ml) bourbon
½ cup (2 oz/60 g) finely chopped pecans
¾ cup (4½ oz/140 g) finely chopped golden
    raisins (sultanas)
1 cup (4 oz/125 g) firmly packed, shredded
    sweetened coconut

FOR THE FROSTING:

6 tablespoons (3 oz/90 g) unsalted butter
1 cup (7 oz/220 g) firmly packed dark brown sugar
½ cup (4 fl oz/125 ml) milk
4–5 cups (12–15 oz/375–470 g) sifted confectioners' (icing)
    sugar, or as needed
¼ cup (1 oz/30 g) pecans, finely chopped

❁ To make the cake, preheat an oven to 375°F (190°C). Lightly coat three 9-in (23-cm) round cake pans with vegetable cooking spray. Insert waxed paper cut to fit the bottom of the pans and lightly coat the waxed paper, then dust with flour.

❁ In a medium bowl, sift together the flour, baking powder and salt. In a separate large bowl, using an electric mixer on medium-high speed, beat the butter and granulated sugar until light and fluffy. On low speed, beat in the flour mixture alternately with the milk in a total of 3 additions, ending with the flour. Beat after each addition until well blended and smooth. Beat in the vanilla.

❁ In another large bowl, using an electric mixer with clean, dry beaters on high speed, beat the egg whites until stiff but not dry. Stir one fourth of the beaten egg whites into the batter until well blended. Then, using a rubber spatula, fold in the remaining egg whites until well blended. Turn the batter into the prepared pans. Bake on the middle oven rack until light golden brown and a toothpick inserted into the center of each layer comes out with just a few crumbs clinging to it, 20–30 minutes. Set the cake layers on wire racks to cool completely in the pans. Remove the cooled cakes from the pans. Peel off and discard the waxed paper.

❁ To make the filling, in a bowl, using an electric mixer on medium speed, beat the egg yolks and granulated sugar until slightly thickened and pale yellow. In a heavy, nonreactive saucepan over low heat, melt the butter. Whisk in the egg mixture and cook slowly, whisking constantly, until thick

enough to coat the back of a wooden spoon, about 15 minutes. Do not let the mixture come to a boil. Remove from the heat and stir in the vanilla, mace, bourbon, pecans, raisins and coconut until well blended.

❁ To assemble the cake, place 1 cake layer on a serving platter. Spread the top evenly with one-half of the warm filling. Top with a second cake layer and spread evenly with the remaining filling. Top with the third cake layer and set aside until ready to frost.

❁ To make the frosting, in a heavy saucepan over very low heat, melt the butter and brown sugar, stirring occasionally, until the sugar has dissolved. Increase the heat to medium and bring to a boil, stirring occasionally. Boil until slightly thickened, stirring constantly, 1 minute. Remove from the heat and let cool for 10 minutes, then transfer the frosting to a medium heatproof bowl. Using an electric mixer on high speed, beat until completely cool. Add the milk and confectioners' sugar and beat until well blended and smooth. Beat in up to 1 cup (3 oz/90 g) more confectioners' sugar, if needed, for desired consistency.

❁ Spread the frosting on the top and sides of the cake and sprinkle the top edge with the chopped pecans.

SERVES 10–12

PEANUT BRITTLE

Peanut brittle has been a favorite confection of the Deep South for nearly a century. This delightful version was inspired by a recipe from Lillian Carter, of Plains, Georgia, mother of former president Jimmy Carter. Use raw (unroasted) peanuts for this recipe. If it isn't peanut season and you're not in peanut country, check your local health food store for the freshest supply, or see Mail Order Sources.

3 cups (1½ lb/750 g) sugar
½ cup (4 fl oz/125 ml) water
1 cup (8 fl oz/250 ml) light corn syrup
3 cups (18 oz/540 g) raw peanuts
2 teaspoons baking soda (bicarbonate of soda)
¼ cup (2 oz/60 g) unsalted butter, at room temperature
1 teaspoon vanilla extract (essence)

❁ Lightly butter two jelly-roll (Swiss-roll) pans, 10½-by-15½-in (26.5-by-39.5-cm) each.

❁ In a medium heavy saucepan over medium-high heat, combine the sugar, water and corn syrup and stir constantly until the mixture comes to a boil. Using a pastry brush dipped in warm water, brush down the sides of the pan above the liquid level. Boil until mixture reaches 230°–234°F (110°–112°C) on a candy thermometer, or until it forms a loose, thin thread when a teaspoonful of the sugar syrup is dropped into a measuring glass of cold water. Add the peanuts and reduce the heat to medium. Cook, stirring, until the mixture turns golden brown and reaches 300°–310°F (150°–154°C) or the hard-crack stage, or until a teaspoonful of the mixture dropped into a measuring glass of cold water and then pressed between your thumb and forefinger separates into brittle threads that shatter easily, 15–20 minutes.

❁ Remove from the heat and stir in the baking soda, butter and vanilla. Stir until the butter melts, then pour onto the prepared pans. Spread the mixture with a buttered metal spatula, then, as it cools, use buttered fingers to pull and spread the mixture to the pan edges. Let cool completely. Using a small mallet, break the brittle into pieces and store between sheets of waxed paper in an airtight container for up to 2 weeks at room temperature.

MAKES 4 LB (2 KG)

The South

BUTTER POUND CAKE WITH ORANGE-MARMALADE GLAZE

The 18th-century version of this recipe called for a pound each of butter, flour, sugar and eggs—hence the name. This one is moist and more delicate in texture than its predecessors, but still possesses the refined, buttery flavor that makes pound cake one of the South's best-loved desserts even today. An orange-marmalade glaze seems well-suited to this cake with English roots—anything richer would mask the beauty of its simplicity.

FOR THE CAKE:

3 cups (9 oz/280 g) sifted unleavened cake flour
2 cups (1 lb/500 g) sugar
½ teaspoon baking powder
¼ teaspoon baking soda (bicarbonate of soda)
½ teaspoon salt
1 cup (8 oz/250 g) unsalted butter, at room temperature
1 cup (8 oz/250 g) lowfat sour cream, at room temperature
5 eggs, lightly beaten
4 teaspoons vanilla extract (essence)

1 cup (10 oz/315 g) orange marmalade, preferably bitter style

❀ Preheat an oven to 325°F (165°C). Lightly coat a 4-qt (4-l), 10-in (25-cm) tube pan, preferably nonstick, with vegetable cooking spray and dust with flour.
❀ To prepare the cake, in a large bowl, using an electric mixer on low speed, mix together the flour, sugar, baking powder, baking soda and salt until thoroughly combined, 30 seconds. Add the butter, sour cream and half of the beaten eggs. Beat on medium speed for 1 minute, using a rubber spatula to scrape down the sides of the bowl. Add the remaining eggs and vanilla extract. Beat until well blended and smooth, 30 seconds longer.
❀ Pour the batter into the prepared pan, smoothing the top. Bake on the middle oven rack until golden brown and a toothpick inserted 1 in (2.5 cm) from the edge of the pan comes out clean, 60–75 minutes. If the cake browns too quickly, cover the top loosely with aluminum foil.
❀ Let the cake cool in the pan on a wire rack for 20 minutes. Then gently loosen the edges of the cake with a thin knife or spatula. Invert onto the wire rack, remove the pan and cool completely. Then place on a cake pedestal or platter.
❀ To make the glaze, in a small, heavy saucepan, heat the marmalade over low heat, stirring constantly, until liquefied enough to pour, about 4 minutes. Starting from the outer top edge of the cake and working toward the inside, pour the glaze in a slow, steady stream over the cake top in a thin, even layer, letting the glaze drip down the sides. Use a moist paper towel to clean the pedestal or platter of any excess glaze. Let cool about 10 minutes and serve.

SERVES 10–12

Tennessee

SPICED JAM CAKE WITH CARAMEL GLAZE

This aromatic layer cake is especially delicious under an old-fashioned caramel icing. If in season, garnish with fresh blackberries.

FOR THE CAKE:

½ cup (4 oz/125 g) unsalted butter, at room temperature
1 cup (8 oz/250 g) granulated sugar
3 eggs, at room temperature
½ teaspoon vanilla extract (essence)

1½ cups (6 oz/185 g) sifted all-purpose (plain) flour
½ teaspoon ground allspice
½ teaspoon ground cinnamon
½ teaspoon ground cloves
½ teaspoon baking soda (bicarbonate of soda)
¼ teaspoon salt
½ cup (4 fl oz/125 ml) lowfat buttermilk, at room temperature
1½ cups (15 oz/470 g) seedless blackberry jam
½ cup (3 oz/90 g) seedless raisins
½ cup (2 oz/60 g) finely chopped black walnuts (see glossary) or pecans

FOR THE CARAMEL GLAZE:

¼ cup (2 oz/60 g) unsalted butter, at room temperature
½ cup (3½ oz/105 g) firmly packed dark brown sugar
¼ cup (2 fl oz/60 ml) milk, or as needed, at room temperature
2 cups (6 oz/185 g) sifted confectioners' (icing) sugar
1 teaspoon vanilla extract (essence)

❀ Preheat an oven to 325°F (165°C).
❀ To make the cake, lightly coat two 8-in (20-cm) round cake pans with vegetable cooking spray. Insert waxed paper cut to fit the bottom of the pans and lightly coat the waxed paper with cooking spray. Flour the waxed paper and sides of the pans.
❀ In a large bowl, using an electric mixer on medium-high speed, beat the butter and granulated sugar until light and fluffy. Add the eggs one at a time, beating well after each addition. Blend in the vanilla.
❀ On a piece of waxed paper, sift together the flour, allspice, cinnamon, cloves, baking soda and salt. Gradually add the flour mixture, then the buttermilk and blackberry jam to the creamed mixture, while beating on medium speed until well blended. Using a rubber spatula, fold in the raisins and nuts.
❀ Pour the batter into the prepared pans and bake on the middle oven rack until the cake begins to pull away from the sides of the pans and a toothpick inserted in the center comes out clean, 45–50 minutes. Cool in the pans for 10 minutes, then remove from the pans to a wire rack and let cool completely. Remove and discard the waxed paper.
❀ To make the glaze, in a medium saucepan over medium-low heat, melt the butter. Add the brown sugar and cook, stirring, for 2 minutes. Add the milk and continue to cook, stirring constantly, until the mixture boils. Remove from the heat and gradually whisk in the confectioners' sugar. Blend in the vanilla. If the glaze gets too thick, add a little more milk and blend quickly.
❀ To assemble, place one cake layer on a serving plate. Top with one third of the glaze. Top with the second cake layer and pour the remaining glaze over the cake, smoothing the glaze with a spatula.

SERVES 12

The South

UPSIDE-DOWN PINEAPPLE GINGERBREAD

In the South, gingerbread is often made in a cast-iron skillet. This one has a pineapple topping—so you have two desserts in one: a gingerbread and an upside-down cake. Top with dollops of Ginger-Scented Whipped Cream. (Follow directions for Chantilly, recipe on page 201, folding in ½ teaspoon ground ginger just before serving.) If you'd like, garnish with finely chopped crystallized ginger.

¾ cup (6 oz/185 g) unsalted butter, at room temperature
1 cup (7 oz/220 g) firmly packed dark brown sugar
6 slices canned pineapple rings (in natural juice), drained
6 perfect maraschino cherries, stemmed, or
   6 perfect pecan halves
1 egg, lightly beaten, at room temperature

Clockwise from top left: Butter Pound Cake with Orange-Marmalade Glaze, Spiced Jam Cake with Caramel Glaze, Upside-down Pineapple Gingerbread

¼ cup (2 fl oz/60 ml) molasses

1½ cups (6 oz/185 g) sifted all-purpose (plain) Southern flour (see glossary) or sifted unleavened cake flour

2 teaspoons ground ginger

1 teaspoon ground cinnamon

¼ teaspoon ground nutmeg

¼ teaspoon ground cloves

¾ teaspoon baking soda (bicarbonate of soda)

¼ teaspoon salt

⅓ cup (3 fl oz/80 ml) boiling water

1 teaspoon vanilla extract (essence)

❋ Preheat an oven to 350°F (180°C). Lightly coat a 9-in (23-cm) round, well-seasoned cast-iron skillet with vegetable cooking spray.

❋ Set the skillet over low heat and melt ¼ cup (2 oz/60 g) of the butter. Add ½ cup (3½ oz/110 g) of the brown sugar and stir until the sugar melts. Continue to cook, stirring, until the sugar mixture is thick and dark brown in color, about 2 minutes.

❋ Working quickly, remove skillet from the heat and arrange the pineapple rings around the perimeter of the hot skillet, placing one in the center. Inside each pineapple ring, place either a single maraschino cherry or a pecan half, flat side up.

❋ In a large bowl, using an electric mixer on low speed, beat together the remaining ½ cup (4 oz/125 g) butter and ½ cup (3½ oz/110 g) brown sugar until light and fluffy, about 1 minute. Add the egg and molasses and continue to beat until well blended.

❋ On a piece of waxed paper, sift together the flour, ginger, cinnamon, nutmeg, cloves, baking soda and salt. In a small cup, combine the boiling water and vanilla. Gently fold the flour mixture into the butter-sugar mixture, alternating with the boiling water mixture. Do not overmix. Pour the batter into the prepared skillet, smoothing the surface with a spatula.

❋ Bake on the middle oven rack until the cake springs back when pressed lightly in the center, 35–40 minutes. Set the skillet on a wire rack to cool for 5 minutes, then invert the cake onto a serving plate. Slice into wedges and serve warm.

SERVES 8–10

Hummingbird Cake

HUMMINGBIRD CAKE

Southern Living magazine of Birmingham, Alabama, figures this *triple-decker cake is their most requested recipe. Originally published in February 1978, it has won countless blue ribbons at county fairs and accolades at church suppers across the South. The story goes that it tastes so good you'll hum when you eat it.*

FOR THE CAKE:

3 cups (15 oz/470 g) all-purpose (plain) flour
2 cups (1 lb/500 g) granulated sugar
1 teaspoon baking soda (bicarbonate of soda)
1 teaspoon ground cinnamon
½ teaspoon salt
3 eggs, lightly beaten
¾ cup (6 fl oz/180 ml) vegetable oil
1½ teaspoons vanilla extract (essence)
8 oz (250 g) canned crushed pineapple, packed in
    unsweetened juice, undrained
1 cup (4 oz/125 g) finely chopped pecans
1¾ cups (10 oz/315 g) mashed ripe bananas, about 3

FOR THE CREAM CHEESE FROSTING:

½ cup (4 oz/125 g) unsalted butter or margarine, at
    room temperature
8 oz (250 g) cream cheese, at room temperature
1 lb (500 g) confectioners' (icing) sugar, sifted
1 teaspoon vanilla extract (essence)
½ cup (2 oz/60 g) finely chopped pecans

❋ To make the cake, preheat an oven to 350°F (180°C). Lightly coat three 9-in (23-cm) round cake pans with vegetable cooking spray and dust with flour.
❋ In a large mixing bowl, combine the flour, granulated sugar, baking soda, cinnamon and salt. Add the beaten eggs and oil and stir until the dry ingredients are moistened. Do not beat. Stir in the vanilla, pineapple and juice, pecans and mashed bananas.

❋ Pour the batter into the prepared pans. Bake on the middle oven rack until a toothpick inserted in the centers comes out clean, about 25 minutes. Cool in the pans on a wire rack for 10 minutes. Then invert onto the wire racks, remove the pans and cool completely.
❋ To make the frosting, in a large bowl, using an electric mixer on medium speed, beat together the butter and cream cheese for 2 minutes. Gradually add the confectioners' sugar, beating on low speed until light and fluffy. Stir in the vanilla and pecans.
❋ Assemble the cake, spreading the frosting between the layers and on the top and sides.

SERVES 15

SHAKER LEMON PIE

In the early 1800s, Shaker missionaries from New York and New England established a religious community in Pleasant Hill, Kentucky. The fellowship lasted little more than a century, but the Shaker influence lives on in their craftsmanship and cooking. You can still try this pie at the Shaker Village, a living history museum. Shaker Lemon Pie uses lemon slices, rind and all, so make it only with the thinnest-skinned, unwaxed lemons.

FOR THE FILLING:

2 large thin-skinned lemons, washed, thinly sliced
    and seeded
2 cups (1 lb/500 g) sugar
4 eggs, lightly beaten

FOR THE PIE PASTRY:

2 cups (8 oz/250 g) sifted all-purpose (plain) flour
1 teaspoon salt
⅔ cup (5 oz/155 g) vegetable shortening
3 tablespoons ice water, plus 2 tablespoons ice
    water if needed

❋ In a nonreactive bowl, combine the lemon slices and sugar. Cover with plastic wrap and let stand at room temperature for 2 hours, stirring occasionally.
❋ Meanwhile, to make the pie pastry, in a large bowl combine the sifted flour and salt. Using a pastry blender, 2 knives or a fork, cut in half of the shortening until the mixture resembles coarse crumbs. Cut in the remaining shortening until it resembles small peas. Sprinkle the 3 tablespoons ice water over the mixture. Stir gently with a fork until the dough begins to come together, adding more of the remaining ice water if needed. The mixture should be moist enough to form a ball but not sticky. Divide the dough in half, shape each half into a ball and flatten slightly. On a lightly floured work surface, roll out one ball into a round about 11 in (28 cm) in diameter. Carefully drape the pastry around the rolling pin and unroll into a 9-in (23-cm) pie pan, without stretching the pastry. Fit the pastry into the pan, trimming the edge even with the rim. Place in the refrigerator. For the top crust, place the remaining dough between 2 sheets of waxed paper and roll out into a circle about 11 in (28 cm) in diameter. Place in the refrigerator.
❋ Preheat an oven to 450°F (230°C).
❋ Add the beaten eggs to the lemon mixture and blend well. Turn into the pie crust, arranging the lemon slices evenly. Cover with the top pie crust. Crimp the edges and cut several slits for steam in the center. Bake 15 minutes, then reduce the heat to 375°F (190°C) and bake until a knife inserted near the center comes out clean, about 20 minutes longer. Cool completely before slicing.

SERVES 8

Deep South

SCRIPTURE CAKE

This cake is basically a variation of the famous American 1-2-3-4 cake (1 cup of butter, 2 cups of sugar, 3 cups of flour and 4 eggs), but its name comes from its clever references to Scripture. Though many households across the United States have made one form or another of Scripture Cake, it is especially prevalent in the Bible Belt of the South. Some treat it like a fruitcake and soak it in liquor, letting the flavors mellow with age before serving. Or you can dust the cake with cocoa and sugar as a fancy snacking cake. The references listed in the ingredient list refer to passages in A New American Standard Translation of the Bible.

3½ cups (14 oz/440 g) sifted all-purpose (plain) flour
   (from 1 Kings 4:22)
2 teaspoons baking powder (from Amos 4:5)
pinch of salt (from Leviticus 2:13)
1½ teaspoons ground cinnamon (from 1 Kings 10:2)
1 teaspoon ground allspice (from 1 Kings 10:2)
1 teaspoon ground nutmeg (from 1 Kings 10:2)
½ teaspoon ground cloves (from 1 Kings 10:2)
1 cup (8 oz/250 g) unsalted butter, at room temperature
   (from Judges 5:25)
2 cups (1 lb/500 g) granulated sugar (from Jeremiah 6:20)
6 tablespoons (4½ oz/140 g) honey (from Exodus 16:31)
6 eggs, at room temperature (from Isaiah 10:14)
1 cup (8 fl oz/250 ml) milk, at room temperature
   (from Judges 4:19)

2 cups (12 oz/375 g) seedless raisins (from Samuel 30:12)
2 cups (12 oz/375 g) dried figs, coarsely chopped (from
   Nahum 3:12)
2 cups (8 oz/250 g) sliced (flaked) almonds, toasted and
   cooled (see glossary) (from Numbers 17:8)
1 tablespoon confectioners' (icing) sugar for dusting
1 teaspoon Dutch-processed cocoa powder (European style)
   for dusting

※ Preheat an oven to 350°F (180°C). Lightly coat a 9-by-13-in (23-by-33-cm) baking pan with vegetable cooking spray and dust with flour.
※ In a large bowl, sift together the flour, baking powder, salt, cinnamon, allspice, nutmeg and cloves.
※ In another large bowl, combine the butter, granulated sugar and honey. Using an electric mixer on medium-high speed, beat until well blended, about 1 minute. Add the eggs one at a time, beating well after each addition. While beating, gradually add the flour mixture, alternating with the milk until well blended, about 2 minutes. Using a rubber spatula, fold in the raisins, figs and almonds until well blended.
※ Pour the batter into the prepared pan and spread evenly. Bake on the middle oven rack until the cake begins to pull away from the sides of the pan and a toothpick inserted in the center comes out clean, 45–50 minutes. Cool completely in the pan on a wire rack.
※ When ready to serve, lightly sift the confectioners' sugar evenly over the cooled cake. Gently place a doily cut to fit on the surface of the cake and sift the cocoa powder over it. Lift carefully to reveal the decorative pattern.

SERVES 12–16

Top to bottom: Shaker Lemon Pie, Scripture Cake

Kentucky

JEFFERSON DAVIS PIE

This pie, a relative of the chess pie (recipe on page 215), is believed to have been created by a former slave named Mary Ann around the time of the Civil War. Mary Ann cooked for a Missouri merchant who admired Jefferson Davis and named this pie for him.

½ cup (4 oz/125 g) unsalted butter, at room temperature
1 cup (7 oz/220 g) firmly packed light brown sugar
1 tablespoon all-purpose (plain) flour
3 eggs, at room temperature
1 cup (8 fl oz/250 ml) light (single) cream, at room temperature
½ teaspoon vanilla extract (essence)
1 teaspoon ground cinnamon
½ teaspoon ground allspice
¾ teaspoon ground nutmeg
½ cup (3 oz/90 g) finely chopped pitted dates
½ cup (3 oz/90 g) golden raisins (sultanas)
1 deep, unbaked 9-in (23-cm) pie shell (see glossary)
Brandied Whipped Cream (see recipe headnote page 216)

❈ Preheat an oven to 350°F (180°C).
❈ In a large bowl, using an electric mixer on low speed, combine the butter and sugar and beat until light and fluffy, 2 minutes. Beat in the flour. Beat in the eggs one at a time, beating well after each addition. Add the cream, vanilla, cinnamon, allspice and nutmeg and beat until well blended and smooth. Stir in the dates and raisins until well blended.
❈ Pour the filling into the pie shell and set the pie pan on a baking sheet. Bake on the middle oven rack until a knife inserted 1 in (2.5 cm) from the center comes out clean, about 45 minutes. If the pie crust or filling browns too quickly, cover loosely with aluminum foil. Do not overbake.
❈ Let the pie cool in the pan on a wire rack for 30 minutes before slicing. Serve warm or at room temperature with Brandied Whipped Cream.

SERVES 8

South Georgia

CHOCOLATE PECAN PIE

Pecan pie is no doubt the quintessential Southern dessert. Here is a deep-dish pecan pie to top all others—laced with chocolate and chock-full of pecans in the luscious filling and even in the crust.

FOR THE PIE PASTRY:

1¾ cups (7 oz/220 g) sifted all-purpose (plain) flour
½ teaspoon salt
6 tablespoons (3 oz/90 g) unsalted butter, cut into ¼-in (6-mm) dice, chilled
¼ cup (2 oz/60 g) vegetable shortening
½ cup (2 oz/60 g) pecan halves
2–4 tablespoons ice water, as needed

FOR THE FILLING:

3 oz (90 g) unsweetened chocolate
½ cup (4 oz/125 g) unsalted butter
4 eggs, at room temperature
1 cup (8 oz/250 g) sugar
1 cup (8 fl oz/250 ml) dark corn syrup
1 teaspoon vanilla extract (essence)
¼ teaspoon salt
3 cups (12 oz/375 g) pecan halves

1 oz (30 g) semisweet chocolate for garnish
8 pecan halves for garnish

praline or chocolate swirl ice cream for serving

❈ To make the pie pastry, in a medium bowl stir together the flour and salt. Using a pastry blender, 2 knives or a fork, cut in the butter and shortening until mixture resembles coarse crumbs. In a food processor fitted with the metal blade or in a blender, finely chop the pecans, but do not pulverize. Stir the chopped pecans into the flour mixture. Sprinkle the ice water over the mixture, 1 tablespoon at a time, as needed, stirring with a fork until the dough just begins to come together but is not sticky. Shape the dough into a flat disk, wrap tightly in waxed paper and refrigerate for 30 minutes.
❈ Meanwhile, to begin the filling, in a small, heavy saucepan over very low heat, melt the unsweetened chocolate and butter, stirring constantly. Transfer to a small heatproof bowl and let cool to room temperature.
❈ Preheat an oven to 350°F (180°C).
❈ On a lightly floured work surface, roll out the chilled dough into a round 10 in (25 cm) in diameter. Lightly moisten the edges of a deep 9-in (23-cm) pie pan with water. Carefully transfer the pastry to the pie pan. Fit the pastry into the pan, fold the edges under and crimp to form an attractive edge. If the pecans cause the dough to break apart, use your fingers to "patch" the pastry into the pan by gently pressing it in place. Refrigerate the pie shell until ready to fill.
❈ To finish the filling, in a large bowl, using an electric mixer on medium speed, lightly beat the eggs. Add the sugar, corn syrup, vanilla and salt and beat until well blended and thickened, about 1 minute. Beat in the cooled chocolate mixture. Stir in the pecan halves until well blended.
❈ Pour the filling into the pie shell and set the pie pan on a baking sheet. Bake on the bottom oven rack until the filling is puffy, the top is crisp with a few cracks and a knife inserted 1 in (2.5 cm) from the edge comes out clean, 1–1½ hours. If the pie crust or filling browns too quickly, cover loosely with aluminum foil. The very center of the pie should be slightly soft, whereas the edges and near center should be set. Do not overbake.
❈ Meanwhile, to make the garnish, in a small, heavy saucepan over very low heat, melt the semisweet chocolate, stirring constantly. Remove from the heat. Dip each of the 8 pecan halves halfway into the chocolate and then place them on a baking sheet lined with waxed paper. Refrigerate until ready to serve.
❈ Let the pie cool in the pan on a wire rack for 30 minutes before slicing. Serve warm or at room temperature. Just before serving, working quickly, place small scoops of ice cream on top of the pie at 8 evenly spaced intervals. Insert a chocolate-covered pecan into each scoop, chocolate tip up. Serve at once.

SERVES 8

Williamsburg, Virginia

PUMPKIN CARAMEL-PRALINE FUDGE ICE CREAM

Chef Marcel Desaulniers, co-owner of the Trellis restaurant in Williamsburg, Virginia, has become known for his truly decadent desserts—he's the author of Desserts to Die For.

FOR THE PUMPKIN ICE CREAM:

2 cups (16 fl oz/500 ml) heavy (double) cream, at room temperature
1 cup (8 fl oz/250 ml) milk, at room temperature
1 cup (8 oz/250 g) sugar
¼ teaspoon ground nutmeg
6 egg yolks, at room temperature
1½ cups (12 oz/375 g) fresh or canned pumpkin purée
¼ cup (2 fl oz/60 ml) bourbon

FOR THE CHOCOLATE FUDGE SAUCE:

Clockwise from left: Chocolate Pecan Pie, Jefferson Davis Pie, Pumpkin Caramel-Praline Fudge Ice Cream

4 oz (125 g) semisweet chocolate, broken into 8 pieces
1 oz (30 g) unsweetened chocolate, broken into 2 pieces
½ cup (4 fl oz/125 ml) heavy (double) cream
2 tablespoons unsalted butter

FOR THE CARAMEL SAUCE:

1 cup (8 fl oz/250 ml) heavy (double) cream
¼ cup (2 oz/60 g) unsalted butter
½ cup (4 oz/125 g) sugar
⅛ teaspoon fresh lemon juice

FOR THE CHOCOLATE-PECAN PRALINE:

1 cup (4 oz/125 g) pecan pieces, toasted (see glossary)
1 cup (8 oz/250 g) sugar
¼ teaspoon fresh lemon juice
1 oz unsweetened chocolate, chopped into ¼-in (6-mm) pieces

❊ To make the Pumpkin Ice Cream, in a heavy, medium saucepan over medium-high heat, combine the cream, milk, ½ cup (4 oz/125 g) of the sugar and nutmeg. Cook, stirring constantly, until the sugar has dissolved and then bring the mixture to a boil.

❊ While the cream mixture is heating to a boil, place the egg yolks and remaining sugar in a large bowl. Using an electric mixer, fitted with a paddle if available, beat on high speed for 2–2½ minutes. Scrape down the sides of the bowl. Continue beating on high until slightly thickened and lemon-colored, about 2½–3 minutes longer. Reduce the mixer speed to low and continue to mix until the cream mixture is boiling.

❊ Pour the boiling cream mixture into the beaten egg yolks and whisk to combine. Pour this mixture back into the saucepan and place over medium-high heat, stirring constantly until temperature reaches 185°F (85°C) on a candy thermometer, about 1 minute.

❊ Remove from the heat and strain through a fine-meshed sieve to a stainless steel bowl. Add the pumpkin purée and bourbon and stir to combine. Place the bowl in an ice water bath and cool to 40°–45°F (5°–7°C), about 15 minutes. When the mixture has cooled, pour into an ice-cream freezer and freeze according to the manufacturer's directions.

❊ Meanwhile, to make the Chocolate Fudge Sauce, place the chocolates in a medium stainless steel bowl. In a small saucepan over medium-high heat and stirring occasionally, heat the cream and butter until boiling. Pour the boiling mixture over the chocolates and let stand 5 minutes, then whisk until smooth. Set aside to cool to room temperature.

❊ To make the Caramel Sauce, in a small saucepan over low heat, heat the cream and butter until the butter melts. In a large saucepan over medium-high heat, whisk together the sugar and lemon juice. Cook to caramelize, whisking constantly, for 4 minutes. The sugar will turn clear as it liquefies, then light brown as it caramelizes. Slowly add the hot cream and butter, whisking briskly to combine. Remove from the heat and pour into a large stainless steel bowl. Set aside to cool to room temperature.

❊ To make the Chocolate-Pecan Praline, place the pecans in a buttered pie pan and spread them out in an even layer. In a large saucepan over medium-high heat, whisk together the sugar and lemon juice. Cook to caramelize, whisking constantly, for 4 minutes. Remove from the heat and add the chopped chocolate, stirring to melt. Immediately pour the caramel mixture over the pecans to cover. Place the pan in a freezer to harden, about 15 minutes. Remove the praline from freezer and chop it into ⅛-in (3-mm) pieces.

❊ To finish, transfer the pumpkin ice cream to a large plastic container. Using a large rubber spatula, fold in the chopped praline. Add the Chocolate Fudge Sauce and give the mixture 2 folds. Then add the Caramel Sauce and give the mixture 5 or 6 folds. Cover the container and place in a freezer for 2–3 hours before serving.

SERVES 10

Fresh Lemon Meringue Pie

FRESH LEMON MERINGUE PIE

Good food accompanied good stories in the Monroeville, Alabama, household in which Truman Capote was reared. One of the writer's favorite desserts—and the inspiration for this recipe—was a lemon meringue pie created by Sook Faulk, the family cook. In Sook's Cookbook, Capote's aunt Marie Rudisill quoted Sook's description of the pie, "I make it sour enough to make a pig squeal." Topped with a soft, billowy, stippled meringue, this Fresh Lemon Meringue Pie recipe has a pure lemon-flavored filling, which, unbeknownst to many, is due to the addition of extra lemon zest, not juice.

1 baked deep 9-in (23-cm) pie shell, cooled to room temperature (see glossary)

FOR THE FILLING:

1 cup (8 oz/250 g) sugar
6 tablespoons (1 oz/30 g) cornstarch (corn flour)
1½ cups (12 fl oz/375 ml) cold water
6 egg yolks, lightly beaten
2 tablespoons unsalted butter, at room temperature
⅓ cup (3 fl oz/80 ml) fresh lemon juice
2 tablespoons grated lemon zest, from 6–10 lemons
¼ teaspoon salt
1 tablespoon (1 envelope) unflavored gelatin powder
¼ cup (2 fl oz/60 ml) boiling water

FOR THE MERINGUE:

1 tablespoon cornstarch (corn flour)
⅓ cup (3 fl oz/80 ml) cold water
6 egg whites, at room temperature
½ teaspoon cream of tartar
½ teaspoon vanilla extract (essence)
½ cup (4 oz/125 g) sugar

❈ Preheat an oven to 350°F (180°C).

❈ To make the filling, in a heavy, medium nonreactive saucepan off heat, whisk together the sugar, cornstarch and water until well blended. Set over medium-high heat. Cook, whisking constantly but gently, until the mixture thickens and bubbles, about 6 minutes.

❈ Immediately remove from the heat. Place the beaten egg yolks in a small bowl and whisk in ¼ cup (2 fl oz/60 ml) of the hot mixture until blended. Whisk this mixture back into the saucepan until well blended. Set the pan over low heat and bring to a simmer. Cook, whisking constantly but gently, until the mixture is very thick and glossy, about 3 minutes longer.

❈ Immediately remove from the heat. Gently whisk in the butter, lemon juice, lemon zest and salt until the butter has melted and the mixture is well blended. Sprinkle the gelatin over a heatproof bowl filled with the boiling water, and let stand for 1 minute to soften. Whisk until the gelatin is dissolved. Then whisk the dissolved gelatin into the filling until well blended. Pour the piping hot mixture into the cooled baked pie shell.

❈ To make the meringue, in a small, heavy saucepan off heat, combine the cornstarch and water and whisk until well blended. Set over low heat and bring to a simmer, whisking constantly but gently, until the mixture has thickened and becomes clear, 4–6 minutes. Remove from the heat and transfer to a small, heatproof bowl to cool completely. Set aside.

❈ In a large bowl, using an electric mixer on medium speed, beat the egg whites, cream of tartar and vanilla until frothy, about 1 minute. Do not overbeat. Gradually add the sugar, 1 tablespoon at a time, while beating on high speed until all the sugar is incorporated and mixture forms soft peaks. Gradually beat in the cooled cornstarch mixture 1 tablespoon at a time. Continue to beat until glossy, stiff, but not dry peaks form, about 2 minutes longer. When the beaters are raised and turned upside down, the peaks should lean over slightly but hold their shape.

❈ Working quickly, transfer the meringue to a pastry bag fitted with a #8 star tip. Working quickly, pipe meringue rosettes on top of the hot lemon filling, working from the outside toward the center and making sure the meringue attaches to the pie crust. Cover the filling completely with two-thirds of the meringue. Pipe the remaining meringue in a second layer of rosettes in the center of the pie to make a rounded top. Alternatively, spread the meringue evenly over the top to the edges of the pie crust with a rubber spatula.

❈ Bake on the middle oven rack until the meringue is golden brown, 25–30 minutes. Set on a wire rack to cool to room temperature. Cover loosely and refrigerate until chilled firm enough to slice, about 2 hours.

SERVES 8

Atlanta, Georgia

RUM-SOAKED DRIED PEACH FRUITCAKE

Calvin Trillin once wrote a column suggesting that there is only one fruitcake in the world and that it changes hands every holiday season because no one really likes this dense doorstop of a dessert. Well, believe it or not, Southerners do. Bakeries from Georgia to Texas turn out thousands of fruitcakes, and most people have an old family recipe somewhere. Fruitcakes come in many hues, from white to midnight black, but this one is an in-between caramel. Rather than using candied fruits, it derives its sweetness from dried peaches, crystallized ginger and rum.

For a special presentation, decorate the top of the cake by holding a paper doily in place while sifting confectioners' (icing) sugar over it. Carefully remove the doily to reveal the lacy pattern. Alternatively, brush the top of the loaf with heated light corn syrup, arrange a row of overlapping dried peach halves cut to form half-moons, and sprinkle with chopped crystallized ginger. For easy chopping of crystallized ginger or dried fruits, lightly coat your knife blade or food processor blade with vegetable cooking spray.

1 cup (4 oz/125 g) coarsely chopped pecans
1½ cups (8 oz/250 g) coarsely chopped dried peaches
1 cup (6 oz/185 g) golden raisins (sultanas)
⅓ cup (2 oz/60 g) finely chopped crystallized ginger
1 cup (4 oz/125 g) sifted all-purpose (plain) flour
1 teaspoon baking powder
½ teaspoon salt
1 teaspoon ground ginger
1 teaspoon ground cinnamon
¼ teaspoon ground nutmeg
½ cup (4 oz/125 g) unsalted butter, at
   room temperature
½ cup (3½ oz/105 g) firmly packed dark
   brown sugar
3 eggs, at room temperature
grated zest of 3 oranges (see glossary)
¼ cup (2 fl oz/60 ml) dark molasses
¼ cup (2 oz/60 g) sour cream, at room temperature
¼ cup (2 fl oz/60 ml) dark rum or bourbon plus dark
   rum or bourbon to taste (optional)

❈ Preheat an oven to 300°F (150°C). Lightly coat a 9-by-5-by-3-in (23-by-13-by-7.5-cm) loaf pan with vegetable cooking spray. Insert waxed paper cut to fit the bottom and lightly coat the waxed paper. Flour the waxed paper and sides of pan.

❈ In a large bowl, combine the pecans, peaches, raisins and crystallized ginger with ¼ cup (1 oz/30 g) of the flour and stir with a fork until well blended.

❈ On a piece of waxed paper, sift together the remaining ¾ cup (3 oz/90 g) flour, baking powder, salt, ground ginger, cinnamon and nutmeg.

❈ In a medium bowl, using an electric mixer on low speed, beat together the butter and brown sugar until light and fluffy, about 1 minute, using a rubber spatula to scrape down the sides of the bowl as needed. Add the eggs one at a time, beating 20 seconds after each addition. Add the orange zest, molasses, sour cream, the ¼ cup (2 fl oz/60 ml) rum or bourbon and the flour and spice mixture. Beat until smooth, about 1 minute. Pour the batter into the bowl containing the dried fruit mixture and stir until well blended.

❈ Pour into the prepared loaf pan, smoothing the top. Place on a baking sheet on the middle oven rack and bake until a toothpick inserted in the center comes out clean and the cake edges pull slightly away from the sides of the pan, 1¼–1½ hours. If the top begins to brown too quickly, cover loosely with aluminum foil. Set the pan on a wire rack to cool for 15 minutes. Then invert the cake onto a serving platter, peel away and discard the waxed paper and let the cake cool completely.

❈ If desired, soak a large piece of cheesecloth (muslin) with more rum or bourbon. Wrap the cooled cake with the cheesecloth and then with a double thickness of aluminum foil. Store the cake in the refrigerator for up to 3 months. Resoak the cheesecloth in more rum or bourbon as the liquor is absorbed or as desired. Rewrap and refrigerate.

❈ Let the cake mellow for 2 weeks before serving. Serve at room temperature.

MAKES 1 LOAF   *Photograph pages 196–197*

On napkin, clockwise: Raspberry Divinity, Benne Drops, Kentucky Cream Candy

minutes. Using a fork, pull the candy to and from the pan until cool enough to handle, about 4 minutes. Shape thickened candy into a ball.

❋ Dip your fingers in cornstarch or rub them lightly with butter. Holding the candy in both hands, pull it as you would taffy, stretching it out about 6–12 in (15–30 cm) in length. Double it over and continue pulling until the candy just begins to lose some of its gloss but is still pliable, about 10 minutes. Put more cornstarch or butter on your fingers if you need it. Then twist the candy into a rope.

❋ Working quickly, cut the rope into 6 equal pieces. Pull each piece out long and thin to about 12 in (30 cm) in length. Butter a pair of sharp scissors and cut the rope into 1-in (2.5-cm) pieces. Place the candy between pieces of waxed paper and leave it in a cool, dry place (don't refrigerate) for 24 hours to become "creamy." Store in a tight tin box for up to 3 weeks.

MAKES ABOUT 6 DOZEN PIECES

South Carolina

BENNE DROPS

What the rest of America calls sesame seeds, South Carolinians call benne seeds, after a West African word. The seeds came to the Low Country during the slave trade of the 1600s and have been used in cookies and candies there ever since.

½ cup (4 oz/125 g) sugar
1 tablespoon unsalted butter
1 tablespoon water
½ teaspoon fresh lemon juice
1 cup (4 oz/125 g) unhulled benne (sesame) seeds, toasted and cooled (see glossary)

❋ Generously butter a heavy-duty baking sheet.

❋ In a small, heavy saucepan over medium heat, combine the sugar, butter and water and stir until well blended and the butter has melted. Cook, without stirring, to the firm ball stage, 244°–248°F (118°–120°C) on a candy thermometer, about 5 minutes. Remove from the heat. Stir the lemon juice and benne seeds into the hot sugar mixture until well blended.

❋ Working quickly, drop the candy mixture by teaspoonfuls about 1 in (2.5 cm) apart onto the baking sheet. Let stand at room temperature until cooled completely and firm. Wrap each candy separately in waxed paper and seal with tape. Store in an airtight container for up to several weeks at room temperature.

MAKES ABOUT 2 DOZEN DROPS

Kentucky

KENTUCKY CREAM CANDY

This recipe is originally from a 1940 cookbook by Kentucky writer Marion Flexner, Dixie Dishes. Pulled cream candies can be tricky to make, so be patient. It may take several tries before you are used to the pace and timing required for sumptuous results. Be sure to invite a friend over to help when it gets time to pull the candy; you'll want an extra pair of hands. Around the holidays it is not uncommon for Southerners to gather for a candy-making party.

3 cups (21 oz/780 g) superfine (castor) sugar
1 cup (8 fl oz/250 ml) water
1½ teaspoons distilled white vinegar
½ teaspoon salt
1 cup (8 fl oz/250 ml) heavy (double) cream
¼ cup (2 oz/60 g) unsalted butter
½ teaspoon vanilla extract (essence)
unsalted butter or cornstarch (corn flour) for pulling the candy

❋ Combine the sugar, water, vinegar, and salt in a large, heavy saucepan. Bring to a boil over high heat, stirring constantly. Remove the pan from the heat and stir until the sugar has completely dissolved.

❋ Reduce the heat to low and stir in the cream until well blended and bring the candy again to a boil. Partially cover the pan and cook to allow the sugar crystals on the side of the pan to dissolve in the steam, 2–3 minutes.

❋ Stir in the butter until melted and raise the heat to medium. Cook uncovered over medium heat, without stirring, until the candy reaches the hard ball stage or registers 258°F (125°C) on a candy thermometer, 20–25 minutes.

❋ Pour the candy onto a lightly buttered jelly-roll pan placed on a rack, or, better still, on a lightly buttered marble slab.

❋ Add the vanilla and blend it into the candy by working it with a spatula. Keep turning the outside edges to the center until the candy has thickened but is still glossy and pliable, 5

The South

RASPBERRY DIVINITY

Though there are several stories as to the name's origin, divinity was probably named, quite rightly, for its divine flavor. The bewitchingly airy candy is a perennial Southern favorite. This version is heightened with the flavor of raspberry, which also gives it a light blush.

2⅔ cups (21 oz/655 g) sugar
½ cup (4 fl oz/125 ml) water
½ cup (4 fl oz/125 ml) light corn syrup
¼ teaspoon salt
2 egg whites, at room temperature
3 tablespoons red raspberry–flavored gelatin powder

❋ Line 2 baking sheets with waxed paper.

❋ Lightly butter a medium, heavy saucepan. Combine the sugar, water, corn syrup and salt in the pan and set over medium heat, stirring until well blended. Cook, stirring often with a long-handled wooden spoon, until the sugar has dissolved, about 8 minutes. Using a pastry brush dipped in warm water, brush down the sides of the pan. Increase the heat to medium-high. Cook, without stirring, to the hard ball stage, 256°F (124°C) on a candy thermometer, about 10 minutes. After the first 5 minutes, brush down the sides of the pan again, and repeat after 3 minutes longer.

❋ Meanwhile, in a medium bowl, using an electric mixer with clean, dry beaters on medium speed, beat the egg whites until frothy. On medium-high speed, beat until stiff but not dry peaks form. Set aside.

❋ Remove the saucepan from the heat and let the boiling subside. On medium speed, beat the egg whites continuously while pouring in the sugar syrup mixture in a slow, steady stream, without stopping until incorporated. Do not pour any down the sides of the bowl. Add the gelatin powder and beat until well blended. Increase the mixer speed to high and beat until stiff peaks form and the mixture begins to lose its gloss and holds its shape when a teaspoonful is dropped onto waxed paper, about 5–8 minutes longer.

❋ Working quickly, transfer the candy mixture to a pastry bag fitted with a #9 star tip. Pipe rosettes of the Divinity about 1 in (2.5 cm) apart on the baking sheets. Alternatively, drop by teaspoonfuls onto the baking sheets, raising the spoon to create a peak on each dollop. Let the candy stand at room temperature until firm. Store in an airtight container between layers of waxed paper for up to 5 days at room temperature. Do not refrigerate.

MAKES ABOUT 4 DOZEN PIECES

❋ To make the cake, in a large bowl, sift together the cake flour, cocoa and baking powder and set aside.

❋ In a separate large bowl, using an electric mixer on medium speed, beat together the butter and granulated sugar until light and fluffy. Beat in the eggs and egg yolk one at a time, beating well after each addition. Beat in the vanilla and salt. Beat in the red food coloring, then the water, using a rubber spatula to scrape down the sides of the bowl, until well blended.

❋ Using the lowest speed, beat in the flour mixture alternately with the buttermilk for a total of 4 additions, ending with buttermilk and blending well. In a glass measuring cup, dissolve the baking soda in the vinegar. Pour in and beat on medium speed until just blended, about 10 seconds, scraping down the sides of the bowl as needed. Do not overbeat. Turn into the prepared cake pans.

❋ Bake on the middle oven rack until a toothpick inserted in the center comes out clean, 25–30 minutes.

❋ Meanwhile, to make the frosting, in a large bowl, using an electric mixer on low speed, beat together the cream cheese, butter and confectioners' sugar for 10 seconds. Then beat on high speed until well blended and smooth, scraping down the sides of the bowl as needed. Add the vanilla and blend well. Cover and refrigerate until ready to use.

❋ Let the cake cool completely in the pans on a wire rack. Assemble the cake, spreading the frosting between the layers and on the top and sides. Using the back of a metal tablespoon, make decorative swirls in the frosting. Refrigerate the cake until ready to serve.

SERVES 8–12

South

RED VELVET CAKE

Though many stories abound as to the origin of this cake, the most accepted version is that it was created at the old Waldorf Astoria Hotel in New York City at the turn of the century. But Southerners have acquired a particular fondness for it, and it continues to show up regularly at church suppers and bake sales. Don't be timid about using the full amount of red food coloring—it is necessary for a truly "red," not pink, velvet cake. The cocoa also adds depth to the cake's red velvet color. This cake is best when made the day of serving.

FOR THE CAKE:

2½ cups (7½ oz/235 g) sifted unleavened cake flour
3 tablespoons Dutch-processed cocoa powder
   (European style)
1½ teaspoons baking powder
½ cup (4 oz/125 g) unsalted butter, at room temperature
2 cups (1 lb/500 g) granulated sugar
2 eggs, at room temperature
1 egg yolk, at room temperature
1 teaspoon vanilla extract (essence)
½ teaspoon salt
¼ cup (2 fl oz/60 ml) red food coloring
3 tablespoons lukewarm water
1 cup (8 fl oz/250 ml) lowfat buttermilk, at room temperature
1 teaspoon baking soda (bicarbonate of soda)
1 tablespoon apple cider vinegar or distilled white vinegar

FOR THE CREAM CHEESE FROSTING:

1 lb (500 g) cream cheese, at room temperature
½ cup (4 oz/125 g) unsalted butter, at room temperature
1 lb (500 g) confectioners' (icing) sugar, sifted
1 teaspoon vanilla extract (essence)

❋ Preheat an oven to 350°F (180°C). Lightly coat two 9-in (23-cm) round cake pans with vegetable cooking spray. Insert waxed paper cut to fit the bottom of the pans and lightly coat the waxed paper with the cooking spray, then dust with flour.

Red Velvet Cake

Left to right: Mango-Blueberry Cobbler, Key Lime Pie

MANGO-BLUEBERRY COBBLER

If you are a south Floridian, a mango tree in your yard can be a curse or a blessing—a curse if you dread the constant clean-up of fallen fruits splattered all over your lawn, a blessing if you can't get enough of the fragrant, sunshiny fruits. Here mangoes are the main ingredient in a blueberry-studded cobbler, a summery dessert or brunch treat made all the more striking with a scoop of strawberry ice cream.

2 cups (8 oz/250 g) sifted all-purpose (plain) flour
1 cup (8 oz/250 g) sugar
½ teaspoon baking powder
¼ teaspoon baking soda (bicarbonate of soda)
¼ teaspoon salt
1 cup (8 fl oz/250 ml) milk, at room temperature
2 eggs, lightly beaten
½ teaspoon lemon extract (essence)
2½ cups (10 oz/315 g) fresh blueberries
2 lb (1 kg) ripe mangoes, peeled and cut into slices ¼ in
  (6 mm) thick
strawberry ice cream for serving (optional)

❀ Preheat an oven to 350°F (180°C). Lightly butter a 9-by-13-by-2-in (23-by-33-by-5-cm) baking dish.
❀ In a medium bowl, combine the flour, sugar, baking powder, baking soda, salt, milk, eggs and lemon extract. Whisk until well blended and smooth. The batter will be thin. Using a rubber spatula, fold in the blueberries until well blended. Pour the batter in an even layer on the bottom of the baking dish. Scatter the mango slices over the top of the batter, letting them sink to the bottom. Do not stir.
❀ Bake on the middle oven rack until the edges are golden brown, 30–35 minutes.
❀ To serve, spoon the hot cobbler into individual dishes or low-stemmed goblets and serve at once. Top with strawberry ice cream, if desired.

SERVES 8–12

KEY LIME PIE

Authentic Key lime pie doesn't look lime green. It's colored pale yellow by the tangy juice of the yellowish limes grown on the Florida Keys since the 1830s. Cooks there started making this classic dessert shortly before the Civil War, using condensed canned milk since fresh milk was unavailable on the islands. Today many Key lime pie recipes call for a graham cracker crust, but the original version used a pastry shell so as not to overpower the delicate filling. Another traditional ingredient—eggs—has been replaced here by cream cheese, which doesn't require baking.

FOR THE FILLING:

1 lb (500 g) cream cheese, at room temperature
3½ cups (28 fl oz/875 ml) canned lowfat sweetened
  condensed milk, undiluted
¾ cup (6 fl oz/180 ml) fresh Key lime juice, squeezed by
  hand, from 10–15 Key limes, or ¾ cup (6 fl oz/180 ml)
  bottled Key lime juice (see glossary)
1 teaspoon grated Key lime zest, from 2–4 Key limes
¼ teaspoon salt

1 baked, deep 9-in (23-cm) pie shell, cooled to room
  temperature (see glossary)

FOR THE TOPPING:

2 cups (16 fl oz/500 ml) heavy (double) cream, chilled
1 teaspoon vanilla extract (essence)
3 tablespoons confectioners' (icing) sugar

❋ To make the filling, in a large bowl, using an electric mixer on medium-high speed, beat the cream cheese and condensed milk until well blended and smooth. Beat in the lime juice, lime zest and salt until well blended. Spoon into the pie shell, smoothing the surface. Cover and refrigerate until completely chilled and set, about 3 hours.

❋ To make the topping, in a medium bowl, using an electric mixer with clean, chilled beaters on high speed, beat the cream and vanilla until soft peaks form. Add the confectioners' sugar and continue to beat until stiff peaks form. Transfer the whipped cream mixture to a sieve set over a bowl to catch any liquid. Cover tightly with plastic wrap and refrigerate for up to 2 hours until ready to serve.

❋ To serve, spread the topping evenly over the surface of the chilled pie and, using a spoon, swirl and peak the topping for a decorative touch. Serve at once.

SERVES 8

Atlanta, Georgia

THE BUCKHEAD DINER'S WHITE CHOCOLATE BANANA CREAM PIE

There are no gum-snapping waitresses named Flo at the Buckhead Diner. After the valet takes your car at the sleek, chrome-clad restaurant, you can order a "meat and three" plate—but the meat loaf is made with ground veal and wild mushrooms, and the mashed potatoes with puréed celery root. So it goes with their desserts. This Banana Cream Pie recipe isn't just bananas but also white crème de cacao, banana liqueur and white chocolate curls, enough to fill 2 pastry shells. To make white chocolate curls, you might want to purchase a large chunk of white chocolate from a pastry shop instead of the smaller bars at the supermarket. The larger the chunk you begin with, the larger and longer the curls will be.

FOR THE PIE PASTRY:

1 cup (8 oz/250 g) unsalted butter, at room temperature
¾ cup (6 oz/185 g) sugar
1 egg
2½ cups (12½ oz/390 g) all-purpose (plain) flour

FOR THE FILLING:

6 egg yolks, at room temperature
5 tablespoons (3 oz/80 g) sugar
¼ cup (1 oz/30 g) cornstarch (corn flour)
2 cups (16 fl oz/500 ml) milk, at room temperature
1 vanilla bean, cut in half
2 tablespoons unsalted butter, cut into 8 pieces
3 oz (90 g) white chocolate, melted

FOR THE WHITE CHOCOLATE CURLS:

12 oz (375 g) white chocolate, at room temperature

8 ripe bananas, sliced ¼ in (6 mm) thick
2 tablespoons fresh lemon juice
2 cups (16 fl oz/500 ml) heavy (double) cream, chilled
3 tablespoons white crème de cacao
3 tablespoons banana liqueur

2 tablespoons Dutch-processed cocoa powder (European style), sifted, for garnish

❋ To make the pastry, in a large bowl, combine the butter and sugar. Using an electric mixer on low speed, blend together but don't cream. Add the egg and flour and mix for 1 minute until dough begins to come together. Remove the dough with floured hands, wrap in plastic wrap and refrigerate for 2 hours.

❋ Meanwhile, prepare the filling. In a bowl, whisk together the egg yolks and sugar until the mixture is pale yellow. Whisk in the cornstarch and set aside. In a small, heavy saucepan over medium-high heat, bring the milk and vanilla bean halves to a boil. Remove the pan from the heat. Remove and discard the vanilla bean. Stir 3 tablespoons of the hot milk into the egg mixture. Return the pan to low heat and, while stirring constantly with a wooden spoon, slowly add the egg mixture to the milk. Cook, stirring constantly, until the mixture thickens and just comes to a boil, then remove from the heat and stir in the butter pieces until melted. Strain the mixture through a medium-meshed sieve into a bowl, cover with plastic wrap and allow to cool 20 minutes. Stir in the melted white chocolate, then cover and refrigerate until ready to assemble the pies.

❋ To make the white chocolate curls, carefully draw a vegetable peeler across the flat surface of room-temperature white chocolate. Refrigerate until ready to assemble the pies.

❋ Divide the chilled pastry dough in half. On a lightly floured work surface, quickly roll out half of the dough into a round about 12 in (30 cm) in diameter and ¼ in (6 mm) thick. Repeat with the remaining dough. Carefully transfer the rounds to two 10-in (25-cm) tart pans and gently fit the pastry into the pans. Trim the edges and prick the interiors all over with a fork. Refrigerate for 30 minutes.

❋ Preheat an oven to 450°F (230°C). Bake the chilled crusts on the middle oven rack until golden, 12–15 minutes. Set aside to cool completely.

❋ To assemble the pies, toss the sliced bananas with the lemon juice. Whip the cream until stiff peaks form. Fold the whipped cream into the chilled filling. Fold in the bananas, crème de cacao and banana liqueur. Fill the pie shells with the banana cream filling and top generously with white chocolate curls. Dust with sifted cocoa powder. Serve at once.

MAKES 2 PIES

The Buckhead Diner's White Chocolate Banana Cream Pie

SAVANNAH CREAM CAKE WITH CANDIED ROSE PETALS

It's a measure of how much Southerners love gardens that they have created recipes for eating flowers. As early as 1847, Sarah Rutledge gave a method for candying flowers in her book, The Carolina Housewife. *This cake, developed by Atlanta food consultant Margaret Ann Surber, continues the tradition. It's a show-stopper of white layers and sherried custard filling based on a cake in the 1933 collection* The Savannah Cook Book.

FOR THE CAKE:

2 cups (6 oz/185 g) sifted unleavened cake flour
1¾ teaspoons baking powder
¼ teaspoon ground nutmeg
¾ cup (6 oz/185 g) unsalted butter, at room temperature
1 cup (8 oz/250 g) plus ⅓ cup (3 oz/90 g) granulated sugar
¾ cup (6 fl oz/180 ml) half & half, at room temperature
1 teaspoon vanilla extract (essence)
2 eggs, at room temperature
2 egg whites, at room temperature

FOR THE CUSTARD:

¼ cup (1 oz/30 g) sifted all-purpose (plain) flour
⅓ cup (3 oz/90 g) granulated sugar
3 egg yolks, at room temperature
1½ cups (12 fl oz/375 ml) heavy (double) cream, at room temperature
⅓ cup (3 fl oz/80 ml) dry sherry

FOR THE TOPPING:

1¼ cups (10 fl oz/310 ml) heavy (double) cream, chilled
2 tablespoons confectioners' (icing) sugar
1 tablespoon dry sherry
15–20 candied, pesticide-free rose petals for garnish

❀ Preheat an oven to 350°F (180°C). Lightly coat two 8-in (20-cm) round cake pans with vegetable cooking spray and dust with flour.
❀ In a medium bowl, sift together the flour, baking powder and nutmeg and set aside. In a small bowl, whisk together the half & half and vanilla until well blended.
❀ In a large bowl, using an electric mixer on medium speed, beat the butter and 1 cup (8 oz/250 g) granulated sugar until light and fluffy. Add the eggs one at a time, beating well after each addition. On low speed, beat in the flour mixture alternating with the half & half mixture for a total of 3 additions, ending with the flour. Beat after each addition until well blended.
❀ In another large bowl, using an electric mixer with clean, dry beaters on medium speed, beat the egg whites while gradually adding the ⅓ cup (3 oz/90 g) granulated sugar in a slow, steady stream until well blended. Continue to beat until stiff and glossy, but not until dry peaks form. Working quickly, using a rubber spatula, stir about one eighth of the beaten egg whites into the batter until well blended. Then fold in the remaining egg whites until well blended.
❀ Divide the batter between the pans and smooth the surface. Bake on the middle oven rack until a toothpick inserted in the centers comes out clean, 25–30 minutes. Set the cake layers on wire racks to cool in the pans for 5 minutes. Then remove from the pans and return to the rack to cool completely.

❀ To make the custard, in a small, heavy nonreactive saucepan off heat, whisk together the flour, the ⅓ cup (3 oz/90 g) granulated sugar and egg yolks until well blended. Slowly whisk in the cream, then the sherry, until well blended and smooth.
❀ Set the saucepan over medium heat and cook, whisking constantly, until the mixture is very thick and begins to bubble, about 5 minutes. Remove from the heat and strain the custard through a fine-meshed sieve into a medium heatproof bowl. Let the custard cool to room temperature. Then cover with plastic wrap laid directly on the surface of the custard to prevent a skin from forming. Refrigerate at least 2 hours or for up to 24 hours before serving.
❀ To make the topping, 30 minutes before serving, in a large bowl, using an electric mixer with clean, chilled beaters on high speed, beat the cream until soft peaks form. Add the confectioners' sugar and sherry and continue to beat until stiff peaks form. Transfer to a fine-meshed sieve set in a bowl. Cover and refrigerate until ready to serve.
❀ To assemble the cake, place 1 cake layer on a cake pedestal or platter. Spread the top evenly with two thirds of the custard. Top with the second cake layer. Using a rubber spatula, fold the remaining custard into the whipped cream mixture. Spread just enough of the topping on the top and sides of the cake, reserving the remainder to pipe decorations. Just before serving, using a #6 star tip, pipe a ring of rosettes around the top edge and base of the cake. Place the candied rose petals on alternating rosettes. Serve at once.

SERVES 10–12

OZARK PUDDING

If Ozark Pudding inspired Huguenot Torte (recipe on page 210), what inspired Ozark Pudding? Author John Egerton traced the recipe to Henrietta Dull's 1928 cookbook Southern Cooking. *Whatever its genesis, the dessert was well established by 1946 when it was served to Winston Churchill and Harry Truman during the prime minister's visit to the president's home state of Missouri.*

2 eggs
1½ cups (12 oz/375 g) sugar
¼ cup (1½ oz/45 g) all-purpose (plain) flour
½ teaspoon baking powder
½ teaspoon salt
½ teaspoon grated lemon zest
1½ teaspoons vanilla extract (essence)
1 Golden Delicious or Red Delicious apple
¾ cup (3 oz/90 g) finely chopped pecans
vanilla ice cream or Cinnamon-scented Whipped Cream (see recipe headnote page 216) for serving (optional)

❀ Preheat an oven to 350°F (180°C). Lightly coat an 8-in (2-cm) square baking dish with vegetable cooking spray and dust with flour.
❀ In a medium bowl, using an electric mixer on medium speed, beat the eggs until light. Gradually add the sugar, beating until well blended. Add the flour, baking powder, salt, lemon zest and vanilla and beat until well blended and smooth.
❀ Peel and core the apple and shred in a food processor fitted with the coarse shredding disk. Alternatively, shred using the large-holed side of a box grater. Stir the apple and pecans into the pudding mixture until well blended. Ladle into the baking dish and bake until lightly browned and set, 25–30 minutes. Set on a wire rack to cool in the baking dish for 10 minutes. Serve warm directly from the dish. Top with vanilla ice cream or Cinnamon-scented Whipped Cream, if desired.

SERVES 4–6

Savannah Cream Cake with Candied Rose Petals

MOONSHINE LOAF CAKES WITH WHISKEY GLAZE

These whiskey-soaked chocolate sponge cakes don't actually contain moonshine, the uncultured corn liquor that very few people still make illegally in the Southern mountains. The recipe relies instead on the complex taste of bourbon. Although the cakes and the glaze both use whiskey, it's doubtful you'll need to appoint a designated driver.

2 cups (8 oz/250 g) sifted all-purpose (plain) flour
¼ cup (¾ oz/20 g) unsweetened Dutch-processed cocoa
    powder (European style)
½ teaspoon baking powder
½ teaspoon baking soda (bicarbonate of soda)
¼ teaspoon salt
1 tablespoon instant coffee
2 tablespoons boiling water
1 cup (8 fl oz/250 ml) milk, at room temperature

1 teaspoon vanilla extract (essence)
1 cup (8 oz/250 g) unsalted butter, at room temperature
2 cups (1 lb/500 g) granulated sugar
3 eggs, at room temperature
2 tablespoons bourbon

FOR THE GLAZE:

¾ cup (2½ oz/75 g) sifted confectioners' (icing) sugar
¼ cup (2 oz/60 g) unsalted butter, at room temperature
4 teaspoons bourbon

❋ Preheat an oven to 325°F (165°C). Lightly coat four 5½-by-3-in (14-by-7.5-cm) miniature loaf pans with vegetable cooking spray and dust with flour.

❋ In a large bowl, sift together the flour, cocoa powder, baking powder, baking soda and salt and set aside. In a small bowl, dissolve the instant coffee in the boiling water. In a medium nonreactive bowl, whisk together the coffee mixture, milk and vanilla and set aside.

❋ In another large bowl, using an electric mixer on medium-high speed, beat the butter and granulated sugar until light and fluffy. On medium speed, beat in the flour mixture in 2

Left to right: Moonshine Loaf Cakes with Whiskey Glaze, Ozark Pudding

WATERMELON-CHARDONNAY ICE

For many a Southerner, diving face-first into a wedge of just-cut, vine-ripened watermelon is one of summer's greatest gustatory pleasures. Most have never seen reason to try to improve upon its natural flavor, except perhaps to give it a shake or two of salt. But Atlanta recipe developer Carol Beller just might have succeeded, by pairing it with fruity Chardonnay in a refreshing watermelon ice.

8 cups (48 oz/1.5 kg) cubed watermelon, seeded
1 teaspoon fresh lemon juice
1 cup (8 fl oz/250 ml) Chardonnay wine
½ cup (2 oz/60 g) confectioners' (icing) sugar
8 miniature watermelon slices for garnish (optional)
8 sprigs of fresh mint for garnish (optional)

❀ Working in batches, if needed, in a food processor fitted with the metal blade, process the watermelon cubes until puréed. Transfer the purée to a medium freezerproof bowl and stir in the lemon juice. Set aside.

❀ In a small, nonreactive saucepan over medium heat, combine the wine and confectioners' sugar. Stir until well blended and bring to a boil. Reduce the heat to medium-low and cook, stirring occasionally, for 2 minutes. Stir the wine mixture into the bowl of watermelon purée until well blended. Let stand until completely cool, then cover with aluminum foil and freeze until solid, at least 8 hours or overnight.

❀ Just before serving, place another medium freezerproof bowl in the freezer. Working quickly, remove the bowl of frozen watermelon mixture from the freezer and, using a dull knife, break up into large chunks. Working in small batches, in a food processor fitted with the metal blade, process until just smooth, not liquefied, transferring the mixture into the bowl in the freezer between batches. Using a spatula, press down the watermelon mixture until firmly packed.

❀ To serve, scoop into short-stemmed glass goblets. Garnish, if desired, with a miniature watermelon slice and a mint sprig.

SERVES 8

Watermelon-Chardonnay Ice

additions. Then beat in the milk mixture in 3 additions until well blended. While beating on low speed, add the eggs one at a time, beating well after each addition. Divide the batter among the miniature loaf pans. Set the pans on a heavy-duty baking sheet. Bake on the middle oven rack until a toothpick inserted in the centers comes out clean, 30–35 minutes.

❀ Set the cakes on wire racks to cool completely in the pans. Then remove the cooled cakes from the pans. Using a pastry brush, brush the top, sides and bottom with the bourbon, using 1½ teaspoons of the bourbon per cake. Wrap each cake tightly with plastic wrap and refrigerate for 1 day to let the flavors mellow before glazing.

❀ To make the glaze, in a small bowl, using an electric mixer on medium-high speed, beat the confectioners' sugar, butter and bourbon until well blended and smooth. Using a rubber spatula, scrape down the sides of the bowl as needed. Spread a thin layer of glaze on top of each cake and let it drip down the sides, then serve.

MAKES 4 MINIATURE LOAF CAKES; SERVES 8

Charleston, South Carolina

PINK LADY CUPCAKES

The basis for these delicious cupcakes is the egg white–lightened batter used in a number of classic, turn-of-the-century Southern cakes, most notably the Lady Baltimore cake. (The lady's leftover egg yolks frequently went into Lord Baltimore cakes.) That towering layered confection was filled and frosted with fluffy, snow-white seven-minute frosting, to which chopped dried figs, raisins and nuts were added. These modernized miniature versions are crowned instead with an equally ladylike strawberry buttercream frosting. If desired, garnish each cupcake with 2 mint leaves and a fresh sliced strawberry.

1 cup (8 oz/250 g) unsalted butter, at room temperature
2 cups (1 lb/500 g) granulated sugar

3½ cups (10½ oz/330 g) sifted unleavened cake flour
¾ teaspoon baking powder
¼ teaspoon salt
1 cup (8 fl oz/250 ml) milk, at room temperature
2 teaspoons vanilla extract (essence)
½ teaspoon almond extract (essence)
8 egg whites, at room temperature

FOR THE FROSTING:

1¼ cups (10 oz/315 g) unsalted butter, at room temperature
2 cups (6 oz/185 g) sifted confectioners' (icing) sugar
½ cup (5 oz/155 g) strawberry jelly

24 small fresh strawberries for garnish (optional)
48 small fresh mint leaves for garnish (optional)

well blended. Divide the batter among the muffin cups. Bake on the middle oven rack until lightly browned and a toothpick inserted in the centers comes out clean, 20–30 minutes. Set the cupcakes on a wire rack to cool in the tins for 5 minutes. Then remove the cupcakes and return to the rack to cool completely.

❋ To make the frosting, in a medium bowl, combine the butter, confectioners' sugar and jelly. Using an electric mixer on low speed, beat until well blended. Then on high speed, beat until smooth and fluffy. Spread the frosting on top of each cupcake and refrigerate until ready to garnish, if desired.

MAKES 2 DOZEN CUPCAKES

Georgia

GEORGIA PEACH ICE CREAM

Georgia has never led the nation in peach production, yet no state is as identified with the sweet, fleshy fruit. It is the Peach State, as its license tag attests. And there is no better use of a Georgia peach than this ice cream, one of the highlights of a Southern summer. After freezing, let the ice cream flavors "ripen" in a freezer for 1–2 hours before serving.

2 cups (16 fl oz/500 ml) light (single) cream
1½ cups (12 fl oz/375 ml) heavy (double) cream
1¼ cups (10 oz/310 g) sugar
4 egg yolks, lightly beaten
1 teaspoon vanilla extract (essence)
2½ lb (1.25 kg) very ripe peaches
1 tablespoon fresh lemon juice
¼ teaspoon salt
2 cups (16 fl oz/500 ml) light (single) cream, chilled

❋ In a medium saucepan over low heat, combine the 2 cups (16 fl oz/500 ml) light cream and the heavy cream and scald but do not allow to boil. Set aside.

❋ In a large bowl, combine ¾ cup (6 oz/185 g) of the sugar and the egg yolks. Using a whisk or an electric mixer on medium speed, beat until the mixture is light-colored and thick enough to form a broad ribbon when the whisk or beater is lifted, about 3 minutes.

❋ Remove and discard any skin from the surface of the scalded cream. Gradually ladle the cream into the egg yolk mixture, whisking or beating after each addition.

❋ Transfer this custard mixture to the top of a double boiler set over simmering water. Simmer, stirring constantly, until thick enough to lightly coat the back of a wooden spoon, 15–20 minutes. Do not allow the mixture to boil.

❋ Remove from the heat and strain through a fine-meshed metal sieve into a large heatproof bowl. Stir in the vanilla until well blended. Cover with aluminum foil and refrigerate for 1 hour.

❋ Meanwhile, peel the peaches and place in a large bowl. Using a potato masher, mash the peaches, leaving a few chunks. Add the remaining ½ cup (4 oz/125 g) sugar, lemon juice and salt and stir until well blended. Cover tightly with plastic wrap and refrigerate for 1 hour.

❋ Just before freezing the ice cream, stir the 2 cups (16 oz/500 ml) chilled light cream into the custard mixture until well blended. Pour the custard mixture into a 4-qt (4-l) ice-cream freezer and freeze according to the manufacturer's directions. When you have churned the custard mixture for half the amount of time given in the directions and the mixture is the texture of soft ice cream, add the peach mixture and stir with a long-handled spoon until well blended. Continue to freeze.

MAKES ABOUT 4 QT (4 L)

Top to Bottom: Pink Lady Cupcakes, Georgia Peach Ice Cream

❋ Preheat an oven to 350°F (180°C). Line 24 standard muffin cups with paper muffin liners.

❋ In a medium bowl, combine the butter and granulated sugar and, using an electric mixer on medium speed, beat until light and fluffy. Add the flour, baking powder and salt. Beat on low speed while gradually adding the milk in a slow, steady stream until well blended. Beat in the vanilla and almond extracts on medium speed until the mixture is well blended and smooth.

❋ Place the egg whites in a large bowl. Using an electric mixer with clean, dry beaters on high speed, beat until stiff, glossy but not dry peaks form. Working quickly, stir one fourth of the beaten egg whites into the batter until well blended. Then, using a rubber spatula, fold in the remaining egg whites until

GLOSSARY

ANDOUILLE
Spicy, smoky sausage essential to many Cajun and Creole dishes.

AVOCADO
Also known as alligator pear. The Florida avocado differs from the wrinkled, dark green California Hass avocado in several ways: It's larger, smoother and brighter green on the outside, and its flesh is sweeter and lighter, in taste as well as in fat and calories. A ripe avocado will yield softly when squeezed. If it's hard, it may need to ripen at room temperature for a day or two, or up to a week before it's ready to use. Avocados brown quickly after cutting, so rub the cut surfaces with a little lemon or lime juice.

BARBECUE
Southerners use this term to refer to meat or poultry that has slowly cooked by the smoke of smoldering coals. Foods that are seared quickly over a much hotter fire are "grilled." In other parts of the country, however, the term "barbecue" is often applied—though Southerners believe incorrectly—to grilled foods as well.

BARBECUE SAUCE
Savory mixtures that enhance barbecued or grilled meat. They may be applied before, during or after the cooking, depending on the type of sauce. The most familiar tomato-based sauce is primarily a table sauce to be added after the meat has been cooked. It may also be used as a finishing sauce—applied on the meat during the last 10 or 15 minutes of cooking. Because tomatoes and sugar tend to burn, it should not be added any sooner. In North Carolina, a very thin, tomatoless, vinegar-based sauce is popular. Many South Carolinians favor a mustard-based sauce that also contains vinegar, sugar and spices. Some barbecuers use a sop, or mop—a very thin liquid that may be no more than beer or vinegar—to baste the meat during the cooking. Others apply a dry rub—a combination of seasonings, usually those in the sauce—that forms a flavorful bark, locking in the juices as the meat cooks.

BEANS
See *Pole beans* and *Shell beans*.

BENNE SEEDS
A West African name for sesame seeds, frequently heard in the Low Country. In the spice section, they are sold in small bottles and are quite expensive. They're much cheaper, and often fresher, if purchased in bulk at an ethnic market or health food store. To bring out their flavor, toast them in a single layer in a dry skillet over low heat until just golden.

BISCUITS
ANGEL BISCUITS: Sweet, rich, fluffy biscuits leavened with yeast.

BEATEN BISCUITS: Crisp and short, almost like crackers, these biscuits were originally made by beating the dough vigorously with a mallet until it blistered; nowadays a food processor can do the trick, saving considerably on muscle power. Beaten biscuits are often served with thin slivers of country ham tucked inside.

BUTTERMILK BISCUITS: The classic Southern biscuit, leavened by the reaction between the baking soda (bicarbonate of soda) and the acid in the buttermilk. The buttermilk also adds a faint tang and helps to tenderize the biscuit. It owes its flakiness to lard or vegetable shortening, its lightness to a soft-wheat Southern flour such as White Lily or Martha White.

SHORTCAKE: Slightly sweetened biscuit dough that is often enriched with egg and/or cream. After baking, it's split, slathered with butter and topped with berries or other fruit and a dollop of whipped cream.

BLANCH
To plunge raw food—usually vegetables or fruit—into boiling water very briefly and then refresh it in ice water. This may be done to brighten the color of vegetables such as broccoli or carrots, to loosen the skins of tomatoes or peaches, or to mellow the flavor of garlic or onions.

BOUDIN
Louisiana sausage that includes pork, spicy seasonings and rice *(boudin blanc),* and sometimes calf's blood, liver, heart and tongue as well *(boudin rouge).*

BOURBON
Bourbon is legally defined as whiskey distilled from fermented mash (at least 51 percent corn) and aged in new charred-oak barrels for at least two years. Most bourbon comes from Kentucky. A close relative, Tennessee whiskey, differs slightly in taste and distilling technique.

CANE SYRUP
Similar to light molasses, with a taste akin to dark brown sugar. It's made by boiling extracted sugarcane juice to the consistency of thick maple syrup. Cane syrup is used in baking.

CANNING
See *Preserving, Canning.*

CAST-IRON SKILLETS
For frying the crispiest chicken and baking the most delicious corn bread—crunchy on the outside and tender on the inside—only this utensil will do. Cooking with cast iron boosts both the iron content and the taste of the foods that are cooked in it. Cast iron is dark and porous, enabling it to absorb more heat than other cookware. Southern cooks take advantage of this especially for making corn bread by first heating a well-greased skillet in the oven and then pouring the batter into the hot skillet. The corn bread is well on its way to forming a wonderfully browned, crunchy crust even before it goes into the oven to bake.

Like a fine wine, cast iron only gets better with age, provided you season it properly and care for it regularly. Here's how: Clean a new pot or skillet with mild dish soap and a stiff brush, never with steel wool or abrasives. Grease the skillet inside and out with vegetable shortening and put it in a preheated 300°F (150°C) oven for 1 hour. Then turn the oven off and let the skillet cool in the oven overnight. Remove from the oven, wipe out the skillet with a barely dampened cloth and store until ready to use. Cast iron will rust if left to soak or to air-dry. After each use, always wash and dry it immediately, then coat with a thin film of vegetable oil before storing. If it does rust, pour some salt over the area, wipe off the salt and reseason the pan.

CATFISH
Spiny, scaleless freshwater fish with long whiskers on the snout, chin and jaw. Most catfish sold today are raised in man-made ponds and fed controlled diets, thus producing a sweeter, milder taste than that of the somewhat wild-tasting river-bottom scavengers caught with a cane pole. Most commercial catfish is cleaned and filleted. Its flaky white flesh adapts well to most cooking techniques, but Southerners still find the traditional preparation irresistible: dredged in seasoned cornmeal, fried and served with hush puppies and coleslaw.

CHICORY ROOT
The white root of a certain variety of chicory (not the kind that goes in salads) that's dried, roasted, ground and brewed with dark roast coffee in a drip pot to make the very strong, distinctively flavored brew loved by Louisianans—especially for dunking beignets.

CHITTERLINGS
Better known as chitlins, they're the small intestines of a pig, which must be thoroughly cleaned before cooking. After boiling, they're often battered and deep-fried.

CHOCOLATE CURLS
To make decorative curls of chocolate, set the bottom edge of a chocolate bar on a work surface and hold it upright with one hand. With the other hand, scrape a vegetable peeler down the side of the chocolate. If the edge of the chocolate is cool, you will get shavings; if it is slightly warm—but not warmer than room temperature—you will get curls. To warm the chocolate just enough to make it supple, hold it very briefly under a lamp or other heat source.

CHORIZO
Spicy Spanish sausage.

CHOW CHOW
Spicy relish of pickled vegetables, also known as piccalilli.

CLARIFIED BUTTER
Best for sautéing because it can be heated to a fairly high temperature without burning. To clarify butter, melt unsalted butter in a small saucepan over low heat without stirring, then skim and discard any white foam that forms. Spoon the clear butter into a container, discarding the milky residue at the bottom of the pan. Clarified butter will keep up to 2 months refrigerated in an airtight container.

CLEANING LEEKS
Leeks are often full of sand when purchased, and must be thoroughly cleaned before using. Remove any wilted leaves, cut off the dark green tops and trim the root end, leaving only the white and light green parts. Slit lengthwise down to where the white begins, give a quarter-turn and slit again. Under cold, running water, wash the leeks thoroughly, fanning the leaves with your fingers to remove all dirt in between. If you are not using the leeks whole, cut them in half lengthwise and rinse under cold water, separating the leaves with your fingers.

CLEANING MUSHROOMS
Mushrooms should be thoroughly cleaned, but don't soak them in water or they will become waterlogged. If they aren't too dirty, wipe them off individually with a damp paper towel. If very dirty, run them quickly under warm water to loosen the dirt, then under cold water. Wipe with a damp cloth, then dry gently with paper towels.

COBBLER
Deep-dish fruit dessert with a biscuit or pastry topping. It usually does not have a bottom crust, though some do.

CONCH
Giant edible sea snail with a knobby, pink and white shell whose firm-textured, briny-sweet meat was once a dietary staple of Key West. In recent years, however, supplies have been depleted, and now most of the conch served in Florida comes from Costa Rica or the Bahamas. It's as popular as ever, tossed in salads, breaded and pan-fried, frittered, stewed and simmered in soups. Like squid, conch can be tough and chewy if you're not careful. Therefore it's usually ground or tenderized by pounding with a ridged mallet before cooking.

CORN BREAD
To tell for sure on which side of the Mason-Dixon line people were raised, ask them how they like their corn bread. If they like it sweet and cakey, you know they're not from the South. Most Southerners wouldn't hear of adding sugar or flour to their favorite bread—rather, they like it thin, dense and crispy, tasting primarily of corn. And it must be baked in a cast-iron pan. Many also insist on using white cornmeal, although white and yellow cornmeal taste pretty much the same. Corn bread comes in various other forms aside from a round, flat loaf. Corn pone is made without eggs or milk and fried in a skillet; corn dodgers are hard sticks made from corn-pone batter; spoon bread is a very soft, puddinglike corn bread eaten with a spoon; hush puppies are deep-fried, onion-flecked cornmeal fritters. Slaves made hoe cakes by baking their corn bread on the blade of a hoe set in an open fire.

CORN FLOUR
Very finely milled yellow or white cornmeal used for coating foods for deep-frying.

CORNMEAL
Dried, ground corn. Most cornmeal is yellow or white, though blue cornmeal from the Southwest has become popular lately. Southerners tend to prefer white cornmeal over yellow even though, besides the color, there is little difference between the two.

COUNTRY HAM
Salt-cured, smoked, aged ham produced in various parts of the rural South. Because it is so salty, it is typically slivered thin and served in small portions either as a first course, tucked into biscuits or added as a flavoring. The most revered country ham is the Smithfield ham, from Smithfield, Virginia, which comes from peanut-fed hogs. Smithfields include both the full butt and the shank bone, which are removed from other hams prior to packing. The hams are coated with black pepper before being hung on racks and smoked in a smokehouse. They are then aged from 6 to 18 months.

Cured country ham, like cured Italian prosciutto, is safe to eat raw. But most people are used to eating a cooked ham and prefer it that way. Often the fat covering the ham is scored and a brown-sugar glaze is added. Boiling it first before baking is highly recommended, because it leaches out some of the salt and keeps the meat moist.

Before cooking country hams, they must be soaked and cleaned. Here's how: Place the ham in a large pot and cover with enough water for it to float. Let soak 12–24 hours, changing the water several times. Remove the ham from the pot and discard the soaking water. Using a stiff brush, scrub the ham vigorously under lukewarm running water to remove any trace of mold or pepper. Wipe it with a damp kitchen towel. The ham is now ready to be cooked.

CRABS
BLUE CRAB: Found in salt and fresh water from Cape Cod to Florida, particularly in the bays and estuaries of the Gulf of Mexico and the Chesapeake Bay. Lump crabmeat from the body of blue crabs in their hard-shell state is excellent for salads, seafood cocktails and crab cakes. The claw meat may be steamed and served as an hors d'oeuvre. When blue crabs molt, they are sold as fully edible soft-shell crabs, which are delectable fried, sautéed or grilled.

STONE CRAB: The huge orange-red and black claws are a seasonal South Florida delicacy, served as either a first course or an entrée, often with a mustard dipping sauce. After the claws are removed, the bodies are thrown back into the water where the crab will grow new claws in about 18 months. The claws should be cooked as soon as they are brought inland; they are usually already cooked when sold. Serve them slightly chilled or at room temperature; if reheated, they'll develop an ammonia taste. The meat is exceptionally sweet and tender; if it has a spongy texture, you know it's been frozen. If you should get some fresh, uncooked claws, cook them in boiling water for about 2½ minutes; do not overcook.

CRACKLINGS
Crisp, browned bits that remain in the pan when fat has been rendered from pork rinds or poultry skin. Pork cracklings are added to corn bread batter to make "cracklin' bread."

CRAWFISH
Fresh-water crustaceans found in South Louisiana lakes, rivers and bayous. Resembling tiny lobsters, they are prized for their tender, sweet white meat. In the Deep South and a few other parts of the country, they are sold live or freshly boiled when in season. They're more widely available peeled and frozen all year-round.

To cook live crawfish: First wash them thoroughly in several changes of cold water. Then place them in a pot of boiling water until they just turn red, as briefly as a few seconds. Let cool and pull off the heads. If desired, reserve the orange fat from the heads for flavoring the dish you're cooking. Remove the meat from the shells by pinching the tail until the meat pops out (this takes a little practice). Eat as is, or use in casseroles or other dishes.

CREOLE MUSTARD
Piquant, light brown mustard made from spicy brown mustard seeds. It's essential to the spicy mayonnaise dressing for the famous salad, shrimp remoulade. Zatarain's Creole mustard is a popular brand.

DEGLAZE
To add liquid (water, broth, wine) to a pan in which food has been cooked, scraping up the browned bits from the bottom of the pan and stirring to dissolve them. The liquid is cooked until reduced to the desired consistency.

FIELD PEAS
A term that encompasses a wide variety of Southern peas, the best known being black-eyed peas. These starchy, earthy-flavored peas are sold fresh, frozen, canned and dried and are a principal component of Hoppin' John, the classic New Year's Day good-luck dish featuring peas, rice, ham hock and spicy seasoning. They are also the basis for hearty salads such as Mississippi Caviar (or Texas or Georgia Caviar, depending on where you're from), a garlicky, marinated mixture of peas and finely chopped vegetables. Other

varieties of field peas are similar and can be used interchangeably in most recipes, but black-eyed peas do have characteristics of their own. Identifying them is often confusing, since the terminology varies from one region to the next.

COWPEAS: Similar to black-eyes, but without the black spot (though in some areas this term is synonymous with black-eyed peas).

CROWDER PEAS: Reddish brown in color, somewhat spherical in shape and without a definite eye.

PURPLE-HULL: Pale, tender, elongated peas with a defined eye, but slightly smaller and firmer than the more familiar black-eyed peas.

WHITE ACRE PEAS OR LADY PEAS: Light-colored and without an eye, these are the tiniest of the field peas.

FILÉ POWDER
Ground dried sassafras leaves widely used in Louisiana to thicken and flavor gumbos and Louisiana stews. Filé can turn gummy or stringy if boiled, so remove the pot from the heat, then immediately sprinkle the filé into the hot mixture, cover the pot and let it stand undisturbed for about five minutes. Then stir to blend it in.

FLAMBÉ
Flaming brandy or some other liqueur to pour over a dish is an easy way to create a showstopper, but it must be done with care. Always remove the dish from the heat source first. Use long fireplace matches and stand back from the dish while you're igniting. Before flaming, warm the liqueur in a small, heavy saucepan, remove it from the heat, ignite, then pour over the dish that has been taken off the heat. Or skim the accumulated fat from the cooking liquids and add liqueur to the pan. When warm, remove from the heat and ignite. The flames will quickly die out.

FRITTERS
Sweet or savory batter-dipped morsels that are deep-fried until crispy.

GARLIC
See *Roasting garlic.*

GOO GOO CLUSTER
A confection of chocolate, caramel, marshmallow and peanuts manufactured by the Standard Candy Company in Nashville since 1912.

GREENS
In the South, this term typically applies not to salad greens but to a variety of dark green, leafy, wild and cultivated vegetables. Turnip greens and collard greens are hardy, strong-tasting winter plants that usually cook for an hour or longer in pork-seasoned broth. Wild greens such as dandelion, watercress, poke sallet and lamb's quarters grow in Appalachia and other mountainous regions. Wild greens are tender and delicate and require only a few minutes of cooking.

GRITS
A corn product made from ground, dried hominy, available in coarse, medium or fine grinds. Though it's typically cooked into a mush and served with butter and salt as a breakfast staple, lately it's been turning up at other times, day or night—mixed with pesto; baked and topped with seafood or quail; even sweetened and topped with fruit for a dessert.

GUMBO
If Louisiana had a state soup, this would be it. It typically begins with a roux and is further thickened either with filé powder or the glutinous pods of okra. Ham or other smoked meats, vegetables, poultry, duck or other game birds, shrimp, crawfish, oysters or other seafood are typical embellishments. Gumbo is ladled into bowls over hot, cooked rice.

HAM
See *Country ham.*

HANDLING HOT CHILI PEPPERS
When handling jalapeños or any hot chilies, wear rubber gloves and do not touch your face, eyes or nose, because the oils from the chilies can burn your skin and mucous membranes. After handling, wash hands, cutting board, knife, and anything else that came into contact with the chili peppers using warm, soapy water. Before cutting fresh chilies, rinse them and pull the stems out under cold, running water. To prepare the chilies for cooking or serving raw, cut the pods in half lengthwise and, using a teaspoon or the small end of a melon baller, scoop out the seeds and the fleshy ribs and discard. Dried chiles should also be stemmed, deribbed and seeded before using, but they do not require washing.

HEARTS OF PALM
Also called swamp cabbage, these ivory-colored, edible centers of Florida palm trees have a flavor similar to artichokes.

HOMINY
Whole kernels of dried corn that have been treated and soaked to remove germs and hulls. White and golden hominy are sold in cans.

HOT CHILI PEPPERS
There are many varieties of fresh and canned hot chili peppers used throughout the South that differ in their color, flavor and heat. Some common varieties are *anaheim, habanero, jalapeño, poblano,* and *serrano.* Because all chilies contain some degree of heat, they should be handled with caution. See *Handling hot chili peppers.*

ICED TEA
For the perfect pitcher of iced tea that's sparkling clear, not cloudy, follow these tips: Use black tea. Use a teapot, which keeps the water hot while brewing and brings out the tea's flavor. Start with freshly drawn cold tap water. Bring it to a boil in a nonaluminum pot or pan. When the water comes to a rolling boil, immediately pour it over tea leaves or tea bags. (Longer boiling make the tea cloudy.) If you like your tea sweet, add sugar to taste while the tea is still hot. Cool the tea to room temperature before pouring over ice. However, some iced-tea connoisseurs insist that the best iced tea is made by pouring hot tea over ice. They may be right. If you use that method, make the tea twice as strong and use more ice to compensate for the melting. Do not refrigerate warm tea. This could also make it cloudy.

JALAPEÑO
A bright green tapered chili about 6 in (15 cm) long and 1 in (2.5 cm) wide. Jalapeños are the most common hot chili in the United States. The ripe form is bright red and slightly sweeter than the green; both red and green jalapeños are good pickled. Because of their heat, they should be handled with caution. See *Handling hot chili peppers.*

JERUSALEM ARTICHOKE
Sometimes called sunchoke, this tan, bumpy tuber resembles fresh ginger, but has a nutty, mellow flavor more akin to the globe artichoke. Southerners prize its crisp, ivory flesh for relishes.

JULIENNE
To cut into even, matchstick-sized strips.

KEY LIMES
Small, yellow citrus fruits that look more like small lemons than limes. Their acid content is so high that pies made with them seldom need gelatin to set. Though Key lime trees flourish in South Florida, most commercial Key limes in U.S. markets are from Haiti. Persian or other green limes may be substituted in recipes calling for Key limes, although they will produce a green pie, rather than the more authentic yellow one, and their flavor will not be the same.

KEY WEST OLD SOUR
Key West table condiment used for seasoning seafood, soups, stews and greens. To make it, strain 2 cups (16 fl oz/500 ml) of Key lime juice into a bottle or cruet. Add 1 tablespoon of salt and 1 or 2 small hot peppers. Replace the top. Let stand in a dark place until it has turned a dark amber color. Condiment will keep indefinitely.

LARD
See *Pork fat.*

LEEKS
See *Cleaning leeks.*

MAYHAW

Tart, bright-red berries (actually members of the rose family) used primarily for jelly and wine making.

MIRLITON

Green, pear-shaped member of the cucumber family also known as chayote, vegetable pear or christophine. Popular in Louisiana, it is often stuffed and baked.

MOLASSES

Boiled sugarcane juice that becomes darker, stronger and less sweet with each boiling. Light molasses, produced after the first boiling, is sweet and mild enough to be used as a condiment as well as a baking ingredient. Dark molasses, produced by the second boiling, is stronger and less sweet, better suited for baking. Blackstrap molasses, produced by the third boiling, is a thick, black, slightly bitter syrup used sparingly in cooking. Unlike its milder counterparts, it has a significant concentration of iron, potassium and calcium.

MOON PIE

Four-inch round snack cake made of graham cracker–like cookies sandwiched with marshmallow cream and dipped in chocolate. There are other coating flavors, too—vanilla, banana, coconut—but Moon Pie enthusiasts generally don't acknowledge them. The cellophane-wrapped snacks have been manufactured in Chattanooga, Tennessee, since 1917.

MUSCADINES

Thick-skinned purple grape that grows during the late summer primarily in the Southeast. Historically one of the first grape varieties to be made into wine, it's also used for making jellies and pie fillings—although this takes some patience; the pulp must be removed from the hulls, and the seeds must be separated from the pulp.

MUSHROOMS

See *Cleaning mushrooms.*

NUTS

See *Toasting nuts.*

OKRA

Fuzzy, ridged, finger-shaped green vegetable, which may be battered and deep-fried, stewed or added to soups. In gumbos especially, it's valued for its thickening properties. The more it's cut or cooked, the more slimy it becomes—so be careful how you prepare it.

OLD BAY SEASONING

A staple seasoning blend of the Chesapeake Bay area used mostly for crab and shrimp boils, although it may also season poultry, meats or salad dressings. It consists of celery salt, mustard, pepper, cloves and other seasonings. If not found in the spice section of your supermarket, check the seafood counter.

PEACHES

There are two basic types of peaches: freestones, which separate easily from the pit; and clingstones, which cling to the pit. Most commercial peaches are freestones, because they are juicier and more tender. The firmer clingstones are used mostly for canning. Though it's fine to eat them skin and all, there is an easy way to skin them while retaining most of the flesh: blanch in boiling water 10–20 seconds, then plunge into ice water. The skins should slip off easily.

PEPPER VINEGAR

In virtually every traditional Southern restaurant, you'll find a bottle of this seasoned vinegar to sprinkle on turnip or collard greens, as well as other vegetables. To make pepper vinegar, slit a dozen or more small hot peppers and pack loosely in a bottle or cruet. Cover the peppers with cider vinegar or white wine vinegar. Set aside for 10 days in a cool, dark place.

PERSIMMON

A puckery, late-ripening orange fruit also known as date plum. In the South, its seeds are ground and used as a coffee substitute. For holidays, persimmons are often made into puddings.

PIE SHELL

To make a deep-dish single 9- or 10-in (23- or 25-cm) pie pastry, in a medium bowl, stir together 1¾ cups (7 oz/220 g) sifted all-purpose (plain) flour and ½ teaspoon salt. Using a pastry blender, 2 knives or a fork, cut in 6 tablespoons (3 oz/90 g) chilled, diced, unsalted butter and ¼ cup (2 oz/60 g) vegetable shortening until it resembles coarse crumbs. One tablespoon at a time, sprinkle 2–4 tablespoons of ice water over the mixture and stir with a fork until the dough just begins to come together but is not sticky. Shape the dough into a flat disk, wrap tightly in waxed paper and refrigerate for 30 minutes. On a lightly floured work surface, roll out the chilled dough into a round 10 in (25 cm) in diameter. Lightly moisten the edges of a deep 9- or 10-in (23- or 25-cm) pie pan with water. Carefully transfer the pastry to the pie pan and fold and crimp the edges to form an attractive edge. This constitutes the recipe for an unbaked pie shell. To bake the shell, cover the pie crust with aluminum foil, poke a few holes in the aluminum foil and press it snugly into the pan. Prick the bottom and sides of the shell with the tines of a fork. Bake in an oven preheated to 350°F (180°C) for 10 minutes, remove the foil and bake an additional 8–10 minutes. Let cool completely on a rack before filling.

PILAU

Any number of recipes for rice pilaf cooked in a broth and embellished with various meats and vegetables.

POACH

To cook foods gently in simmering, not boiling, liquid.

POLE BEANS

Green beans that are longer, flatter and tougher than string beans, but have a wonderful flavor when cooked long and slowly until meltingly soft. Be sure to remove the strings before cooking. Salt pork or some other pork fat is its favored seasoning.

POMPANO

Flat, silvery-skinned saltwater fish of the jack family found mostly along the Gulf Coast and Florida coastline. Mark Twain once called it "delicious as the less criminal forms of sin." A fatty fish with a mild yet distinctive flavor, it takes well to sautéing, broiling, baking and grilling. Its most famous preparation is *en papillote* (baked in parchment paper), a dish created at Antoine's in New Orleans.

PORK FAT

Though politically incorrect in this age of cholesterol-consciousness, Southern cooks still revere pork fat for its unique flavoring and cooking properties.

BACON: Smoked fat from the belly of the pig.

FATBACK: Salted slab of fat from the back of the pig, containing no meat at all.

HAM HOCK AND HOG JOWL: Both commonly used for flavoring cooking water for vegetables, particularly for the black-eyed peas that are served on New Year's Day for good luck.

LARD: Rendered from fresh pork fat. Used cold like shortening, lard produces extraordinarily flaky, flavorful biscuits and pie crusts. When melted, it becomes an ideal medium for frying the crispiest chicken. It may be found in the dairy sections of supermarkets, but purists recommend asking the butcher for leaf lard—a sheet of fat pulled from around the kidneys and saddle of the pig's belly.

SALT PORK: Salt-cured, fat-streaked side meat similar to bacon, but not smoked.

STREAK O' LEAN: Fat that is ribboned with meat, like bacon.

PORK RIBS

To some Southerners, pork ribs are as essential to a Memorial Day or Fourth of July cookout as turkey is to the Thanksgiving table. These are the basic types for barbecuing:

COUNTRY-STYLE RIBS: Shoulder end of a bone-in loin, with leaner meat than other ribs. Without the extra fat, they are more likely to dry out and toughen, so be careful not to overcook.

LOIN OR BABY BACK RIBS: Shorter than spareribs, they are also typically meatier and costlier.

SPARERIBS: America's most popular rib, this elongated slab cut from just behind the pork shoulder is mostly bone and little meat—but it still makes for pleasurable gnawing.

POT LIKKER

The nutrient-rich cooking liquid left in the pot after greens have simmered for a lengthy time. It's often served in a separate bowl with corn bread for dipping.

PRALINE

A flat, cookie-shaped confection made of sugar, cream and/or butter. There are white, pink and cream praline variations; sometimes they are made with nuts, usually pecans. Most often associated with New Orleans, it is popular throughout the South.

PRESERVING, CANNING

Home preserves and canned goods must be put up in sterilized jars and made using sterilized equiptment. To sterilize the jars, boil them gently in water to cover for 10 minutes; leave them in the water until you are ready to fill them. In order to process any preserves for shelf-stable storage, further important steps must be followed for the safety of the product. Please contact your local County Cooperative Extension office found under your County Listings in the local Yellow Pages. This office provides current information from the USDA and Land Grant University System for safe home-preserving procedures.

REDEYE GRAVY

Gravy with a broth-like consistency made from the pan juices of fried slices of country ham, to which coffee or water is added. It's often served over ham and grits.

RENDER

To heat a solid fat slowly until liquefied.

ROASTING GARLIC

Garlic's flavor becomes mellow and nutty and it softens to a buttery consistency when roasted in its own skin, which keeps it from burning. The cloves may be separated and added to the roasting pan along with meats and vegetables. Or the whole heads may be roasted. To roast a whole head of garlic, snip off the tip of the head, barely exposing the cloves. Remove the papery outer layer of skin without separating the cloves. Place the head or heads in a small baking dish or on a double layer of aluminum foil. Drizzle with olive oil and season to taste with salt and pepper. Add a sprig of thyme or rosemary, if desired. Cover the dish, or fold up the ends of the foil around the garlic, and bake in a preheated oven at 350°F (180°C) for 1–1½ hours, until the garlic is very soft. Remove garlic from the skins by squeezing the ends. Roasted garlic may be mashed and spread on French bread like butter or used as a condiment on roasted meats or as a flavoring in other dishes.

ROUX

A mixture of flour and fat slowly cooked together in a skillet to form a rich, brown paste of differing hues (depending upon the recipe) that serves as the foundation for gumbo and other Cajun and Creole classics.

SAUTÉ

To cook quickly in a hot pan with a small amount of butter or oil.

SCUPPERNONGS

White Muscadine grapes.

SHELL BEANS

Beans with edible seeds that must be shelled from their tough, stringy pods. Most are purchased dried or canned. The dried beans must be soaked overnight before cooking. Usually the water they are cooked in is flavored with pork, but this isn't a necessity. Various regions of the South have their favorites: Louisianans rely on kidney beans and small red beans for their red beans and rice; Floridians, particularly those of Cuban or Spanish heritage, favor black (turtle) beans and, to a lesser extent, garbanzo beans (chick-peas) for soups. In the Deep South, pale green, soft-textured lima beans—or their close relative, the slightly larger, more delicate butter bean—are a standard vegetable plate component. Appalachians like their pork-simmered pinto beans for dunking corn bread; and in Memphis, white beans or navy beans, are flavored with pork and sweetened with brown sugar for barbecue beans.

SHRIMP

To peel raw or cooked headless shrimp, pull off the legs, then, starting from underneath, peel off and discard the shell. Pull off the tail, or for presentations such as shrimp cocktail, leave the "fan" of the tail intact. To devein, using a small, sharp paring knife, make a shallow cut along the back of the shrimp and remove and discard the black vein underneath.

SIMMER

To cook liquid over low heat below the boiling temperature, so that just a few small bubbles appear on the surface.

SORGHUM SYRUP

Strong-tasting syrup, similar to dark molasses, produced from sorghum grain, an Old World grass grown for both animal forage and syrup making.

SOUTHERN FLOUR

The key to biscuits and shortcakes that are airy on the inside and semicrisp on the outside is low-gluten flour milled from soft winter wheat. White Lily is the brand most Southerners recommend. Though once found only in the South, it is becoming increasingly available in many metropolitan areas as demand grows.

SQUAB

A young pigeon with dark, moist, delicate flesh once available only to hunters in the South and elsewhere. Today they are farm-raised, mostly in California. The birds weigh about ¾–1 lb (375–500 g), and can be stuffed and roasted whole, or split and grilled or broiled.

STOCKS

Long-simmering, well-seasoned stocks can be made from meat, poultry, fish or vegetables. Though time-consuming, they're easy to make and can be frozen for future use. Canned broth may be substituted for stock in most recipes, but be aware that most commercial broth is very salty.

BEEF OR LAMB STOCK: In a roasting pan, roast 4 lb (2 kg) beef or lamb bones (with some meat on them) in a preheated oven at 450°F (230°C) for 30 minutes, turning once. Place the bones in a large pot and add 2 onions, peeled and halved; 3 whole carrots; 3 whole celery stalks; 1 bay leaf; a few parsley sprigs; 1 teaspoon salt and ½ teaspoon cracked peppercorns. Discard the fat from the roasting pan. Deglaze the pan with 2 cups (16 fl oz/500 ml) water and add to the pot of water. Bring to a boil over medium-high heat, then reduce the heat to low and simmer gently, partially covered, for about 5 hours, skimming off any foam that rises to the surface during the first 30 minutes. Strain the stock through several thicknesses of cheesecloth (muslin) and let cool, uncovered. Makes about 3 qt (3 l).

CHICKEN STOCK: In a large pot, place about 4 lb (2 kg) chicken pieces (backs, wings, necks and the remains of a roasted chicken). Add 2 onions, peeled and halved; 2 whole carrots, 2 whole celery ribs; four parsley sprigs; 1 bay leaf; 6 cracked peppercorns; 1 teaspoon dried thyme; and 1 teaspoon salt. Pour in enough water to cover the ingredients by 1 in (2.5 cm). Bring to a boil over medium-high heat, then reduce the heat to low and simmer gently, partially covered, for about 4 hours, skimming off any foam that rises to the surface during the first 30 minutes. Strain the stock through several thicknesses of cheesecloth (muslin) and let cool, uncovered. Makes about 3 qt (3 l).

FISH STOCK: Rinse about 4 lb (2 kg) of white-fleshed fish heads and meaty skeletons under cold running water. Place in a large pot and add 2 onions, peeled and sliced; 2 carrots, peeled and thinly sliced; 2 celery ribs, sliced; 1 bay leaf, 8 cracked peppercorns; and 1 teaspoon salt. Add 2 cups (16 fl oz/500 ml) dry white wine and enough water to cover the ingredients by 1 in (2.5 cm). Bring to a boil over medium-high heat, reduce the heat to low and simmer, uncovered, for about 45 minutes, skimming off any foam that forms on the surface. Strain the stock through several thicknesses of cheesecloth (muslin) and let cool, uncovered. Makes about 3 qt (3 l).

PORK STOCK: The simplest method uses just ham hocks and water. In a large saucepan, pour 2 qt (2 l) water over 2 split ham hocks. Cook over low heat for 2 hours, until ham hocks are fork-tender. Add more water to the pot, if necessary, so that by the end of cooking time you have about 6 cups (48 fl oz/1.5 l) of stock.

SHRIMP STOCK: In a medium saucepan, place the shells from 6 oz (185 g) of shrimp and add 5 cups (40 fl oz/1.25 l) water. Bring to a boil over medium-high heat, reduce the heat to medium low and simmer 8-10 minutes. Strain, reserving liquid and discarding shells. Makes 1 quart.

VEGETABLE STOCK: Vegetable scraps such as carrot ends, celery leaves, potato peelings, onion skins, pea pods and the stems of mushrooms, parsley, spinach and broccoli can take on a new life when used for soup stock. Leftover cooking water from vegetables may also go into the stock pot. Avoid rotten or moldy vegetables and very strong-tasting vegetables such as beets and cabbage. The more variety, the better. Cover the vegetables with 1 in (2.5 cm) water. Bring to a boil over medium-high heat and then reduce the heat to low and simmer for only 20 minutes. Strain, reserving the liquid and discarding the vegetables.

SWEET POTATO

There are two dominant types of this tuber. One is yellowish with a dry, faintly sweet flesh, and has been cultivated in the Southeast since the 1600s. The other is moister with a dark orange flesh. It was brought to this country from Puerto Rico in the 1930s and marketed as a "Louisiana yam," even though it bears little resemblance to true yams—large, hairy, tropical tubers found in some Latin markets. The confusion actually started long before that, with the arrival of slaves who called sweet potatoes by the Gullah word "nyam," meaning "to eat."

TABASCO SAUCE

A thin, red, hot sauce made from the tongue-searing hot peppers first cultivated on Avery Island, Louisiana. During the Civil War, Edmund McIlhenney, a prosperous New Orleans banker, created the brew with his only possession left after the Union Army destroyed his plantation: chili peppers. He crushed them into a mash and added vinegar and Avery Island salt. After aging the mixture in oak barrels, he packed the fiery liquid in old cologne bottles and within a year had sold several thousand. Today more than 50 million bottles of Tabasco sauce are sold in the United States alone. In Southern cooking, it's as indispensable as salt and pepper and almost as versatile.

TASSO

Highly seasoned Cajun smoked ham.

TEA

See *Iced tea*.

TOASTING NUTS

Spread the nuts on a baking sheet and toast, stirring often, in a preheated oven at 350°F (180°C) for about 7–13 minutes for pecan halves; about 3–5 minutes for chopped pecans; about 5–10 minutes for whole almonds; about 4–7 minutes for sliced almonds. Be careful not to let the nuts burn; almonds should be light brown and pecans should have a golden brown cast with a pleasant "toasted" aroma when done. Transfer the nuts at once to paper towels to cool.

TOMATOES

To peel a tomato, immerse it into boiling water for a minute or so, or until the skin cracks, then plunge it into ice water. Slip the tomato out of its skin. If it's still hard to peel, return it to the boiling water for a few more seconds. After peeling, core the tomato by cutting out a small cone around the stem. To seed the tomato, cut it in half horizontally and squeeze gently until the seeds fall out. Use your finger or a small spoon to remove any stubborn seeds.

VIDALIA ONIONS

Sweet, mild onions grown in South Georgia, available from late April through June, and briefly in October and November when limited supplies are brought out of storage. Mature Vidalias are somewhat flat, golden-brown bulbs that come in a variety of sizes. In early spring, baby Vidalias are available in limited areas and by mail-order; they have tender, white bulbs and dark green tops like large scallions. To substitute for mature Vidalias, try Maui, Spanish Sweet, Texas 1015 SuperSweet or Walla Walla onions.

WHITE CHOCOLATE

Because it contains no chocolate liquor, it's really not chocolate. Rather, it contains cocoa butter, milk solids, sugar and flavorings. Cheaper brands may replace some, or even all, of the cocoa butter with vegetable shortening. For maximum flavor, use brands with all cocoa butter. To melt white chocolate, use a double boiler set over low heat—it can burn very easily. To make decorative white chocolate curls, see *Chocolate curls*.

YAM

See *Sweet potato*.

ZEST

The colored part of citrus peel, zest does not include the bitter white pith just underneath the surface. The zest can be removed with a simple tool known as a zester by drawing its sharp-edged holes across the fruit's skin to remove the zest in thin strips, or by using the fine holes on a hand-held grater. Alternatively, remove strips of zest with a vegetable peeler, taking care not to remove any white pith. Thinly slice the strips with a small, sharp knife. Zest adds a fresh, intensely citrus punch to sauces, marinades and numerous baked goods.

COOK'S GUIDE

Recipe terms used in *The South the Beautiful Cookbook*:

All eggs called for are large eggs.

Range of skillet sizes referenced: small 7–8 in (18–20 cm), medium 10–12 in (25$\frac{1}{N}$30 cm), large 12–14 in (30$\frac{1}{N}$35 cm).

Range of saucepan, saucepot and Dutch oven sizes referenced: small 1–2 qt (1–2 l), medium 2–6 qt (2–6 l), large 6–10 qt (6–10 l), very large 10–12 qt (10–12 l), extra large 5–8 g (20–32 l).

ACKNOWLEDGMENTS

Mara Reid Rogers, Jim Auchmutey and Susan Puckett thank all of the talented chefs, celebrities and authors who contributed their recipes; and the creative and discriminating culinary professionals who helped test recipes: Hillary Davis–Tonken, Carol Beller, Linda Hogue, Susan Mack, Margaret Ann Surber and Anne Byrn. A special thanks goes to Nathalie Dupree, Daphne Eaton, John Egerton, Edna Lewis, Susan Nicholson, Ray Overton III, Irene Smith and Eugene Walter. Thank you to the entire Weldon Owen crew, especially to Anne Dickerson, Genevieve Morgan, Hannah Rahill and Desne Border for "going the extra mile"; to the photographers and the food styling team; and to Collins Publishers San Francisco for the opportunity and fun this project provided.

The photographer and stylists gratefully acknowledge the following individuals and companies for their generous support (all in San Francisco unless specified): Cyclamen Studios, Julie Sanders Design, Berkeley; Ward Finer; Bea and Marty Glenn; Nancy Glenn; Rosie Ella Glenn-Finer; Harry Paul Glenn-Finer; Judy Goldsmith and Bernie Carrasco; J. Goldsmith Antiques Prop Shop; Missy Hamilton; Jill, Chris, Peter and Nicholas Lynch; The Gardener; Sydney Johnson; Todd Johnson; Sue Fisher King; Anabel Rose Glenn-Schuster; Roberta Glaser; Mimi Koch; Merna Oeberst; Makenna Salaverry; Susan Pascal; Dan Schuster; Virginia Breier Gallery; Wilkes Home at Wilkes Bashford; Fillamento; Aude Bronson Howard, New York; As You Like It, New Orleans; Marcia Michaels; Cindy Luna, Millfield, Ohio; Alan Goldfarb Blown Glass, Burlington, Vermont; Wolfe Rudman; Zia, Berkeley.

Weldon Owen extends a special thanks to Lila and Bill Jaeger.

ILLUSTRATION GUIDE

CONTENTS

The development of wrought-iron architectural adornments in the South was, literally, the result of a "melting pot" of British, French and German blacksmithing techniques. In a trade traditionally passed down from father to son or master to apprentice, American smithing was born in a transference of skills from Old World to New World. Truly ornamental applications of wrought-iron in the forms of balconies, railings, fences, gates and grilles were a development of the late eighteenth century. This flower-centered medallion, the centerpiece in scrollwork from the landing of a stairwell, is an example from the early architecture of Charleston, South Carolina.

INTRODUCTION

Difficult to secure and costly, on account of its resistance to moisture and its superior malleability, Swedish iron was almost exclusively employed in wealthy Charleston, South Carolina. This rendering of an ornate nineteenth-century wrought-iron over-throw, featured in the park at City Hall in Charleston, demonstrates the shell and lyre motifs popular in English ornamental

ironwork. To shape the numerous scrolls, craftsmen plunge an iron rod into a coal-burning furnace until it turns cherry red. They then use hammers and tongs to bend and twist the hot metal around the horn of an anvil. Joining the discrete scrolls by forge welding creates a single piece of metal as strong as each of the contributing parts.

DEEP SOUTH

This relief from the buttress of a gate in Mobile, Alabama, shows the interesting marriage of cast iron and wrought iron: while the center circle and palmettes anchoring this design have been poured in a single mold, the scrolls that frame it are separate pieces of iron riveted together.

THE PIEDMONT

Although a detachment of Sherman's invading troops occupied the Gordon-Banks House when it stood in Milledgeville, Georgia, during the Civil War, it survived unscathed. Constructed in the

1820s, the entry hall of the finely detailed residence serves as a model for this wrought-iron design. The house was completely renovated and moved to Newnan, Georgia, in 1969.

LOUISIANA

Cast-iron work appeared in the Lower Garden District of New Orleans, Louisiana, by 1849, and became immensely popular once people discovered its capability of rendering all types of designs, including those never before accomplished in metal. Costs were

reasonable since a mold could be used countless times and, once hardened, the single piece of sculpted iron was virtually indestructible. With this innovation, metal workers were able to embellish their designs with even more intricate, delicate patterns than ever before—this modeling from the balcony of the Pontalba Building in New Orleans demonstrates their ability to create light, airy lace in iron.

UPPER SOUTH

Decorative weather vanes adorn homes and farms all across the countryside in the rolling, grassy hills of Kentucky and Tennessee. This trotting-horse weather vane, celebrating the proud animals for which this area is famous, was designed and manufactured in 1880. The original, measuring 24 inches high and 51½ inches wide, was made of gilded copper and has a handsome, worn blue-green patina.

TIDEWATER

The streets of Charleston, South Carolina, are lined with a procession of strikingly beautiful buildings; Federal, Colonial, Italianate,

Victorian, Gothic Revival and Art Deco, they are all superbly preserved. The homes in old Charleston are unique in that the entrances are guarded by distinct yet harmonious sets of fine wrought-iron gates. Every single gate has its own design, showcasing the vast variety of possible shapes and textures. This scroll lyre pattern is taken from a residence at 133 Church Street.

HIGHLANDS

During Colonial times, blacksmiths were the figurative hearth of rural communities, making, repairing and sharpening virtually all the tools required for farm life: from kitchen instruments and hinges for the home, to plow points and ox yokes for working the fields, to horseshoes for farriers. This cast-iron traveler, or wheel-race, was used all over Appalachia by wheelwrights to determine the cir-

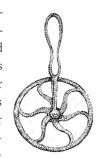

cumference of tires for buggies and carriages. Once measured, they would "sweat on the tire" by heating the metal band before hammering it onto the wooden rim, then douse it in water to shrink and permanently tighten the wheel.

FLORIDA

Southerners' love of adornment can be glimpsed throughout the South in the profusion of arches, columns, parapets and porticos. Marking the entrance to a Mediterranean Revival home in Jacksonville, Florida, this wrought-iron gate is evidence of their fondness for elegant architectural accents.

MAIL-ORDER SOURCES

Many of these mail-order sources have catalogs that offer a wide range of products. This source listing is arranged according to their unique specialities.

DESSERTS AND CANDIES

Chattanooga Bakery
P.O. Box 111
Chattanooga, TN 37401
(615) 267–3351 or (800) 251–3404
Moon Pies

Moravian Sugar Crisp Co., Inc.
Route 2, Box 431
Friedberg Road
Clemmons, NC 27012
(919) 764–1402
Moravian cookies, ginger crisps, sugar crisps and other assorted cookies

Standard Candy Company
Mail Order Department
P.O. Box 101025
Nashville, TN 37210
(615) 889–6360 or (800) 231–3402
Goo Goo Clusters, Goo Goo Supremes and King Leo Stick Candy

DRIED BEANS AND NUTS

The Bean Bag Bulk Foods
818 Jefferson Street
Oakland, CA 94607
(510) 839–8988
Many varieties of dried beans and related seasonings

Missouri Dandy Pantry
212 Hammons Drive East
Stockton, MO 65785
(800) 872–6879
Black walnuts

Nuts D'Vine
P.O. Box 589
Edenton, NC 27932
(919) 482–2222 or (800) 334–0492
Peanuts and peanut oil

Sunnyland Farms
P.O. 8200
Albany, GA 31706–8200
(912) 833–3085
Pecans

W. B. Rodenberry Co., Inc.
P.O. Box 60
Cairo, GA 31728
(912) 377–1431
Boiled peanuts

FISH AND SHELLFISH

Bucksnort Trout Ranch
Route 1, Box 156
McEwen, TN 37101
(615) 729–3162
Smoked trout and trout caviar

The Farm at Mt. Walden
515 Main Street
The Plains, VA 22171
(703) 253–9800
Smoked trout

Pickwick Catfish Farm
Highway 57
Counce, TN 38326
(901) 689–3805
Smoked catfish

Joe's Stone Crab Restaurant
Take Away
227 Biscayne Street
Miami Beach, FL 33139
(305) 673–4611 or (800) 780–CRAB
Stone crab claws

Handy Soft Shell Crawfish
10557 Cherry Hill Avenue
Baton Rouge, LA 70816
(504) 292–4552
Soft-shell crawfish

Vieux Carre Foods, Inc.
P.O. Box 50277
New Orleans, LA 70150
(504) 822–6065
Shrimp and crab boil and other Louisiana fare

GAME AND POULTRY

The International Home Cooking Catalog
(800) 237–7423
Game

Ottomanelli's Meat Market
281 Bleeker Street
New York, NY 10014
(212) 675–4217
Game

Manchester Farms, Inc.
P.O. Box 97
Dalzell, SC 29040
(803) 469–2588 or (800) 845–0421
Quail

Maple Leaf Farms
P.O. Box 308
Milford, IN 46542
(219) 658–4121
Duck

Palmetto Pigeon Plant
P.O. Drawer 3060
Sumter, SC 29151
(803) 775–1204
Squab, poussin and pheasant

GRITS AND OTHER CORN PRODUCTS

Adams Milling Company
Route 6, Box 148A
Napier Field Station
Dolthan, AL 36303
(205) 983–4233
Grits milled from whole-kernel corn and other corn products such as water-ground cornmeal

Callaway Gardens Country Store
Pine Mountain, GA 31822
(404) 663–5100
(800) 262–8181
Grits stone-ground from whole-grain corn

Hoppin' John's
30 Pinckney Street
Charleston, SC 29401
(803) 577–6404
Stone-ground cornmeal, grits and corn flour and other items, including a multitude of cookbooks

HAMS

Gwaltney of Smithfield
P.O. Box 489
Smithfield, VA 23430
(800) 678–0770
Smithfield hams

The Smithfield Companies
P.O. Box 487
Smithfield, VA 23430
(804) 357–2121 or (800) 628–2242
Smithfield hams

The Honeybaked Ham Company
P.O. Box 370
Carrollton, GA 30177
(800) FOR-A-HAM
Honeybaked hams

Robertson's Country Meats
P.O. Box 56
Finchville, KY 40022
(502) 834–7952 or (800) 678–1521
All-natural sugar-cured country hams

S. Wallace Edwards and Sons
P.O. Box 25
Surry, VA 23883
(800) 222–4267
Older-cure country hams and small packages of boneless country ham slices

JUICES, JAMS AND JELLIES

Nellie and Joe's Inc.
P.O. Box 2368
Key West, FL 33045
(305) 296–5566
Bottled Key lime juice

Southern Touch Foods Corporation
P.O. Box 2853
Meridian, MS 39302–2853
(800) 233–1736
Muscadine juices (including one made with the Scuppernong variety of the Muscadine grape), jams, jellies, preserves and syrups

A. M. Braswell Jr. Food Company, Inc.
P.O. Box 485
Statesboro, GA 30458
(no phone orders)
A large line of jams, jellies, pickles and relishes, including artichoke relish and pear preserves

The Mayhaw Tree
P.O. Box 144
Colquitt, GA 31737
(800) 677–3227
Mayhaw jelly, syrup and other goodies

KITCHENWARE

Cumberland Grocery Store
Route 3
Crossville, TN 38555
(615) 484–8481
A store and a catolog filled with old-fashioned merchandise, such as cast-iron corn stick pans, pickle crocks and hand-crank ice-cream freezers

Williams-Sonoma
Mail-Order Department
P.O. Box 7456
San Francisco, CA 94120–7456
(415) 421–4242 or (800) 541–2233
A vast array of kitchenware including miniature cast-iron corn stick pans, and specialty food items such as White Lily® Flour, Virginia bacon, lemon curd and candied rose petals

MUSHROOMS

Aux Delices des Bois
4 Leonard Street
New York, NY 10013
(212) 334–1230 or (800) 666–1232
Wild edibles, including mushrooms and other
seasonal specialties such as ramps

Low Country Exotic Mushroom Farm
P.O Box 867
John's Island, SC 29457
(803) 559–9200
Mushrooms

RICE

Konriko Company Store
P.O. Box 10640
New Iberia, LA 70562–0640
(800) 551–3245
Wild Pecan Rice, with its pecanlike flavor and
wonderful aroma, is the result of crossbreeding
Louisiana long-grain rice with several Indochinese
aromatic rice species

SAUSAGES

Aidells Sausage Company
1575 Minnesota Street
San Francisco, CA 94107
(415) 285–6660
Andouille and other sausages

Baltz Brothers
1612 Elm Hill Pike
Nashville, TN 37210
(615) 360–3100
Hickory–smoked sausage and bacon

Comeaux's Grocery
1000 Lamar Street
Lafayette, LA 70501
(800) 323–2492 or (800) 737–2666
Boudin blanc and *boudin rouge* sausages

Poche's Meat Market & Restaurant
Route 2, Box 415
Breaux Bridge, LA 70517
(318) 332–2108
Andouille sausage and more

SEASONINGS AND SAUCES

K-Paul's Louisiana Mail Order
824 Distributors Row
P.O. Box 23342
New Orleans, LA 70183–0342
(800) 457–2857
Chef Paul Prudhomme's Magic Seasoning
Blends, cookbooks, videos, cast-iron skillets
and local foods such as jellies and Louisiana-
grown rice

Louisiana General Store
The Jackson Brewery
620 Decatur Street
New Orleans, LA 70130
(800) 237–4841
Filé powder and many more ingredients for
Cajun and Creole cuisines

Char-Broil
P.O. Box 1300
Columbus, GA 31902
(800) 241–8981
Barbecue sauces, utensils, cookers and more

Exclusively Barbecue
P.O. Box 3048
Concord, NC 28025
(800) 948–1009
Barbecue sauces, grills and apparel

Flamingo Flats
P.O. Box 441
St. Michaels, MD 21663
(800) 468–8841
A wide selection of barbecue sauces

Great Barbecue Sauce Catalog
9538 Hickory Falls Way
Baltimore, MD 21236
(800) 672–8237
Many barbecue sauces, including celebrity
sauces

Great Southern Sauce Company
5705 Kavanaugh Blvd.
Little Rock, AR 72207
(800) 437–2823
Many types of condiments including barbecue
sauces

Hot Stuff
227 Sullivan Street
New York, NY 10012
(212) 254–6120
A myriad of sauces, including hot sauces and
barbecue sauces

Mo Hotta, Mo Betta
P.O. Box 4136
San Luis Obispo, CA 93403
(800) 462–3220
A large selection of sauces, including barbecue
sauces

Tabasco Country Store
McIlhenny Company
Avery Island, LA 70513–5002
(800) 634–9599
Tabasco brand hot pepper sauce and other
products

Trappey's Fine Foods, Inc.
P.O. Box 13610
New Iberia, LA 70562–3610
(318) 365–8727 or (800) 365–8727
Hot sauces

SOUTHERN FLOUR

The White Lily Foods Company
P.O. Box 871
Knoxville, TN 37901
(615) 546–5511
White Lily® Flour

SWEET ONIONS

Bland Farms
P.O. Box 506
Glennville, GA 30427–0506
(800) 843–2542
Vidalia onions and baby Vidalias

Frank Lewis Co.
100 North Tower Road
Alamo, TX 78516
(210) 787–9971 or (800) 477–4773
Fresno Sweet onions

Humphrey's Gift Fruit
P.O. Box 1436
Los Fresnos, TX 78566
(800) 828–4458
Texas 1015 SuperSweet onions

Lone Star Farms
P.O. Box 685
Mercedes, TX 78570
(800) 552–1015
Texas 1015 SuperSweet onions

Planters Three
P.O. Box 92
Wadmalaw Island, SC 29412
(800) 772–6732
Wadmalaw Sweet onions

SWEET POTATOES

Garber Farms
Route 1, Box 9
Iota, LA 70543
(318) 824–7161 or (318) 824–4953
The dark orange-fleshed, sweeter, moister type
of sweet potato that Southerners fondly refer to
as "yams"

SYRUP

C.S. Steen Syrup Mill, Inc.
P.O. Box 339
Abbeville, LA 70510
(318) 893–1654
Cane syrup

Golden Kentucky Products
P.O Box 246
Livingston, KY 40445
(606) 453–9800
Cane syrup and sorghum syrup

TEA AND COFFEE

Charleston Tea Plantation
6617 Maybank Highway
Wadmalaw Island, SC 29487
(800) 443–5987
American Classic™ tea

Community Kitchens
P.O. Box 2311
Baton Rouge, LA 70821–2311
(504) 381–3900 or (800) 535–9901
Community coffee, Creole mustard and other
Louisiana specialities

The Company Store
1039 Decatur Street
New Orleans, LA 70116
(504) 581–2914
Café du Monde coffee

INDEX